Migration across Time and Nations

Migration across Time and Nations

POPULATION MOBILITY
IN HISTORICAL CONTEXTS

EDITED BY
Ira A. Glazier
AND
Luigi De Rosa

HOLMES & MEIER
New York • London

Photo credits: The Bancroft Library (page 9); The Library of
Congress (cover, pages 77, 269, 303).

First published in the United States of America 1986 by
Homes & Meier Publishers, Inc.
30 Irving Place
New York, N.Y. 10003

Great Britain:
Holmes & Meier Publishers, Ltd.
Pindar Road
Hoddesdon, Hertfordshire, EN11 OHF

Book design by Ellen Foos

Library of Congress Cataloging-in-Publication Data
Main entry under title:

Migration across time and nations.

    Papers presented at a session of the Eighth
International Congress on Economic History held in Budapest
in 1982.
    1. Emigration and immigration—History—Congresses.
2. Migration, Internal—History—Congresses. I. Glazier,
Ira. II. De Rosa, Luigi, 1922–   .   III. International
Congress on Economic History (8th : 1982 : Budapest,
Hungary)
JV6021.M53   1986   325'.09   85-17615

ISBN 0-8419-0994-6

Manufactured in the United States of America

Dedicated to the memory of
Arcadius Kahan, a great
scholar who devoted his
life to the study of
human migration

Contents

Looking Ahead

Migration across Time and Nations

Introduction
Ira A. Glazier and Luigi De Rosa

This volume contains papers presented at the session on "History, Models and Methods in Migration Research" at the Eighth International Economic History Congress in Budapest in 1982. Here are twenty-two essays of unquestioned relevance for the study of migration, understood not only as population movements across international boundaries but also as demographic movements within a single state. It is important to note that, although the essays devote ample space to illuminating different aspects of these movements, they do not have and, indeed, could not have a purely descriptive character, given the aims of the panel; they deal rather with the problems of analysis and interpretation as well as suggest new methods for the study of the migratory process.

These studies show the true geographical dimensions of migration movements that involved populations far beyond the frontiers of Continental Europe. At one time or another, Asia, Africa, America, Australia, as well as Europe, were all affected. A. J. H. Latham, for example, discusses two great currents of Asian migration: the flow from India to Burma, Ceylon, Malaysia, Mauritius, Fiji, the Caribbean, and East Africa; and the flow from China to Burma, Malaysia, the Dutch East Indies, Siam, French Indonesia, and the Philippines, in addition, of course, to the secondary movements from China and India to the United States, Australia, New Zealand, Cuba, and Hawaii. The two streams, the Indian moving eastward and the Chinese moving westward, came together in Malaysia. Although they are difficult to quantify, Latham estimates the number of Chinese in Southeast Asia at about 2½ million at the outbreak of World War I and net Indian migration to Southeast Asia between 1834 and 1932 at 6 million. The Indian case is particularly significant because overseas migration occurs simultaneously with internal migration. The study by M. S. A. Rao has special relevance here, and his analysis of internal migration of India since 1820, the reasons for its growth and the results to which it gave rise, makes an important contribution to our understanding of Indian migration, and is rendered even more valuable by his conclusions concerning the relations between migration, development, and deprivation in the subcontinent. In Southeast Asia, where Indian, Chinese, and European élites were the main protagonists in the migration process, the growth and development of the preindustrial city of Batavia is carefully documented and analyzed by Frank Spooner and confirms the character and effects of great demographic movements, particularly of the Chinese, who played an important part in the history of the region in the seventeenth and eighteenth centuries.

It is, nevertheless, North and South America in the nineteenth and twentieth centuries that provide the great stage for the migration drama, where migration assumes extraordinary dimensions, and where it has left a legacy of social and economic problems that are still relevant for our time. While for the other continents migration was a means of relieving demographic pressure by moving surplus population to regions of lower density, in North and South America the problem was one of providing a labor force to work the vast areas of open land waiting to be brought under cultivation.

The migration phenomenon assumes its most dramatic form in the United States, where rapid economic growth due to historically high rates of labor productivity and capital accumulation in the nineteenth century provided an extraordinary impulse to immigration. It is hardly surprising then that most of these studies deal with the origin, structure, and destination of successive waves of migration to the United States, particularly to the ports of New York, Boston, and Philadelphia. Migration to South America is not entirely neglected, however, as the study by Kristin Ruggiero on Italian emigration to Argentina demonstrates.

Migration to the United States is considered from three perspectives: (1) in terms of the flows of groups or individuals coming from

Europe; (2) in terms of the status and occupation of the emigrants in country of origin; (3) in terms of the status they attained in the United States. The three perspectives are rarely considered entirely independently of each other. In general, we study at least two of these perceptions with respect to a single migratory process. In view of the large number of emigrant groups analyzed here—Dutch, British, Irish, Swedish, German, Italian, Yugoslavian, Hungarian, German Jewish, and East European Jewish—we have not only a reasonably complete picture of this extraordinary European diaspora and of the various nationality groups that came to be represented in the American melting pot but, above all, an opportunity for a deeper and more profound analysis of the economic and social history of Europe.

The analysis by Robert P. Swierenga, for example, of Dutch emigration to the United States is enlightening, not only for what it reveals about the social and occupational composition of the emigrant population and political and economic reasons for emigration as well as about areas of settlement and occupations in the United States, but because it challenges the traditional view that international migration necessarily results in downward occupational mobility over the short run. Swierenga's study, based on linked-files combining data sets on the pre- and postmigration periods, shows that Dutch immigrants achieved a marked degree of occupational change and rising occupational status in the United States.

This emphasis on the interrelations between demographic change and political and economic factors in the sender country emerges also in the studies of Shaul Stampfer and Avraham Barkai on Jewish emigration from Germany and Eastern Europe. Barkai analyzes Jewish *Binnenwanderung* and emigration and their social and economic impact on German Jewry—those who emigrated as well as those who stayed behind—with a keen awareness for the importance of internal social, political, and economic realities. Stampfer studies the differential propensity to emigrate among the various regions of the Pale, and finds that *landsmanshaften* membership is a good indicator of the relative size of the migrant population from a particular region. The studies of Cormac Ó Gráda on Irish emigration, Ivan Čismić on Yugoslavian emigration before World War II, Julianna Puskás on emigration from Hungary and the Austro-Hungarian Empire, and Luigi Di Comité on Italy all emphasize the interrelations of demographic and socioeconomic factors. Walter D. Kamphoefner's work on the relationship between emigration rates, population density, and economic specialization shows that protoindustrialization and deindustrialization were important factors in German emigration in the first half of the nineteenth century. The degree of socioeconomic mobility that German immigrants achieved in America is only understood if one starts by investigating the occupational and social composition of the emigrant group in Europe. Kristin Ruggiero's study of Italian emigration to Argentina points out correctly that while overpopulation, underproduction, land scarcity, and agrarian crises are often offered as motives for emigration of Italian peasants, other factors of a social and political nature remain to be studied.

Migration movements can also occur within a single state. Jana Englová analyzes population movements in the Hapsburg Empire using the Austrian census of 1900. She finds that 51.3 percent of the population born in Bohemia still lived in their native parishes in 1900. Thus half the population emigrated from their place of birth, 30 percent from their native district (of which 23 percent were in Bohemia and 7 percent in the Austrian provinces). Prague and its environs and the coal mining districts of northern Bohemia were the most important centers of population influx. Emigration from the Austrian provinces, however, was of a much smaller magnitude; only 15 percent moved to parishes in other districts of the same province while over 6 percent moved to other provinces.

In addition to the studies that illustrate the migration process in various countries, others offer information on source materials, on new methods and techniques in the field, as well as critical surveys of the migration literature for many of the countries under study. Several contributions suggest new approaches to research that go beyond the conventional treatment of the migration theme that will be of interest to scholars as well as to the nonspecialist reader. The study by Kleiner, Sørenson, Dalgard, Moum, and Drews represents a methodology still largely unknown outside the Anglo-Saxon world of scholarship and raises critical questions for further work. Robert C. Ostergren's study of Swedish migration provides a very helpful survey of results obtained by combining techniques of the so-called Swedish school, particularly of the Uppsala group, with American methods, and makes a compelling case for longitudinal studies in transatlantic migration. Julianna Puskas's study on emigration from the Austro-Hungarian Empire demonstrates the great possibilities of microhistory for analysis of social and geographical mobility across continents. Of no less importance is the work of Jacques Dupâquier on geographical and social mobility in France in the nineteenth and twentieth centuries. Adapting methods developed by Louis Henry on family reconstitution, Dupâquier presents a progress report on research on internal migration. The study, based on a sample of 3,000 families for which he has collected data on age, birth, family size, migration distance, and frequency of return migration, allows him to compare the social and professional status of emigrants and nonemigrants and to study the links between geographical and social mobility.

Several studies are based on empirical data from the ship passenger lists, a source used by Swierenga in his study of Dutch emigration, by Ó Gráda for Irish emigration in the pre-Famine period, and by others. The fact that the manuscripts of the U.S. ship passenger lists have recently been rediscovered and that a large-scale project is under way at the Balch Institute to put information on these lists into machine-readable form, opens unusual opportunities for research on a wide range of problems, and not only demographic problems connected with migration. Sune Åckerman has recently observed that migrational processes need to be studied in depth but that depth is elusive at the level of aggregate statistics. It is quite clear then that these lists will become increasingly important for the study of migration in the years to come. The ship lists have been preserved for all the major U.S. ports between 1820 and 1930.

Charlotte Erickson's analysis of the strengths and weaknesses of the passenger lists ˙n her study of British and Irish emigration is essential and indeed indispensable for anyone interested in these lists as a research tool. She has found that they offer the basis for a more accurate estimate of the number and nationality of immigrants than those in the official published sources and much new data on occupations, family structure, age, and sex of the migrating population, as well as facilitate longitudinal studies that link immigrants to their place of origin and destination. An example of the possibilities for linkage with the passenger lists can be seen in Deirdre Mageean's study of the influx and assimilation of Ulster emigrants into the urban and social life of Philadelphia between 1847 and 1865.

Of no less interest, however, are the growth and formation of the little homelands in the great metropolitan cities of America. The "little Italies" deserve particular attention as Rudolph J. Vecoli shows in his study of the Italian community in Chicago. Vecoli gives us a history of that community and, by analyzing the geographical origins of Italian immigrants, provides us with an explanation of the customs, traditions, and mentalities that they express as a group having specific origins and characteristics that they try to preserve in their new settlement. Thus we have a different and original interpretation of the immigrant's choice of neighborhood and occupational preference. Vecoli believes that the assimilation of Italians into American social life is less the result of economic forces than of such factors as contingency, cultural preference, and personal inclination and that the history of a single community, and of its growth and disintegration, would contribute to a much improved understanding of the role of ethnicity in the cultural geography of the American city.

Thus international migration, international demographic movements, and assimilation of migrant populations in their new place of settlement, provide over a long period the real key to the understanding of society and, in particular, to the comprehension of American society. From this perspective, United States census data can make an important contribution to the study of migration as they contain information on the geographical origins and conditions of the immigrant population as well as on their movements within the United States. The study of Ann R. Miller is an outstanding example. Using microlevel samples from the 1900 U.S. Population Census, she analyses variations in age and occupation of native-born migrants over time, the effects of internal migration on the structure of employment and economic growth, and the extent to which the migrant differs from the nonmigrant population. She offers then a method that enables us to evaluate the enormous changes that are a constant and continuing feature of American society. And if we pay attention to what she says, it is clear that census data can make a very important contribution to the study of international and internal migration and not only in quantitative terms.

Finally we see in the study by John Day and Serge Bonin on internal migration in Sardinia in the eighteenth century that cartographical analysis can be an important aid in migration research. The maps are used very ingeniously to illustrate changes in population density, the number and type of villages, the state of the harvests, numbers of live stock, and so forth.

It is hoped that from these brief remarks the reader will gain some idea of the extraordinary richness of this collection and will understand the reasons that the publisher and editors have decided to publish it. In releasing it to the public, we hope that it will stimulate many more studies on migration. The multiplication of these studies will confirm our conviction that it is population movements that have been responsible in every epoch and in every part of the world for the rebirth of society, unleashing new and powerful energies over immense spaces so that weary peoples might satisfy basic human needs. The benefits have been as great for the countries of destination as for the countries of origin.

THE MIGRATION
MOVEMENTS TO
SOUTHEAST ASIA
AND AFRICA

1

Southeast Asia: A Preliminary Survey, 1800–1914

A. J. H. Latham

This essay should be read in conjunction with the chapters on population and migration in my books *The International Economy and the Undeveloped World, 1865–1914*, and *The Depression and the Developing World, 1914–1939*.[1] These outline the two main flows of migrants in Southeast Asia, from India and China. Indian migrants went to Burma, Ceylon, British Malaya, Mauritius, Fiji, the Caribbean, and East Africa, of which the first three were most important. The migrants went by sea, and were mostly employed in tropical plantations. Burma was the exception, and there the immigrants worked in the rice mills, on the docks, and harvesting rice. Indian migration was largely temporary, and often only seasonal, and Davis in the definitive study estimates that between 1834 and 1932 30 million left, of which 24 million returned, a net loss of approximately 6 million.[2] Chinese migrants went to Burma, Malaya, the Dutch East Indies, Siam, French Indo-China, and the Phillipines, with smaller flows to the United States, Australia and New Zealand, Cuba, and Hawaii. It was in Malaya that the flow of Indians eastward met the flow of Chinese westward. This Chinese migration has not been quantified so far, although

Purcell in his classic study does suggest that the Chinese were more numerous than the Indians in all the countries of Southeast Asia except Burma, and, by implication, Ceylon.[3] A rough estimate would suggest that at the outbreak of World War I, the Chinese population in Southeast Asia beyond China was about 2½ million. Siam led (792,000), followed by Malaya (693,000), the Dutch East Indies (563,000), French Indo-China (293,000), Burma (122,000), and the Phillipines (43,800).[4] The Chinese also went by sea, but their occupations in their new countries were more varied than those of the Indians. Mining, particularly tin mining, was of great importance in Malaya, Siam, and the Dutch East Indies, but the Chinese were also heavily involved in the rice trade, including milling, and the cultivation of sugar, coffee, rubber, pepper, and tobacco. They were also engaged in railway building and general crafts and trade.

The destination of the emigrants, and their activities in their countries of destination, have been given more attention than their origins. Who were the migrants, and why did they go? It is to these questions that the rest of this paper will be addressed.

With respect to Indian migration, Davis argued:

> It is doubtful if economic conditions in India have had any effect at all; we may assume, indeed, that the pressure to migrate, in an economic sense, has always been great enough to provide a stream of emigrants much larger than the actual stream, given the opportunity. In other words, the demand has been less than the supply.[5]

This view is explicitly challenged by Dharma Kumar in her work on Madras Presidency. She says it is not true that there was an ever-present pressure to migrate, checked only by government restrictions and the availability of opportunities abroad. For there were often spurts in migration after famines, such as the increase in migration from Madras after the great famine of 1874–78. But she does accept that movements in demand for labor abroad were more important than internal forces. She narrates that South Indian Tamils had been employed in the Straits Settlements as domestic servants and agricultural laborers before 1800, but it was the development of coffee plantations in Ceylon after 1830 that led to the systematic recruiting of indentured laborers in 1839. Thereafter probably 90 percent of migration from India to Ceylon was from Madras. Emigration reached a peak in 1877 following the great famine of 1874–78 but fell between 1880 and 1890 with the collapse of the coffee plantations. It revived as tea and rubber plantations were started.

Burma was the other main destination for migrants from Madras. Much of the migration to both countries was seasonal, but this cannot be distinguished from the statistics. It was a peculiarity of Ceylon that whole families went for short periods, as there was work there for women and children. Centers of migration changed in response to factors such as famines. In 1857 Tanjore, Trichinopoly, South Arcot, Vizagapatam, Rajahmundry, and Ganjam were the main origins of migrants, whereas in 1860–61 and 1861–62 they were Madura and Tinnevelly. In 1872 the main migration was from Godavari, Vizagapatam, Ganjam, Madras and Chingleput, whilst in 1881 it was from Madura, Tanjore, and Tinnevelly. In 1895, migration to Mauritius and Natal was largely from North Arcot and Chingleput. Generally speaking the coastal districts of Andhra supplied migrants to Burma, and the Tamil coastal districts, with South Arcot, to Ceylon. So Kumar's assertion that natural disasters such as famines were important appears to be confirmed. But in trying to get closer to the people who went, she is only able to say that, although migrants to Ceylon were mainly from the lower castes, including the agricultural labor castes, the evidence is too uncertain a basis for trying to estimate how many belonged to each category of caste. However, she is able to say that in 1834 migrants to Bourbon and Mauritius from Godaveri were washermen and weavers thrown out of work by the closing of the East India Company's factories, and in 1838 migrants from Godaveri to Mauritius were weavers, discharged sepoys, agricultural laborers, and "inferior servants." Weavers, washermen, tailors, and barbers went to Burma from Rajahmundry in 1840, and in 1863 the migrants from Vizagapatam to the French Colonies and Mauritius were mostly weavers, and there were no agricultural laborers. So it is clear that, although famine played its part, so did other sorts of economic distress.[6] The fact that weavers are mentioned so often confirms that one of the forces behind migration was the dislocation of the handloom cotton industry, as has often been asserted.[7]

Hugh Tinker, in his recent study on Indian migration, strangely makes no reference to Davis or Kumar, although he does locate the origin of more of the emigrants. From 1834 to about 1870 a large part of the flow via Calcutta was made up of Dhangars from Chota Nagpur, plus the down and outs of Calcutta and the nearby districts of the Twenty-Four Parganas. The Dhangars, known as "hill coolies," were the aboriginal inhabitants of the district, and the various invaders of India from the Indo-Aryans to the Mughals had not penetrated there. They were non-Hindus, and beyond the caste system, and had no dietary taboos. They and their neighbors the Santals were heavily recruited for the sugar plantations of Demerara and Mauritius. From the 1850s less were recruited because of their high death rate on the sea voyage, and because they began to find work on tea plantations to the north, and from the 1870s in coal mines close to their

Figure 1.1: Origins of Indian Emigrants

Main Districts of Recruitment

Note : each group is listed in order of concentration of recruitment

SOUTH INDIA

The Tamil Districts

A. Trichinopoly
B. Madura
C. Ramnad
D. Salem
E. Tanjore
F. Chingleput
G. North Arcot
H. South Arcot
I. Malabar
J. Tinnevelly

Telugu Districts

K. Vizagapatam
L. Ganjam
M. East Godavari
N. West Godavari
O. Guntur
P. Nellore

Bombay Presidency

Q. Ahmadnagar District

NORTH INDIA

Hill Coolie Districts

1. Santal Parganas
2. Hazaribagh
3. Ranchi
4. Manbhum
5. Birbhum
6. Singhbhum
7. Palamau

Bihari Districts

8. Shahabad
9. Patna
10. Gaya
11. Muzaffarpur
12. Champaran
13. Saran
14. Darbhanga
15. Monghyr

Districts of United Provinces

16. Ballia
17. Ghazipur
18. Azamghar
19. Fyzabad
20. Basti
21. Gonda
22. Gorakhpur
23. Banaras
24. Mirzapur
25. Jaunpur

Calcutta Metropolitan Area

26. Twenty Four Parganas

Source: Tinker, *A New System of Slavery,* p. 40.

14

home region. As the supply of hill coolies declined, drifters were persuaded to emigrate from the ports of Calcutta, Madras, and Bombay. These included cooks, footmen, washermen, grooms, coachmen, dancers, musicians, prostitutes, and simple countryfolk who had come to the city as bearers and burden carriers. Their recruitment began to concentrate on the region around Banares, from where migrants had been coming since a famine in the 1840s. In 1857 the main districts sending migrants to Calcutta were Banares itself, Asamgarh, Gorakhpur, and Jaunpur in the North-West Provinces, later the United Provinces, and Ghazipur, Muzaffarpur, Champaran, Shahabad, Patna and Gaya in Bengal Presidency, later Bihar. Others came from Hazaribagh and Chota Nagpur. The people of the Banaras districts were landless laborers who had lost their holdings to superior castes, because of the exactions placed upon them. In Bihar, a kind of semislavery existed by which poor people sold their services, and sometimes those of their children, for years ahead, just to exist. To them, migration was a preferable alternative. In 1883 two-thirds of the recruits via Calcutta were from the North-West Provinces and Oudh, a sixth from Bihar and Bengal, and a few from the Punjab, a pattern that lasted until the indenture system gave way to the contract system in the early years of the new century. As the Biharis increasingly found work in the factories of Calcutta, and the jute fields of eastern Bengal, an increasing proportion of migrants came from the United Provinces. In 1904 62 percent from Calcutta were from there, and another 17 percent from the Central Provinces, which had not previously been visited by the Calcutta recruiters. Only 6 percent were from Bihar. Increasingly recruiters concentrated on Fyzabad, Basti, and Gonda of the United Provinces, which were often exposed to famine, drought, and flood.

In the 1840s, demand from Mauritius was met to some extent from Bombay, but mainly from Madras. In the Tamil district Tinker suggests that the landless laborer could barely survive. The Untouchables, who made up almost a fifth of the population of Tamilnad, were almost slaves and welcomed any escape. The main recruiting areas were Tanjore, Trichinopoly, and South Arcot, and there was a flow from the Telegu districts of Visagapatam, Ganjam, and Rajahmundy. There were also probably Puliars and Mandavars, the aboriginal hill tribes of the region between Cochin and Travancore on the west coast. During the 1870s the flow from Madras grew as demand from Ceylon increased, and expanded further in the 1880s as Burma drew more people from the Telegu districts around Vizagapatam. In the 1880s about 60 percent of Madras emigrants went to Ceylon, nearly 30 percent to Burma, and the rest to Mauritius, the Straits Settlements, Natal, and the Caribbean. Only from the turn of the century did Malaya become a major destination, with the rubber boom, most of the laborers coming from Madras. In the early years of the new century migration was high from there, many being Untouchables.

Information about the social and caste composition of migrants from Calcutta is more complete than from Madras. In 1872–73 2,521 emigrants were from high castes, 4,974 from agricultural castes, 1,537 were artisans, and 5,309 were low caste. There were also 2,910 Muslims. In 1883, of the 7,695 Hindus embarked, 1,995 were Brahmans or other high-caste people, 2,454 were agriculturists, 456 artisans, and 2,790 low caste. So the emigration was a representative sample of the rural population of North India, excluding the trading, clerical, and priestly castes, and many of the really downtrodden, the sweeper folk, the lowest of the Untouchables. Overall, Tinker's view is that emigration depended on the need of people to obtain relief from an intolerable situation, so it coincides with Davis's view. Migrants came from the most overcrowded agricultural districts in India, where crop failure could bring sections of the village community close to starvation. Where Tinker differs from Davis, and comes closer to Dharma Kumar's position, is in arguing that departures were heaviest when harvests were poor. In 1860–61 there was a famine in the North-West Provinces, and a high departure from Calcutta. In 1865–66 famine in Bihar and Orissa brought high migration again from Calcutta, as did the scarcity in 1873–75 in Bihar, Oudh, and the North-West Provinces. There was famine in South India in 1874–78, bringing heavy migration from Madras.[8]

Burma was the leading destination for Indian emigrants, and Michael Adas has outlined their origins. Most were from Madras and Bengal, and he suggests that in the last twenty years of the century 60 percent came from Madras and between 25 and 30 percent from Bengal. Between 1891 and 1901 the Madras emigrants came from Tanjore, Ganjam, Godavari, Vizagapatam, Madras City, South Arcot, and Kistna on the east coast. But migrants from Bengal were more evenly spread out. Chittagong provided about 40 percent, and there were large numbers from the Puri district of Orissa, from Shahabad and Patna in Bihar, and from Calcutta and its neighborhood.

Adas asserts that the majority of Indians in Burma were from agricultural castes, or castes whose occupation was related to agriculture. The laborers on the wharves, in the rice mills and paddy fields, came almost entirely from these groups. North Indian agricultural castes were represented by the Kurmis from Bihar and the Jats, and there were Ahirs of upper India and Gwalas of Bihar, branches of the large north Indian cowherding caste. But the largest agricultural castes were the Untouchable castes of South India. Most important of these were the Pallis or Vanniyans, and the Paraiyans of the Tamil south, and the Malas from the Telegu districts. The other agricultural castes from South India were the "clean" Sudras, including the Kammas and Reddis, also called Kapus of the Telegu-speaking areas, and the Vellalas of Tamilnad. Many Kallans, professional thieves who had become big landholders in some Tamil districts, also went to Burma. The numerous Tamil and Telegu laborers made the Hindus predominant, in 1872 there being equal numbers of Hindus and Muslims, but in 1901 Hindus were 67 percent of the Indian population and Muslims 31 percent. The sex ratio of the Indian community was 4:1 and, due to caste restrictions on women traveling, it was higher in some groups, such as the migrants from Orissa, where it was 320:1. Many of the low-caste women from Oriya and Telegu were prostitutes. Few immigrants were from nonagricultural castes, but Kayasthas from North India and Brahmans held many of the posts in the provincial government. Brahmans were also prominent in the law, education, and medicine. Sikhs and Rajputs filled the army and police force, and Banias, Chatris, and Marwaris from the north were in finance and trade. So were the Nattukottai Tamil Chettiars, the Telugu Chetties, and Telugu Komatis from the south. Dhobis and Kahars provided domestic service.

The higher caste groups migrated for direct economic gain, but for the lower groups there were social reasons as well. The agricultural castes of the south were very poor, and the Malas of the Telegu areas and the Paraiyans of Tamilnad were Untouchables. The Palli or Vanniyan caste of the Tamilnad was not untouchable, but was as poor. Until 1843 Pallis and Paraiyans who were farm workers were almost slaves in many places, including Tanjore and South Arcot, and could be sold or mortgaged, a condition inherited by their children in many cases. Conditions were less hard in Telegu areas, but some Malas were held in hereditary service, for debt. Malas, Pallis, and Paraiyans who were free laborers were often worse off than those in service, as they found regular employment only during the busy seasons, finding casual employment on roads and public parks where they could at other times. When there was scarcity, they found jobs on government works, emigrated, or died. Migration gave them clear economic gain, even when there was no famine. In Burma, wage rates were paid according to work done, not to caste. In 1887 the highest wages in Madras Presidency were in Vizagapatam, where an agricultural laborer could expect Rs 72 per year. In Rangoon, industrial workers got Rs 270. Deducting Rs 30 for passage both ways, his net gain would be Rs 168. Although an agricultural worker only got Rs 180 a year, his net gain would still be Rs 78. So although the cost of living was higher in Burma, there were still clear economic advantages in migrating to work, and this advantage increased for those unlucky enough not to be in Vizagapatam.

Crucial to the migration to Burma was the introduction in 1861 of the first regular steamship service between Calcutta, Akyab, and Rangoon. But Burma attracted migrants even though Ceylon was closer for many, because the opportunities were better there, on the wharves, in the rice mills and paddy fields. Despite the underlying advantage in migration, specific events caused sudden surges. In 1865–66 there was large-scale emigration from Vizagapatam due to famine, and in 1885–86 and 1886–87 migration rose because of floods in Godaveri and Tanjore. In 1889 there was again famine around Vizagapatam, and in 1889–90 and 1890–91 there was famine in Ganjam. From 1890–91 to 1892–93 migration continued high because of floods in Tanjore, Godavari, and Shahabad, cholera in Ganjam, and in 1892 there were food shortages in Vizagapatam, and general scarcity in all Madras Presidency. There was a sharp rise in migration between 1895–96 and 1896–97, the period of the Great Famine. In 1898–99 and 1899–1900 migration was again high due to floods in South Arcot and Tanjore, plague in Shahabad, and cholera in Puri. The rise after 1902–3 resulted from floods, plague, and scarcity in Shahabad, floods in Patna and South Arcot, and a cyclone in Godavari. The increase in 1910 and 1911 came after severe food shortage and epidemics in Sultanpur, Fyzabad, and other areas of the United Provinces between 1907 and 1910. In addition a cyclone struck Ganjam, and floods caused shortages in Shahabad.[9]

Sandhu has indicated that migration to Malaya dates back to the early years of the nineteenth century. The early indentured laborers worked on sugar plantations, but nearly a third of them had not been agricultural workers, but weavers, oil millers, washermen, and cooks, and broke down when put to work. The government of India only allowed indentured migration from Madras Province and mostly they came from Tanjore, Trichinopoly, Madras, and sometimes Salem and Coimbatore. This was because Negapatam was the main port of exodus, and the recruiters operated chiefly in its hinterland. Madras occasionally was used, and illegal migration came from Karikal, Pandicherry, Cuddalore, Porto Novo, and Nagore.

Migration was low for much of the nineteenth century as both Burma and Ceylon offered better opportunities, the wage rate in Burma being double that in the Straits. The introduction of a regular steamship service in the 1870s helped, but the real breakthrough came in 1887 when a steamship subsidy cut the rate from Rs 15 to Rs 8, from Negapatam to Penang. Migration was to the sugar areas of Province Wellesley, Perak, and Negri Sembilan. But at the beginning of the new century the sugar industry collapsed due to competition from Europe and Java, leaving rubber plantations as the main employers. Indentured labor died out with the sugar plantations, and was replaced by free contract labor. A few hundred northern Indians were recruited in the early 1900s, Sikh and Rajput plate layers from the Punjab and Rajputana, Mahrattas from Bombay Province, Oriyas from Hydrabad State, and Bengalis from the Ganges valley, but most of the free laborers were Tamils and Telegus from the south, and some Malayalis from the Malabar coast. They came from North Arcot, Trichinopoly, Tanjore, Salem, Chingleput, and South Arcot. They were mostly from the lower castes, especially the Untouchables.

There were a few independent migrants, and the Northern Indians were the first commercial migrants, being Bengalis, Parsis, and Gujaratis. From the turn of the century they were overtaken by Sinhis, and Sikhs, with some Marwaris. But the majority of commercial immigrants also came from the south, Muslims from Malabar and the Coromandel Coast, and Chettiar Hindus. Mostly the commercial immigrants were salesmen, pedlars, traders, and shopkeepers. Merchants, financiers, and contractors of substantial means were a tiny minority, principally Chettiars, and Marakkayar Muslims of the Madras coast, and Parsis, Sinhis, and Sikhs. Indians also came to work in government departments, and there were skilled workmen, clerks, teachers, and doctors. Most of them also came from South India, Malayalis, and Tamils. There were some Bengalis from Calcutta and Dacca in this group, and some Punjabis. Many Sikhs from the Punjab were employed in the army and police force, as were Pathans, Punjabi Hindus and Muslims, Rajputs and Mahrattas.[10]

Migration from India to Burma, Ceylon, and Malaya, is shown on figures 1.2, 1.3, and 1.4. They show plainly the link between famine or disaster, and peaks in emigration. Yet underlying trends seem to have been more linked to demand for labor in the receiving countries. The rise in migration to Malaya as the rubber boom got under way brings this point out very clearly. The trough in migration to Ceylon in the 1880s supports this, it being the period of the collapse of the coffee industry. So migration seems to have taken place when there was a marked difference between economic opportunities in India and the country of destination. Burma, Ceylon, and Malaya received immigrants in that order of magnitude, because that was the order of magnitude of the opportunities between those countries. But despite differentials between India and the countries of destination, two other factors were important—the cost of transport and natural disaster. Migration increased as transport costs fell with cheaper steamship services, and in times of famine or disaster there were big increases in migration. As for the idea that the collapse of the domestic cotton industry was a force, this seems substantiated to a degree, particularly in the first half of the century. Weavers do seem to have migrated in large numbers. But the overwhelming majority of migrants in the

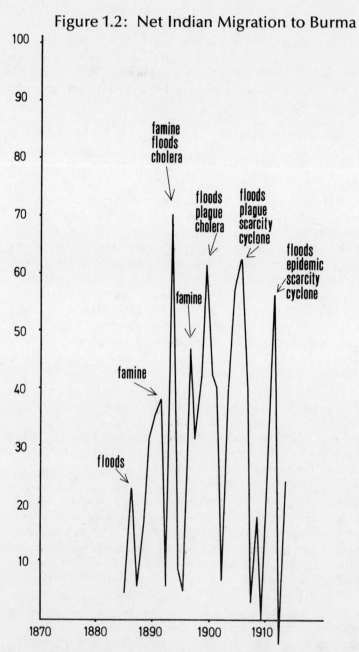

Figure 1.2: Net Indian Migration to Burma

Source: Siok-Hwa Cheng, *The Rice Industry of Burma, 1852–1940* (Kuala Lumpur: University of Malaya Press, 1968), p. 262. Adas, *Burma Delta*, pp. 96, 163.

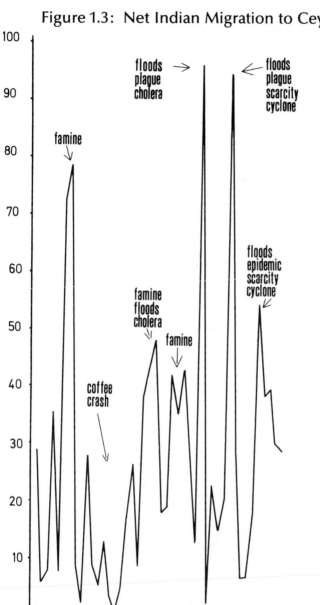

Figure 1.3: Net Indian Migration to Ceylon

Source: D. R. Snodgrass, *Ceylon: An Export Economy in Transition* (Homewood, Illinois: Richard D. Irwin, 1966), p. 308.

Figure 1.4: Net Indian Migration to Malaya

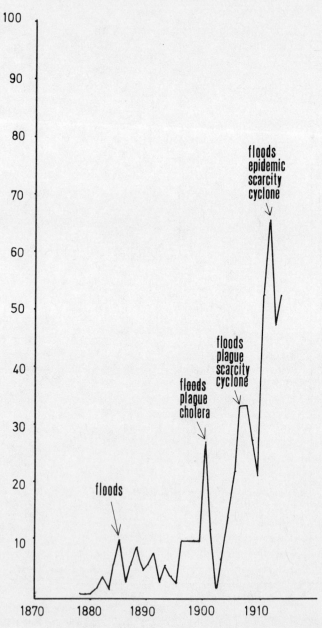

Source: Sandhu, *Indians in Malaya*, pp. 315–16.

Figure 1.5: Origins of Chinese Emigrants

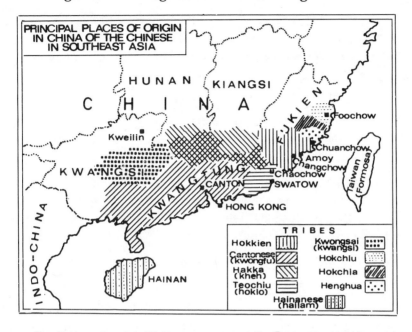

PRINCIPAL PLACES OF ORIGIN
IN CHINA OF THE CHINESE
IN SOUTHEAST ASIA

HUNAN   KIANGSI

C H I N A   FUKIEN   Foochow

Kweilin   Chuanchow
Amoy
K W A N G S I   Changchow Taiwan (Formosa)
KWANGTUNG   Chaochow
CANTON   SWATOW
HONG KONG

INDO-CHINA

HAINAN

TRIBES
Hokkien
Cantonese (kwongfu)
Hakka (kheh)
Teochiu (hoklo)
Hainanese (hailam)
Kwongsai (kwangsi)
Hokchiu
Hokchia
Henghua

The Hakkas often inhabit the same areas as the Cantonese, Hokkien, and other tribes.
The following authorities, among others, have been followed: (1) Linguistic Map of China, THE GEOGRAPHICAL JOURNAL, vol. cii, no. 2 (August 1943) p. 5; (2) Ta Chen, op. cit. p.23; (3) W.J. Cator, THE ECONOMIC POSITION OF THE CHINESE IN THE NETHERLANDS INDIES (Oxford, Blackwell, 1936) p.28(map).

Source: Purcell, *Chinese in Southeast Asia, p. 9.*

second half of the century were agricultural workers. The extent to which they were affected by the changes in cotton growing and home spinning through yarn imports from Lancashire, and later Bombay, is as yet unresearched.

If Indian migration is not well served by scholars, Chinese migration fares worse. Purcell's magnificent study has been mentioned, but it tells us little about the causes of Chinese migration and the fluctuations in flow over time. The main groups were the Kwong-Fu, Hokkien, Hakka, and Teochieu, from Kwantung and Fukien provinces, and the Hailams from Hainan. Of these only the Hokkien and Teochieu spoke mutually intelligible dialects. What drove them to migrate, and how did they choose their destinations?

Here Skinner's study of the Chinese in Siam throws more light than any other source. He suggests that the introduction of the sweet potato and peanut by the beginning of the seventeenth century led to population expansion in Kwantung and Fukien, where there was abundant hilly land unsuitable for rice. At the middle of the nineteenth century, China, then overpopulated, was moving out of a period of peace and prosperity, when underpopulated Siam was moving into a period of peace and prosperity. The Taiping rebellion of 1848–65 caused emigration as the rebels operated in Kwantung and Fukien, leaving famine and disease behind them. When the movement collapsed, many of its followers fled abroad. From 1855 Siam experienced enormous economic expansion through the production of rice for export, and although the Siamese were prepared to grow the paddy, they were content to leave the milling, transport, and marketing, to the Chinese immigrants. The Chinese also flocked in to work in the tin mines of Southern Siam, the teak sawmills, and to build canals and railways. Bangkok wage rates were the highest in the Far East. The Chinese grew sugar, vegetables, and fattened pork, and were artisans, retailers, wholesalers, and providers of personal services. Bangkok was the chief center of Chinese concentration, and the Chinese were probably half the population for much of the nineteenth century. The Teochieu were the leading revenue farmers and rice mill owners, with the Hokkiens next. The Teochieu also dominated most branches of trade, especially the rice trade, and the trade in other local products, besides imported textiles and Western foodstuffs. They were the leading pawnbrokers. It was the mechanization of rice milling that really explains the expansion of the Chinese population, as the mills were largely owned by Chinese who brought in workers to operate them. The entire rice trade was in Chinese hands, once the paddy had been bought from the Thai at the paddy fields.

Of vital importance to the distribution of the various Chinese clans overseas was the pattern of shipping services from their nearest port of departure. The establishment of Hong Kong in 1842 with its far-flung shipping connections, channeled the Kwong-Fu to distant places such as Australia and New Zealand. Because Canton and Amoy were treaty ports open to foreign shipping from 1842 to 1858, when Swatow and Hainan ports were not, the pattern of Kwong-Fu and Hokkien emigration in Southeast Asia was established before the Teochieu, Hakka, and Hailam emigrants were generally available. The Hokkien and Kwong-Fu dominated everywhere except Siam and Cambodia. Only when emigration from Hong Kong and Macao to Peru, Cuba, the United States, the Hawaiian Islands, Australia, and other distant places was stopped in 1882 was the stream of Kwong-Fu migrants redirected to Southeast Asia. Because by 1870 regular steamship services ran from Amoy to Singapore and Manila, but not to Bangkok, the Hokkien were disproportionately directed to the Philippines, and the areas served by Singapore, Malaya, South

Siam, Java, Sumatra, and Burma. However, Hainan was close to foreign shipping, so for the first three-quarters of the nineteenth century the Hailams could get as far as Bangkok by junk. But Swatow was the nearest port of departure for the Hakkas and Teochieus, and it was not until regular steamship services began between Swatow and Bangkok in 1882 that they began to come to Siam in numbers. When regular steamship services from Haikow to Bangkok began in 1886, more Hailams flooded into Siam. So the introduction of steamshipping between South China and the recipient countries between 1865 and 1886 determined the migration of the various Chinese clans. Recruitment procedures in China became regularized in the 1880s, and malpractices in the passenger traffic from Chinese ports were suppressed.

Nineteenth-century Chinese emigrants were "contract" or "indentured," "credit ticket," and free. The indentured or contract migration was associated with the coolie traffic to the West Indies and Peru, the Dutch East Indies, and Malaya. Siam migrants mostly went by credit ticket, passage payments being made by friends or relatives for whom the newcomer worked until the debt was paid. This became over the years a very organized business, with agencies linking those needing hands in Bangkok to potential migrants in China, via subagencies linked to lodging houses. Skinner suggests that 6,000 to 8,000 a year were emigrating to Siam in the 1820s, and this rose gradually to 16,000 in the 1880s. From 1882 most migrants went on European steamers, and the Chinese customs returns became more accurate. There was a high turnover, as in the case of Indian migration, and the relaxation of emigration controls increased the rate of return, as people no longer had broken laws to leave in the first place.

Skinner's figures are shown on figure 1.6. They are based on the Swatow-Bangkok, and Haikow-Bangkok migrations. The relatively high level of the early 1880s was due to the new steamer services between Bangkok and Swatow, and the sharp reduction in fares. Between lines going to the Straits and to Bangkok there was a price war that pushed rates down. When the lines colluded, rates rose and the migration fell away. From 1884 to 1888 migration remained low because the labor market was flooded in Bangkok from the previous rush, and in 1884 French hostilities hindered migration from Hainan.

A ban on the credit-ticket system at Swatow in 1888 hindered migration, but it was compensated for by a big increase from Hainan when steamer passages really began. This continued into 1889, and was augmented by a bigger flow from Swatow, where the credit-ticket ban was enforced less rigorously. The decline in 1891 was due to business depression in Bangkok. The law prohibiting emigration and return from China was finally repealed in 1893, and the rise of 1894 was the result of demand

Figure 1.6: Net Chinese Migration to Siam

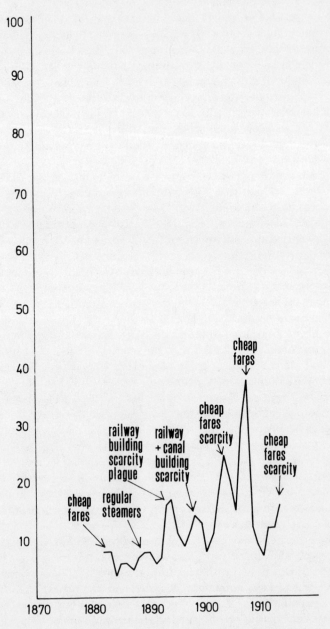

Source: Skinner, *Chinese Society in Thailand*, p. 61.

for laborers on the railway from Bangkok to Ayutthaya at a time when the sweet potato crop failed in Chaochow.

The same year bubonic plague in Hong Kong led to Singapore's being closed to Chinese ports, and migrants were diverted to Bangkok. When Singapore reopened in 1895 the numbers going to Bangkok declined again. The rise from 1897 was related to demand for workers on railway and canal construction, and in the rice mills. In 1898 and 1899 poor crops in Hainan caused increased migration, but plague in Swatow and Haikow led to a fall due to quarantine restrictions. In 1901 migration recovered as regulations were lifted, and in 1902 food shortages and high prices in Swatow and Hainan caused more to migrate. The year 1903 saw a spectacular rise as there was a price war between the lines on the Bangkok-Swatow route, but when this ended in 1904 prices rose and migration fell.

Price wars in 1906–7 and 1907–8 also brought high migration. When they ended and prices rose, migration again declined. The big increase in 1909–10 and 1910–11 was due to bad crops in Hainan, and another fare war on the Bangkok-Swatow run. The year 1910 also saw the end of all legal obstacles to emigration from China. But net figures were affected by high departures from Siam for 1910–11 because of the introduction of an annual tax on Chinese there, and racial tension between Chinese and Thai. This coincided with good harvests in Hainan in 1911–12 and 1912–13, the 1912 harvest being the best rice harvest there for twenty years.

From this it can be seen that the emigration rate was very responsive to circumstances in China and Siam. In China, the state of the crops was the most important factor, whilst in Siam the demand for labor was paramount. Migration was also very sensitive to the cost of passage. The lower the price, the more the migrants. Most of the migrants to Siam were poor, and had been agricultural workers or peasants in China. They went to Siam as laborers. Their chief motivation was desire for economic improvement, but often they were driven out by particular natural disasters.[11]

Wickberg's book on the Chinese in the Philippines confirms that the steamship links determined the clans which dominated a particular region. In the Philippines, the establishment of regular services between Amoy, Hong Kong, and Manila in the 1870s gave the Hokkiens preeminence, followed by the Cantonese. The voyage only took three days, and steerage rates were low. The Chinese were importers of rice. There was a kinship migration as Chinese who had established themselves sent home for teen-aged sons or nephews, and there was coolie immigration, as foreign businesses needed men for labor gangs, or door-to-door salesmen.[12] Wang Gungwu confirms that the Hokkiens were the majority in the Philippines, and also in Java, although it was the Hokkiens and the Teochieus in the

Straits.[13] Certainly the Hokkiens were the largest group in the Dutch East Indies, where they were the most active and most successful traders. There were Teochieus, who specialized in agriculture, there. The Hakkas were also there. They came from the barren mountainous region of Kwantung, and were not a maritime group. They were forced to migrate through poverty, and were the poorest of all the migrant groups from China. They went first to the outer islands of the Dutch East Indies, to work the mines, and to this day are the major influence in Chinese society in the former gold-mining districts of West Borneo. The contemporary dialect of the tin-mining island of Bangka is derived from Hakka. The Kwong-Fu too were mine workers and went to Bangka. They were usually wealthier and had more skills than the Hakka.[14]

So although much more research needs to be done on the Chinese migration movement, we do have a little more understanding of the forces behind it. As with the Indians, adversity and economic opportunity were the key factors, with cheap steamship fares playing a part. A study dealing with Chinese emigration in the interwar years commented that, on the basis of the replies of a large sample of emigrant families, clearly adversity was the driving force, the attraction of opportunities overseas being the principal motivation in a smaller number of cases. Natural calamities such as floods played a prominent role.[15] It has been suggested that the disintegration of the domestic cotton industry in China was a key factor in the migration, as has been alleged in the case of India. It was not so much the problems of the weaving industry that provoked migration, but the import of yarn, first from Lancashire, then from Bombay, and later from Japan. Those peasants whose subsistence margin depended on the income from growing cotton and spinning yarn were driven below the subsistence level when this income disappeared, and migration became their only hope.[16] But there is nothing to confirm or deny this idea. So, as in India, where weavers certainly did leave, it may have been part of the story.

At the end of the day, the migrant communities of India and China before World War I, were acting with economic rationality to the opportunities created by the expanding international market. If often adversity drove them out, cheap fares and the availability of economic opportunity determined where they went.

References

1. A. J. H. Latham, *The International Economy and the Undeveloped World, 1865–1914* (London: Croom Helm, Ltd., and Totowa, N.J.: Rowman and Littlefield, 1978), pp. 103–21. A. J. H. Latham, *The Depression and the Developing World, 1914–1939* (London: Croom Helm, Ltd., and Totowa, N.J.: Barnes and Noble, 1981) pp. 132–51.

2. Kingsley Davis, *The Population of India and Pakistan* (Princeton, N.J.: Princeton University Press, 1951), pp. 13, 99.

3. Victor Purcell, *The Chinese in Southeast Asia* (London: Oxford University Press, 1951), p. 691.

4. Latham, *International Economy*, pp. 105, 109, 113; Latham, *Depression*, pp. 143–44; G. William Skinner, *Chinese Society in Thailand: An Analytical History* (Ithaca, N.Y.: Cornell University Press, 1957), p. 79.

5. Davis, *Population and India*, p. 99.

6. Dharma Kumar, *Land and Caste in South India: Agricultural Labour in the Madras Presidency during the Nineteenth Century* (Cambridge: Cambridge University Press, 1965), pp. 128–39.

7. Latham, *International Economy*, pp. 109, 150.

8. Hugh Tinker, *A New System of Slavery: The Export of Indian Labour Overseas, 1830–1920* (London: Oxford University Press, 1974), pp. 46–60, 118–20, 273.

9. Michael Adas, *The Burma Delta: Economic Development and Social Change on an Asian Rice Frontier, 1852–1941* (Madison, Wisc.: University of Wisconsin Press, 1974), pp. 85–102, 162.

10. K. S. Sandhu, *Indians in Malaya: Some Aspects of Their Immigration and Settlement, 1786–1957* (Cambridge: Cambridge University Press, 1969), pp. 57–99, 115–25.

11. Skinner, *Chinese Society in Thailand*, pp. 29–35, 47–53, 57–67, 78–80, 104–15. 136; Charles A. Price, *The Great White Walls Are Built: Restrictive Immigration to North America and Australia, 1836–1888* (Canberra: Australian National University Press, 1974).

12. Edgar Wickberg, *The Chinese in Philippine Life, 1850–1898* (New Haven, Conn.: Yale University Press, 1965), pp. 103, 119–23, 169–72, 177.

13. Wang Gungwu, *A Short History of the Nanyang Chinese* (Singapore: Eastern University Press, 1959), pp. 30–31.

14. G. William Skinner, "The Chinese Minority," in Ruth T. VcVey (ed.), *Indonesia* (New Haven, Conn.: Yale University Press, 1963), pp. 102–3.

15. Ta Chen, *Emigrant Communities in South China: A Study of Overseas Migration and Its Influence on Standards of Living and Social Change* (New York: Institute of Pacific Relations, 1940), pp. 259–61.

16. Latham, *International Economy*, pp. 109, 150, 157; Albert Feuerwerker, *The Chinese Economy c. 1870–1911* (Ann Arbor, Michigan: Michigan University Press, 1969), pp. 17–58; Ta Chen, *Emigrant Communities*, p. 99.

2

Batavia, 1673–1790: A City of Colonial Growth and Migration

Frank Spooner

The foundation of a colonial capital marks an important moment in the economic balance of the continents—and no less, as the decades pass, in the structure of human settlement. The arrival of Europeans in Asia proved no exception, for their strategy of colonial trade soon created foci of both influence and attraction. The early initiative of the Portuguese opted for Goa to take over the pepper trade of the Malabar coast. Other European enterprise settled for Manila, Macao, Pondicherry, Calcutta—all of which represented significant commitments of time, men, and money. Among these vintage assets, Batavia found its place and grew through commercial expansion and human renewal into a major city of settlement among the peoples, creeds, and powers of Asia.

Batavia (now Djakarta) was founded on 30 May 1619 by Jan Pietersz. Coen, the governor-general of the Verenigde Oostindische Compagnie (United East India Company—VOC). From an earlier concession (1610) by the king of Jakarta,[2] he made a fortress at the mouth of the river Chiliwong, adjacent to an old Javan settlement—and the good fortune of Djakarta. The VOC could then consolidate the new southern sea route from the Cape of Good Hope and gain control of the Sunda Strait, one of the two channels of access to the Malay Archipelago and the South China Sea.[3] In no time at all, Batavia held off attacks and transformed the old community into one of the great cities of the world. By the 1770s, it was the second city of the Netherlands world-system,[4] behind Amsterdam to be sure, but three times the size of Rotterdam, four times that of The Hague, and on a par with some of the bright lights of Europe: Madrid, Lyons, Venice.[5] Almost without saying, the city quickly adopted the style of the Netherlands, translated into a tropical setting, with walls and bastions, stadhuis and armories, tree-lined canals, churches, markets, banks, and soon, too, one of the finest botanical gardens in the five continents. First and foremost, Batavia marked Dutch power and prestige in a network of trade stretching from Persia to the Moluccas and from Ceylon to Japan.[6] It won recognition as Queen of the Orient; but for others it remained in grim silence the Dutchman's grave.

The formation of this system of trade and influence was largely settled within a half century of the foundation of Batavia, by the date for the beginning of this study. With Ceylon (1640) and Malacca (1641) firmly in hand the VOC held the strategic routes of Asia. Sea power completed the investment of the Archipelago, and one after another rulers and colonial powers soon came to terms of dependence or exclusion; in 1657–63, Ternate and Tidore; in 1667, the Treaty of Breda excluded the English East India Company from the profitable Moluccas; in 1668, the Treaty of Bongaja broke the monopoly of Macassar over Sumbawa.[7] And then the infiltration of Java and its adjacent islands proceeded apace. To the west, the port and market of the old muslim sultanate, Bantam, succumbed after the war of 1682–84. To the east, the same exercise of dominance saw the acquisition of Preanger (1677). The Treaty of 1705 furthered the breakup of the muslim sultanate of Mataram and put Java under the control of the VOC, confirmed in the subsequent Treaty of Surakarta (1755). By the middle of the eighteenth century, the Archipelago had settled into three great zones: to the north with Sumatra and Borneo; to the east with the islands of Celebes and the Moluccas; and then the heartland of Java. Few of the islands managed to survive in independence. Under the aegis of trade and navy, the system of the VOC adopted the complexion of a multi-ethnic, multiconfessional, multilingual empire.

The assertion of power dismantled many old associations, or rather continued the resettlements that had progressed over the centuries. Batavia became a notable center of attraction. In 1775, William Herbert noted that "the road is always full of ships, of all the Indian nations, who come hither to trade."[8] At the close of the eighteenth century, the profits of the VOC in the city were not always high, for a balance of trading such as in December

1779[9] gave Batavia a mere 9½ percent return on capital compared with more favorable results from India (Surat 118.5 percent; Ceylon 122.7 percent; Bengal 151.5 percent). Even Java (with 73.6 percent) and Amboina (with 73.5 percent) offered better prospects.

Over the years, the city absorbed streams of migrants from Asia. Like so many preindustrial settlements, it survived on suppliants from a wide hinterland. The pull factors of trade and the push factors of political and social reformation combined to mingle tribes and societies. The experience of Batavia, therefore, relayed older circuits and contacts among the varieties of lineage, customs, and bondage. Islam had long since spread a carpet of distinctive civilization. Portugal had formed a structure of mercantile customs and language to leave an indelible human witness. Ethnic strata, already complex, found further expression in floating populations lost to their origins but now opting for a place in the fresh systems of colonial enterprise. The population of Batavia emerged as a living document of such huge and multifarious transformations. This evolution affected the urban shape and plan; the size and growth of numbers; and the location and ethnic composition of the inhabitants. The city became a meeting place for old and elaborate civilizations to take another shape in history.

The fortress of Batavia at the mouth of the Chiliwong River dominated the early development of the city.[10] Until 1741 it remained the residence of the governor-general, and at the same time flourished both as the center of administration in Asia, and as the strongbox for the valuables of the VOC. It molded the old, adjacent community of Jakarta into the style of a Dutch town, not a "dam-town," but astride the river—the *Grote Rivier*—the axis of the settlement.

The progression was astonishing, sustained by the impetus of colonial expansion invested with the techniques of urban engineers from the Netherlands. The manuscript map of 1629 puts the settlement in perspective.[11] The fortress occupied the shore, protected by a moat of tidal water and reached by a bridge. At that time, the city had an irregular shape but was already endowed with walls and canals, notably the Tijgersgracht. The main settlement came on the right bank, opposite the English house.[12] Beyond the walls to the east lay patches of swamp and scrub; to the west rice fields. The river meandered through to the sea, offering access to trade. Later maps in the seventeenth century show the river to have been straightened,[13] and this can also be seen in figure 2.1. The accuracy of detail in the 1629 version admittedly leaves much to be desired, but the original shape (rather than the position) of the river course is clear enough. On the left-hand bank to the west, the port facilities of the

Company, the Chinese wharf, timber-yard, and hospital. Pedro Barreto de Resende in his *Livro do Estado da India Oriental* (c. 1634) indicates anchors, timber, guns, and a crane.[14] Beeckman's painting (1656) gives a view across the fish market and river.[15] And later, James Cook on his voyage of discovery (1770) declared that for ship repairs no marine yard could match the facilities of Batavia.[16] To the south, the *voorstad* (suburb) occupied the loop of the river. The descriptions convey a picture of growing size, spreading beyond the walls, toward the east with the River Antjol, but also to the south and west. The inner city had acquired a formal, geometric plan; the main river was supplemented by side canals to the east and west parallel to the river, skirting the walls, and emptying into the sea. These waterways created a virtual delta.

The inner city soon lived up to this allotted space. There was some possibility of extension in the direction of the sea, for Batavia suffered from a problem besetting many preindustrial maritime cities: the accumulation of silt.[17] The disturbances of mud through canal building added to the scour of the river and the debris brought down by earthquakes. Successive maps point to the real cost to the city. That of 1681 already featured the spreading mudflats and mangrove swamps well advanced from the old shoreline.[18] In the mideighteenth century (see figure 2.1) the outport of Batavia stretched well beyond the old fort, no longer surrounded by a moat of seawater but now part of the canal system. A breakwater guarded access to the channel and fairway. At the same time, typical husbandry soon drained the new land and provided it even with residences and pleasure gardens.

The limits to the city created the twin problems of crowding and pollution. As the size of the population grew, so the pressure on the inner city increased. Stagnant water in the canals became breeding grounds for disease, above all malaria: the epidemic of 1731–32 was a notable case;[19] and that of 1778 carried off 300 citizens a week.[20] The description by some that the city was a Dutchman's grave had more than literary license.

From early days the Company was alert to the dangers and earmarked levies for cleansing the river and canals—in 1633, for example,[21] and, after 1698, for extensive river operations. In the three decades to 1730, some 531,558 guilders[22] were laid out in clearing the blocked fairway.[23] The removal of the bar required dredging machines, in operation from 1703 to 1714.[24] Another 188,809 guilders were spent on the canals both in and outside the city. Further work in 1742, after the riots of 1740, aimed to deal with the canals and the sandbank in the estuary.[25] A later project of 1778–79 to improve the flow of water through the city and its precincts brought experts from the Netherlands; but their efforts were hampered by tidal water and ultimately proved disappointing. Access by ships through

Figure 2.1: Batavia in 1629 and 1762

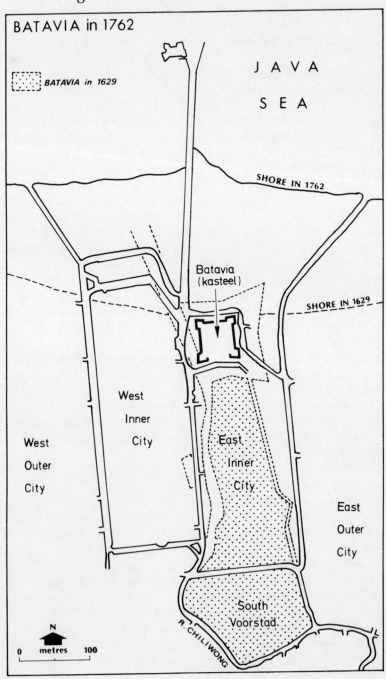

BATAVIA in 1762

BATAVIA in 1629

J A V A

S E A

SHORE IN 1762

Batavia
(kasteel)

SHORE IN 1629

West
Inner
City

West
Outer
City

East
Inner
City

East
Outer
City

South
Voorstad

R. CHILIWONG

N

0   metres   100

the breakwaters half a mile out to sea required the unremitting labor of gangs of slaves.[26] All added up to a serious effort to maintain, to restore the flagging fortunes of the city and make it once more a powerful center of trade.[27] At the going technology, Batavia faced the built-in retardation that often dogged the commercial survival of preindustrial cities.

How then did the number of inhabitants in Batavia increase? Our data derive, at least in part, from the policy of the authorities to control the inhabitants as the population lived up to the resources within the walls. In 1657, Joan Maetsuyker, the governor-general (1653–1678), organized the city into quarters. Each block had a *wijkmeester* (block master) and was numbered and lettered. In addition, the city was divided into zones: an east side; a west side; and the suburb to the south, originally "outside the city" but now brought in as the south inner city.[28] The incomplete record of these divisions in 1657 gives five sections, as shown in table 2.1.

Table 2.1
CITY ZONES—1657

	Zone	*No. of blocks*
1	East side	7
2	(presumably also East side)	[9]
3	West side	13
4	South/voorstad	[1]
5	Outside the south/voorstad	15

By the early eighteenth century, the situation had settled: table 2.2 shows number of blocks under *wijkmeesteren* who were named in the report of 1730.[29]

Table 2.2
CITY ZONES—1730

Zone	*No. of blocks*
Inner city	
East side	16
West side	13
South/voorstad	1
Outer city	
East	18
West	13

The counts were made separately for inner and outer Batavia, and these were each copied onto large sheets for despatch with the returning fleets to the Netherlands. The report for 1673 appears to be one of the first surviving records, but by the turn of the century the reports were an annual routine.

The list for the inner city was closed on 31 December; that for the outer city a month later. In 1720, for example, Frederick Repertus authenticated the latter reports, which he "reconciled" with the main lists of the block-masters returned to the college of the *Heeren* (Masters).[30] In consequence, a month's discrepancy exists between the two lists in making totals for the city, but as they appeared annually there is reasonable internal consistency. As in any colonial situation, the control and tabulation of large and fluctuating numbers of people of different societies and creeds presented a huge problem, and has no doubt led to margins of error. Nevertheless, from early days the VOC appointed heads or consuls of the different ethnic groups, and this aided the accuracy of the reports. Even so, as Alfred Sauvy has often said, the going demography was little more than prestatistical;[31] but the counts for Batavia have special interest in listing the inhabitants by location, ethnic group, sex, and age. This forms the basis of the present study. In order to ascertain the trends, I have taken sample years at decade intervals.[32] The first four (1673, 1680, 1691, 1701) improved in coverage. After 1701, the reports became routine administration and arrived regularly in the Netherlands.

Over the whole period 1673–1790, there is consistent information for the inner city. In 1673 the three zones contained 18,895 inhabitants (see table 2.3). The rate of growth from the original foundation no doubt followed a logistic curve and tended to a limit with the opening of the eighteenth century. By 1710, the numbers leveled out to 20,860. Then came a further increase to 23,340 in 1730 (maximum in 1728: 24,082). At this level, the inner city reached its boundary. The 1730s showed a sagging trend, and by 1739 the numbers were back to those of 1710. Then came a first recession following the riot and massacre of October 1740. The count of 1740 showed a drop of a third of the population. Apart from a slight recovery in the 1750s (1760: 16,785), the numbers in the inner city continued to decline so that by 1790, the returns gave a figure of 8,138, a third of the peak of 1728. The south side was apparently less affected: it started the century with a share of 8.4 percent, but by 1790, had increased this to 24.1 (see figure 2.2 and table 2.4).

As the inner city declined, so the growing population found its quarters beyond the walls or in the outer city. The totals in the first two samples, 1673 and 1680, probably underestimated the numbers of Javanese/Balinese and slaves living in these zones. However, the count of

1691 returned a total of 47,728 almost equally divided between east and west. By 1720 the total had grown to 90,088 and the balance remained for some time. Then, through the 1730s, as the immigration of Chinese increased, the west side grew. This side suffered most after the events of 1740, but within a decade had recovered. By 1780 the outer city counted 129,943, of whom two-thirds lived on the west side.

The combined totals for the inner and outer cities thus show growth through the eighteenth century but with two reverses: first, in the break of 1740, but the progression had regained its trend-path by 1760; second, the decline at the close of the century. The total population reached 151,759 in 1779. The recession derived no doubt from a number of causes, partly from disruptions during the Fourth Anglo-Dutch War (1780–1784); but also from water-borne epidemics, which specialist canal engineers from the Netherlands were unable to remedy. When renewed growth came in the nineteenth century, the focus moved in particular to Weltevreden, a new area of settlement in the south linked to the old city by the Molenvliet. Early in the next century, Batavia could claim a population of over a quarter of a million (1924: 282,069), so that some of its rapid expansion came under the direction of the VOC.

Table 2.3

POPULATION OF BATAVIA BY ZONES

	Inner city				Outer city			Total
	East	West	South	Total	East	West	Total	
1673	7,905	9,852	1,138	18,895	5,183	3,030	8,173	27,068
1680	8,535	9,873	1,674	20,082	2,560	8,098	10,658	30,740
1691	8,129	10,907	[1,710]	[20,746]	23,671	24,057	47,728	[68,474]
1701	8,014	11,040	1,746	20,800	24,422	24,550	48,972	69,772
1710	7,880	10,725	2,255	20,860	26,254	32,507	58,761	79,621
1720	8,549	11,083	2,664	22,296	34,185	33,607	67,792	90,088
1730	9,158	11,271	2,908	23,337	36,144	44,612	80,756	104,093
1740	6,285	6,497	1,353	14,135	37,512	34,994	72,506	86,641
1750	5,318	6,462	2,498	14,278	36,799	43,898	80,697	94,975
1760	6,188	7,351	3,246	16,785	36,553	72,840	109,393	126,178
1770	4,226	5,989	2,944	13,159	40,724	83,145	123,869	137,028
1780	4,450	5,749	2,452	12,651	32,502	97,441	129,943	142,594
1790	2,438	3,737	1,963	8,138	45,084	81,515	126,599	134,737

Note: In the count of 1691 there is no mention of the voorstad. However, the trends in the east and west sides of the city seem consistent; so I have entered a figure of 1,710 (the average of 1680 and 1701), which has accordingly raised the totals to 20,746 (inner city) and 68,474 (total population).

Table 2.4

DISTRIBUTION OF THE POPULATION OF BATAVIA BY ZONE
(PERCENTAGES)

	Inner city				Outer city		
	East	West	South	Total	East	West	Total
1691	11.87	15.93	2.50	30.30	34.57	35.13	69.70
1701	11.49	15.82	2.50	29.81	35.00	35.19	70.19
1710	9.90	13.47	2.83	26.20	32.97	40.83	73.80
1720	9.49	12.30	2.96	24.75	37.95	37.30	75.25
1730	8.80	10.83	2.79	22.42	34.72	42.86	77.58
1740	7.25	7.50	1.56	16.31	43.50	40.39	83.69
1750	5.60	6.80	2.63	15.03	38.75	46.22	84.97
1760	4.90	5.83	2.57	13.30	28.97	57.73	86.70
1770	3.08	4.37	2.15	9.60	29.72	60.68	90.40
1780	3.12	4.03	1.72	8.87	22.79	68.34	91.13
1790	1.81	2.77	1.46	6.04	33.46	60.50	93.96

This growth made Batavia a cosmopolitan city, under the rule of an élite of
Europeans. Like other preindustrial cities, it relied on migration from
outside and absorbed populations formed from earlier dominant cultures.
The very nature of colonial success implied the disruption of existing
societies and their circuits of migration. New flows to Batavia soon made
their presence in the lists of the wijkmeesteren, which bore witness to a
city of ethnic groups.

In pride of first place came the Dutch. At least, in the early counts,
for after 1700 those living in the inner city were named as Europeans; in
the outer city, they remained *Nederlanders*. This distinction probably reflected an important characteristic of the VOC, which came to rely increasingly on the services of aliens. In 1691, they formed a fifth of the
company's servants; in 1778 two-thirds, including many German sol-
diers.[33] This tendency finds confirmation in the lists of burgesses. In the
eighteenth century the candidates came from Germany, Switzerland,
Scandinavia, Poland, Russia, the southern Netherlands, France, Sur-
inam, the Cape colony, from Asia itself.[34] In the decade 1750–59, out of a
total of 351 new burgesses only 29 percent named a birthplace in the
Netherlands. They were often a skilled élite: Breuning notes that a large
part of the contingent provided craftsman services: in 1674, about 240 out
of 340 came into this category.[35]

However, as the city grew, the Europeans became or rather remained
an increasingly small minority that kept its place with some difficulty. In
1691, they represented 3.54 percent, in 1701, 3.12 percent of the population; at the end of the century the count of 1790 showed them to have a

Figure 2.2: Batavia: population

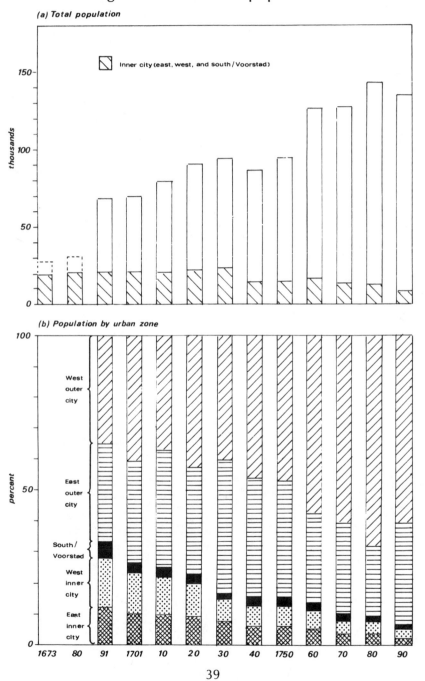

(a) Total population

☒ Inner city (east, west, and south / Voorstad)

(b) Population by urban zone

West outer city

East outer city

South / Voorstad

West inner city

East inner city

1673 80 91 1701 10 20 30 40 1750 60 70 80 90

39

Figure 2.3: Batavia: migration

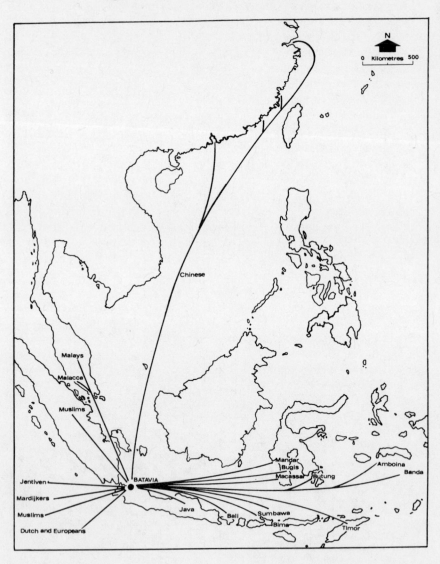

mere 0.89 percent. In absolute numbers they were down to half the total in 1691. The fall was most apparent in the inner city for, while 78.07 percent of the Europeans lived there in 1691, only 58.65 percent did so in 1790. No doubt the unhealthy old quarters were to blame, for the Europeans tended to prefer the east side, which held the largest numbers of the five zones. But the count of 1790 showed a change for the first time, heralding a move to the growing residential zone in the south.

The counts of men, women, and children (separate totals for boys and girls, both over and under fourteen years of age) give some insights into the family structures of the expatriates. Colonial service tended to favor single male migrants, and the Europeans in Batavia proved no exception. Although at first the VOC encouraged the family, unfavorable conditions gradually militated against this. In 1701, the ratio of men to women was 1.36 (see table 2.5); in 1760, 2.84; and in 1790, 2.32. In the same line, the ratio of children over fourteen to women moved from 0.56 in 1701 to 0.26 in 1790. And the shift was even more dramatic for children under fourteen: 0.89 to 0.38, respectively. Total children to women moved from 1.45 to 0.65 over the same period. This may explain, along with the high mortality among Europeans, the prominence of payments from Batavia to the various *weeskamer* (orphan asylum) in the Netherlands.

After the Netherlanders came the Eurasians: *mestiezen*. At first, the VOC established rigorous codes of conduct for its servants. In 1615 they could not marry without the permission of the governor-general; in 1635 and 1636 Eurasian women were forbidden to arrive with their husbands; in 1645 marriage between Christians and non-Christians was forbidden; and concubinage was likewise prohibited.[36] However, the entries for mixed race were a significant, although declining, part of Batavia's population (see figure 2.4 and tables 2.6 and 2.7). They hovered around a thousand for most of the period but after 1760 fell away to reach 413 in 1790. Initially, most lived in the inner city, but in the middle decades of the eighteenth century there was a rough equality between inner and outer zones, with the latter gaining toward the 1780s.

Table 2.5

EUROPEANS—SEX AND FAMILY RATIOS

	Men to women	All children to women	Children over 14 to women	Children under 14 to women
1701	1.36	1.45	0.56	0.89
1730	1.74	1.19	0.42	0.76
1760	2.84	1.19	0.33	0.85
1790	2.32	0.65	0.26	0.38

Figure 2.4: Batavia: population by ethnic groups

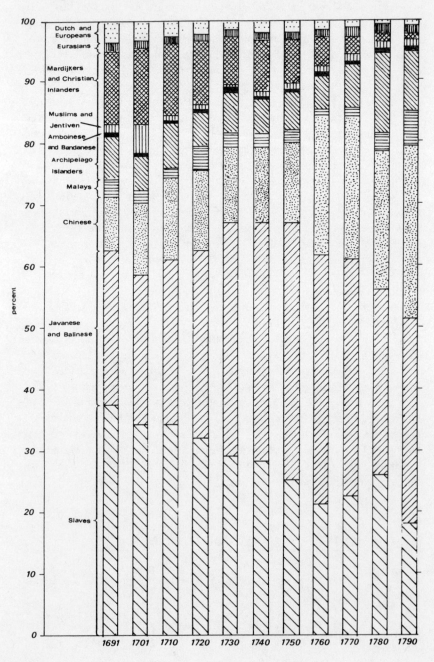

Table 2.6

POPULATION OF BATAVIA BY ETHNIC GROUP

Groups	1691	1701	1710	1720	1730	1740	1750	1760	1770	1780	1790
Dutch/Europeans	2,362	2,175	2,084	1,971	1,677	1,695	1,833	2,034	1,511	1,025	1,197
Eurasians	986	927	1,012	1,147	1,126	1,029	1,046	1,101	893	608	413
Mardijkers/Christian Inlanders	7,883	8,604	9,021	8,970	7,929	7,081	6,789	6,330	5,222	3,922	2,895
Chinese	5,668	8,137	10,710	11,724	12,873	10,774	12,255	28,348	32,009	32,238	37,682
Muslims/Jentiven	838	3,196	677	644	568	829	1,026	1,461	1,752	1,419	1,611
Amboinese/Bandanese	440	438	261	387	789	234	249	588	399	754	706
Islanders from Bima, Bone, Bonerate, Butung, Macassar, Mandar, Sumbawa, Timor	4,634	3,683	5,934	5,201	6,699	5,159	5,982	6,609	9,624	18,513	13,128
Malays	1,954	1,588	1,267	3,526	2,661	1,726	1,986	1,537	1,891	4,120	7,593
Javanese/Balinese	16,718	17,050	21,397	27,569	39,442	33,485	39,834	51,396	52,629	42,788	44,682
Slaves	25,281	23,974	27,258	28,949	30,329	24,629	23,975	26,773	31,098	37,207	24,830
Total	*66,764	69,772	79,621	90,088	104,093	86,641	94,975	126,178	137,028	142,594	134,737

*Unadjusted total (see table 2.3).

43

Table 2.7

DISTRIBUTION OF THE POPULATION OF BATAVIA BY ETHNIC GROUP (PERCENTAGES)

Groups	1691	1701	1710	1720	1730	1740	1750	1760	1770	1780	1790
Dutch/Europeans	3.54	3.12	2.62	2.19	1.61	1.96	1.93	1.61	1.10	0.72	0.89
Eurasians	1.48	1.33	1.27	1.27	1.08	1.19	1.10	0.87	0.65	0.43	0.31
Mardijkers/Christian Inlanders	11.81	12.33	11.33	9.96	7.62	8.17	7.15	5.02	3.81	2.75	2.15
Chinese	8.49	11.66	13.45	13.02	12.37	12.43	12.91	22.47	23.36	22.61	27.97
Muslims/Jentiven	1.25	4.58	0.85	0.72	0.55	0.96	1.08	1.16	1.28	0.99	1.19
Amboinese/Bandanese	0.66	0.63	0.33	0.43	0.76	0.27	0.26	0.46	0.29	0.53	0.52
Islanders from Bima, Bone, Bonerate, Butung, Macassar, Mandar, Sumbawa, Timor	6.94	5.28	7.45	5.77	6.43	5.95	6.30	5.24	7.02	12.98	9.75
Malays	2.93	2.27	1.59	3.91	2.55	1.99	2.09	1.22	1.38	2.89	5.63
Javanese/Balinese	25.04	24.44	26.87	30.60	37.89	38.65	41.94	40.73	38.41	30.01	33.16
Slaves	37.86	34.36	34.24	32.13	29.14	28.43	25.24	21.22	22.70	26.09	18.43

As for the sex and family ratios (see table 2.8), there was a marked contrast with the Europeans. The presence of women was clear; but the ratios of children to women not appreciably different from those of the Europeans. If the totals of Europeans and Eurasians are combined, the ratio of men to women at once appears to have been more favorable.

Third in the lists came the *Mardijkers*. Of Portuguese origin, they may have migrated from Malacca, some no doubt as prisoners. Others probably originated from Ihdia—Malabar, Coromandel, Arakan, Bengal—and even from Angola. The map of 1681 listed a special Malabar quarter in the inner city.[37] Sometimes they were former slaves or indentured laborers who had managed to buy their freedom; sometimes Muslims, but converted to Christianity.[38] In the lists from the 1780s they appeared as Christian Inlanders, perhaps originating from southwest or eastern Java. Invariably, the Mardijkers spoke Portuguese;[39] and the establishment of Portuguese churches was an indicator of this human flotsam: the *Binnenkerk* (Inner Church) (January 1673) and the *Buitenkerk* (Outer Church) (October 1695). A similar group, the *Pampangers*, of Spanish origin usually from Manila, were not mentioned separately, but may have been included in this category. In the seventeenth century the Mardijkers were an important group as the VOC prized the Portuguese from their outposts and strongholds: they formed 12.33 percent of the population in 1701. With a total of 9,021 in 1710, they were still the third largest group. However, they were often unruly,[40] and their position weakened: by 1790 they figured only as 2.15 percent of the total. The larger part lived in the outer city; and within the walls their numbers declined appreciably in the eighteenth century from 2,207 in 1701 to a mere 571 in 1790, hardly a quarter of the earlier total.

In sex and family ratios they were similar to the Eurasians, and a group apart (see table 2.9). Women outnumbered men when the numbers were high, but with the decline in the eighteenth century this ratio tended to improve so that, at the close, the ratio approximated to that of the Eurasians.

Table 2.8

EURASIANS—SEX AND FAMILY RATIOS

	Men to women	All children to women	Children over 14 to women	Children under 14 to women	European and Eurasian men to women
1701	0.60	1.80	0.66	1.14	1.10
1730	0.62	1.36	0.57	0.79	1.22
1760	0.66	1.13	0.44	0.69	1.76
1790	0.80	0.60	0.29	0.31	1.77

Table 2.9

MARDIJKERS/CHRISTIAN INLANDERS—SEX AND FAMILY RATIOS

	Men to women	All children to women	Children over 14 to women	Children under 14 to women
1701	0.76	1.40	0.57	0.83
1730	0.76	1.34	0.61	0.73
1760	0.67	1.01	0.39	0.62
1790	0.80	1.10	0.55	0.55

Table 2.10

MUSLIMS/JENTIVEN—SEX AND FAMILY RATIOS

	Men to women	All children to women	Children over 14 to women	Children under 14 to women
1701	1.09	1.16	0.41	0.75
1730	0.97	1.72	0.50	1.22
1760	0.98	1.48	0.76	0.72
1790	0.92	1.00	0.42	0.58

The group of Muslims or Arabs—*Mooren*—originated from a wide area, probably southern India and Coromandel, or from Kalinga and elsewhere, all part of the huge incursion of the Koran into southern Asia. They also came from dispersed areas in the Archipelago, perhaps from Sumatra and the other islands. They mingled with Jentiven, often from the same areas, but not belonging to the Muslim faith. Sometimes, they engaged in the cotton trade from Bombay to the eastern archipelago, which offered a good market for cloth.[41] The numbers formed a small part of the population and tended to fluctuate, at a high in 1701 (4.58 percent), and low in 1730 (0.55 percent). Some lived in the inner city, usually on the west side; but the larger part drifted to the west outer city.

In contrast to the Mardijkers, they appeared to have had more family structure (see table 2.10). The imbalance between men and women was less noticeable. And, at least until the mideighteenth century, there was a higher proportion of children under fourteen in relationship to the number of women.

Among the different origins, the islands of the Archipelago provided perhaps the most complex and interwoven flows of migrants. The curfew order imposed by the governor-general (31 May 1697 and renewed in 1730) listed "Malays, Bugis, Macassars, Saleiers, Papuans, Malabaren, Cassers, . . . Boutonders, Amboinese, Bandanese, Ternatese, Papangers, Bimanese" and other aliens, together with the local "Jacatrase" both inside and outside the city.[42] The Bugis, an important group, probably came from the area of Bone in the densely populated south-west Celebes. Some of the islanders, however, were small in number.

In the early counts, these groups were often listed together. In 1701, Muslims, Malays, Javanese, and Balinese were joined by Bugis and migrants from Amboina, Banda, Macassar. Inside the city walls, Malays went with Javanese, Balinese with Macassars; outside, Macassars appeared with Bugis. Only in the late 1750s did these various groups in outer Batavia appear separately. In the list of 1780, only Christian Inlanders, Malays, and Muslims remained inside the city; the islanders and Javanese found a place outside.

The Amboinese and Bandanese were hardly more than a few hundred, regularly below one percent of the total population. The map of 1681 indicates a separate quarter for Bandanese, but in the eighteenth century they settled invariably in the outer city, at first mainly on the west side but from the count of 1770 moving progressively to the west.

With such small samples, the sex/family ratios (see table 2.11) fluctuated widely but apparently were not unfavorable.

The Malays also originated no doubt from a wide area of the extensive Malacca empire, which in addition to the Peninsula included parts of Siam and Sumatra. In 1720 they reached 3,526 or 3.91 percent of the total population. At the close of the eighteenth century, however, they numbered 7,593 (1790) or 5.63 percent of the total. A small part lived in the inner city but the larger part outside, at first on the west side but in the counts of 1780 and 1790 increasingly to the east.

The sex and family ratios appear more balanced (see table 2.12), both for men to women and for children to women; but at the same time, the samples are generally small.

A further group of Archipelago islanders originated from various parts of the dismantled empire of Macassar. Small numbers came from the islands of Bima, Sumbawa; and also from Timor. Others arrived from Celebes: Butung, and the densely settled southwest—Macassar, Mandar,

Table 2.11
AMBOINESE/BANDANESE—SEX AND FAMILY RATIOS

	Men to women	All children to women	Children over 14 to women	Children under 14 to women
1701	1.78	1.10	0.54	0.56
1730	0.89	1.57	0.70	0.87
1760	1.02	1.38	0.64	0.74
1790	0.86	1.20	0.53	0.67

Table 2.12

MALAYS—SEX AND FAMILY RATIOS

	Men to women	All children to women	Children over 14 to women	Children under 14 to women
1701	1.19	1.26	0.57	0.69
1730	1.06	1.23	0.45	0.78

Table 2.13

ARCHIPELAGO ISLANDERS—SEX AND FAMILY RATIOS

	Men to women			Children over 14 to women			Children under 14 to women		
1701	0.89			0.38			0.39		
1730	1.15			0.61			0.63		
	(1)	(2)	(3)	(1)	(2)	(3)	(1)	(2)	(3)
1760	0.86	1.03	1.09	0.66	0.72	0.66	0.53	0.75	0.78
1790	1.00	1.33	1.34	0.78	0.73	0.79	0.67	0.58	0.43

(1) Bima, Mandar, Sumbawa, Timor
(2) Macassar
(3) Bugis

and the Bugis from the region of Bone.[43] Often they were Muslims. The early lists confined attention to the Bugis and Macassars; but after 1760 a more detailed classification was regularly given. A few lived in the inner city. None appeared there in the count of 1750, and in the separate lists after 1760, only Macassars in 1760 and 1770. There are no indications in the second half of the eighteenth century that Bugis settled in the inner city. In general, they preferred the west side, but the count of 1790 showed a remarkable shift to the east. Other islanders from Bima, Butung, Sumbawa, . . . regularly lived outside. The numbers in this combined group increased in the eighteenth century, reaching 18,503 in 1780; but fell back to 13,128 in 1790.

The ratios in the counts of 1760 and 1790 (see table 2.13) show a growing proportion of men to women, especially from Celebes when taken in the separate lists. At the same time, the proportions of children tended on average to be somewhat higher than for others from the Archipelago.

There remain three main components of the population of Batavia: the indigenous Javanese and Balinese; the Chinese; and the slaves.

At the beginning, the lists for the inner city linked the Javanese with Malays and the Balinese with Macassars. But in the important totals for the outer city, Javanese and Balinese appeared together. After 1760, they were allocated to separate lists. The undercounting in the early lists of 1673 and 1680 was largely due to a shortfall in the totals of these groups. Their origins and arrival in Batavia are not very clear; once established their growth was impressive.[44] By 1701, they were second with a total of 17,050 or 24.44 percent of the total population. The next four decades continued this development so that by 1730 they numbered 39,442 or 37.89 percent. Although most of them were relegated beyond the walls, the pressure on the city clearly gave the authorities cause for anxiety. The order of 31 May 1697, renewed in 1730, imposed a curfew at nine o'clock and forbade the carrying of kris and side-arms.[45] The pressure combined with that from the Chinese to create a basis for the riots of October 1740.[46] In the count of December 1740/January 1741, this group lost some 6,000; but the trend picked up to 52,629 or 38.41 percent of the total in 1770. A decline then set in, reaching 44,682 in 1790 or 33.16 percent of the total. For the last three samples, it is possible to distinguish the two groups in the outer city, where the majority settled (see table 2.14).

The Javanese thus outnumbered the Balinese by more than two to one. However, from early days very few of either group lived in the inner city; in the counts of 1780 and 1790 none were so listed. In the outer city, they were widely spread, at first preferring the east side but after the mideighteenth century, moving more to the west.

In sex and family ratios (see table 2.15), the combined data appear to

Table 2.14

JAVANESE AND BALINESE—TOTALS IN THE OUTER CITY

	Javanese	Balinese
1770	36,440	15,986
1780	28,402	14,386
1790	32,395	12,287

Table 2.15

JAVANESE (1) AND BALINESE (2)—SEX AND FAMILY RATIOS

	Men to women		Children over 14 to women		Children under 14 to women	
	(1)	(2)	(1)	(2)	(1)	(2)
1701	2.02		0.47		0.68	
1730	1.92		0.49		0.63	
1760	1.75	1.21	0.88	0.74	0.90	0.79
1790	1.46	1.13	0.72	0.62	0.59	0.61

indicate an imbalance at the beginning of the eighteenth century, with the gap closing toward the end. In each of the later samples, the ratio of men and women was more favorable for the Balinese; but the Javanese appeared to have the slight advantage in family/children structures.

Next in importance were the Chinese. They proved to be a powerful force, and perhaps typical of developments in southeast Asia. Among the various residents in the city, the Chinese alone were classed as aliens.[47] At the original foundation of the city, they were already important. The VOC ordered them at once to nominate a consul or Bencon.[48] He carried some weight, for he sat on the *College van Schepenen* (Counsel of Founders), at least until 1666, and played an important role at the time of the 1740 riots.[49]

The Chinese merchants thrived on the annual trade with China: annual fleets of junks left Canton, Amoy, Foochow, Hangchow, and other ports, with cargoes of tea, silk, porcelain, drugs, aromatics—and, no doubt, migrants. They usually arrived in January/February and sailed home in July. For example, between 19 January and 11 February 1710, nine junks arrived from Amoy, Tonkin, and Canton. In 1790, nine arrived with a complement of 1,969, of whom 1,059 remained in Batavia.[50] Although the authorities were careful to list arrivals and departures, the numbers grew in the city with impressive speed and almost without restraint.

The Chinese also played a significant part in the workforce, both as entrepreneurs who employed slaves and also as laborers. Some idea of their complex activity can be had from the legislation aimed to regulate the community after 1740. The order of 21 November 1760 consolidated the acts of 31 December 1750, 17 October 1752, and 23 June 1758 and put the Chinese in the inner and outer cities under four "consular" lieutenants.[51] The first looked after those in the sugar mills; the second those in the liquor distilleries, oil presses, brick works, limekilns, and timber yards; the third those living in the inner city; while a fourth or junior lieutenant had charge of Chinese working on the estates or plantations. The Chinese community thus covered a wide range of the economy of both Batavia and the surrounding region.

During the whole of the seventeenth century, the community continued to grow: there were some 2,300 in 1632, and in 1691 the numbers reached 5,668. In the eighteenth century, this growth was consistent. However, unlike the Javanese/Balinese, they formed at first an important group in the inner city (see tables 2.3 and 2.4 and figure 2.5), where the total of 4,685 in 1737 represented 31.30 percent of all Chinese. This contingent in the inner city, already under pressure, often exceeded the numbers envisaged by the Company. The majority in the outer city worked in the sugar mills;[52] and included poorer groups without means of

Figure 2.5: Batavia: Chinese and the 1740 massacre

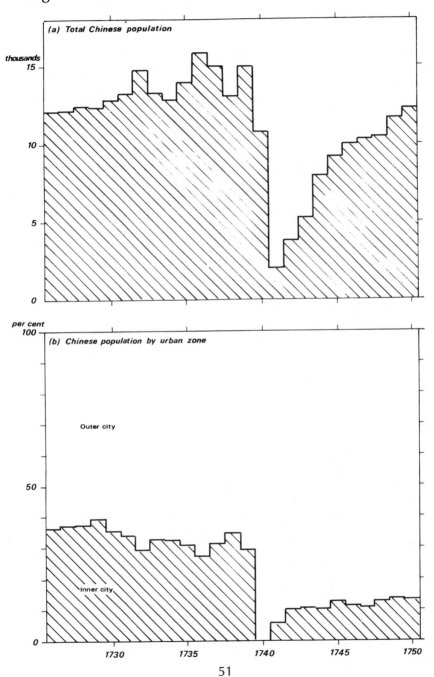

Table 2.16
CHINESE—SEX AND FAMILY RATIOS

	Men to women	All children to women	Children over 14 to women	Children under 14 to women
1701	1.65	1.32	0.36	0.96
1730	1.73	1.45	0.48	0.97
1760	2.68	1.24	0.62	0.61
1790	2.40	1.49	0.83	0.66

support who quickly slipped into robbery and house-breaking.[53] From 1729, all Chinese were required to have a residence permit *(permissiebrief)*. On 25 July 1739, the Raad van Indië (Council of the Indies) ordered all Chinese without permits to be deported to Ceylon. In October, the situation deteriorated further, aided no doubt by the presence of large numbers of Javanese and Balinese; and by a clash of personalities in the administration. In the night of Saturday 8 October several thousand poor Chinese attacked the outer posts of the city. On Sunday 9 October the governor-general ordered a search of Chinese houses for arms; and soon plunder and massacre followed. The next day some 500 Chinese in the prisons of the VOC and city were put to death, apparently with the tacit acquiescence of the governor-general.[54] The count at the end of the year gave only seven Chinese in the south voorstad: 6 women and a girl under fourteen. From 1739 over 4,000 had disappeared: some no doubt took to the hills. In the outer city, the numbers held up at 10,774. A year later, however, after the departure of the junks for China, the gravity of the disaster became clear. The inner city had 112 and the outer city only 1,826 Chinese. With 1742 the numbers began slowly to recover, but more than a decade passed before the movement regained the trend of expansion. By 1790, the total number of Chinese reached 37,682 (27.97 percent of the population), the largest single ethnic group in Batavia—that is, if we divide the Javanese from the Balinese. This time, however, the outer city accommodated the growth. From the counts of 1760 the Chinese concentrated in the *campong* (settlement) to the southwest. By 1790, 84.37 percent of the Chinese lived in the west outer city. A major urban migration had taken place, one that was to last.

How did the sex and family ratios respond to these violent changes? First, they were marked by a growing imbalance of men to women (see table 2.16): the increase in numbers was achieved with more single men. Nevertheless, those Chinese women who were in Batavia appeared to provide for families more stable than in many other cases.

Finally, the third important group: slaves *(lijfeigenen)*. Bondage, an old trade of the Arab world, remained in Muslim Asia. Colonial systems survived with both domestic service and intensive cultivation. The VOC in general and Batavia in particular were no exceptions to this. Madagascar provided slave labor for the farms of the Cape. The VOC accounts regularly included slaves among the assets of the *comptoirs* (company accounts). In 1690, for example, 6,392 slaves were on the Company's books valued at f. 273,700–15–1. Ceylon had 3,665; but Batavia came second with 1,333.[55] Sometimes they came from southern India and Arakan; at other times from the Archipelago Islands, where war and rivalries disrupted societies. Bali was a notable source.[56] Often the slaves were domestic servants and on occasion returned to the Netherlands with their owners: in 1724, for example, 3 men and 6 women slaves sailed as passengers in the returning fleet.[57] Other slaves worked in the plantations and sugar mills. After the riots of 1740, the Raad van Indië was obliged to take charge of numerous slaves left abandoned by their Chinese owners.[58]

Batavia appeared at first virtually a slave city. The total number of slaves at the beginning of the eighteenth century made them the largest single group. In 1691 there were 25,281 (37.86 percent of the population). The numbers remained substantial for much of the following century. In 1790, they remained the third group in order of size (table 2.17).

Initially, almost half the slaves lived in the inner city: in 1730, 49.15 percent of the total. After 1740, those in the outer city grew more rapidly, so that in 1790 some 81.10 percent lived there. This change may point to the Chinese as important slave owners, for in 1790, 51.24 percent of the slaves were located in the west outer city, the site of the Chinese *campong* (settlement).

What can be said of the sex and family ratio of the slaves? The listings were different from the other ethnic groups for they give only men, women, and children. The ratios are given in table 2.18.

While the ratio of women was better than many ethnic groups, the ratio of children was by far the lowest. This could be explained by the age of the slaves; perhaps many were young, hardly more than house-boys.[59] However, the data give little indication of this.

Table 2.17

SLAVE POPULATION

	No. of slaves	Percentage of total population
1701	23,974	34.36
1730	30,329	29.14
1760	26,773	21.22
1790	24,830	18.43

Table 2.18
SLAVES—SEX AND FAMILY RATIOS

	Men to women	Total children to women
1701	1.30	0.35
1730	1.36	0.33
1760	1.22	0.33
1790	1.34	0.44

A final commentary on the lists: the problem of children in general. There are the ratios of boys to girls, divided at the age of fourteen years of age. The data vary considerably, but it is remarkable that while the ratios of the European children in both age groups revealed a clear preponderance of girls, those from the islands, and particularly from Java and Bali, showed the reverse. The Chinese also shared this characteristic. Apparently, unliberated girls in these cases were at a disadvantage.

And the problem of the total numbers of children to women, and presumably to families or households. The figures returned by the lists are disquietingly low and may, if correct, offer a commentary on urban and commercial complexes in a tropical, agrarian hinterland. Did the economic and social structures militate against the large family? Was the urban deficit of this section of the population a matter of mortality? Or of infanticide? Or indeed of the sale of children into bondage? The documents offer little in the way of satisfactory explanation.

In conclusion, the evolution of the population of Batavia from the late seventeenth to the late eighteenth century shows three main traits. First, the city developed into a focus of commercial expansion and administration. In time, it outgrew the future of the Company. A phase seemed to culminate in the 1770s, tending to limits set by the "colonial market" and the urban potential of both the inner and outer cities. At that time, the city rivaled in size some important centers of Europe.

Second, the exertion of Dutch influence soon disrupted older societies and liaisons, creating a fresh sphere for ethnic and social mobility. The city became preeminently cosmopolitan in character and contended with the tropical location by using numerous slaves. Initially, the population reflected the relays from earlier dominant cultures, absorbing Muslims and above all Portuguese Mardijkers. However, as maturity progressed, Batavia came to rely increasingly on the strata of the Archipelago—and the Chinese.

Third, the ethnic structure of the population emphasized two leading characteristics of southeast Asia: the impressive growth of the indigenous peoples, in this case, the Javanese and Balinese; and the exceptional vitality and enterprise of the Chinese. In view of the extensive area from which migrants originated, it would seem that Ravenstein's law—that numbers are inversely correlated with distance traveled[60]—has uncertain relevance. The growth of Javanese and Balinese in the city can certainly be associated with shorter trajectories. And the élite of Europeans made the long haul from the continent by the trade winds via the Cape and south Indian Ocean. However, the concept carries less conviction for the Chinese. At the close of the eighteenth century, these appeared as the largest single ethnic group, but many arrived from China over long distances by land and sea. An alternative explanation could look to the increase of population in mainland China and the marginal efficiencies of labor in eighteenth-century Asia. In this, the theories of Ernst Wagemann on relative growth promise to be a better guide for Chinese infiltration into the Archipelago.[61] And to that great *socio-drame*, Batavia offered one witness among many.

Notes

1. Hereafter cited as VOC.

2. H. A. Breuning, *Het voormalige Batavia*, Amsterdam, 1954, p. 13.

3. J. Heers, *Rivalité ou collaboration de la terre et de l'eau? Position général des problèmes*, in *Les grandes voies maritimes dans le monde, XVe–XIX siècles*, Paris, 1965, p. 16.

4. I. Wallerstein, *The modern world-system*, New York, 1974, esp. chap. 4.

5. R. Mols, *Introduction à la démographie historique des villes d'Europe du XIVe au XVIIIe. siècle*, 3 vols., Leuven, 1955, II:508–23.

6. K. Glamann, *Dutch-Asiatic trade, 1620–1740*, The Hague, 1958, pp. 7–11.

7. For an excellent survey, see B. H. M. Vlekke, *Nusantara: A history of Indonesia*, The Hague, 1959, pp. 157–221; and J. Kennedy, *A history of Malaya, A.D. 1400–1959*, London, 1962, pp. 58–59.

8. W. Herbert, *A New Directory for the East Indies*, London, 1759, p. 130.

9. *Algemeen Rijksarchief, The Hague, Koloniaal Archief* (hereafter *ARA, KA*) 3427, fo. 1800.

10. See map of 1629, *ARA, Collectie Leupe* 1182; Breuning, pp. 12–13.

11. *ARA, Collectie Leupe* 1178.

12. Breuning, pp. 12–13.

13. Ibid., pp. 28, 34, 42, 126.

14. Ibid., p. 28.

15. Breuning, p. 129.

16. Vlekke, p. 189.

17. F. Spooner, Risks at sea: Amsterdam insurance and maritime Europe, 1766–1780, Cambridge UP, 1983, chapter 4.

18. Map of Batavia (1681) in the Geography Department Collection, University of Durham.

19. Vlekke, p. 212.

20. Archives des Affaires Etrangères, Paris, Correspondence Politique, Hollande, 536, fo. 139ro., letter, Grand to Vergennes, Amsterdam, 3 May 1779.

21. Breuning, p. 50.

22. ARA, KA, 2,033, fo. 528.

23. Ibid., Resolutiën, 23 October 1703, 11 March 1704, 16 July 1714.

24. Ibid., 2,033, fo. 527.

25. Breuning, op. cit. p. 29.

26. Cited by Vlekke, p. 186.

27. ARA, KA, Resolutiën, 3 April 1742.

28. ARA, KA, 1,111, fos. 113–14.

29. Ibid., 2,044 (1730).

30. Ibid., 1828 (26 October 1720).

31. A. Sauvy, Théorie générale de la population, 2 vols., Paris, 1952–54, I, esp. pp. 1–7.

32. In this study, the samples by decades are from ARA, KA, 1,181, 1,243, 1,534, 1,675, 1,828, 2,044, 2,374, 2,644, 2,864, 3,174, 3,454, 3,762. Penny Summerfield and John Steele kindly saw the data through the computer in Durham.

33. J. S. Furnivall, Netherlands India: A Study of a plural economy, Cambridge UP, 1939, p. 18.

34. ARA, KA, 3,174, fo. 2,081; and see 2,662, fo. 648, Lijste van alle's Compagnies Dienaren als 't zedert Primo Januarij 1751 tot dato 17 xber deselvs jaars alhier in Burger vrijdom zijn gesteld; and 2,685, fo. 857; 2,694, fo. 542; 2,701, fo. 769; 2,720, fo. 822; 2,737, fo. 245; 2,760, fo. 867; 2,784, fo. 972; 2,805, fo. 664; 2,836, fo. 2,125.

35. Breuning, p. 84.

36. Ibid., 48; ARA, KA, Resolutiën, 11 September 1635 and 17 September 1736.

37. See note 18.

38. Breuning, 45–70; Vlekke, pp. 150, 157–58, 190; G. Huet, "La communanté portugaise de Batavia," Revista Lusitana, XII (1909). See also illustration in F. de Haan Oud Batavia, 2 vols., Batavia, 1922, vol. 2, L, 2b.

39. D. Lopes, A expansão da lingua portugêsa no Oriente durante los séculos XVI, XVII, e XVIII, Barcelos, 1936.

40. Vlekke, p. 190.

41. Breuning, p. 44 et seq.

42. ARA, KA, 2,014, fo. 7,649; see also J. P. Kleiweg de Zwaan, De rassen van de Indische Archipel, Amsterdam, 1925.

43. For a description of the varieties in Celebes, see M. Kornrumpf, *Mensch und Landschaft auf Celebes*, Breslau, 1935.

44. Breuning, p. 44.

45. *ARA, KA*, 2,014, fo. 7649.

46. Vlekke, p. 29.

47. The inhabitants of Batavia were placed in four main categories: Company servants, burgesses, aliens, and slaves/*lijfeigenen*.

48. Vlekke, p. 155.

49. J. E. Wils, Jr., *De VOC en de Chinezen in Taiwan, China en Batavia in de 17de en 18de eeuw* in M. A. P. Meilink-Roelofsz, ed., *De VOC in Azië*, Bussum, 1976, pp. 180–81.

50. *ARA, KA*, 1,660, fo. 1,513; 3,762, fo. 2,940; see also 1782, fos. 1,718, 1,723 for the imperial edict concerning the sailings of junks. For the origins of Chinese migrants in the nineteenth century, see V. Purcell, *The Chinese in South-East Asia*, Oxford UP, 1952, p. 9.

51. Ibid., 2,864, fos. 980–85, 21 November 1760, Article 39.

52. Wils, p. 181.

53. *ARA, Staten Generaal, Resolutiën*, 30 October 1741; and *Rijsarchief in Zeeland, Middelburgsche Commercie Compagnie*, 1624, *Relaas*; see also J. T. Vermeulen, *De Chineezen te Batavia en de troebelen van 1740*, Leiden, 1938.

54. *ARA, Staten Generaal, Resolutiën*.

55. *ARA, KA*, 1,355, fo. 617 et seq.

56. Vlekke, p. 200.

57. Ibid., 1895, fo. 1,299.

58. Ibid., 2377, fo. 3,403.

59. See C. R. Boxer, *Jan Compagnie in Japan, 1600–1850*, 2d ed., The Hague, 1950, p. 142, for a color print of an *Opperhoofd* and his slave (c. 1780).

60. E. G. Ravenstein, "The Laws of Migration," *Journal of the Statistical Society*, 48 (1885): 198–99.

61. For the theories of E. F. Wagemann in *La población en el destino de los pueblos*, Santiago, 1949, and *Economía mundial*, 2 vols., Santiago, 1952–54; see F. Braudel, "La démographie et les dimensions des sciences de l'homme," *Annales: économies, sociétés, civilisations* 15 (1960), esp. pp. 494–503.

3

Migration, Agricultural Development, and Deprivation: A Case Study of a Tribal Situation in India

M. S. A. Rao

It is commonly agreed that migration is an important factor in economic development in developing countries. Historically, the process of colonization through military conquests, extension of planters' and traders' frontiers, missionary activities, and slave trade has involved different forms of both overseas and inland migration that were responsible for development in some areas and for certain sections, but underdevelopment in others and deprivation for still other sections of the population. Outside this context of traditional process of colonization and imperialism, economic development has occurred within a country resulting in regional imbalances. Some Marxian scholars have characterized the development process in terms of capitalist mode of production, capitalist world economy, center-periphery and metropolis-satellite dependency. However, this is an oversimplified analysis. The Indian agrarian situation is characterized by multiple modes of polarization.

This essay develops a more open framework of development—deprivation in the democratic political framework. The agents of economic

58

development have been a category of people with capital, technical know-how, and organizational skills. They have migrated to areas where new opportunities for development opened up. Besides the stream of entrepreneurs—industrial, commercial, and agricultural—there is the stream of migrants consisting of workers and laborers who form an essential component of development. In the process of economic development, the migrant entrepreneurs tend to have a greater share in the benefits than the migrant workers and laborers. Second, the migrant entrepreneurs have also exploited the locals. Hence, development in its trail has given rise to relative deprivations. While the process of development has received much attention, the study of its consequences has suffered from neglect.

This essay aims to examine both the process of development and its consequences in the context of migration with special reference to colonization of cultivators from the plains and the consequent deprivations of the tribals in Andhra Pradesh. This is, first, a situation of agricultural colonization and development and not industrial or commercial development. Second, the pattern of migration is rural-rural and not rural-urban.

Agricultural Colonization

Agricultural colonization is one type of colonization that normally means settlement on virgin soil by a migrant community. The migration may be either overseas or inland, and the process of settlement may vary with the nature of economic and political relations between the migrants and the locals. Four situations may be distinguished in this regard. In the case of European colonization of America, Africa, and Asia, agricultural colonization mainly consisted of establishment of large plantations and farms. Here the process of migration and settlement was part of imperialism. Second, agricultural colonization may be part of a government program. The state takes the initiative in settling different types of groups and categories such as the refugees, nomads, economically backward sections, tribals, former military men as part of rehabilitation programs. This type of planned and sponsored colonization can occur either by claiming semi-forest land or by settling people in large irrigation project areas. Farmer (1957, 1974) has described such a process of agricultural colonization in Ceylon and India. Similar schemes of colonization can be found elsewhere too, for instance, Latin America (Dozier 1969) and Africa (Amin 1974: 111–12).

Besides the situation of sponsored migration, there are situations of voluntary migration with different implications for the relationship between migrants and locals. Hence, third, peasants and farmers may voluntarily migrate, instead of their being sponsored, to flow-irrigated regions, buy land from the locals, and establish their camps. Since the migrant farmers will have bought the land legally from the locals, the latter do not feel alienated from their land, although they may feel jealous of the success of the migrants who have the capital and the skills of organization. The fourth situation of agricultural colonization is that where the peasant-farmers have migrated voluntarily to areas reserved for the tribals and established their camps and villages. Unlike the third situation, here the migrants are not legally allowed to buy or lease-in land from the tribals. Still they do it through various means resulting in land alienation of the tribals.

This essay is confined to the last situation of migration and agricultural colonization in the tribal area of West Godavari District in Andhra Pradesh, a state in southeast India.

Polavaram Taluk of West Godavari District

Ecologically West Godavari District is divided into lowland delta area and upland dry area. In 1960 the upland area in which the Polavaram *taluk* (village headquarters) lies was found suitable for the cultivation of light-soil, flue-cured virginia tobacco, which has a large and expanding export market. The taluk consists of 135 villages of which 102 are located in the Agency area, and 33 are situated in the plains. Agency is a Scheduled Tribal area governed by special laws relating to land, education, employment, and other aspects. For instance, the Agent, equivalent to a Collector of a District, is in charge of collecting revenue and administering both civil and criminal laws.

Koyas are the dominant tribe in the Agency. In 1971, they formed 55.1 percent of Agency population. Out of 44.9 percent of nontribal population, scheduled castes constituted 32.0 percent and the rest (12.9 percent) were caste Hindus. The Christian missionaries were unable to convert the Koyas, but succeeded in converting about 50 percent of the scheduled castes. The major nontribal cultivating and land-owning castes are the Kapu, Kamma, Raju (cultivators), Komati (merchant), Setty Bala-jiga (distiller), and Gollas or Yadavas (cowherds and goatherds).

Early History

During the early period of British occupation, from 1765 to 1828, there was one lineage of Hill Reddi, a tribe that owned three estates—Polavaram and Cutala in Polavaram taluk and Kothapalli estate across the Godavari river in Chowdavaram taluk. The British administration made arrangements, sometimes combining and at other times dividing the estates, that were expedient for collection of revenue. In this process they interfered with the legal ownership of estates, which caused resentment. Thus Mangapati Devu's stepmother, who was the legal guardian of her minor heir to Cutala estates, rebelled against the administration in 1790, which was no doubt quelled by superior military force.

Another cause of resentment of the *zamindars* (tribal chiefs) was the increase in the revenue demanded by the administration each year. Some of the British officers who visited the zamindari area saw the rich alluvial land on the banks of Godavari and were convinced that the zamindars were collecting more revenue than they gave to the East India Company. They also noticed the royal style of the zamindars, which meant for them lavish and wasteful expenditure. When more revenue was demanded, the zamindars were reluctant to pay, and many of them became defaulters and the estate revenue fell into arrears. The last resort for the administration was to use military force, confining the zamindars in their forts, forcing them to pay the arrears. Under such circumstances of humiliation the tribal zamindars revolted against the administration.

The usual pattern of revolt for the zamindars was to escape from the fort into the forests in the adjoining Nizam territory, build up an army, and attack the police stations, and engage in guerilla warfare against the military in the forests. In 1799 Mangapati Devu, the zamindar of the three estates (Polavaram, Gutala, and Kothapalli) who was considered to be a regular payer of revenue, fell into arrears and revolted against the administration. He did not surrender as did his two other brothers, and he could not be captured either. The estate was confiscated and was given to a cousin of Mangapati Devu on a permanent settlement in 1802. However, the estate again fell into arrears and came into the auction market finally in 1827. This ended the political supremacy and economic dominance of the tribal zamindars in Polavaram taluk. It also marked the beginning of a steady increase in the migration of the plainsman into the tribal territory, exercising control over diverse productive resources that were hitherto in the hands of the Hill Reddis and Koyas. It was the second step in the deprivation process, the first step being the interference by the administration.

Between 1827 and 1947, one can identify four major forces that altered the socioeconomic conditions of the tribal areas in Polavaram: (1) The change in nature of the zamindari system with the permanent settlement and the consequent immigration of the plainsmen; (2) the increasing inroads that the administration made through the forest, *abkari* (liquor), and civil and criminal laws; (3) the series of tribal revolts as response to the indiscriminate interference by the administration, and (4) Ryotwari (peasant) settlement of villages.

First Phase of Immigration

All these forces encouraged in different ways the migration of the plainsmen into the tribal area. The first phase of migration of peasants from the plains occurred around 1820 when a number of zamindaris either in whole or in parts came into the auction market and the highest bidder got the rights of ownership. Thus the Gutala zamindari passed into the hands of a rich Vaisya (businessman caste) of Manyam lineage in 1827. Raja Manyam Venkataratnam was originally a resident of Yanam on the coast, which was under the French occupation. He later moved to Kakinada before he finally settled in Rajahmundry. He encouraged the Kapus of Elur and Rajahmundry to migrate and settle the villages in his zamindari. He gave them semiforest land and asked them to clear it and bring it under cultivation. The Koyas who were already there had to move to the interior regions. The Kapu peasants took along with them the agricultural laborers and service castes, and in this process the existing villages grew in size and new villages came into being. However, the Koyas did not come into violent conflict with the new migrants. They held the administration responsible for their conditions of relative deprivation.

The administration made steady inroads into the control of the productive resources of the tribal areas by passing forest laws in 1882 and abkari laws in 1864. Large areas of forests were reserved, making them inaccessible to the tribals in many ways. Their economy, which was mainly based on forest, was upset. They had to pay a tax on *podu* (slash-and-burn) lands. There were restrictions on tapping toddy (country liquor) from any palm tree, and on collecting the forest products for trade. The abkari laws encouraged the migration of distiller castes who had bought the license to tap, distill, and sell liquor. The distillers easily had the tribals indebted to them, as the latter loved toddy and developed a taste for other types of distilled liquor. They acquired the land of the Koya customers in lieu of petty debts. This was similar to the practice of the merchants and money lenders, who had acquired tribal land. The tribals only lost more and more of their land in this process.

The response of the tribals to rack-renting of the zamindars was violent. Two major revolts broke outside Polavaram but inside the Godavari Agency, one in 1879 and another in 1922. The Rampa rebellion of 1879 in North Uttar Pradesh was the result of rack-renting and oppression of the Rampa zamindars, the general discontent of the tribals against the forest and abkari laws, and the civil and criminal laws that supported the merchants and zamindars who attached cattle, produce, and land in satisfaction of their debts. The 1922, Alluri Seetharama Raju's rebellion was also against the administration's laws, which made the tribals alienated from productive resources. In particular it was against the forced labor demanded by the British officers to construct a road in the tribal area. The administration was able to quell the revolts only after getting several military reinforcements.

The British did realize the severity of the tribal problem soon after the 1879 Rampa rebellion. The revised rules of India Act XXIV of 1839 were made applicable in the Godavari Agency in 1874 (Scheduled Area Act, *Madras Manual* 1885: I, 69). The British also made certain concessions to the tribals in respect of forest and abkari laws, and established direct contacts with the zamindars *(muthadars)* (feudal lords) and ryots (farmers). In 1917, the Agency Tract Interest and Land Transfer Act was introduced. Under this act no tribal could sell his land to a nontribal without permission.

With the failure of the Permanent Settlement Act of 1802–3, the old zamindaris were parceled into small blocs and sold for arrears. In the absence of bidders, the government took possession of them and made a survey of land and settled them. Thus the first Ryotwari settlement was done in 1899 and a resettlement was made in 1933. The government villages were called *Izara* villages, and the revenue was collected directly through the village head *(munsif)*, who was assisted by the village accountant *(karnam)*, peons *(taliaris)*, and others. Thus in Polavaram taluk different types of tenure villages coexisted: there were the zamindari villages, gift for service *(inam)* villages and lands, gift to Brahmins and temples *(agraharam)* villages, and government *(Izara)* villages. Cultivators, merchants, and others who had influence with the administration could move into the Agency area and buy land with permission. Rich zamindars from the delta area bought large chunks of land in the semiforest area, in order to graze their cattle. Thus the Izara and zamindari villages received more migrants consisting of the peasants and laborers from the plains.

Second Phase: Developmental Migration

The second phase of migration of farmers from the plains occurred in the postindependence period. Land in the Agency came into the market in thousands of acres in the 1950s. The nontribal who owned land in large quantity began to sell in anticipation of the forthcoming land-ceiling legislation. The beneficiaries here were primarily the Kammas, who migrated from the delta area of West Godavari District and established colonies in different remote villages. The migrants also "bought" land from the Koyas.

The stream of migration of Kammas in the 1950s was of a different character from the earlier migration of peasants before 1947. While the latter was one of subsistence, the former was of development. The Kamma migrants who moved from the delta area in the 1950s had the necessary capital and organizational and technical skills of development agriculture. They lost no time in exploiting the natural resources. The colonizers cleared the jungle, removed the boulders, and brought land under plough. They initially faced the horrors of malaria, the fear of wild animals, and fear of serpents, but soon overcame these fears. They put up pumps, lifted water from the streams running below the field level, and irrigated their lands. It had not occurred to the Kapu and Raju peasants who were in the Agency area for generations to use the water resources in this way. The Kamma colonizers thus brought about significant agricultural development in the region.

The buyers knew that they had to spend a lot on reclaiming land for cultivation. But for that reason the land was very cheap—about Rupees 100 or less per acre. This was in contrast to the high price of land in the delta area, where the man-land ratio was very high. If the peasants could sell one acre in the delta area, they could buy ten areas in the upland semi-forest area where there were potentialities of improvement including irrigational facilities.

Third Phase: Tobacco Rush-Commercialization of Agriculture

The third phase of migration started when light-soil, flue-cured virginia (FCV) tobacco was introduced in Polavaram taluk in 1960 as both land and water were suitable. The Kamma migrants who were already there were the first to take advantage of this opportunity. The FCV tobacco cultivation generated a further demand for land. But the 1959 legislation prevented the nontribals from buying land from the tribals. Hence the former started leasing in land from the latter. The tribals were not interested in cultivating barn tobacco as this season (December to April) overlapped with the toddy season. They preferred tapping and drinking toddy to growing tobacco. Second, they got cash income by leasing out their land. The lease rate varied from Rs. 300 to 600 per acre per season. The nontribal farmers who leased in land made enormous profit (about Rs. 3,000 per acre).

The "tobacco rush" resulted in both extension of commercialized agriculture by the farmers who had already migrated and also a fresh wave of migration of nontribal farmers either as transients (for the tobacco season) or as residents. However, for the tribals, it meant further loss of land and control over the exploitation of the vast benefits from commercialized agriculture. Although the nontribal farmers were "tenants" from the point of tenure position, they were the real exploiters in terms of production relations reaping vast profits. The tribals who were the landowners came to be exploited by the tenants as a major share of the benefits of the tobacco economy went to the latter.

Land Alienation

Complete data for all the 102 Agency villages regarding the extent of land under the possession of the nontribals are not available. In any case the land leased-in by the nontribals cannot be known from the land records, as the transactions are informal or *benami* (in some other name). On the basis of my investigations in 19 villages, it may be estimated that about one-third of the cultivable land is under the possession and control of the nontribals. However, the land owned and leased-in by the nontribals is of the best quality.

An all-India study of land alienation among the tribals (Dubey and Murdia 1977) fails to give an all-India estimate of land alienation, due to the paucity of data. But it indicates that the incidence is very high. According to census figures, between 1961 and 1971, the percentage of cultivators in tribal population decreased from 68.15 to 57.16 percent. But the percentage of agricultural laborers among them increased from 19.73 to 33 percent.

According to enterprising Kamma farmers in Polavaram "there are still about 2,000 acres of unreserved semi-forest land in the Agency which can be developed but the Agency laws are against the non-tribals and we are asked to surrender our land." The special deputy collector says that the law is in favor of the tribals, and in his decisions he goes strictly by the documents. If a nontribal is unable to produce documentary evidence of having purchased or acquired the land before 1917 and is in continuous possession of it, the land automatically goes to the tribal. This is in accordance with Land Transfer Regulation Act of 1970. The law is also against any kind of transfer-share *(palu)*, lease *(kaulu)*, mortgage *(bhogya)* or sale *(kraya)*. Between July 1, 1977 (the date on which the special deputy collector assumed office), and April 1, 1978, he had heard about 500 litigations involving 2,400 acres, and he had restored 1,261 acres to 126 tribals, by evicting the nontribals (interview: Elur, April 1, 1978).

Migration, Agricultural Development, and Deprivation in a Tribal Village—Kanakapalli

Before we consider the administrative measures to alleviate the conditions of relative deprivation, we may provide one specific case study of a village (Kanakapalli) that is located in the heart of the tribal area, illustrating the process of migration, development, and the consequent situation of deprivation already generally described. Kanakapalli is a government village, in the Buttayagudem Developmental Bloc. The geographical area of the village *panchayat* consists of six hamlets spreading over 6,458 acres, with a cultivable area of 2,910 acres, a cultivable waste of 2,000 acres, and 1,547 acres of wasteland. The social composition of the village shows that it is still predominantly a Koya village with 73.4 percent of tribal population of 2,388 persons distributed over 708 households. But in terms of ownership and cultivation of land, the Koyas own and/or cultivate only 17.4 percent of the cultivable area of 2,910 acres, the rest being owned and/or cultivated by the nontribals. Among the nontribals, the Kamma migrants own nearly 40 percent of the total cultivable land.

The way that the Kammas came to settle in the new site of Kanakapalli shows the pattern of migration. The village was first settled in 1899 for revenue. At that time it consisted of 120 households with a population of 572 spread over ten hamlets. It was predominantly a tribal village with a few households of Rajus, Kapus, Setti, Balajigas, Gollas, and Malas. Most of the land was owned by Koyas and Koya Nayakas.

The first major land alienation of the tribals took place in 1920 when a wealthy Kshatriya (Raju) zamindar of the Godavari delta "bought" about 1,000 acres of semiforest in the village in order to graze his cattle. He had a herd of 600 cattle that he sent every year during July and November with a team of twenty herdsmen to Kanakapalli, covering a distance of forty miles. The herd would return home after the paddy harvest when dry fodder was available to the cattle.

In the 1930s four Raju (Kshatriya caste) migrants from Chittur District bought about a hundred acres of land from the zamindar who had bought grazing land in the village. Later some persons belonging to Distiller, Merchant, and Herdman castes also came to own land in the village. All these cultivators, however, practiced subsistence agriculture, which was not different from that of many tribals, although some of the tribals practiced shifting cultivation, hunting, fishing, and food gathering. The Koya did not feel relatively deprived at this point of time with the migration of the plainsmen. There was enough land for them, and the gains of the migrants were not distinctly marked.

But the nature of the stream of migrating Kammas (a major cultivating caste) in 1949–50 was quite different. Initially thirteen households, belonging to one village in the delta region, together bought 900 acres of land from the descendants of the zamindar who had originally bought 1,000 acres of grazing land. The Kammas migrated because they thought that the land that they had in Chityala would not be sufficient for their children and grandchildren. The land value in 1949 in Chityala was Rs. 1,000 per acre. Although many of them had 30 to 60 acres there, they preferred to sell their land and migrate, mainly because of the perception of long-term advantages. If they sold 1 acre in Chityala they could buy 10 acres in Kanakapalli, and the Kamma migrants did this. Kammas are very enterprising and highly foresighted. They are committed to land and its cultivation, and are very sensitive to market conditions.

The preparedness of the Kammas to buy land and move to Kanakapalli was complementary to a set of conditions responsible for the land coming into the market. After independence and especially the police action in Hyderabad, the Andhra Pradesh government promulgated the land-reform measures. The major objectives of the land reforms were the abolition of the intermediaries like the zamindars and Inamdars, the transfer of land titles to tenants, and the imposition of a ceiling on the size of land holdings. While the measures were being debated in the Assembly, the nontribal zamindars and big landowners got the message and started selling land in large chunks.

Thus in the 1950s land came into the market in a big way, and Kammas in the delta area, where the land-man ratio was high, rushed to the Agency area, "bought" land and established their "colonies" in several villages. In Kanakapalli the pioneer settlers were young (in the age group of twenty to forty). They cleared the jungle full of boulders and stones, bushes and trees. This released the snakes all around. They also had to face the fear of wild beasts and malaria. Without exception everyone suffered from malaria. They called a doctor from Chityala and encouraged him to settle down in the village. They also bought him a horse. In this process a few Kammas returned home. But after the first three years of hard work and three successive good crops, more Kamma families joined them. They also brought more families of farm servants. By 1965, a Kamma colony had grown on the new site of the village with thirty-four households. About forty migrant Mala and Madiga laborers set up their huts near the Koya hamlet.

Kinship and affinal ties played an important part in the colonization process of the Kammas. Over a period of twenty years (from 1950 to 1978) the pattern of migration shows the predominance of affinal ties. The Kammas have three preferential marital alliances: mother's brother's daughter, elder sister's daughter, and father's sister's daughter. Exchange of women among close-knit kindred provides an effective link for migration. The system of dowry is highly prevalent among the Kammas, and the status of a person is measured by his capacity to pay a high dowry to get a bridegroom belonging to a family of high economic status. An important part of the dowry is the land that is given to the daughter. The son-in-law has only rights of management and not ownership. This acts as an incentive for him to move to the wife's place of residence, in case he has strained relations with his brothers. Similarly when a woman becomes a widow, she has the option to return to her father's or brother's village and her son can cultivate the land, which is in the name of his mother under the guidance of his mother's brother, who is his potential father-in-law. Based on the same logic of expanding network of kindred links, the process of dispersal (out-migration) of Kammas to neighboring villages has also started. The kindred network, inheritance of land, and land payment in dowry have thus provided the structural framework for migration of Kammas to Kanakapalli.

As a result of collective colonization and entrepreneurship, the Kamma migrants were able to bring about a high degree of agricultural development in Kanakapalli. They brought about 1,400 acres of semiforest land under cultivation. They introduced the capitalist mode of production in spirit but combined it with precapitalist modes in different ways. They have invested in oil pumps, now electric pumps (tube wells), tractors, fertilizers, pesticides, and improved seeds, and in improving land and water resources and management. There were two streams in the village running well below the land level. The Kammas lifted water from the two streams by electric pumps, improved tanks, installed tube wells. With such improvement in irrigational sources, they started growing paddy but combining it with millet, pulses, jingilly, chilli, and country tobacco. They established the Kanaka Durga Service Cooperative Society in 1961 to obtain credit, fertilizers, and other inputs. With all this infrastructure the agricultural production of the village increased tenfold in three decades (1950–1980).

In 1968 the Indian Leaf Tobacco Development Company of the former Imperial Tobacco Company introduced a new variety of cigarette tobacco called light-soil, flue-cured virginia (LSFCV). The Kammas of Kanakapalli were one of the first to grow LSFCV as they already had experience growing FCV on black cotton soil in their place of origin in Kovoor taluk. In 1978, the Kamma farmers owned forty-seven out of fifty-three barns in the village.

Cultivation of LSFCV made it necessary that the Kammas continually seek suitable land with irrigational facilities since barn tobacco cannot be grown on the same plot every year. There is a competitive demand for leasing-in land as buying land legally from the tribals is out of the question. In 1978, twelve Kamma farmers had leased-in forty-five acres from the Koyas in the village and another forty acres from the Koyas of the two neighboring villages. Thus they have made huge profits from tobacco cultivation.

Many Koyas lack both skills and interest in growing tobacco, although a few of them have started growing it since 1976. The tobacco season overlaps with the toddy season, and the Koyas prefer to realize a certain cash income by leasing out their land and at the same time have all the time for themselves to enjoy the toddy season. The lease rate in the Kanakapalli area for growing barn tobacco is Rs. 400 to 500 per acre per season. But some of the Koyas who have acquired the skills and who are interested in growing barn tobacco resent the clever Kamma migrants who have become very affluent. The government gives the tribals easy credit and other supplies to grow tobacco. For instance, only the tribals are entitled to get a loan for installing a rig, which is a special tube well that can go below the rockbed to reach the water level. A former Koya Member of the Legislative Assembly in Kanakapalli resented the way the entrepreneurial Kammas have amassed wealth at the cost of the tribals, encroaching on their land and having many tribals as their farm servants. In 1978 there were only 47 tribals out of 85 farm servants who were working at the migrant Kamma farms. About 60 tribals have migrated out of the village to other villages in the plains in search of jobs.

The foregoing account of the process of migration and colonization of the Kamma farmers in Kanakapalli shows that Kammas have been able to bring about significant agricultural development, including commercialization of agriculture. However, along with development there is deprivation of the tribals in terms of land alienation, joining the ranks of farm servants and agricultural wage laborers, and out-migration in search of jobs. The conditions of relative deprivation of the tribals have been further worsened because of the stringent forest laws, which prevented their access to forest and other resources such as game, fishing, food and nonfood gathering, and free extraction of toddy, but encouraged the nontribal contractors to exploit the forest resources.

Under such circumstances, the government introduced several measures in order to alleviate the conditions of relative deprivation accompanying the agricultural development brought about mainly by the migrant farmers.

Administrative Measures to Alleviate Conditions of Deprivation

The state government has taken several measures to alleviate the conditions of relative deprivation of the tribals. The Agency Land Transfer Regulation Act of 1970 prohibits any kind of land transaction between the tribals and the nontribals and also holds all earlier transfers after 1917 null and void. The Andhra Pradesh Scheduled Tribes Relief Regulation of 1970 writes off the accumulated interest. Under the Andhra Pradesh Scheduled Area Ryotwari Settlement Regulation II of 1970 the last batch of the 29 former zamindari and other remote villages were surveyed and settled for the first time in 1975. The settlement officer in most cases has resorted the land to the tribals. In 1977 a special deputy collector was appointed to restore land to the tribals in accordance with the 1970 act. This legislation along with the intensive tribal development programs in regard to agriculture, horticulture, sericulture, animal husbandry, employment, and education have, to some extent, retrieved the Koyas from the position of land alienation and relative deprivation.

A trend in this direction is seen in the Buttayagudam Development Bloc, where 34 Koyas have started growing FCV since 1976. There are in all 41 out of about 900 barns in the bloc owned by the tribals. If this trend continues, the feeling of alienation that they have been left out of the gains from the new commercial economy will be reduced to a considerable extent.

With the possibilities of irrigation facilities and commercialization of agriculture, there is an increasing demand for labor. Tribals are only beginning to acquire new skills of paddy and tobacco harvesting. About one-third of the Koyas work as farm servants and casual agricultural laborers. Many Koyas like to work as farm servants rather than casual laborers because the former provides a sense of security and gives them an advantage of a cash loan from the farmers whenever they want. As farm servants they are not required to learn the skills of harvesting and stringing of tobacco leaves or harvesting tobacco.

The immigration of the plainsmen—cultivators, laborers, and all—has to some extent resulted in the out-migration of the tribals from the Agency. In 1971, 42.52 percent of the total number of tribals living in West Godavari District were found residing outside the Agency area, i.e., on the plains. A majority of 85.18 percent of the tribals living on the plains resided in rural areas. They are employed as agricultural laborers, farm servants, domestic servants, and as unskilled workers in various construction and repair works. The out-migration of the tribals from the Agency area is due to several factors. There is a shrinkage of job opportunities for the tribals in the Agency area with increasing restrictions of using and selling forest resources. They are dispossessed of podu and other lands. Generally they lack skills to engage in paddy- and tobacco-harvesting operations. Here the migrant cultivators prefer migrant laborers who are highly skilled, regular, and more reliable than the tribals. For the same reason the forest developers prefer migrant laborers from the plains to the local tribals in cutting bamboo, felling trees, cutting wood, and road construction. It should be noted here that out-migration of the tribals in itself is not undesirable as long as it is developmental in nature. But in this context they are forced out of their habitat as a result of the colonization of nontribals.

General Discussion on Migration, Development, and Deprivation

On the basis of the foregoing case study, we can consider the general theoretical problems concerning migration, development, and deprivation indicated in the introduction. First, there is the framework of a set of related concepts such as core-semiperiphery-periphery, metropolis-satellite dependency; economic development-underdevelopment; capitalist world economy; colonialism and internal colonialism. Wallerstein (1979: 285–93) argues that capitalism is the only mode of production in which the maximization of surplus creation is rewarded per se through the market structure. It is the state system that encrusts, enforces, and exaggerates the patterns. Capitalism has regularly required the use of state machinery to revise the pattern of the worldwide division of labor. The core states become stronger than the peripheral states. In capitalism the surplus value of the proletarian is appropriated by the bourgeois. The proletarian is located in the periphery and semiperiphery and the bourgeois in the core. One of the mechanisms that has affected the process of surplus appropriation is the manipulation of controlling flows over state boundaries, which results in uneven development. Core, semiperiphery, and periphery are conceptual tools in analyzing forms of class conflict in the capitalist world economy.

Gunder Frank (1967: 8–21) had argued earlier that in this system of dependency of the periphery on the core, there was a stepwise linkage of national and international metropolises. At each step of the way up, the economic surplus from each of the minor and major satellites gravitated up or into the capitalist world's metropolitan center. This initiated a process of the underdevelopment of the satellite on the one hand and the economic development of the metropolis on the other.

This framework of analysis claims that such a process of development of capitalist world economy is a global one and its pattern of development is the center-periphery or metropolis-satellite dependency system. However, it is a very simplistic assumption, because it associates the exploitative and the exploited groups with different territorial units and, second, it posits only one direction of flow of labor from the periphery and pattern of dominance of the center. In the light of the data presented above it is clear that a development-deprivation situation can develop within a single area with the immigration of entrepreneurial farmers and the deprivation of the autochthons who in Polavaram are tribals. But in other situations it would be different groups under the term "sons of the soil": the Maharashtrians in Bombay, Assamese in Assam, Mulkis in Hyderabad, and Kannadigas in Mysore (see Weiner 1978).

While the center-periphery argument is weak in respect of its universal applicability of migration trends and location of different groups involved in development, the political aspect as it is considered has also its limited validity. The part played by the entrepreneurial migrant farmers is no doubt closely related to the policies of administration. The state is intimately connected with the nature of economic development opportunities that open up in an area and the nature of migration of different groups. The part played by the state further is directly relevant in its forest and tribal policies. The manner in which these forces have operated in Polavaram taluk both in pre- and post-Independence periods has been illustrated. However, the center-periphery, metropolis-satellite hypothesis ignores the intervention of the state in promoting developmental policies to rectify the imbalances in development. In this respect the land restoration policy of the government, preventive laws, and the developmental schemes for tribals are important.

Another related aspect of the Marxian analysis of development relates to modes of production debate in the context of Indian agriculture. Recently Alice Thorner (1982) has meaningfully summarized the debate on whether classes and modes of production in India can be characterized as semifeudalism or capitalism. In the light of data presented in this essay, there are not only multiple modes of production but different combinations. Still the slash-and-burn agriculture, hunting, fishing, food gathering, nonfood gathering and selling, with ideas of shared work, control, and egalitarian redistribution rather than ownership, are prevalent among the Koyas. Although the migrant Kamma farmers show a spirit of entrepreneurship in their practice of development agriculture, their mode of production is far from being capitalistic. There is greater dependence on family labor, farm servants, semiattached laborers than on free-floating wage laborers. Second, the farmers are not big land owners but medium and small landholders. The first-generation big landholders in the 1950s have become medium and small landholders in the 1970s thanks to large-size families and nonprimogeniture or ultimogeniture system of property inheritance. This has resulted in fragmentation of holdings, some of which are even uneconomical. Such a process has given rise to a multitier agrarian system rather than a simplistic two-class system. Further, the caste and tribe factors blur the question of polarization of classes. Third, the center and state policies are clearly against buying or leasing-in land from the tribals in the region, which prevents any expansion of capital accumulation in the form of land.

If by these facts, the mode of production is not capitalistic, has the consequence been one of class conflict? The course of migration and development is such that it has not led to class formation in the sense of class for itself. On the contrary, there is ethnic formation based on tribal and nontribal identities. The nontribals are the migrants, and the tribals are the autochthons. The former are the exploiters, and the latter the exploited. In fact, the Naxalite political reform movement, led by the Marxist-Leninist Communist Party of India in Srikakulam tribal area of Andhra Pradesh thrived on ethnic conflict that transcended internal "class" differences among the tribals and the nontribals. In Polavaram and other Agency tracts of Andhra Pradesh tribals form the mainstay of the Naxalite movement. However, in Polavaram, the tribals are disillusioned with the Naxalite nontribal leaders who organize them against the migrant landlords but disappear from the scene. Either they are rounded up by military police or go into hiding. Such a situation forces the tribals once again to depend on the landlords for work, subsistence, and loans for rituals. Without self-organization, they either become farm servants of landowners or move out of the Agency in search of work. All this empirical evidence points to the fact that there is no class formation but increasing patron-client relationship on the one hand and ethnic formation on the other that is expressed in frequent tribal and nontribal conflicts. The conflict is also a conflict between migrants and the autochthons. Thus both ethnic and territorial identities coincide.

The evidence for ethnic conflict instead of class conflict can be seen in other regions, under similar conditions of migration and development-deprivation. Myron Weiner (1978) has produced evidence from Assam, Chota Nagpur in Bihar, Mulkis movement in Hyderabad. All these illustrate different forms of ethnic conflict based on diverse patterns of development-deprivation. At the root of the ethnic conflict is the opposition between the autochthons and the aliens. It is, however, necessary to stress that all migrations do not result in ethnic formations and conflicts, but only those where there is competition and where the migrant groups have become successful as a result of their having greater access to economic and political resources, and an attempt on their part to establish their cultural, economic, and political dominance. Under conditions of such acute forms of deprivation, conflict gets articulated through social and cultural movements based on defined ideologies.

In the tribal context, there have been messianic and millenarian movements, and cargo cults all over the world in developing countries (see Fuchs, 1965; Raghaviah, 1971; Roy, 1970; Suresh Singh, 1966; Bharadwaj, 1977; Mahapatra, 1968, 1972; Rao 1979, 1980, 1981). Such tribal movements are also to be found in the developed countries like the United States and Canada. It is seen that various American Indians and Eskimos have organized themselves into movements resisting different forms of exploitative processes by the nontribals. All these are different kinds of responses to acute conditions of relative deprivation.

To conclude, the analysis of development process in the tribal Agency tract in terms of the Marxist laws of motion of capitalist development is not true to empirical facts. Such a framework is more misleading than enlightening for the process of development. On the contrary the framework that is presented here, namely, development-deprivation, is open and flexible to identify the trends, nature, and direction of the process of development and the consequences in terms of deprivation as the basis of an ideology of social, cultural, ethnic, and political movements. Development-deprivation framework at the same time takes into account the sources and patterns of conflict and the wider economic, social, and political forces in their dynamic interrelationships.

References

Amin, Samir. 1974. *Modern Migrations in Western Africa*. London: Oxford University Press.

Bharadwaj, Copal. 1977. "Socio-Political Movements Among the Tribes of India." In S. C. Dube, ed., *Tribal Heritage of India*. New Delhi: Vikas.

Dozier, C. L. 1969. *Land Development and Colonization in Latin America*.

Dubey, S. N., and Ratna Murdia. 1977. *Land Alienation and Restoration in Tribal Communities in India*. Bombay: Himalaya Publishing House.

Farmer, B. H. 1957. *Pioneer Peasant Colonization in Ceylon: A Study of Agrarian Problems*. Oxford: Oxford University Press.

————. 1974. *Agricultural Colonization in India Since Independence*. London: Oxford University Press.

Frank, Andre Gunder. 1967. *Capitalism and Underdevelopment in Latin America*. New York: Monthly Review Press.

Fuchs, Stephen. 1965. *Rebellious Prophets: A Study of Messianic Movements in Indian Religions*. Bombay: Asia Publishing House.

Mahapatra, L. K. 1968. "Social Movements Among Tribes in Eastern India with Special Reference to Orissa," *Sociologus*, 18:1.

————. 1972. "Social Movements Among the Tribes of India," in K. Suresh Singh, ed., *Tribal Situation in India*. Simla: Indian Institute of Advanced Study.

Raghaviah, V. 1971. *Tribal Revolts*. Nellore: Andhra Rashtra Adimajati Sevak Sangh.

Rao, M. S. A. 1979. *Social Movements and Social Transformation: A Study of Two Backward Classes Movements in India*. New Delhi: Macmillan.

————. ed. 1980. *Social Movements in India*. vol 2. Delhi: Manohar.

————. 1981. "Prophecy and Heritage in Social and Cultural Movements," *Social Action* 31 (April–June), pp. 174–81.

Roy, S. C. 1970. *The Mundas and Their Country*. Bombay: Asia Publishing House (First edition published in 1912).

Singh, Suresh K. 1966. *Dust Storms and Hanging Mist: Story of Birsa Munda and His Movement.* Calcutta: Firma K. L. Mukhopadyay.

Thorner, Alice. 1982. "Semi-Feudalism or Capitalism? Contemporary Debate on Classes and Modes of Production in India," *Economic and Political Weekly* 17, no. 49, pp. 1961–1968; ibid., no. 50, pp. 1993–1999; ibid., no. 51, pp. 2061–2066.

Wallerstein, Immanuel. 1979. *The Capitalist World-Economy.* Cambridge: Cambridge University Press.

———. 1974. *The Modern World-System: Capitalist Agriculture and the Origins of European World-Economy in the Sixteenth Century.* New York: Academic Press.

Weiner, Myron. 1978. *Sons of the Soil: Migration and Ethnic Conflict in India.* Delhi: Oxford University Press.

THE MIGRATION
MOVEMENTS TO
THE UNITED STATES
AND ARGENTINA

4

Across the Briny Ocean: Some Thoughts on Irish Emigration to America, 1800–1850

Cormac Ó Gráda

That the emigration from Ireland was already substantial in the years between Waterloo and the Great Famine is nowadays universally conceded. Then as later it was the most favored means of population control. By contrast with the post-Famine record, however, the reluctance or inability of the Irish to move in still greater numbers to distant lands remains an important historiographical theme.[1] The image of peasant multitudes clinging to home, "like sailors to the mast or hull of a wreck,"[2] is given point by the million or more fatalities of the Famine. It must not be forgotten, though, how small emigration from Europe in general was before 1845. Between the Discoveries and that date it is estimated that no more than five million or so Europeans settled in the New World, half of them after 1815.[3] Of the latter, Ireland supplied one-third, ten times more than her population share. No other country contributed as much. In addition perhaps another six hundred thousand Irish made Great Britain their home between 1815 and 1845.[4] Though post-Famine rates put earlier emigrations in the shade, by contemporary standards the pre-Famine Irish

Table 4.1

SOURCES FOR IRISH EMIGRANTS TO AMERICA, 1803–1848

Year	Destination	Source[8]	Number of Emigrants
1803–06	North America	Public Record Office, London	3,603
1819–20	U.S.A.	U.S. Congressional Papers	1,423
1830–39	North America	Ordnance Survey Memoirs (R.I.A., Dublin)	1,834
1822–39	Boston	U.S. Immigration Archives	7,000
1820–48	New York	U.S. Immigration Archives	30,534

must be characterized as "highly mobile" rather than *adscriptus glebae* (bound to the soil).[5]

The extent, nature, and consequences of the pre-Famine outflow have been discussed and debated over the years by Adams, Cousens, Jones, McDonagh, and others.[6] For such a historically significant phenomenon, the literature is small but of high quality. From the standpoint of this essay, perhaps the well-known emphasis on the different regional base and social structure of the pre-Famine emigration, and on the tendency of families rather than individuals to dominate, is more relevant. The claim that Catholic emigrants were disproportionately few early in the century, and Adams's point that the outflow was becoming both larger and more proletarian on the eve of the Famine, are also important. My main purpose is to round out somewhat more the profile of the pre-Famine emigrant through the use of contemporary passenger lists and allied material and to review some economic aspects of the emigration in light of the data.

"Who Were the Irish Emigrants to America Before 1845?"

The data base for this essay is information on the age, sex, occupation (usually), and regional origin (sometimes) of over thirty thousand pre-Famine emigrants.[7] (See table 4.1.)

The 1819–48 United States lists used here all have their origin in the same administrative concern: safeguarding the lives and welfare of the passengers who made the crossing. An act of March 2, 1819, required the master of a vessel arriving at any U.S. port from another country to present a list of passengers to the collector of the local customs district. The master was supposed to swear the list in the collector's presence.[9] The 1803–6 lists are a byproduct of legislation to prevent the emigration of sailors during the Napoleonic Wars.[10] The 1830s Ordnance Survey Memoirs data refer to one northern Irish county only: they are due to a scheme—abortive as it turned out—to accompany the survey with detailed socioeconomic and antiquarian reports for each area.[11] While probably incomplete in their coverage, in no case is there a presumption that these data are grossly misleading.

Computer frequency counts and cross-tabulations produced the results summarized in tables 4.2 to 4.11, which form the basis of our discussion. Let us review the more important findings.

1. All lists imply that proportionately *more children* and people over thirty-five emigrated before 1845 than later in the century (tables 4.2 and 4.3). Overall, fewer women left than men, but for those who traveled unaccompanied, the male concentration is rather remarkable. The number of unaccompanied men exceeded women by two to one among the Boston and New York immigrants of the 1820s and 1830s, but the ratio was almost four to one in 1819–20 and nine to one in 1803–6. This pattern evidently contrasts sharply with the post-Famine picture, but is quite in line with the nineteenth-century norm for other European nationalities. The factors that held down the emigration of Irishwomen early on in the century, and made it blossom later on, are imperfectly understood; however, candidates include the relatively harsh life of women in post-Famine Ireland, the increasing demand for domestic servants in America during the second half of the century, and the vast size of the emigration itself.[12] Finally, the data illustrate a feature seemingly common to all Irish nineteenth-century emigrations across the Atlantic: unaccompanied women left at an earlier age than unaccompanied men, many of them in their late teens.[13]

According to Adams, "The Irish preferred to emigrate in families when they could." In the case of all groups examined here, "family" emigrants, in the sense of people of the same surname traveling together, outnumbered unaccompanied emigrants. The lists imply a stronger unaccompanied element, though, than might be inferred from a reading of the existing literature. Nor were the family units that left typical: on average they were smaller than the family in the population at large. Some groups were big, but a substantial majority were of two or three people. The lists show that even in 1803–6 almost 70 percent of all emigrants left in parties of one to three people, while 75 percent of the Boston emigrants traveled in parties of three or less. Moreover, the lopsided sex ratio of the outflow indicates that only a minority of those unaccompanied can have paved the way for the rest of their households. Finally, the prevalence of units of one to three *may* suggest that the majority of emigrants came from a poorer background, but only if Adams's unsupported assertion about preferences holds.[14]

The lists produce a large and, at first, bewildering, catalogue of occupations, which I have reduced to six broad categories (tables 4.4 and 4.5). The results should be interpreted with caution: the 1803–6 data are

Table 4.2
AGE OF DISTRIBUTION OF IRISH EMIGRANTS TO AMERICA, 1800–1900
(in percentage)

Age	1803–5*	1819–20†	1820–46‡	1822–39§	1847–8‡	1865†	1900†	1841 Population
0–14	13.4	27.8	18.4	19.5	20.5	16.9	8.6	32.8
15–19	11.3	9.6	15.6	11.7	15.1	45.1	50.0	10.8
20–24	25.3	21.9	31.1	28.0	30.2	45.1	50.0	9.6
25–34	30.6	25.1	24.8	31.1	21.2	25.7	25.2	14.5
35–44	11.4	8.1	5.7	6.3	8.0	7.2	5.4	11.0
45 +	8.1	7.4	4.6	3.4	5.0	5.1	3.8	21.3

Sources: Note 8
*North America
†United States
‡New York
§Boston

Table 4.3
EMIGRANTS' AGE AND SEX, 1800–1850

Age	1803–5 Unaccompanied M	F	1803–5 Family M	F	1819–20 Unaccompanied M	F	1819–20 Family M	F	1822–39 Unaccompanied M	F	1822–39 Family M	F	1820–46 Unaccompanied M	F	1820–46 Family M	F	1847–48 Unaccompanied M	F	1847–48 Family M	F
0–14	15	8	214	185	19	7	114	104	60	43	598	573	260	257	1,985	1,986	72	60	585	544
15–29	154	24	112	100	39	25	37	55	184	299	104	205	936	1,178	642	987	208	235	221	269
20–24	432	60	207	174	144	42	82	89	810	407	303	376	3,188	1,650	1,303	1,437	628	398	379	396
25–34	424	54	337	241	182	36	101	91	867	235	541	462	2,470	794	1,473	1,308	469	182	361	294
35–44	124	12	148	107	55	12	63	70	153	32	134	111	477	111	420	388	124	57	148	161
45+	54	12	124	90	5	4	30	14	49	34	69	78	212	128	389	393	51	41	116	101
	1,023	172	1,142	897	444	127	427	423	2,123	1,050	1,749	1,805	7,543	4,118	6,212	6,499	1,112	973	1,810	1,765

83

particularly suspect, and probably a goodly proportion of those described therein as "laborers" were in fact semiskilled or skilled artisans. For the rest, it is likely that some of those termed "farmers" in the lists were simply laborers, though I have not attempted to adjust for this. A cautious guess, then, is that perhaps about a third of the men who left before 1820 were farmers or farmers' sons, about a tenth white-collar (gentlemen, merchants, and so forth), and the remainder about equally divided between laborers and artisans. The Boston and New York immigrants were less skilled, and only a small proportion of them listed as farmers.[15]

In all lists, artisans are more heavily represented among emigrants than in the population as a whole. This, on the face of it, may look like a "human capital" or "skill" drain, a possibility that worried some contemporary critics of pre-Famine emigration. Quick conclusions from the data are not warranted, however, since presumably *some* proportion of these artisans—particularly in the textile sector—were structurally unemployed, and their specific skills, therefore, rendered worthless. This after all was an era of unprecedented structural transformation in both Britain and Ireland.[16] In the Boston lists, though not in the others, artisans outside the textile sector tended to be concentrated in the older age groups, an indication, perhaps, of redundant skills. Interestingly, few former employers are to be found in the lists. The Boston data, for instance, give one "ironfounder," four "manufacturers," twenty-seven "merchants," and seven "brewers" and "distillers."

The County Derry Ordnance Survey Memoirs are silent on some of the issues discussed so far, but are alone in containing the religious affiliations of emigrants. They indicate that during the 1830s Presbyterians and other Dissenters left in greater numbers than their share in the population would predict, and Catholics and Established Church members less. The same pattern was found for neighboring County Antrim by Adams.[17] The lists also prompt a look at differences in destination across religious affiliation, controlling for area of origin within the county. To avoid the problem of empty or very small cells, I have grouped all parishes providing data into three areas (table 4.6). A common pattern within any area might then be regarded as evidence that people of all creeds used the same information flow about the New World in choosing their destination. However, at this level of disaggregation the differences are significant on standard statistical criteria.

The 1803–6 lists provide details too on port of destination. Crosstabulations by province of origin yield no interesting patterns in this case, but the data suggest that unaccompanied emigrants were rather more prone to go to New York, and families to the more traditional ports such as Baltimore and Philadelphia. Further, as Maldwyn Jones has already

Table 4.4

OCCUPATION AND EMIGRANTS' FAMILY STATUS
1803–5, 1819–20, 1822–39, and 1820–46

Occupational Category	1803–5 (U.S.)		1819–20 (U.S.)		1822–39 (Boston)		1820–46 (New York)	
	Unaccompanied	Family	Unaccompanied	Family	Unaccompanied	Family	Unaccompanied	Family
Laborers, servants	626 (45.6)	378 (28.1)	124 (31.7)	60 (20.5)	1,191 (60.0)	840 (66.6)	5,554 (60.7)	3,499 (52.5)
Textile workers	88 (6.4)	379 (28.2)	49 (12.3)	54 (18.5)	125 (6.3)	107 (8.5)	977 (10.7)	847 (12.7)
Farmers	433 (31.6)	516 (38.3)	105 (26.3)	129 (44.2)	150 (7.6)	109 (8.6)	1,093 (11.9)	1,056 (15.8)
Other artisans	17 (1.2)	11 (0.8)	52 (13.0)	27 (9.2)	435 (21.9)	184 (14.6)	1,181 (12.9)	1,042 (15.6)
White collar	206 (15.0)	61 (4.3)	66 (16.5)	22 (7.5)	82 (4.1)	22 (1.7)	193 (2.1)	136 (2.0)
Other	2 (0.0)	1 (0.0)	3 (0.8)	0 (0.0)	3 (0.2)	1 (0.1)	151 (1.7)	83 (1.2)
	1,372 (100.0)	1,346 (100.0)	399 (100.0)	292 (100.0)	1,926 (100.0)	1,261 (100.0)	9,149 (100.0)	6,663 (100.0)

Table 4.5

OCCUPATIONS OF IRISH EMIGRANTS TO BOSTON AND
NEW YORK, COMPARED TO THE CENSUS DATA, 1841
(Percentages)

Occupational Category	Boston		New York		Census 1841	
	Male	Female	Male	Female	Male	Female
Laborers, servants	62.7	78.6	60.5	63.3	55.4	33.7
Textile workers	3.5	11.1	7.0	24.4	7.1	59.3
Farmers	10.4	0.5	15.7	9.2	20.7	1.9
Other artisans	20.5	8.1	13.3	2.3	10.5	0.7
White collar	2.7	1.0	3.6	0.8	4.9	3.4
Other	0.2	0.7	—	—	1.5	0.4

pointed out,[18] the lists show New York to have been the main port of disembarkation for Irish immigrants already by the 1800s. During the 1820s and 1830s New York handled at least thirty times as many Irish immigrants as Boston.

The Boston lists show that the great majority of its Irish arrivals proceeded not directly from Ireland, but via the Canadian Maritime ports.[19] Of 7,000 emigrants, over 5,400 took the Canadian route, arriving for the most part in dribs and drabs by smaller ships, some of which seem to have specialized in the traffic. Only 216 arrived directly from Ireland. The Canadian crossing was the third-class route of the day.[20] The role it played in the Boston immigration may mean that the Irish who went there were of a lower socioeconomic status than those who preceded them to the States in the 1800s and the 1810s, if not also those who were traveling to New York in the 1820s and 1830s.

Tables 4.7 and 4.8 provide some insight into the changing composition of the Atlantic emigration over time. The New York and other lists suggest that the unaccompanied component, and the female proportion of it, were increasing; the occupational data suggest a rising proportion of laborers, and fewer artisanal and textile workers. Overall the data are in broad agreement with Adams's claim of a lowering of the socioeconomic status of the emigrants after 1835 or so.[21]

Adams and Cousens have highlighted the Ulster element in pre-Famine emigration.[22] Only the 1803–6 lists provide comprehensive county-of-origin data: they confirm Ulster's preeminence at that juncture, with, interestingly enough, the western counties of Donegal and Tyrone to the fore in relative terms (table 4.9). Of the 3,215 whose county origins can be traced, almost 80 percent came from Ulster, and another 12 percent from Leinster. Only Sligo of the Connacht or Munster counties supplied an appreciable number of emigrants, though Sligo was arguably within the west Ulster orbit.

The New York lists (table 4.10) give the county origins of some eleven thousand emigrants. Ulster's share turns out to have still been disproportionately large, but had fallen to only 37 percent in 1820–46. Connacht's share, though always small, rose over time.

Some Economic Implications

Comparing the usual cost of a passage—£4 to £8—and the annual earnings of a pre-Famine laborer—£10 to £15—explains the resiliency of the hypothesis that a "poverty trap" prevented the poorest in Ireland from leaving in those years. The 1803–6 data are at least consistent with this: Ulster, the richest of the four provinces, accounted for the lion's share of the emigrants, and nonlaborers comfortably outnumbered laborers. The New York data too suggest that Ireland's poorer districts yielded disproportionately small pre-Famine emigrant flows. Qualitative evidence arguing in the

Table 4.6

THE DESTINATION OF COUNTY DERRY EMIGRANTS OF
1835–38 BY RELIGION
(in percentages)

Destination	Dissenters	Roman Catholic	Established Church
A. *West Derry*			
New York	19.3	28.3	14.3
Philadelphia	43.7	16.2	9.5
Quebec	25.3	40.3	47.6
St. John's	11.7	14.9	28.6
B. *South Derry*	*Roman Catholic*	*Other*	
New York	45.8	20.4	
Philadelphia	14.7	18.3	
Quebec	32.4	45.5	
Other	7.1	15.8	
C. *East Derry*			
New York	15.6	11.0	
Philadelphia	7.8	27.0	
Quebec	55.8	51.6	
Other	20.8	10.4	

Source: See note 8.

Table 4.7

THE CHANGING COMPOSITION OF EMIGRATION OVER TIME: SEX AND FAMILY STATUS, NEW YORK, 1820–48

Period	Unaccompanied		Total	
	Male	Female	Male	Female
1820–29	870 (77.2)	257 (22.8)	1,586 (62.2)	963 (37.8)
1830–34	1,306 (69.7)	567 (30.3)	2,344 (59.1)	1,623 (40.9)
1835–39	2,177 (64.4)	1,206 (35.6)	3,936 (57.0)	2,968 (43.0)
1840–46	3,196 (60.5)	2,088 (39.5)	5,894 (53.8)	5,063 (46.2)
1847–48	1,612 (62.4)	973 (37.6)	3,422 (55.6)	2,738 (44.4)

Table 4.8

OCCUPATIONS, NEW YORK, 1820–48

Occupation	1820–34	1835–46	1847–48
Laborers, servants	1,956 (48.0)	7,097 (60.4)	2,719 (60.2)
Textile workers	352 (13.5)	1,272 (10.8)	591 (13.1)
Farmers	687 (16.9)	1,472 (12.5)	506 (11.2)
Other artisans	691 (16.9)	1,532 (13.0)	580 (12.8)
White collar	117 (2.9)	212 (1.8)	70 (1.6)
Other	74 (1.8)	160 (1.4)	49 (1.1)

same direction is plentiful. Nevertheless the "poverty trap" hypothesis needs more careful definition, since it was not merely the fare but—more importantly—other transactions costs of the move, and the poorer prospects facing Irish-speaking peasants from the south and west in America kept down the numbers wanting to leave.[23] A comparison with contemporary European data indicates that, not only the Famine, but greatly reduced travel and job search time, altered the balance after midcentury.[24]

The passenger lists give no straightforward answer to the question "were the emigrants the most talented and ambitous?" As we have just seen, the lists are elusive even on the simpler problem of useful skills and training. A priori reasoning is of little help in predicting who emigrated. On the one hand, insofar as people who were relatively productive in Ireland in agriculture and other sectors earned incomes related to their specific complementarities with respect to other inputs, there is some theoretical presumption that they would stay. On the other, if emigration is regarded as a lottery, wherein the "best" leave because the odds of their improving their lot are better, the outcome is reversed.

Our data provide the raw material for one crude test of the educational or literacy level of the emigrants relative to the population as a whole—not exactly what we want, yet relevant, nevertheless. Demog-

Table 4.9
EMIGRANTS' PROVINCE OF ORIGIN, 1803–5

	Unaccompanied	Family	Total
Leinster	217	185	402
Munster	35	48	83
Ulster	936	1,612	2,548
Connacht	100	82	182
	1,288	1,927	3,215

Table 4.10
NEW YORK EMIGRANTS' PROVINCE OF ORIGIN, 1820–1848

	1820–34	1835–46	1847–48
Leinster	897 (38.8)	2,361 (38.8)	590 (21.5)
Munster	357 (15.4)	706 (11.6)	375 (13.7)
Ulster	904 (39.1)	2,237 (36.7)	1,114 (40.6)
Connacht	156 (6.7)	787 (12.9)	663 (24.2)
	2,314	6,092	2,742

raphers have long noted the association between economic backwardness and illiteracy on the one hand, and "age-heaping" in censal returns on the other. In poorer countries a disporportionately large number of people give their ages rounded to the nearest zero or five. The Irish census of 1841, the first to publish year-by-year age information, suffers from notoriously extreme age-heaping.[25] A comparison of the 1841 data and those taken from the emigrant lists should, by extension, tell us whether those who left were more or less "backward" than the average. Many measures of age-heaping have been proposed,[26] but we simply define I here as a relative age-heaping index, where

$$I = \frac{\Sigma w_i \pi_i}{\Sigma w_i \pi_i^*}$$

Here w_i equals the share of emigrants aged i in the emigrant flow, and π_i and π_i^* the proportion of those in age-bracket i (e.g., 20–24 years) who reported their age as a multiple of ten (e.g., twenty) in the lists and the census, respectively. When I is unity the population at large and the emigrants age-heaped equally; if I is greater than one, the emigrants heaped more.

The results, calculated from the data in table 4.11, give $I_{1803-6} = 1.06$, $I_{1819-20} = 0.99$, $I_{1822-39} = 1.11$, and $I_{1820-46} = 1.13$. No comfort here,

Table 4.11
VALUES OF π FROM IRISH PASSENGER LISTS 1803–1839, THE 1841 AND 1851 CENSUSES, AND SWEDISH PASSENGER LISTS 1820–1850

Ireland, 1803–6		
Age	π	n
20—4	.260	874
30—4	.631	374
40—4	.690	158
50—4	.716	95
Ireland, 1819–20		
20—4	.212	358
30—4	.697	132
40—4	.704	54
50—4	.611	36
Ireland, 1822–39		
20—4	.269	1,910
30—4	.672	772
40—4	.829	199
50—4	.771	83
	π^*	π^*
Irish Census, 1841, 1851	*1841*	*1851*
20—4	.308	.338
30—4	.498	.517
40—4	.576	.661
50—4	.617	.604
Sweden, 1820–50	π	n
20—4	.261	471
30—4	.341	422
40—4	.465	243
50—4	.380	100

then, for the "brain drain" argument. It might be countered that the lists reflect the ship master's carelessness rather than the passengers' lack of numeracy. Certainly a perusal of some of the lists would give some support to this view, but a comparison with the Swedish pre-1850 data, culled from the same source as some of my own lists, suggests that the passengers' numerical ability was indeed being captured.[27]

From an economic standpoint, the notion that emigration was beneficial in the long run, since those who left eventually did well, and the law of diminishing returns worked in favor of those who stayed is an appealing one. For the pre-Famine period, especially, it has a plausible ring to it. Nevertheless, emigration has had its cogent critics, and one of their strongest points is that the self-selected character of the outflow could have hurt the stay-at-homes. There are two main reasons for this, the first of which has been discussed. The second source of putative loss, stemming from the unbalanced age-structure of the emigration, can receive only summary treatment here.[28]

Just as the arrival of "ready-made" workers conferred a human capital boon on nineteenth-century America,[29] it has long been recognized by European writers that the age-selectivity of emigration could simultaneously injure the sending country. The "loss" follows from the emigrant often spending his unproductive years at home running up debts against family and fellow citizens but supplying credits in turn under another flag. Whether remittances provided adequate compensation is an open question.[30]

Setting age distribution from our passenger lists and the 1841 census side by side (table 4.2) is in itself evidence of a potential problem here. More concretely, we may assume that the average emigrant who left before the age of thirty or thirty-five years had not fully repaid his debts. Full calculations of the loss from this source require assumptions about consumption and earnings at different points over the life cycle, and about remittances. They also require somewhat restrictive assumptions about the nature of the intergenerational transfers that took place. Preliminary estimates of the loss, taking account too of emigration to places other than the United States, range from 0.5 to 2 percent of contemporary national income. Not a large proportion, certainly, but appreciable in a faltering economy.

The profile of the New York emigrants of 1847 and 1848 reported in tables 4.2, 4.3 and 4.4 differs less markedly from those who preceded them in the late 1830s and early 1840s than might be expected. True, they were somewhat more likely to be under fifteen or over thirty-five years of age, and less likely to travel alone; they may also have been less skilled. Moreover, a full sample of Famine emigrants may accentuate the differences. But if these results provide even an approximate description of the outflow, they add an intriguing insight to our understanding of the workings of the Famine. For if the emigrants continued to be disproportionately male and young, the structure of the surviving population implies that the excess deaths of the Famine years were more likely to have been the women, the very young, and the elderly. It is possible, too, that the age and sex structure of the Famine emigration, by leaving behind those most at risk, increased the human toll of those years.[31]

Notes

1. For a quick introduction to the subject see G. Ó Tuathaigh, *Ireland before the Famine, 1798–1848* (Dublin, 1972), pp. 140–42. On the inability/unwillingness to emigrate, e.g., J. C. Beckett, *The Making of Modern Ireland, 1603–1923* (London, 1966), p. 344; O. MacDonagh, *A Pattern of Government Growth, 1800–60: The Passenger Acts and Their Enforcement* (London, 1961), pp. 24–27; P. Taylor, *The Distant Magnet: European Migration to the United States* (London, 1971), pp. 34–35.

2. MacDonagh, 25, quoting William Cobbett.

3. C. McEvedy and R. Jones, *Atlas of World Population History* (Harmondsworth, 1978), pp. 30–31.

4. Compare Ó Tuathaigh.

5. J. K. Ingram, "Considerations on the State of Ireland," *Journal of the Statistical and Social Inquiry Society of Ireland*, IV, part xxvi (1864), 14.

6. W. F. Adams, *Ireland and Irish Emigration to the New World from 1815 to the Famine* (New Haven, 1932); S. H. Cousens, "The Regional Variation in Emigration from Ireland between 1821 and 1841," *Institute of British Geographers, Transactions and Papers* 37 (1965), 15–30; M. Jones, "Irish Emigration, 1783–1815," in E. R. R. Green (ed.), *Essays in Scotch-Irish History* (London, 1969), pp. 48–68; O. Mac-Donagh.

7. Compare C. Erickson's well-known "Who Were the Emigrants from England and Scotland in the Late Nineteenth Century?" in D. V. Glass and R. Revelle (eds.), *Population and Social Change* (London, 1972).

8. The 1803–6 lists come from British Museum, Additional Ms. 35932, "Passengers from Ireland to America." The 1819–20 lists were published in U.S. State Department, *Letter from the Secretary of State, with a Transcript of the List of Passengers Who Arrived in the United States from 10/1/19 to 9/30/20* (Washington, 1821). The other U.S. lists are deposited in the National Immigration Archives, Balch Institute, Philadelphia: the National Library, Dublin, has microfilm copies. The Ordnance Survey Memoirs (hereafter cited as OSM) are held in the Royal Irish Academy, Dublin.

Brian Trainor, Public Record Office of Northern Ireland, kindly provided me with the 1803–6 and 1822–39 data in typed, easily codable form. Joel Mokyr allowed me to use his New York emigrants file (fully explained in his *Why Ireland Starved: A Quantitative and Analytical History of the Irish Economy 1800–1850* (forthcoming, 1982), chap. 7). My thanks to them both.

9. The legislation and its background are explained in United States Immigration Commission, *Abstracts of Reports*, vol. 2 (Washington, 1911), pp. 589–91.

10. R. Jones.

11. J. H. Andrews, *A Paper Landscape: The Ordnance Survey in Nineteenth-Century Ireland* (Oxford, 1975), pp. 144–79.

12. R. E. Kennedy, Jr., *The Irish: Emigration, Marriage, and Fertility* (Berkeley, 1973), pp. 66–85; J. J. Lee, "Women and the Church since the Famine," in M. MacCurtain and D. Ó Corráin (eds.), *Women in Irish Society: The Historical Dimension* (Westport, Conn., 1979), pp. 37–45.

13. On the age and sex of European emigrants to the Americas during the nineteenth century, cf. United States Immigration Commission, pp. 5–8; I. Ferenczi, *International Migrations: Statistics* (New York, 1929).

14. The average size of the emigrating Boston "family," for instance, was just over three. Compare F. J. Carney, "Aspects of Pre-Famine Irish Household Size: Composition and Differentials" in L. M. Cullen and T. C. Smout (eds.), *Comparative Aspects of Scottish and Irish Economic and Social History 1600–1900* (Edinburgh, 1978), pp. 32–46. An exception to the pattern outlined here is provided by Peter Robinson's planned emigration of 1823–25, which carried about three thousand Irish, mainly from Cork, to Upper Canada. This emigration was overwhelmingly a family emigration, for reasons clearly explained in W. Cameron, "Selecting Peter Robinson's Irish Emigrants," *Social History/Histoire Sociale* 9, no. 17 (1976), 29–46. This latter emigration, it might be noted, much more closely resembled contemporary Scottish Highland emigration than the usual Irish pattern. My cursory inspection of Scottish passenger lists suggests more young people and women, and a higher proportion of family emigrants. See, e.g., Home Office, London, 102/18 (lists of passengers aboard the *Sarah* and *Dove* bound for Pictou, Nova Scotia, in 1801); Public Archives, Canada, MG 40 C 10 (lists of passengers aboard the *Commerce* out of Greenock in 1820). Scottish emigration is discussed at some length in M. Flinn (ed.), *Scottish Population History* (Cambridge, 1977), pp. 93–96, 435, 443–47, but more relevant to the present discussion is M. Flinn, "Malthus, Emigration and Potatoes in the Scottish North-west, 1770–1870," in L. M. Cullen and T. C. Smout (eds.), especially pp. 57–58.

15. On difficulties with interpreting the 1803–6 lists, see R. Jones.

16. The disastrous effect on Irish industry and protoindustrial employment may be gauged from a comparison of the occupational details given in the censuses of 1821 and 1841. See C. Ó Gráda, "Demographic Adjustment and Seasonal Migration in Nineteenth-century Ireland," in L. M. Cullen and F. Furet (eds.), *Ireland and France: Towards a Comparative Study of Rural History* (Paris, 1981).

17. Adams; J. H. Johnson's "Population Movements in County Derry during a Pre-Famine Year," *Proceedings of the Royal Irish Academy*, vol. 60, Section C (1959), 141–62, also uses the OSM data to answer several related questions.

18. "Irish Emigration, 1783–1815," 60.

19. On the role of the Maritime ports in Irish immigration, see J. S. Martell, *Immigration to and Emigration from Nova Scotia, 1815–38* (Halifax, 1942); H. Cowan, *British Emigration to British North America* (Toronto, 1928).

20. There was a fourth-class route to Boston: an indeterminate number of immigrants made their way there from the Maritimes by foot. See O. Handlin, *The Uprooted* (New York, 1951), pp. 59–60.

21. Adams, chap. 5.

22. Ibid., 118–20, 188, 221; Cousens.

23. On the implausibility of the "poverty trap" argument after 1850 see C. Ó Gráda, "On Some Aspects of Nineteenth-century Irish Emigration," in L. M. Cullen and T. C. Smout (eds.). The importance of seasonal migration from the west and south before 1845 means that the passage money alone—for single young men at least—was no insuperable obstacle to emigration.

24. The huge rise in emigration from England, Germany, and the Scandinavian countries in the 1850s is documented in I. Ferenczi, 377–80.

25. As noted by the census commissioners themselves, and discussed in J. Lee, "Marriage and Population in pre-Famine Ireland," *Economic History Review*, 21 (1968), 289–90.

26. S. Shrycock and J. S. Siegel, *The Methods and Materials of Demography* (Washington, 1973), pp. 700–4. For further analysis along the same lines, using other measures, see J. Mokyr and C. Ó Gráda, "Emigration and Irish Poverty before 1845," *Explorations in Economic History*, forthcoming.

27. The Swedish data are taken from N. W. Olsson, *Swedish Passenger Arrivals in New York* (Chicago, 1967).

28. It is discussed in more detail in J. Mokyr, *Why Ireland Starved*, chap. 7; C. Ó Gráda, "On Some Economic Aspects of Pre-Famine Emigration" (unpublished, February 1981); J. Mokyr and C. Ó Gráda.

29. L. Neal and P. J. Uselding, "Immigration, A Neglected Source of American Economic Growth: 1790 to 1912," *Oxford Economic Papers*, 24 (1972), 68–88; P. J. Hill, *The Economic Consequences of Immigration into the United States* (New York, 1975).

30. W. Farr, *Vital Statistics* (London, 1885), pp. 59–64; A. Marshall, *Principles of Economics: Variorum Edition* (London, 1961), II, p. 622; F. Kapp, *Immigration and the Commissioners of Emigration* (New York, 1870), pp. 144–47.

31. Phelim Boyle of the University of British Columbia and I are currently engaged in a study of these issues.

5

Dutch International Migration and Occupational Change: A Structural Analysis of Multinational Linked Files

Robert P. Swierenga

The economic progress of European immigrants to the United States is one of the major questions in the literature (Thomas, 1978; Kirk and Kirk, 1978b; Hudson, 1976). Using occupation and wealth as indices of socioeconomic status, researchers have developed cross-sectional and longitudinal data sets to compare American ethnic groups spatially at one point in time or to follow wage earners over time once they were established in the United States (Thernstrom, 1974, 220–61; Hershberg, 1981, 461–91).

But few studies have explored occupational change as a result of the overseas emigration process itself. To do so requires a comparison of the "last job" in the country of origin with the "first job" in the country of destination. The social geographers Ostergren (1979), Gjerde (1979), and Hudson (1976) and historians Kamphoefner (1978) and Conzen (1976) have demonstrated the feasibility of such international occupational mobility studies in a number of Scandinavian and German case studies. But their data bases were small and usually limited to a few Old World villages that were tied through chain migrations to particular Midwestern frontier communities.

This essay examines occupational changes among overseas emigrants for an entire nationality group, the Dutch, for the years 1840 through 1870. All officially registered emigrants throughout the Netherlands who were bound for the United States in these thirty years are included. Emigrants can thus be compared by decadal cohorts, age, rural-urban origin, social class, religion, and geographic region. In short, by studying a total immigrant population one can capture the full diversity of the group rather than be limited to subgroups that may be homogeneous.

Hypotheses

Migration scholars have hypothesized that, all things being equal, international migration is likely to result in downward occupational mobility, at least in the short run, because of language difficulties and the imperfect transferability of credentials and job skills (Chiswick, 1977). Within a few years, as the new arrivals gain a tolerable competency in English, adapt to American job practices, and obtain needed credentials, they begin to experience upward mobility. This model posits a U-shaped pattern of immigrant occupational change, with an initial sharp decline followed by steady advance, until the newcomers reach and even surpass their original level.

The extent of occupational change in the migration process, however, is directly dependent on the labor and land market opportunities, and the similarity of occupational structures in the sending and receiving countries and particularly in the local communities involved. The greater the differences, the sharper the decline. If the two countries are alike in most respects, we can hypothesize that occupational skills are readily transferred and that immigrants would suffer little status loss and might actually improve their position from the outset. Immigrants from English-speaking countries (the British Isles and Canada) have generally followed this pattern. But when the two countries differ substantially in language and culture, as is the case of emigrants from Continental countries, the initial deterioration would be more intense.

This hypothesis, which derives from modern studies of occupational status change among emigrants, must be modified to take into account the greater land and labor opportunities in the United States in the nineteenth century that stood in stark contrast to overcrowded, stagnant Europe. Until the closing of the farmers' frontier in the 1890s, European peasants and rural day laborers frequently were able to obtain their own farms because of generous American land policies. In such situations, despite wide differences between countries of origin and destination, emigrants would experience an immediate rise in status from landless laborer to farm proprietor. Indeed, in such circumstances, the U-shaped pattern might be inversed. If the first immigrants could monopolize the available land, they would experience a sharp rise in status, whereas latecomers, closed out by high land prices, would suffer an initial decline (Doyle, 1982).

The comparative economic opportunities and level of development in the respective sending and host communities thus affect job transferability and status changes. The Netherlands, for example, lagged behind the United States in industrial development in the midnineteenth century, but this affected Dutch immigrants only slightly because they did not enter the American labor market in the conventional two-stage process. Rather, the Dutch bypassed eastern seaboard factories, opting instead to go directly to the farm lands of the Midwest (Swierenga, 1982).

Empirical Analysis

The data base for this essay is a linked nominal file of Dutch overseas emigrants in the years 1835–70 and Dutch-born households in the United States population censuses of 1850, 1860, and 1870. The Dutch records are the official emigration lists compiled annually by local officials beginning in the mid-1840s, under the direction of the Interior Ministry (Swierenga, and Stout, 1975). They provide a wealth of social, economic, and geographical data, including name, place of birth, sex, age, occupation, religion, economic and tax status, presumed reason for emigrating, and intended general destination. When the premigration biographical data are combined with the postmigration information in the well-known U.S. population censuses, the resulting profile of individual immigrant families is rich indeed.

The Netherlands was not a high emigration country, ranking only tenth among European nations in the volume of overseas emigration (Swierenga, 1982). Approximately 15,000 Dutch families and single adults emigrated to the United States in the thirty years of this study. By searching the U.S. population censuses of all counties and cities with at least 50 Dutch-born persons, I was able to trace about 4,000 households (approximately one-third).

The linkage procedure was done by hand, according to a careful set of rules which have been described elsewhere (Swierenga, 1981). The wide-ranging search was greatly facilitated by the clustered settlement pattern of the Dutch in the Great Lakes region. The primary settlement region was within a fifty-mile radius of the southern Lake Michigan shoreline from

Muskegon, Holland, and Grand Rapids on the eastern side to Chicago, Milwaukee, and Green Bay on the western side. Secondary fields were central Iowa (Marion County) and the New York City region including northern New Jersey.

Subsequently, of course, the Dutch dispersed themselves over a wider area of the Great Plains and Far West in search of cheap farmland. But few European immigrant groups of comparable size have clustered more than did the clannish Dutch. In 1850, 72 percent of the nearly 9,000 Dutch immigrants in the United States lived in only 16 counties (out of 1,626 counties nationwide); in 1870 after 25 years of continuous migration and a spreading out across the land, 56 percent of all Dutch immigrants still resided in only 18 counties (out of some 2,300 counties nationwide), and 40 percent lived in a mere 55 townships and city wards (Swierenga, 1982).

The biases in the linked file are not fully known. As in other studies, however, the most likely missed links involved isolated families or single adults living outside of known Dutch communities, especially those who settled in the large cities where the census marshals were extremely careless in recording names. If names are unrecognizable, linkage is problemmatic. Single persons were also more difficult to link than families, because of the lack of comparable data for other family members. The "lost" immigrants ranged in numbers from 14 percent in 1850 to 38 percent in 1870. Many were single young men. Others were fringe types—unchurched, adventurous, malcontents, and members of racial and religious groups with an international institutional character, specifically Roman Catholics and Jews. Thus, the linked file on which this essay rests is biased toward Protestants and especially those who emigrated in family or community groups and followed common migration streams to rural colonies or urban Dutch neighborhoods.

The Dutch Emigration Context

Changing socioeconomic and politico-religious conditions provided the impetus for Dutch overseas migration. The nation suffered a series of setbacks in the early nineteenth century that set the stage for the emigration of 400,000 Hollanders in the century prior to World War I (Griffiths, 1979; DeJonge, 1981; Mokyr, 1976). The first blow struck when Napoleon conquered Holland and attempted to rationalize the stagnant, antiquated Dutch economy and integrate it into the larger French-Belgian system. In 1814, with Napoleon's defeat, the Congress of Vienna created the United Netherlands by combining Belgium (the Southern Provinces) and Holland, the intent being to form a buffer against French aggression. But the hybrid economic and political union lasted only fifteen years, until 1830, when the Catholic and largely French-speaking Belgians, who were more advanced economically, successfully revolted against predominantly Protestant Holland. The North at first used military force to try to prevent the loss of half a kingdom, but Belgian resistance and a British trade embargo led to a costly armed truce in 1839.

The war caused a general economic recession in the late 1830s and virtually bankrupted the Dutch government, prompting King William I to abdicate the throne in 1840. Before taking this positive step, the aristocratic and strong-willed William had also instigated a massive revolt against the national *Hervormde* (Reformed) Church by his heavy-handed suppression of evangelical reformers (Oostendorp, 1964). These dissenters, called Separatists, emigrated to the United States by the thousands in the years 1846 to 1850, thus enhancing an emigration mentality among Hollanders that had already been nurtured by heavy German Rhineland emigration to the United States.

But socioeconomic problems were paramount in Holland (Stokvis, 1977; Borgman, 1959). The Napoleonic and Belgian wars left the country in a weakened state, suffering from high taxes, unemployment, chronic pauperism, and a general feeling of disillusionment and bitterness. This was the situation when potatoes and rye, the basic food crops, failed three years in a row in the mid-1840s and brought the Netherlands to the brink of famine (Bergman, 1967; Terlouw, 1971). Potatoes had long been a dependable, cheap food, but prices now rose 250 percent. The number of persons on government poor relief tripled, protests erupted in market towns, and pillaging increased in the countryside. Without potatoes from their small garden plots, the laborers lost their ability to survive without government doles.

Agricultural conditions in themselves, however, do not account fully for Dutch emigration. Another factor was the lagging economic modernization. It was after 1890 before the Netherlands belatedly underwent economic "take-off" (DeJonge, 1971). Displaced rural laborers, therefore, had difficulty finding alternative opportunities in the industrial sectors of the economy. Meanwhile, skilled workers in the traditional small-scale protoindustries in inland regions, such as textiles, sugar refining, metals, and paper making, also were forced to adapt to mechanization or suffer a sharp economic decline. Understandably, the rural day laborers and craftsmen were prime candidates for emigration to the United States, where abundant Midwestern farm lands beckoned and wage rates far exceeded those in the Old Country.

Dutch labor migration to the United States thus responded, as one would expect, to structural determinants in both countries resulting from differing levels of land supply, wages, and industrial jobs. Emigration simultaneously alleviated the conditions of labor oversupply and food shortages in the Netherlands at midcentury, and in the United States it ameliorated problems of labor scarcity, high wages, and unused lands in a period of rapid economic development.

General Character of the Emigration

The socioeconomic patterns of Dutch emigration, which can be determined from the official lists compiled by Dutch officials, reveal an emigration of young lower-middle-class rural families and single male adults. Of the more than 60,000 registered emigrants in the period 1835–1880, only 20 percent lived in the Randstad cities (Amsterdam, Rotterdam, and The Hague), in provincial capitals, or in lesser urban municipalities. The remaining 80 percent were from rural villages and the countryside. Farmers and farm laborers comprised 26 percent (10 points above the national average in 1859), day laborers—some of whom doubtless also worked in agriculture—made up another 39 percent (20 points above the national average), 21 percent were village craftsmen, 4 percent worked in the industrial sector, mainly in textiles and small instruments (table 5.1). Only 10 percent held white-collar positions. This was 30 points below the national average. Blue-collar workers thus made up less than half of the Dutch labor force in 1859, but they comprised two-thirds of the emigrant labor population.

Economically, two-thirds of the emigrant families were classified in the documents as middling in status, a fifth were needy, and one in eight was well-to-do. The average age of all Dutch arrivals in the States was 23.1 years, adult males outnumbered females by a ratio of six to four, and more than three-fourths of all immigrants left with family members (Swierenga, 1980). This high family involvement, plus the concentrated settlement behavior, indicates a chain migration pattern.

As one would expect in a preindustrial migration, the Dutch had a noticeable lack of occupational diversity, and *none* of the new industrial jobs is found among the top twenty occupations (table 5.2). The three most common occupations—unskilled day laborers, farmers, and farm hands—accounted for nearly 60 percent of the adult male work force. Almost nine out of ten (86 percent) of the emigrant males worked in fewer than twenty occupations. Apart from the top three, only carpenters and merchants accounted for more than 3 percent of the emigrant work force. Merchants, clergymen, government officials, and teachers were the only nonblue-collar occupations among the top twenty. Nor does the pattern change substantially over time, at least before 1880.

Emigration was also place-specific and varied greatly between the

Table 5.1
OCCUPATIONS BY INDUSTRIAL SECTOR, DUTCH EMIGRANTS, 1835–1880

Sector	1835–1859		1858–1868		1869–1880		Total	
	Row N	Row %	Row N	Row %	Row N	Row %	Row N	Col. %
Primary								
Farmers	1,245	44	779	28	813	29	2,837	16
Farm Laborers	540	31	465	27	738	42	1,743	10
								26
Secondary								
Preindustrial Crafts:								
Building trades	653	43	371	25	484	32	1,508	8
Food processors	261	33	295	37	235	30	791	4
Metal workers	162	49	76	23	93	28	331	2
Wood workers	487	49	234	23	273	23	994	5
Clothing Trades	148	40	113	30	112	30	373	2
								21
Industrial:								
Textiles	160	60	56	21	49	18	265	2
Iron and Steel	6	35	5	29	6	35	17	0
Engineers	14	37	12	32	12	32	38	0
Watch/Instrument	134	38	96	27	122	35	352	2
Printers	4	16	11	44	11	40	26	0
Misc.	14	25	17	30	26	46	57	0
								4
Laborers (unspecified)	2,176	31	2,256	32	2,673	38	7,105	39
Tertiary								
Clerical	24	19	41	32	64	50	129	1
Commercial	310	37	218	26	300	36	828	4
Officials, government	31	15	98	46	82	39	211	1
Professional	148	26	212	38	199	36	559	3
Gentlemen/Students	44	44	25	25	31	31	100	1
Service	29	52	10	18	17	30	56	0
								10

Note: The categories are those employed by Charlotte Erickson, "Who Were English Emigrants of the 1820s and 1830s? A Preliminary Analysis" (unpublished paper, 1977). The 2,043 individuals with no occupation or trade or not employed are excluded.
Source: R. P. Swierenga, Netherlands Emigration Data File.

Table 5.2

TWENTY MOST FREQUENTLY LISTED OCCUPATIONS,
DUTCH EMIGRANT MALES, 20 YEARS AND OLDER, 1835–1880

Rank	Occupations	N	Cumulative Percentage	Rank 1835–57	Rank[a] 1858–68	Rank[b] 1869–80
1	Laborer	5,712	36	1	1	1
2	Farmer	2,668	53	2	2	2
3	Carpenter	880	58	3	4	3
4	Farmhand	851	63	4	3	4
5	Merchant	580	67	5	5	5
6	Tailor	356	69	6	9.5	7
7	Shoemaker	343	71	7	11	8
8	Sailor	287	73	11	8	6
9	Baker	275	75	9	12	9
10	Blacksmith	257	77	10	14	10
11	Weaver	234	78	8	13	18
12	Soldier	200	79	11	5	17
13.5	Clergyman	198	80	14	9.5	13.5
13.5	Painter	198	81	12	16	11
15	Mason	175	82	13	18	13.5
16	Govt. official	166	83	21	7	12
17	Teacher	154	84	15	15	15
18	Miller	115	85	16	21.5	19
19	Clerk	101	86	23	17	16
20	Wagonmaker	88	86	18	19	20

[a] Period 1–Period 2 $R_s = .61$ $p < .01$
[b] Period 1–Period 3 $R_s = .74$ $p < .001$
Source: R. P. Swierenga, Netherlands Emigration Data File.

major soil regions of the Netherlands: the dairy areas of the west central area, the inland sandy soil regions, and the sea clay areas along the North Sea (see figures 5.1 and 5.2). Over half (57 percent) of all emigrants originated in the rich sea clay soil areas; a third (32 percent) hailed from the thin sandy soil areas, and only 11 percent came from dairy regions (table 5.3). The dairy farms were small, single-family operations. Dairy farmers enjoyed stable prices and technology had little impact, so the propensity to emigrate was almost nil. Agriculturalists in the inland sandy regions also had less pressure to emigrate, because land reclamation in the nineteenth century and improved soil productivity (due to the introduction of artificial fertilizers) allowed several generations of farmers to keep their married sons at home by subdividing their farms.

By contrast, the sea clay regions along the North Sea coast of the provinces of Zeeland, Groningen, and Friesland led in the development of

Figure 5.1: Emigration Rate 1835–1880, per 1,000 Average Population 1830–1878

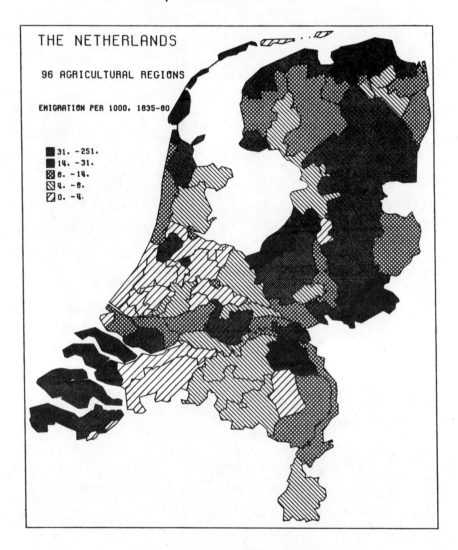

THE NETHERLANDS

96 AGRICULTURAL REGIONS

EMIGRATION PER 1000, 1835-80

31. -251.
14. -31.
8. -14.
4. -8.
0. -4.

Source: R. P. Swierenga, Netherlands Emigration Data File.

Figure 5.2: Agricultural Regions and Provincial Boundaries, the Netherlands

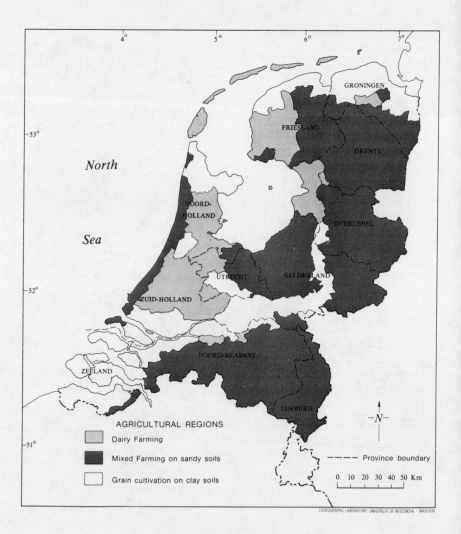

Source: *Verslag van de Landbouw, 1875.*

commercial farming, cattle breeding, and participation in international markets. Agriculture was highly specialized and the farm owners were more entrepreneurial-minded in the coastal areas than elsewhere. The clay soil farms were especially large and prosperous by Dutch standards. They employed numerous farm workers who comprised a landless proletariate. Formerly the laborers were part of a patriarchal and mutually dependent, communal society. But with the introduction of capitalist economics in the eighteenth century, farmers sought higher profits by changing from stock raising to grain farming, by introducing scientific agricultural practices, by consolidating ancient holdings, and by cutting the work force and reducing farm workers to the status of independent day laborers. The laborers, who had formerly been members of the farmer's family group, became strangers to be hired as needed during peak seasons of planting and harvesting. The workers thus became especially vulnerable to periodic food crises. This occurred in the mid-1840s when rising potato and grain

Table 5.3

OCCUPATIONAL CLASS BY ECONOMIC REGION,
DUTCH EMIGRANT HOUSEHOLD HEADS AND SOLITARIES,
1835–1880

	Economic Region							
Occupational Class[a]	Dairy Area		Sandy Soils		Clay Soils		Row Totals	
	N	%	N	%	N	%	N	%
High white collar[b]	176	24	251	34	312	42	739	4
Low white collar[c]	370	31	286	24	524	44	1,180	6
Farmer	278	10	1,828	66	679	24	2,785	15
Farm laborer	27	2	223	16	1,117	82	1,367	7
Skilled/Semi-skilled	775	17	1,711	38	1,989	44	4,475	24
Unskilled	337	4	1,513	20	5,893	76	7,743	42
Column Totals	1,963	11	5,812	32	10,514	57	18,289	98

$X^2 < .001$ C = .43

[a] The occupational social class categories follow the codebook of Lynn Hollen Lees, "Patterns of Lower-Class Life & Irish Slum Communities in Nineteenth-Century London," in Stephen Thernstrom and Richard Sennett, eds., *Nineteenth-Century Cities: Essays in the New Urban History* (New Haven: Yale University Press, 1969), pp. 359–85.

[b] Includes professionals, subprofessionals, owner-entrepreneurs, submanagerials, gentlemen, and students.

[c] Includes clericals, civil service employees, merchants, shopkeepers, and pedlars.

Source: R. P. Swierenga, Netherlands Emigration Data File.

prices brought hunger to the workers and windfall profits to the farmers. These distressed workers, forever immortalized in Vincent Van Gogh's painting "The Potato Eaters," were thus the prime candidates for overseas migration. Over 80 percent of all emigrant farm laborers originated in the clay soil regions, compared to only 24 percent of the farmer emigrants (table 5.3).

In sharp contrast, 66 percent of the emigrant farmers tilled sandy soil, compared to only 16 percent of the farm laborers. Over three-quarters of all emigrant unskilled laborers also left sea clay areas. Many of these were likely working in agriculture or related industries.

Comparing Last and First Occupations: Emigrant Cohorts and Behavioral Characteristics

The linked file of Netherlands emigration records and U.S. census lists permits tracing the occupational progress of the immigrants at three stages in the period 1841–1870: within ten years after the transatlantic move, between ten and twenty years, and from twenty to thirty years after the removal. The data analyzed here are for male household heads and single adults active in the labor force. Female heads, mainly widows, numbered only 1 percent of the linked file and were omitted from the analysis.

The primary records include specific occupations, but for purposes of comparison these were classified into an a priori seven-category, vertical ranking, based on occupational prestige. The categories, ranked from higher to lower, are high white-collar (professional, owner, manager, gentleman), low white-collar (clerk, merchant, shopkeeper, peddler), farmer (or farm operator), skilled and semiskilled laborer, unskilled nonfarm laborer, farm laborer, and jobless.[1]

The findings show a marked degree of occupational change and rising occupation status among the Dutch immigrants.[2] In the first emigrant cohort (1841–50) portrayed in table 5.4, 52 percent of the 700 household heads and single adults changed from one major occupational group to another between their last position in the Netherlands and their "first" occupation reported in the 1850 census. Of these, 32 percent climbed and 20 percent skidded to a lower rank. The most notable change was the shift into the farmer class: One-half of the 31 farm laborers became farmers, as also did one-third of the 181 skilled craftsmen, and 40 percent of the 183 unskilled nonfarm laborers. The lure of the land is indeed striking. The number of farmers among the emigrants nearly doubled (from 195 to 347, including 22 jobless emigrants who became farmers). On the other hand, one-fifth of the immigrant farmers and skilled craftsmen fell to the rank of unskilled day laborers by 1850. The low white-collar group suffered the

Table 5.4

OCCUPATIONAL MOBILITY FROM LAST TO FIRST JOB, 1850: DUTCH MALE IMMIGRANT HOUSEHOLD HEADS AND SINGLE ADULTS, 1841–1850

| Level of "Last" Job | Level of "First" Job | | | | | | | | Percent Unchanged | Percent Climbing | Percent Skidding | Total Person/Ranks Climbing | Total Person/Ranks Skidding | Total Person/Ranks Gain |
	High White Collar	Low White Collar	Farmer	Skilled	Unskilled	Farm Laborer	Jobless	N						
High White Collar	7	2	6	1	2	0	0	18	39	—	61	—	25	−25
Low White Collar	3	4	28	5	15	0	0	55	7	5	87	3	83	−80
Farmer	0	3	149	6	36	0	1	195	76	2	25	3	82	−79
Skilled	2	3	61	76	39	0	0	181	42	36	22	73	39	34
Unskilled	1	0	66	18	97	0	1	183	53	46	1	154	2	152
Farm Laborer	0	0	15	1	15	0	0	31	0	100	0	62	—	62
Jobless	2	1	22	2	10	0	0	37	0	100	—	131	—	131
Totals	15	13	347	109	214	0	2	700	48%	32%	20%	426	231	195

N.A. 135   C = .58   tau − b = .25   gamma = .34
Source: R. P. Swierenga, Netherlands Emigration-U.S. Census Linked Data File.

largest loss in status, with 48 out of 55 moving down. However, 28 of these 48 became farmers who doubtless considered this change a positive one (on this point, see Doyle, 1982, 188).

The 1851–60 emigrant cohort (N = 1,195) had a more sanguine outcome than the 1841–50 group (table 5.5). Again 52 percent changed occupations, but 38 percent climbed in job status, compared to 32 percent in the first cohort. The chief gainers were unskilled day laborers, farm workers, and the jobless, who moved up to the farmer class. None of the 95 farm laborers or unemployed in the Netherlands remained in that status after emigrating. Every one moved up, with a third or more becoming farmers or farm operators, a fifth joining the skilled workers or low white-collar groups. The relatively small number of white-collar emigrants again suffered extreme losses, with 93 percent of the high white-collar group and 84 percent of the low white-collar group skidding. A fifth of the farmers and skilled workers also skidded.

The 1861–70 cohort (N = 1,447) had somewhat less occupation changes and fewer immigrants climbed, but the difference was only 4–5 points (table 5.6). The pattern of change was virtually identical to that of the earlier cohorts. Those in the three lowest ranks climbed and those in the top three ranks skidded, with the number of farmers growing by a third. Again, all 99 farm laborers escaped that lowly status; nearly half became farmers or skilled craftsmen.

When occupational changes of immigrants living in the United States 0–9 years are compared with those in the United States 10–19 years and 20–29 years (i.e., the 1840–50 cohort in 1860 and in 1870, and 1851–60 cohort in 1870) the results show a marked improvement in occupational status (table 5.7). The percentage of immigrants climbing the status ladder increased from a third to a half, and those skidding decreased by nearly one-half, to 10–12 percent. The ratio of "person-ranks" climbing to skidding rose from 1.8:1 to 4.4:1 to 6.5:1 for the 1841–60 emigrant cohort in 1850, 1860, and 1870 respectively, and from 2.7:1 to 6.3:1 for the 1851–60 emigrant cohort in 1860 and 1870 respectively. Thus, within ten years after emigration, half the Dutch in the United States had improved their occupational status compared to their premigration status, and a third remained in the same rank as before emigrating.

Farmers always had the highest degree of occupational stability. The various cohorts ranged between 64 and 87 percent persistency. The latest cohort of 1861–70 had the lowest rate (64 percent) of farmer persistence (table 5.8). This first emigrant cohort had 76 percent persisting in farming in 1850, 78 percent in 1860, and 87 percent in 1870. The second cohort of 1851–60 had 77 percent persisting among farmer emigrants in 1860 and 80 percent in 1870.

Table 5.5

OCCUPATIONAL MOBILITY FROM LAST TO FIRST JOB, 1860: DUTCH MALE IMMIGRANT HOUSEHOLDS AND SINGLE ADULTS, 1851–1860

Level of "Last" Job	Level of "First" Job								Percent Unchanged	Percent Climbing	Percent Skidding	Total Person/ Ranks Climbing	Total Person/ Ranks Skidding	Total Person/ Ranks Gain
	High White Collar	Low White Collar	Farmer	Skilled	Unskilled	Farm Laborer	Jobless	N						
High White Collar	1	1	3	4	4	0	1	14	7	—	93	—	41	−41
Low White Collar	5	4	18	12	19	0	0	51	7	9	84	5	99	−94
Farmer	1	3	191	6	48	0	0	249	77	1	22	5	102	−97
Skilled	2	11	82	144	50	0	1	290	50	33	18	110	52	58
Unskilled	1	7	180	73	228	0	0	489	47	53	0	458	0	458
Farm Laborer	0	2	24	15	27	0	0	68	0	100	0	137	0	137
Jobless	1	4	11	4	7	0	0	27	0	100	—	96	—	96
Totals	11	32	509	258	383	0	2	1,195	48%	38%	14%	811	294	517

N.A. = 36   C = .52   tau − b = .19   gamma = .26
Source: R. P. Swierenga, Netherlands Emigration–U.S. Census Linked Data File.

Table 5.6

OCCUPATIONAL MOBILITY FROM LAST TO FIRST JOB, 1870: DUTCH MALE IMMIGRANT HOUSEHOLD HEADS AND SINGLE ADULTS, 1861–1870

Level of "Last" Job	Level of "First" Job								Percent Unchanged	Percent Climbing	Percent Skidding	Total Person/Ranks Climbing	Total Person/Ranks Skidding	Total Person/Ranks Gain
	High White Collar	Low White Collar	Farmer	Skilled	Unskilled	Farm Laborer	Jobless	N						
High White Collar	7	0	3	5	2	0	0	17	41	—	59	—	29	−29
Low White Collar	4	6	12	9	23	0	1	55	11	7	82	4	104	−100
Farmer	1	1	175	16	78	0	1	272	64	1	35	3	176	−173
Skilled	1	5	56	136	60	2	2	262	52	24	24	69	70	−1
Unskilled	2	12	161	128	420	3	2	728	58	42	1	494	7	487
Farm Laborer	0	1	22	22	54	0	0	99	0	100	0	168	0	168
Jobless	0	3	2	6	2	0	1	14	7	93	—	45	—	45
Totals	15	28	431	322	639	5	7	1,447	52%	33%	15%	783	386	397

N.A.=26   C=.58   tau−b=.23   gamma=.33
Source: R. P. Swierenga, Netherlands Emigration-U.S. Census Linked Data File.

110

Table 5.7
SUMMARY OCCUPATIONAL MOBILITY DATA, LAST TO FIRST JOB: DUTCH IMMIGRANT MALE HOUSEHOLD HEADS AND SINGLE ADULTS, 1841–1870

	1850	1860	1870
1841–1850 Emigrant Cohort			
Percentage Unchanged	48	38	35
Percentage Climbing	32	49	55
Percentage Skidding	20	12	10
Ratio Climbing: Skidding	1.8:1	4.4:1	6.5:1
(person/ranks)			
N	700	643	551
Statistics			
Pearson's C	.58	.51	.46
Kendall's tau-b	.25	.17	.10
Gamma	.34	.26	.16
1851–1860 Emigrant Cohort			
Percentage Unchanged		48	39
Percentage Climbing		38	51
Percentage Skidding		14	10
Ratio Climbing: Skidding		2.7:1	6.3:1
(person/ranks)			
N		1,195	1,032
Statistics			
Pearson's C		.52	.48
Kendall's tau-b		.19	.14
Gamma		.26	.21
1861–1870 Emigrant Cohort			
Percentage Unchanged			52
Percentage Climbing			33
Percentage Skidding			15
Ratio Climbing: Skidding			2.0:1
(person/ranks)			
N			1,447
Statistics			
Pearson's C			.58
Kendall's tau-b			.23
Gamma			.33

Source: R. P. Swierenga, Netherlands Emigration-U.S. Census Linked Data File

111

Table 5.8

OCCUPATIONAL MOBILITY FROM PREMIGRATION JOB TO
U.S. FARM OPERATOR, 1841-1870: DUTCH IMMIGRANT MALE
HOUSEHOLD HEADS AND SINGLE ADULTS

Premigration Occupation	U.S. Farmers and Farm Operators (percentage)		
	1850	1860	1870
	%	%	%
1841–1850 Emigrant Cohort			
High white collar	23	33	31
Low white collar	51	44	56
Farmer	76	78	87
Skilled	34	51	54
Unskilled	36	60	76
Farm Laborer	48	90	87
Jobless	59	72	78
1851–1860 Emigrant Cohort			
High white collar		21	36
Low white collar		31	40
Farmer		77	80
Unskilled		37	54
Farmer Laborer		35	71
Jobless		41	44
1861–1870 Emigrant Cohort			
High white collar			18
Low white collar			22
Farmer			64
Skilled			21
Unskilled			22
Farm Laborer			22
Jobless			14

Source: R. P. Swierenga, Netherlands Emigration-U.S. Census Linked Data File.

The other blue-collar emigrants also consistently climbed the agricultural ladder to farm operator, especially those in the first two cohorts, who emigrated before 1860 at a time when farm land remained available in or near the Dutch colonies. Among farmer laborers in the 1841–50 emigrant cohort, 90 percent had become farm operators by 1860. And 71 percent of the 1851–60 cohort also became farmers by 1870. The unskilled laborers and jobless emigrants had similar successes. Within ten years 60 percent of the unskilled workers in the 1841–50 cohort had become farm operators and within twenty years 76 percent had gained this coveted status. Even a third to a half of the skilled craftsmen became farm operators within twenty years.

Conversely, as table 5.8 also shows, the white-collar workers benefited far less from migration to the United States. Over two-thirds of both the high and low white-collar workers skidded. Many, however, became farm operators, probably by choice, as is clear from the fact that 51 percent of the low white-collar workers entered farming from the 1841–50 cohort and 40 percent of the 1851–60 cohort were farming within ten to twenty years.

Old Country social background characteristics of the Dutch immigrant work force may also have influenced occupational mobility (table 5.9). The factors of religion, geographical origin, social class, and age were analyzed in terms of occupational ranking changes. Religion proved to be irrelevant. Dutch Reformed and Roman Catholic emigrants had identical rates of job changes and also identical proportions climbing and skidding within the first ten years. Concerning the regional and class variables, the

Table 5.9

SUMMARY OCCUPATIONAL MOBILITY DATA, "LAST" TO "FIRST" JOB: DUTCH MALE IMMIGRANT HOUSEHOLD HEADS AND SINGLE ADULTS, 1841–1870

(0 to 9 years since Emigration)

Netherlands Background Variables	Percent Unchanged	Percent Climbing	Percent Skidding	Ratio Climb: Skid[a]	N	C	Tau-b	Gamma
Religion								
Protestant	49	35	16	2.2:1	2,967	.55	.24	.33
Catholic	49	35	16	2.4:1	360	.55	.13	.18
Agricultural Region								
Commercial Farming	49	38	13	2.8:1	1,934	.53	.21	.30
Mixed Farming	49	32	19	1.9:1	1,122	.51	.15	.21
Dairying	48	27	25	1.1:1	273	.59	.21	.28
Cultural Region								
Urban	43	31	26	1.1:1	319	.59	.15	.21
Rural	50	35	15	1.4:1	3,022	.51	.24	.33
Social Class								
Well-to-do	60	22	19	1.3:1	631	.59	.24	.36
Middling	44	41	14	3.0:1	2,547	.48	.17	.24
Needy	41	51	8	5.8:1	1,020	.45	.08	.13

[a] The ratio is based on the total "person-ranks" climbing and skidding. The number of persons climbing or skidding one rank is multiplied by 1, the number moving two ranks is multiplied by 2, etc., up to 7 ranks.

Source: R. P. Swierenga, Netherlands Emigration-U.S. Census Linked Data File.

Table 5.10

SUMMARY OCCUPATIONAL MOBILITY DATA, LAST AND
FIRST JOB, BY AGE COHORT: DUTCH IMMIGRANT MALE
HOUSEHOLD HEADS AND SINGLE ADULTS, 1841–1870

	1850 Age Groups			*1860 Age Groups*			*1870 Age Groups*		
	−30	31–40	41+	−30	31–40	41+	−30	31–40	41+
1841–1850 Cohort									
% unchanged	41	47	51	32	38	46	26	36	46
% climbing	40	37	23	63	49	35	65	54	39
% skidding	19	16	25	6	13	19	9	10	14
1851–1860 Cohort									
% unchanged				38	52	53	32	41	47
% climbing				52	33	29	64	49	36
% skidding				10	15	17	4	10	17
1861–1870 Cohort									
% unchanged							43	54	57
% climbing							45	29	26
% skidding							12	16	17

Source: R. P. Swierenga, Netherlands Emigration-U.S. Census Linked File.

groups that had the most to gain from the decision to emigrate had a higher
proportion rising in job status and a lower rate of status loss. Immigrants
from the hard-pressed, commercial farming regions (clay soils) did 5–6
points better than those from the more stable, mixed farming (sandy soils)
regions and 11–12 points better than those from the prosperous dairy
regions. Half as many emigrants from commercial crop regions skidded as
did those from dairy areas (25 percent compared to 13 percent). Similarly,
urban emigrants fared much worse than did rural folk; 26 percent skidded
compared with 15 percent of the rural emigrants. Among social classes,
the well-to-do likewise had the highest rate of status loss and the needy the
highest rate of status gain. Fifty-one percent of all emigrants classed as
needy, that is, on the public dole, gained one or more occupational status
ranks within ten years after arriving in America.

Within each of the emigrant cohorts, age also strongly affected occupational change in the migration process. The youngest emigrants consistently fared better than the middle aged, and the middle aged did better
than the older ones (table 5.10). Of those under thirty years of age at the
time of emigrating, 40 percent of the 1841–50 cohort experienced status
improvement compared to only 23 percent of those over forty years of age.
In the 1851–60 cohort, 52 percent of those under thirty were upwardly

mobile, in contrast to only 29 percent of the over-forty aged group. Similarly, in the 1861–70 emigrant group, the figures were 45 percent and 26 percent, respectively. The percentage of emigrants losing status likewise varied by age at emigration, with about 10 percent of those under thirty years and 17 percent of those over forty years slipping in occupational ranking. The thirty-one to forty-year-old emigrants had occupation shifts more similar to those over forty than under thirty years of age. Among all emigrant cohorts, the under-thirty age group improved in occupational ranking more than the over-forty group by a range of 17 to 28 points—a spread of 42 to 45 percent in favor of the young. The younger emigrants also skidded by 6 to 13 points (32 to 76 percentage points) less than the over-forty age group.

The age differential was even more pronounced among emigrants in the United States more than ten years. The longer the period after emigrating, the better the younger emigrants fared in their occupational status. By 1860, 65 percent of the 1841–51 emigrant cohort under thirty years of age had risen in job status; only 6 percent had skidded. Among the 1851–60 emigrants, 64 percent had improved by 1870 and only 4 percent had declined. The comparable mobility figures for emigrants over forty years old are 35 percent climbing and 19 percent skidding for the 1841–50 cohort by 1860, and 36 percent climbing and 17 percent skidding among the 1851–60 emigrants by the year 1870. Emigration was clearly a young man's game, judging from these statistics.

From this evidence, it is no surprise that the young, rural, lower class, day laborers emigrated eagerly and in larger numbers than did the wealthy, urban, middle-aged and elderly. Nonetheless, the salient fact is that *all* social and economic subgroups benefited from emigration. Consistently, the proportion enjoying a rise in occupational status was twice as great as those suffering a decline. And always, about half—mostly farmers—held their ground and did not change from one occupational group nor rank to another.

Destination and Job Change

The place of settlement doubtless influenced occupational mobility as much as timing and behavioral characteristics. Labor and land opportunities differed in each settlement community. However, since more than three-fourths of the midnineteenth century Dutch immigrants settled in frontier communities with similar structural characteristics, the major distinctions can be found between urban and rural settlements. Three different Midwestern Dutch communities have been studied, namely Holland, Michigan (Kirk, 1978a), Grand Rapids, Michigan (Vanderstel, 1978), and Pella, Iowa (Doyle, 1982). Grand Rapids was a major light industrial and commercial center; Holland was a small commercial and service village integrally related to surrounding Dutch farms; and Pella was a rural farm settlement with a central village. In Holland "at least half and more commonly 60 percent or more experienced occupational movement," according to Kirk (1978a, pp. 89–90); in Grand Rapids, the rate of change ranged between 50 and 57 percent in the three census years 1850–70 (Vanderstel, 1978, pp. 126–29). In the farming community of Pella, however, less than 40 percent changed occupations (Doyle, 1982, pp. 185–88). Doyle attributes the higher job retention rate in Pella to Dutch conservatism and the more open circumstances of settling in a new farm settlement. As a closed community with limited opportunities for land ownership after the first settlers had monopolized the available land, however, Pella may have had a lower rate of job change precisely because it offered fewer opportunities than the more urban Michigan communities.

Most of the upwardly mobile Dutch immigrants in Holland, Michigan, were blue-collar workers in the old country who became farm owners in America. The percentage of blue collar emigrants before 1850 who achieved this cherished goal of farm ownership increased from 3 percent in the 1850 census to 27, 44, and 47 percent respectively in 1860, 1870, and 1880 (table 5.11). The rates for the 1850s cohort were 10, 27, and 28 percent respectively in 1860, 1870, and 1880. The 1860s cohort fared better, with 20 and 38 percent achieving farm ownership by 1870 and 1880 respectively. Obviously, the major avenue for upward mobility among Dutch immigrants in the Holland colony was from blue-collar jobs to farm ownership. Most of the upwardly mobile were under thirty years of age.

Grand Rapids, a predominantly native-American community, also attracted Dutch immigrants from manual and skilled occupational backgrounds, but more than half of these took up jobs at similar or lower status levels (table 5.12). By 1860, after a decade of adjusting to American life, one-third of the Dutch immigrants in Grand Rapids had advanced to higher status jobs. The vast majority (70 percent) had been unskilled laborers in the old country. Unlike the Holland colony, therefore, where numerous blue-collar workers became farm owners, their counterparts in Grand Rapids remained blue-collar workers after migrating overseas. Holland was a Dutch settlement carved out of virgin forests. Grand Rapids was a thriving city of native Americans, surrounded by developed farms. The Grand Rapids Dutch, therefore, lacked the opportunity to obtain cheap farms in the early years. But long-run prospects in the growing industrial city of Grand Rapids were superior to those of Holland. After two to three decades, Dutch rates of upward mobility increased in Grand Rapids more than in Holland. The large city offered more opportunity for occupational advancement than the rural village on the shores of Lake Michigan.

Table 5.11

SUMMARY OCCUPATIONAL MOBILITY DATA FOR THOSE LIVING IN THE HOLLAND COMMUNITY FOR WHOM OCCUPATIONAL DATA FROM THE NETHERLANDS WAS AVAILABLE USING COLLAPSED OCCUPATIONAL CATEGORIES

	1850	1860	1870	1880
	Those leaving the Netherlands before 1850			
Percentage mobile	60.0	68.5	64.9	70.2
Percentage upwardly mobile	2.2	6.8	8.8	10.6
Percentage downwardly mobile	25.6	9.6	3.5	0.0
Percentage urban to rural	28.9 (3.3)*	49.3 (27.4)*	50.9 (43.9)*	55.3 (46.8)*
Percentage rural to urban	3.3	2.7	1.8	4.3
Sample	90	73	57	47
	Those leaving between 1850 and 1859			
Percentage mobile		55.0	36.4	64.3
Percentage upwardly mobile		0.0	4.5	35.7
Percentage downwardly mobile		10.0	0.0	0.0
Percentage urban to rural		45.0 (10.0)*	31.8 (27.3)*	28.6 (28.6)*
Percentage rural to urban		0.0	0.0	0.0
Sample		20	22	14
	Those leaving between 1860 and 1869			
Percentage mobile			56.7	53.8
Percentage upwardly mobile			10.0	3.8
Percentage downwardly mobile			6.7	7.7
Percentage urban to rural			23.3 (20.0)*	38.5 (38.5)*
Percentage rural to urban			16.7	3.8
Sample			30	26

*Figures in parentheses represent the proportion of immigrants who moved from an urban blue-collar position in the Netherlands to the farm operators category in the Holland Community.

Source: Table 27, p. 90, in Gordon W. Kirk, Jr., *The Promise of American Life: Social Mobility in a Nineteenth Century Immigrant Community, Holland, Michigan, 1847–1894* (Philadelphia: American Philosophical Society, 1978).

117

Table 5.12

TRANSOCEANIC DUTCH OCCUPATIONAL MOBILITY:
NETHERLANDS AND KENT COUNTY (GRAND RAPIDS),
MICHIGAN, 1850–1870

	1850 Census (%)	1860 Census (%)	1870 Census (%)
Upwardly Mobile	17.4	32.7	22.9
Downwardly Mobile	34.8	24.3	26.5
Same Status	47.8	43.0	50.6
Sample	23	107	354

Source: Compiled from table 5.16, 5.17, 5.18, pp. 126, 127, 129 in David Gordon Vander Stel, "The Dutch of Grand Rapids, Michigan: A Study of Social Mobility in a Midwestern Urban Community, 1850–1870" (M.A. thesis, Kent State University, 1978).

In the isolated frontier community of Pella, Iowa, changes in occupational status were less frequent than in either Michigan settlement. The clerical leader of the colony of 1,000 souls had deliberately selected the region because cheap land was available for the many farmers in his group. The high proportion of adult males who took up occupations similar in status to their Old Country positions reflects the fact that many Pella colonists were Dutch farmers who intended to farm in America, hopefully on a larger scale, by taking advantage of cheap prairie land prices. More than one-third of the Pella settlers were Old Country farmers who continued their professions in Pella. Only one-tenth of the Pella farm operators had been blue-collar workers before emigrating (table 5.13). In the Holland colony, this proportion was several times higher.

These three local studies suggest several conclusions. First, the economic composition of the intended destination attracted particular types of emigrants. Farmers sought opportunities for land ownership on a larger scale than the small family plots in the Netherlands. Some blue-collar workers sought land, too, but closer to villages and cities where they could combine farming with other jobs. Other unskilled workers chose to settle in larger cities where industrial jobs were available.

More importantly, the effect of immigration on occupational status was largely determined by the economic nature of the receiving community. Growing industrial towns attracted blue-collar workers, and farm settlements drew farmers and farm laborers. In the first decades of settlement, the rural migrants enjoyed greater stability and had a minimal loss of status. But within a generation, the Dutch in the expanding cities surpassed their kin in the rural colonies. By 1880 Grand Rapids offered more opportunity for advancement than Holland, and Holland held out more promise than Pella. Land was expensive and in short supply by 1880 in the Dutch colonies, and the only remedy was to found daughter colonies.

Conclusion

The research findings reported here do not support the U-shaped model of short-run, downward mobility among non-English-speaking emigrants, followed by a steady advance until they reach and surpass their original level. Even though the U.S. economy was more diverse and advanced than the Dutch economy, and hence the hypothesized status decline should be all the greater, nevertheless 80–90 percent of the Dutch immigrants either remained in the same occupational category or improved their status. Of the first emigrant cohort of 1841–50, the proportion of those climbing in rank, in relation to those skidding in status, increased from 3:2 in 1850 to 4:1 in 1860 to 5:1 in 1870. The initial status decline on the part of 20 percent of the emigrants was greater by 10 points than was the case twenty years later, but there was no overall decline.

Neither does the inverse U-shaped pattern fit the Dutch experience, at least within the first thirty years after emigration. Each passing decade saw a growing proportion within each cohort rising in occupational status. Within ten years, one-third climbed; within twenty years, one-half had improved themselves; and within thirty years, more than half did so. The trend line is steadily upward, without a decline. In individual communities, such as Pella, Iowa, where farmland had become scarce and expensive within twenty years, the inverse U-shaped pattern occurred, but so long as cheap land remained available elsewhere, new Dutch colonies were

Table 5.13

TRANSOCEANIC DUTCH OCCUPATIONAL MOBILITY,
ENTRY OCCUPATION ONLY, NETHERLANDS AND LAKE
PRAIRIE TOWNSHIP (PELLA), IOWA, 1850–1895

	Immigrant Cohorts			
	1847–50	1851–60	1861–70	1871–95
	(%)	(%)	(%)	(%)
Upwardly Mobile*	9.3 (7.0)	19.6 (9.8)	26.7 (26.7)	14.3 (7.1)
Downwardly Mobile	14.0	17.6	13.3	14.3
Same Status	76.7	62.8	60.0	71.4
Sample	43	51	15	14

*Figures in parentheses represent the proportion of immigrants who moved from a blue-collar position in the Netherlands to the farm operators category in the Pella community.
Source: Compiled from research data of Richard J. Doyle, doctoral candidate, Kent State University. I am grateful to Mr. Doyle for permitting me to use his research material.

founded for latecomers and the children of the first arrivals. For most of the Dutch immigrants at midcentury, the American dream of success became a reality.

Notes

1. See Hershberg, et al. (1976) on the problematics of occupational classification to measure social mobility. The social-occupational class categories follow Lees (1969). Semiskilled workers were combined with skilled workers because they comprise only 8 percent of the skilled/semiskilled category and mainly include apprentices in the skilled trades, plus a few shovel workers.

2. As a check against the possibility that some immigrants in the first year or two after arrival may have reported to census marshals their Old Country occupation, while actually holding a different occupation at the time of the census, I compared job changes among immigrants who had been in the United States two years or less, two through five years, and six through nine years (table 5.14). The results show such a similar pattern of stability and change across the various occupational levels for the three immigrant cohorts, that the possibility of widespread misreporting of occupations is unlikely. The percentage of immigrants whose occupational levels remained unchanged declined by only 7 points (52 to 45 percent) between immigrants of two years and those of six through nine years. The percentage climbing in prestige level rose from 28 to 41 percent, and the proportion declining dropped from 19 to 14 percent. The trends in both direction are to be expected, given the longer period of time in which to become established in the new environment.

References

Akerman, Sune (1970). *Nordic Emigration: Research Conference in Uppsala September 1969*. Uppsala: Soderstrom & Finn.

Bergman, M. (1967). "The Potato Blight in the Netherlands and Its Social Consequences." *International Social Science Journal* 12:390–431.

Boogman, J. C. (1959). "The Dutch Crises in the Eighteen-Forties," pp. 192–203 in J. S. Bromley and F. H. Koosman (eds.), *Britain and the Netherlands: Papers Delivered to the Oxford-Netherlands Historical Conference, 1959*. London: Chatts & Winders.

Chiswick, Barry R. (1977). "A Longitudinal Analysis of the Occupational Mobility of Immigrants," pp. 20–26 in Industrial Relations, Research Association Series, *Proceedings of the Thirtieth Annual Meeting, December 28–30, 1977, New York City*.

Conzen, Kathleen Neils (1976). *Immigrant Milwaukie: 1836–1860: Accommodation and Community in a Frontier City*. Cambridge, Mass.: Harvard University Press.

DeJonge, J. A. (1971). "Industrial Growth in the Netherlands, 1850–1914," *Acta Historiae Neerlandica* 5:159–212.

Doyle, Richard L. (1982). *The Socio-Economic Mobility of the Dutch Immigrants to Pella, Iowa, 1847–1925*, Ph.D. dissertation, Kent State University.

Gjerde, Jon (1979). "The Effect of Community on Migration: Three Minnesota Townships, 1885–1905," *Journal of Historical Geography*, 5:403–22.

Griffiths, Richard T. (1979). *Industrial Retardation in the Netherlands, 1830–1850*. The Hague: Maritimes Nijhoff.

Hershberg, Theodore, ed. (1981). *Philadelphia: Work, Space, Family, and Group Experience in the 19th Century*. New York: Oxford University Press.

———, et al. (1973). "Occupation and Ethnicity in Five Nineteenth-Century Cities: A Collaborative Inquiry." *Historical Methods Newsletter* 7:174–216.

———, and Robert Dockhorn (1976). "Occupational Classification," *Historical Methods Newsletter* 9:59–98.

Hudson, John C. (1976). "Migration to An American Frontier." *Annals*, Association of American Geographers, 66:242–65.

Kamphoefner, Walter D. (1978). Transplanted Westfalians: Persistence and Transformation of Socioeconomic and Cultural Patterns in the Northwest German Migration to Missouri, University of Missouri, Columbia: Ph.D. dissertation.

Katz, Michael B. (1972). "Occupational Classification in History," *Journal of Interdisciplinary History* 3:63–88.

Kirk, Gordon W. Jr. (1978a). *The Promise of American Life: Social Mobility in a Nineteenth-Century Immigrant Community, Holland, Michigan, 1847–1894*. Philadelphia: American Philosophical Society.

———, and Carolyn Tyirin Kirk (1978b). "The Immigrant, Economic Opportunity and Type of Settlement in Nineteenth Century America," *Journal of Economic History* 38:226–34.

Lees, Lynn Hollen (1969). "Patterns of Lower-Class Life and Irish Slum Communities in Nineteenth-Century London," pp. 359–85 in Stephen Thernstrom and Richard Sennett (eds.), *Nineteenth-Century Cities: Essays in the New Urban History*. New Haven: Yale University Press.

Mokyr, Joel (1976). *Industrialization in the Low Countries, 1795–1850*. New Haven and London: Yale University Press.

Oostendorp, L. (1964). *Scholte: Leader of the Secession of 1834 and Founder of Pella*. Franeker; the Netherlands: Wever.

Ostergren, Robert (1979). "A Community Transplanted: The Formation Experience of a Swedish Immigrant Community in the Upper Middle West," *Journal of Historical Geography* 5:189–212.

Swierenga, Robert P. (1983a). *Dutch Emigrants to the United States, South Africa, South America, and Southeast Asia, 1835–1880. An Alphabetical Listing by Household Heads and Independent Persons*. Wilmington, Del.: Scholarly Resources, Inc.

———. (1983b). *Dutch Immigrants in U.S. Ship Passenger Manifests, 1820–1830: An Alphabetical Listing by Household Heads and Independent Persons*. Wilmington, Del.: Scholarly Resources Inc.

———. (1982). "Exodus Netherlands, Promised Land America: Dutch Immigration and Settlement in the United States," pp. 127–47, in J. W. Schulte

Table 5.14

OCCUPATIONAL MOBILITY FROM LAST TO FIRST JOB BY NUMBER OF YEARS SINCE IMMIGRATION, FIRST GENERATION DUTCH MALE HOUSEHOLD HEADS AND SINGLE ADULTS, 1841–1870

| Level of "Last" Job | Level of "First" Job | | | | | | | | | | | Total Person/ Ranks Climbing | Total Person/ Ranks Skidding | Total Person/ Ranks Gain |
	High White Collar	Low White Collar	Farmer	Skilled	Unskilled	Farm Laborer	Jobless	N	Percent Unchanged	Percent Climbing	Percent Skidding			
Two Years or Less Since Immigration														
High White Collar	6	2	3	2	3	0	0	16	38	—	62	—	26	−26
Low White Collar	6	4	23	4	25	0	1	63	6	10	84	6	111	−105
Farmer	1	2	166	9	66	0	2	246	68	1	31	4	149	−145
Skilled	1	1	66	95	47	2	2	215	44	32	24	73	57	16
Unskilled	1	1	87	55	246	0	1	391	63	37	0	236	2	234
Farm Laborer	0	0	15	2	20	0	0	37	0	100	0	69	0	69
Jobless	2	2	5	3	6	0	0	19	0	100	—	66	—	66
Totals	17	13	365	170	413	2	7	987	52	28	19	454	345	109

N.A. = 23   C = 29   Tau−b = .30   gamma = .41

Three Through Five Years Since Immigration

High White Collar	6	0	7	4	2	0	0	19	32	—	68	—	34	-34
Low White Collar	4	6	25	13	23	0	0	71	8	6	86	4	120	-116
Farmer	1	4	249	13	70	0	0	337	74	1	25	6	153	-147
Skilled	2	7	88	170	70	0	0	337	50	29	21	108	70	38
Unskilled	2	9	202	109	344	3	1	670	51	48	1	548	5	543
Farm Laborer	0	1	25	23	52	0	0	101	0	100	0	177	0	177
Jobless	1	5	25	5	8	0	0	44	0	100	—	339	—	339
Totals	16	32	621	337	569	3	1	1,579	49	36	15	1,182	382	800

N.A. = 140 C = 55 Tau−b = .22 gamma = .30

Six Through Nine Years Since Immigration

High White Collar	3	1	2	4	3	1	0	14	21	—	79	—	29	-29
Low White Collar	2	4	10	9	9	0	0	34	12	6	82	2	55	-53
Farmer	0	1	100	6	26	0	0	133	75	1	24	1	58	-57
Skilled	2	10	45	91	32	1	0	181	50	32	18	71	34	37
Unskilled	1	9	118	55	155	1	0	339	46	54	0	322	157	165
Farm Laborer	0	2	21	13	24	0	0	60	—	100	0	121	0	121
Jobless	0	1	5	4	5	0	0	15	0	100	—	47	—	47
Totals	8	28	301	182	254	3	—	776	45	41	14	564	333	231

N.A. = 34 C = .52 Tau−b = .18 gamma = .26

Source: R. P. Swierenga, Netherlands Emigration-U.S. Census Linked File.

Nordholt and Robert P. Swierenga, eds., *A Bilateral Bicentennial: A History of Dutch-American Relations.* New York: Octagon Books.

————. (1981). "Dutch International Migration Statistics, 1820–1880: A Comparative Analysis of Linked Multi-National Nominal Files." *International Migration Review* 15:445–70.

————. (1980a). "Dutch Immigrant Demography: 1820–1880." *Journal of Family History* 5:390–405.

————. (1980b). "Local Cosmopolitan Theory and Immigrant Religion: The Social Basis of the Antebellum Dutch Reformed Schism," *Journal of Social History* 14:113–35.

————. and Harry S. Stout (1975). "Dutch Immigration in the Nineteenth Century, 1820–1877: A Quantitative Overview," *Indiana Social Studies Quarterly* 28:7–34.

Stokvis, Pieter R. D. (1977). *De Nederlandse Trek naar Amerika, 1846–1847* [The Dutch Trek to America, 1846–1847]. Leiden: Universitaire Pers.

————. (1976). "The Dutch-American Trek, 1846–1847: A Reinterpretation," *Immigration History Newsletter* 8:3–5.

Terlouw, Frida. "De Aaardappelziekte in Nederland in 1845 en Volgende Jaren," *Economische en Sociaal-Historisch Jaarboek* 34:263–308.

Thernstrom, Stephen (1973). *The Other Bostonians: Poverty and Progress in the American Metropolis, 1880–1970.* Cambridge, Mass.: Harvard University Press.

Thomas, Brinley (1973). *Migration and Economic Growth: A Study of Great Britain and the Atlantic Economy.* Cambridge University Press, 2d edition.

Treiman, Donald J. (1976). "A Standard Occupational Prestige Scale for Use with Historical Data," *Journal of Interdisciplinary History* 7:283–304.

Vanderstel, David Gordon (1978). "The Dutch of Grand Rapids, Michigan: A Study of Social Mobility in a Midwestern Urban Community." M.A. thesis, Kent State University.

6

Swedish Migration to North America in Transatlantic Perspective

Robert C. Ostergren

The historiography of Swedish migration to America has a long and distinguished record. Indeed, many would regard the Swedish migrations as perhaps the best documented and best analyzed of the mass transatlantic migrations of the nineteenth and early twentieth centuries. This is due in large part to the superb quality of Swedish demographic data, which has made the country an important laboratory for the statistical study of migration from as early as the beginning of this century. The seminal example of the early work is Gustav Sundberg's extensive statistical documentation of the emigration, which is still routinely cited as a most remarkable contribution to migration studies, useful in its data as well as its interpretive essays (Emigrationsutredningen, 1908–13).[1] Similarly, Swedish geographer Helge Nelson's study of the geographic distribution and demographic condition of Swedes in America has become a classic (Nelson 1943), along with Dorothy Thomas's contribution, based on Swedish data, to the econometric analysis of international migration (Thomas 1941).

Impressive as these early studies are, it has been a more recent period of scholarship, the 1960s and the 1970s, that has seen the most innovative use of the Swedish data resource and the most systematic treatment of the migrations. The most vigorous element in this period has been the so-called Uppsala group, although there have been many others in Sweden and America who have added to the general outpouring of research publication. From its inception in 1962 the work of tnis group of scholars has been coordinated to a high degree ard strongly attuned to theoretical problems and models in the social sciences. Much of its work, therefore, is marked by a unity of thematic material and methodologies that make it a remarkably systematic examination of a historical phenomenon.

The intense Swedish activity of this period also had a quickening effect on the tempo of research in America. American scholarship on Swedish immigration and settlement in America had always been more prolific than the Swedish work on emigration. However, partly because American immigration history was bound to the overriding cultural problems of assimilation and ethnicity and partly because it was dominated by amateur historians of Swedish background, American efforts were traditionally oriented to the issues of assimilation, Americanization and ethnicity. The effect of the new Swedish initiatives of the 1960s and 1970s, along with new interest in the study of immigration in American social science history, was to generate a more professional and analytical effort on the American side, although it was never as productive as the Swedish nor was it as oriented on the whole to the social sciences. Leadership clearly rested with the Swedish social science historians during this period.

Recent pronouncements, however, by both Swedish and American scholars, suggest that this highly productive and unique phase is drawing to a close (Barton 1978; Runblom and Tedebrand 1979). The relatively high degree of funding available in the 1960s and the early 1970s has diminished considerably, and many researchers have moved on to other things. The commentators note that, while there is still research to be undertaken, much of it on the American side, it largely consists of investigating the few areas that have received inadequate treatment. Further, because of the nature of documentary evidence on the American side, current research will take a more humanistic form.

The aim of this essay is to critically evaluate the scholarship of the 1960s and 1970s and to question whether we have really reached the point of diminishing returns. It emphasizes the work of the Uppsala group and Swedish scholarship over the American, which is rightly so, but most importantly it examines the interface between Swedish and American research; a troublesome area that has potential, nonetheless. Although the works of the last decades have sought to understand the entire Swedish migration experience from emigration to settlement and adaptation in a new environment, this essay argues that there are yet important research opportunities, in that aim, that not only have been missed, but amount to more than the tying up of loose ends.

Swedish Migration Research and the Uppsala Group

Any discussion of the achievements of the 1960s and 1970s must acknowledge the central role played by the "Uppsala Group," a body of more than thirty scholars attached to a migration research project based at the University of Uppsala. Officially entitled "Sweden and America after 1860: Emigration, Remigration, Social and Political Debate," the project was launched in 1962 as a response to the issues raised in a paper delivered by Frank Thistlethwaite at an international conference of historians at Stockholm in 1960 (Thistlethwaite 1960). In that paper, Thistlethwaite challenged European historians to enter the study of international migration, a field then dominated by social scientists. While the scholars of the Uppsala group were certainly not the only European historians to accept Thistlethwaite's challenge, they were rather unique in the organizational approach that they employed—the cooperative research project. This approach, which was becoming fashionable in Nordic academic circles at the time, allowed the study group to collectively formulate theoretical problems and issues, which were then systematically and comparatively tested in the empirical studies of the individual members. Such an approach greatly increased the interchange of ideas and methodologies between researchers and hopefully produced a more comprehensive outcome than that which would have been produced by more individualistic efforts.[2]

An important attribute of the Uppsala research program was the broad range and explorative character of its theoretical underpinnings. Thistlethwaite's recommendation that historians broaden their perspective and avail themselves of the social sciences had an effect, as did the general trend toward the social sciences in the 1960s. The group made every effort to be interdisciplinary in approach, amassing a seemingly eclectic melange of nonhistorical theoretical ideas to inform their empirical research. Such diverse ideas as the phase-shift relations of growth curves, innovation-diffusion processes, demographic and econometric migration models, central place theory, center-periphery relationships, socialization models and various behavioral and perceptual perspectives populate their publication record.[3]

Empirically, there was an effort to comprehensively cover the migration experience. Thistlethwaite admonished his audience to regard the Atlantic migrations as "a complete sequence of experiences whereby the individual moves from one social identity to another." To the Uppsala group this meant a range of specific studies that would add up to an overall view of the mass emigration complex. The initial studies ranged, accordingly, from the treatment of premigration conditions in Sweden to the exploration of assimilation patterns in America and the documentation of remigration patterns back to Sweden. Later, however, there was a definite concentration of effort on the Swedish side of the migration experience, turning eventually to the important issues of relating emigration to Swedish internal migration and demographic processes.

The corpus of work produced by the Swedish migration historians from the inception of the Uppsala project to its termination in 1976 has been reviewed many times, perhaps most thoroughly by Semmingsen (Semmingsen 1978). Members of the group have themselves reviewed and explained the progress of the research. Long-time project leader Sune Åkerman did so at San Francisco in 1975 (before the same organization addressed by Thistlethwaite fifteen years earlier) and in the final report of the project, which appeared in 1976 under the title, *From Sweden to America: A History of the Migration* (Åkerman 1975: 1976). While no summary can do justice to the richness of the Swedish research, what follows is a categorical assessment of the major accomplishments from the vantage point of 1982.

I will begin by briefly delimiting five general areas in which the Swedish research has made a substantial contribution to our understanding of the migrations, each of which is treated more fully in the succeeding paragraphs:

1. The first contribution is a careful skepticism toward econometric explanations of the short- and long-term fluctuations in transatlantic migration founded on aggregated data. This skepticism is based on the results of empirical testing of the macroeconomic models at the local and individual level and is further informed by efforts to apply behavioral models at this level.

2. A second contribution is a rather thorough exploration of Swedish attitudes towards emigration as a social and political phenomenon, which persuasively discounts the effect of government policy and the transport sector (shipping companies and migration agents) on the volume and orientation of the migration stream.

3. A third is the provision of empirical evidence demonstrating the fundamental importance of information flow, kinship, and local migration tradition in generating and maintaining rather permanent migrational linkages between source areas in Sweden and receiving areas in America.

4. A fourth is a tentative inquiry into the settlement process by which Swedish migrants took permanent homes and entered American society that emphasizes the relationship between economic and demographic structure in emigration and settlement areas and the persistence of Swedish America at least at the cultural and institutional level well into the twentieth century.

5. The fifth contribution is a strong conceptualization of the relationship between external and internal migration during the initial phases of industrialization and urbanization in Sweden.

In the 1960s the major explanatory models of migration in the social sciences were based on rather mechanical, econometric analyses of international migration flows. These analyses were built on the belief that migration could be explained from the study of business and labor market cycles based on aggregated data in sending and receiving nations; the central issues being the relative importance of push versus pull factors. In Thistlethwaite's 1960 assessment of research frontiers in migration history, these studies were characterized as pace-setting advances that gave the social sciences such a predominant role in the field. It was, therefore, quite natural that they would have a considerable impact on the early formulation of research issues in Sweden. A special attraction was the fact that high-quality Swedish data offered exceptional advantages in this kind of research (Quigley 1972; Kälvemark 1972).

The Uppsala studies essentially sought to test aspects of the econometric theses, particularly those of Brinley Thomas (Thomas 1954), at the scale of the microstudy. The careful skepticism toward econometric analyses already mentioned emerged from this testing process. Detailed regional studies by Rondahl and Tedebrand, for example, demonstrated a poor fit between the international patterns suggested by econometricians and what appeared to be happening at the local level. Such results caused them to seriously question the relevance of weighted national statistics in assessing migrational motivation (Rondahl 1972; Tedebrand 1972). Nilsson, in his study of Stockholm's emigration between 1880 and 1892, also expressed reservations, pointing out that there were in fact profound differences in the structure of Swedish and American life. While American conditions certainly changed over the years, the perception of them obtained through the media in Sweden was generally dismal and totally overshadowed in impact by the continuously poor conditions prevailing in Sweden, which casts doubt on the notion of a significant American pull factor based on the economic cycle. It was possible that the cycle of economic conditions in Sweden and America could not be viewed comparatively (Nilsson 1970). Before long, Swedish research in general began to raise the possibility that the econometric models oversimplify a complex process. Their reliance on aggregated statistical compilations to produce a facsimile of the economic situation confronting potential emigrants actually produced a set of information that was far beyond that available to the individual who made the decision to emigrate (Åkerman 1978a; Erickson 1980).

In order to capture the decision-making process more accurately, studies at the local or individual scale, which could be based on concrete data, were advocated. In addition, there was an effort to explore new dimensions and alternative approaches to the classical economic debate. This was led by Sune Åkerman, who sought to integrate the economic, social, and even psychological dimensions of the decision to emigrate (Åkerman, 1972a; Åkerman, Cassel, and Johansson 1974). The research was based on a social indicator model devised by Dutch sociologist J. E. Ellemers (Ellemers 1964). The idea was to identify the economic, social and psychological factors that cause people to move and, in particular, to view the interrelationships of these factors as a value-added process that builds to a threshold at which emigration begins. Although technically criticized for its use of the AID scanner technique (Automatic Interaction Indicator), the approach has significantly focused attention on the motivational complexities of the individual's acceptance of the migration opportunity (Gullberg and Odén 1976).

New emphases on the psychological dimension of decision making at the individual level were reinforced by the rather negative results of another line of inquiry that explored the ability of broad external determinants like national attitudes, governmental policy, and the transport sector to influence migration. While the role of transport was generally thought to be quite important, since its cost and capabilities would logically have adverse or encouraging effect on migration streams, it soon became apparent that these factors did not vary greatly during the period of mass emigration from Sweden. Brattne's study of Swedish emigrant agencies during the 1880s found that even when elastic prices did occur, they had no real influence on the volume of emigration (Brattne 1973). Norman observed that the tempo of activity by migration agents followed the curve of emigration rather than dictated it, and Ljungmark's study of the campaign to attract Swedish emigrants to certain colonization districts in Minnesota owed its success more to the prescence of Swedes who earlier settled in the state than to the activities of the agents themselves (Norman 1974; Ljungmark 1971). The efforts of agents to encourage colonization in Canada, where there were few Swedes, met with little success as did efforts to influence the fluctuations in the flow of immigrants over time. Similarly, Kälvemark found national policy and liability to military service to have been of relatively little consequence in the long run (Kälvemark 1972). These studies, in effect, served to direct attention to the process of migration as it occurred at the scale of individuals or groups of individuals moving from point to point and away from the study of macroscale influences.

A number of researchers pursued longitudinal studies that were aimed at establishing the pattern of interaction between Sweden and America. These studies emphasized the importance of information flow, kinship, and local traditions of migration in the determination of transatlantic migration patterns. Geographers had long suggested that the acceptance of innovation—in this case the idea to emigrate—was a matter of information spread or diffusion (Hägerstrand 1947). Local studies of the acceptance of the idea to emigrate underlined the importance of the concept and suggested that the most important stimulus was the trusted information communicated by relatives, friends, and acquaintances. Also important was the establishment of a local migration tradition (Åkerman, Kronber, and Nilsson 1977). The Swedish material shows a marked tendency for local or regional variation in the intensity of emigration. Some areas never really participated in the emigration, while others built up high rates early and often maintained a substantial outflow over time (Norman 1974; Wiren 1975). The conclusion to be drawn was that emigration resulted where there was first of all a potential inclination to move, second, a flow of information conducive to the gradual acceptance of the decision to emigrate, and finally the possibility of continued communication at the interpersonal level between the sending population and the population of emigrés in receiving areas (Åkerman 1978b).

Evidence from the American side, demonstrating the frequent settlement concentration of emigrants of particular regional or local backgrounds, supported the idea that a certain "stock effect" was important in determining the direction of migration flow, choice of initial place of settlement, and subsequently the continuation of flow (Norman 1974); Tedebrand 1972). Indeed, an important part of the entire process was the establishment of what Sune Åkerman has called "the axes of migration" between places on both sides of the Atlantic (Åkerman 1975). People and information flowed over these axes, according to the dictates of a self-generating mechanism that in many ways was isolated from external influences. Detailed studies show that these cross-Atlantic linkages facilitated the gradual movement of families, sometimes over a considerable period of time. There is evidence that the process was not only based on kinship but on age cohorts as well. In other words, emigration can be seen as a means of fulfilling the need on the part of an age cohort, that is, coming of age in a community, to set up marriages and households in a situation of limited economic opportunity (Åkerman, Kronberg, and Nilsson 1977). Since this need is fulfilled by colonization over a particular axis of migration, the action may be viewed as a rather conservative response to the situation, in that it resists disintegration of the local social fabric by simply extending the existing community to another place.

In fact, one of the strongest conclusions of the Swedish research that examined the American experience of the emigrants is the close connection between the premigration and postmigration circumstances of individuals. Hans Norman, in his study of immigrant settlements in western Wisconsin, found similarities in economic structure between the immigration districts and the sending areas in Sweden to which they were linked (Norman 1974). There is ample evidence that emigrants commonly gravitated toward the same means of livelihood in America as they had known in Sweden. There was also significant transplantation of cultural baggage and social custom. An important key to the parallelism of development between migration-linked areas on both sides of the Atlantic is the issue of repatriation. Tedebrand's study of the remigration of emigrants from Västernorrland discovered that 80 percent returned to the same parish from which they originally emigrated and one-half of these emigrated again. The repatriation pattern suggests that the axes of migration contained considerable counterflows that linked, in a fashion, the labor markets in places on both sides of the Atlantic and ensured in the process a degree of parallel development (Tedebrand 1972).

Other lines of investigation into the American experience of the Swedish emigrants have been more tentative. No strong conclusions have resulted from the Swedish effort to look into the urban life of Swedish emigrants in America (Beijbom 1971). The urban immigrant experience has attracted vigorous research efforts within American social science history, but the Swedish migration historians have not pursued these issues in America, although the influence of the American scholarly concern with mobility is apparent in Swedish research on urban migrants in Sweden (Åkerman 1977). Lindmark's study of postmigration Swedish America did succeed in documenting instances of "maintenance phenomena" (group coherence, language retention, institutional stability) well into the 1930s, which turns back the stereotypical notion that Swedes were easily assimilated (Lindmark 1971). But, in general, the American studies by Swedish scholars have lacked depth and possessed limited conceptual frameworks, which make this the uncertain frontier, so to speak, of the Swedish effort.

As Semmingsen has noted, the focus of Swedish research gradually shifted away from the study of the emigration and its American aftermath to the study of the relationship between emigration and internal migration within Sweden (Semmingsen 1978). Extensive research in this area marked the closing years of the project and represents one of the main achievements of the group. It extended the scope of the research from the study of emigration per se to the study of Swedish mobility in general, arguing that emigration was only a part of a general social and spatial mobility occurring in Sweden in the latter part of the nineteenth century and had to be viewed in the broader context (Åkerman 1978a). An early aspect of this shift was a lively debate over whether urban emigration should be treated as an independent phenomenon or as part of a "stage migration." Nilsson's study of emigration from Stockholm held the view that, although Stockholm's emigrants were largely born in the countryside, many had moved frequently before their emigration and most had resided in Stockholm for a period of time before their emigration. They were, therefore, essentially an urbanized population, not a rural population gradually making its way out of the country by stages (Nilsson 1970). The evidence, however, is not conclusive, and considerable debate ensued that served to focus attention on the relationship between external and internal migration (Semmingsen 1978). Also important in this role was the notion of an "urban field of influence," which suggested that the immediate hinterlands of expanding urban centers were less prone to emigration than the districts outside these zones because the expanding centers provided alternatives to emigration for nearby populations (Norman 1974).

By and large, however, the Swedish studies found the relationship between external and internal migration to be rather inconsistent (Åkerman 1978a). The best solution was to break the internal migration down into two types—circular movements and effective migration streams. In the first case, internal movement is largely over short distances. It responds to local conditions, short trends and, in the long run, tends to produce a sort of spatial equilibrium. The latter case is typified by long distance rural to urban migration resulting from real and long-term economic dislocations. It is closely related to emigration in that it can prepare a rural population for emigration or it can produce a climate for emigration in urban receiving areas (Rondahl, 1972). Nilsson's study of Stockholm, for instance, reveals that people from the city's rural surroundings who moved into town were generally disinclined to emigrate, engaging instead in circular movements between their nearby home districts and the city. Long-distance in-migrants, on the other hand, were more inclined to emigrate, often in conjunction with surges of emigration in their home districts (Nilsson 1970). Important to this understanding is the notion that both emigration and effective internal migration move through phase shifts, the characteristics of which can coincide or be quite different at any given point in time. Emigration, for instance, often has an early phase, in which the base is rather broad, consisting of families from rural areas. At the same time, the base of the effective internal migration may be quite narrow. The converse can also be true, usually late in the migration cycle, when the international labor market may dictate a narrow industrial base for emigration while internal migration is broadly based (Åkerman 1978a).

Ultimately, the Uppsala historians return the question to the psychological dimension of migration. Citing the so-called rural-industrial barrier—a marked aversion on the part of rural populations toward moving permanently to industrial centers, which appears in several studies—they conclude that, in the final analysis, we are dealing, not with physical barriers to migration, but with mental ones (Tedebrand 1972; Norberg and Åkerman 1973; Åkerman 1978b). The key to understanding the migrational process lies in being able to isolate the psychological situation of the individual in the context of his changing milieu. Much of the Swedish research points to an emphasis on social and psychological factors, however difficult they may be to analyze.

American Research

American research on Swedish immigration lacks the cooperative direction of its Swedish counterpart. To be fair, one should say that it has not been as well supported financially nor has it enjoyed data resources that are as accessible and useable. As a result, the initiatives are more disparate, and the conclusions form a less coherent picture. In addition, recent American research has been somewhat confined in its direction by its association with past scholarship and the concerns of American historiography in general.

A clear distinction between American and Swedish research is the fact that the American has a more sizeable base of early twentieth-century literature to build on. As early as the 1910s, writers took an avid interest in the situation of the Swedish element in the United States. Much of the very early writing took place in a climate of heightened public tension over the question of continued immigration to America. It tried, therefore, to emphasize the innate ability of Swedish immigrants to assimilate themselves into American life. Swedes, of course, belonged to the "Old" immigration, which was viewed at the time as racially superior to the "New" immigration from southern and eastern Europe, and those who wrote about Swedish immigrants wanted no one to confuse this fact (Babcock 1914; Otley 1940). By the 1930s, scholarship became more "professional" and the racial overtones disappeared. It continued, however, to deal largely with the problem of Americanization from an assimilationist point of view, although the scope of investigation broadened considerably (Stephenson 1932; Ander 1933; Benson 1956).[4] This period also saw the

emergence of "support societies," such as the Augustana Historical Society (1930) and the Swedish Pioneer Historical Society (1948), that pro-
moted and subsidized the publication of Swedish-American history
(Barton 1978a).

While American research in the 1960s and 1970s has enjoyed the
advantage of this sizeable base literature, it has also been constrained by
the ideological nature of what had already been written. The 1960s,
therefore, were a decade in which scholars attempted to redress the views
of the old assimilationist school with new evidence of an "ethnic maintenance factor" and a persistent "Swedish America" (Salisbury 1978). This
trend, like the one before it, mirrored contemporary themes in American
historiography, which in the 1960s took up the causes of ethnicity and
cultural pluralism. Therefore, it must be understood that the American
approach has been firmly rooted in the long-standing debate over the
ethnic factor in America and, as a consequence, has tended to be less
concerned with an overall understanding of the processes or mechanisms
of the transatlantic migration complex.

In the 1970s, however, the issue of geographic and social mobility
became an important research problem and, in that development, American research took a turn that was more relevant to the direction of Swedish
research. For scholars of Swedish immigration, the impetus came in part
from the Swedish example. Indeed, most American review essays published in the 1970s commented favorably on the Swedish emphasis on
migrational processes (Barton 1978a, 1978b; Salisbury 1978; Lindgren
1979). The impetus also came from the new interest in the mobility of
immigrant groups then current in American social science history. Americans had always been characterized as being highly mobile (Billington
1966; Pierson 1972). American historians took this generalization a step
further during the 1970s by comparatively looking at the mobility of
ethnic, social, and occupational groups.

Related to the issue of mobility is the idea of community. The
traditional view among American historians was that immigrants to the
United States were more community-oriented than Old Americans (Malin
1935; Hansen 1940). Immigrants were thought to have valued the security
associated with close settlement in contiguous communities and, therefore, were more residentially persistent once they had settled in America.
This argument was largely dispelled in the 1960s by studies that found
immigrant groups and Americans to have been equally mobile (Throne
1959; Curti 1964; Bogue 1963). The many studies of American migration in
the early 1970s generally confirmed this revision and led to a general
disregard for the role of community as well (Thernstrom 1973; Katz 1975).
The revisionist view, however, may well have dismissed the relationship

between mobility and community too quickly. Too many scholars were clearly skeptical of the relationship from the beginning and, methodologically, they often aggregated data into categories that masked the effect of community. The disregard for community in these studies has more recently been attributed to an ideological preoccupation with economic motivation (Henretta 1977, 1978).

An important segment of the American research on the mobility of Swedish immigrants has, in fact, dealt with the juxtaposition of the ideas of mobility and community. The thrust has been to link them far more than the revisionist historians of the 1960s and 1970s were inclined to do. In large part, this approach has been led by geographers, who quite naturally are predisposed to begin with settlement patterns. As we have seen, Swedish settlement patterns in America, especially on the agricultural frontiers, were characterized by clustering—a result of the frequent establishment of "migration axes" that linked districts on both sides of the Atlantic. Not only did Swedish immigrants cluster as an expression of nationality, their clustering often reflected provincial and even parish origins. This clustering seemed an obvious prerequisite to community formation, and early studies sought to determine the degree to which communities were formed and maintained. Residential persistence (the converse of mobility) was seen as an expression of satisfaction or attachment to the community and analyzed as a measure of community strength (Rice 1973; Ostergren 1973). A major difference between this and the mobility studies already referred to is the fact that data were now being grouped by settlement cluster—a geographic unit far more relevant to community than city wards and townships.

Although based on a small number of instances, these studies demonstrated a positive relationship between residential persistence and the degree to which settlement clusters were representative of restricted source areas in Sweden. If residential persistence is, indeed, a surrogate for the strength of affinity in immigrant settlement clusters, the formation of stable communities among Swedish immigrants seems to have depended on the establishment of rather specific migration axes capable of transplanting culturally homogeneous and often kinship-related populations to specific places in America (Ostergren 1980). This, in turn, was dependent upon local settlement conditions. Settlement frontiers that moved rather quickly and offered uniformly available land were not conducive to this kind of community formation, whereas settlement areas that filled slowly and offered latecomers the possibility of establishing themselves among their own kind were conducive (Rice 1978a; Ostergren 1981a). Also important was the establishment of a strong institutional focus, a role commonly filled by the ethnic church (Rice 1973; Ostergren 1973).

The demonstration of such a strong relationship between mobility and community is not as great a contradiction of other research as it may seem. As pointed out, the basis of data aggregation was decidedly different in these studies, which makes the different results explicable. In addition, because of the microscale of these studies, persistence was more carefully measured than in other studies that simply matched census manuscripts at ten-year intervals to determine the proportion of individuals who persisted from one census to the next.[5] Here the inclusion of diverse sources made it possible to subtract that portion of the population that died and to determine who was temporarily absent. Persistence was also viewed in the context of the household rather than the individual (Ostergren 1979). High levels of mobility were certainly a feature of American life, especially among the sons and daughters of established households. But, if the household persists from one generation to the next, that is a measure of commitment to the community regardless of the number of offspring that may have left home. In fact, mobility among the second generation in these Swedish settlements was quite high, but this need not be viewed as a denial of community and kinship loyalty, for many moved to new settlement clusters further west that contained similar kin structures. In that sense, they remained part of a community that could be defined as a series of migration-linked clusters (Gjerde 1979).

The upshot of this is that one facet of the migration/settlement process for Swedish immigrants (as well as for many other groups) was the establishment of "transplanted communities." This was a phenomenon that did not occur everywhere. Thousands of Swedish immigrants never came in contact with one of these settlements. But these settlements were numerous enough, especially on the agricultural frontiers of the American Midwest, to constitute a significant variant of the process. In a real sense, the study of these communities and the postsettlement migration behavior of the people who formed them is a logical extension of the Swedish research effort. The idea of a transplanted community recalls the "parallelism of development" between migration-linked areas on both sides of the Atlantic suggested by some of the Swedish studies. Further, the emphasis on relating the affinitive ties of community membership and resistance to migration recalls the Swedish emphasis on the psychological factor.

With regard to the psychological factor, the existence of these settlements raises the possibility of examining in depth the question of how the migration and settlement experience affected the lives of the migrants themselves, because they provide an opportunity for the historian to follow individuals through the whole migration process. Åkerman has written that in order to understand the migrational process, we must "investigate in some detail *who* the migrants were, *when* they left, *when*

they departed and *where* they arrived, *under what circumstances* the migration took place, and *from which social and economic context* the migrants were
'uprooted'" (Åkerman 1978a). These settlements with their clear transatlantic linkages allow that kind of longitudinal study to be extended to the
American scene. For American researchers this raised the possibility of
comparing the premigration and postmigration experiences of immigrant
settlers.

Research completed so far suggests that, for the immigrants who
settled in "transplanted communities," there was both a continuity and a
divergence of experience with their European past (Rice 1977; Ostergren
1979; Gjerde 1979). Continuity of experience was greatest in the area of
social and cultural relationships, while divergence was the rule in economic relationships. Because the immigrant community offered a degree
of isolation from American life, the fabric of social and cultural life from
the Old World was often preserved for the immigrant, at least through the
lives of the first generation. Religious and cultural traditions were rigidly
observed, the language was maintained, and social relationships, such as
marriage patterns and inheritance strategies, were maintained (Ostergren
1979, 1980; Rice 1978b). At the same time, the immigrants entered an
economic environment in which they could not remain isolated (Rice 1977;
Ostergren 1979). In order to provide for their families, rapid adaptation to
the American economic system was essential, and here the experience
with the past diverged, although the occupation of the migrant probably
remained the same. In a sense, the immigrant lived simultaneously in two
worlds; one a social world in which traditional ties with church, family,
and homeland were perpetuated, and the other an economic world in
which rapid adaptation to new circumstances and new relationships with
American tradesmen introduced rapid change. The key to the immigrant's
future status depended to a large extent on the shifting interface between
these two worlds (Ostergren 1981a).

The Potential for Future Research

In 1960 Thistlethwaite called for an understanding of the whole transatlantic migration experience. Much has been done in the Swedish and
American study of nineteenth-century migration between the two countries to achieve that aim. A major problem, however, has been the tendency for American and Swedish scholars to work at this goal from the
context of circumstances on their respective sides of the Atlantic. Americans have tended to view Swedish immigration against the problems of
American society, focusing on the issues of assimilation or cultural pluralism. The Swedes, while ranging further afield in their efforts, have also

concentrated on issues relevant to their society, ultimately concentrating on the task of placing the emigration in the context of general social and economic change in nineteenth-century Sweden. Consequently, there has been a persistent chasm between research efforts on both sides of the Atlantic. Åkerman acknowledged the difficulties of the situation in 1975 when he wrote, "Yet despite this progress in European research it remains difficult to link findings on the European background of mass migration with studies of the assimilation process in North and South America. There are several reasons for this. One is that American scholars are more oriented towards ethnic studies—a most popular speciality nowadays. This is, of course, valuable, but does little to help realize Frank Thistle-thwaite's exception of a study of the entire migration process" (Åkerman 1975).

This essay has suggested that longitudinal studies of the emigrants who formed "transplanted communities" on Midwestern agricultural frontiers could serve as one means of closing the gap between American and Swedish research. Not only do they allow in-depth analysis of what happened to the emigrants and their descendants, they also allow us to trace the fortunes of those (and their descendants) who were left behind. In addition to placing the entire migration experience of a group of people under scrutiny, such studies also place these people in the context of sending and receiving areas, that have well-defined relationships with each other and the larger societies of which they are a part. Implicit in this context is a model against which the experiences of both individuals and group can be gauged.

In this model, the sending community can be thought of as having divided, sending out a fragment of itself to form a daughter settlement in America (fig. 6.1). This period of intense emigration is followed by a time of adjustment in both mother and daughter settlements. Those who left for America had to respond to their encounter with a new environment and the stresses of community formation and maintenance in an alien society. Meanwhile the old community had to respond to the mass emigra-tion of a segment of its whole, absorbing the resources of those who left and redressing the conditions that caused them to leave. Throughout this period of adjustment, there is a flow of people and information back and forth across the Atlantic that both links and influences these adjustment processes. Examples of this might be the parallel establishment of noncon-formist religious establishments in both communities or the resurgence of emigration or remigration in response to changes in the labor market on one side or the other. However, with the emergence of a new generation that did not directly experience the emigration or the premigration period, the linkage between the places becomes weaker, as does continuity with

Figure 6.1: A Model of Community Transplantation

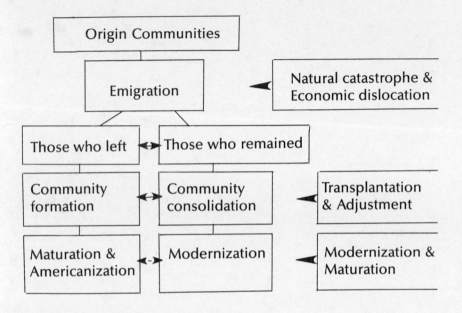

the cultural and social past. Both communities now have to deal with new pressures and changes in their respective societies as they enter the modern era of industrialization and urbanization. Although communication linkages and sporadic migration persist, the consciousness of the two communities begins to diverge.

The approach, of course, has considerable problems that must be acknowledged and dealt with. One is the problem of linkage. Substantial differences exist between Swedish and American source materials. Swedish population records were continuously recorded and are replete with cross-references as to local movements, marriages, and so forth. From them, remarkably complete reconstructions are possible. American population records exist in the form of periodic censuses ten years apart. This means that individuals are easily lost in the American records. Immigrants could pass through settlements without a trace. Even for those who resided there long enough to be counted, it is often not possible to fully reconstruct what happened to them between censuses. In order to keep these data problems manageable, most longitudinal studies completed to date have been small-scale efforts (Åkerman 1975). A second problem is that of representativeness. One may quite legitimately question how representative the "transplanted community" model is of the migration complex (Åkerman 1975). We are well aware that the character of the mass migrations of the nineteenth century varied enormously. They were at times dominated by landed farmers, at times by young members of a growing rural proletariat. At other times skilled urban workers were important and so on. Too much emphasis on this model, which essentially belongs to the earlier phase of famine-induced family emigration from the Swedish countryside, runs the risk of deemphasizing other phases.

New data-handling technologies and new source materials, however, have begun to alleviate the record linkage problem. We have now become more accustomed to machine handling of population linkage and family reconstitution. Swedish researchers, for instance, have invested in a computerized data base to support new demographic research in selected parts of Sweden (Sundin 1979). Historian Robert Swierenga has developed techniques for linking migrants recorded in Dutch and American population records. Further, with appropriate effort the dataless time period between American censuses can often be filled in by gleaning supportive material from other sources, such as church records, tax rolls, and property lists. This is a painstaking process, but if patiently done, reconstitutions as complete as those assembled from the Swedish data are possible. In fact, due to increased emphasis on the preservation of archival material, the range of American source materials is constantly expanding (Barton 1978b).

The problem of representativeness is not easily shrugged off. The proportion of Swedish migrants who passed through communities of this type is not high and, for the most part, they belonged to a particular phase of the migrations. Yet the process that created the transplantations was a process central to much of the migration. Even the most culturally heterogeneous Swedish settlements and urban neighborhoods in America commonly had a kinship-related group representing a particular district or province at their core or had several such groups among the later arriving contingents. In his studies of southern Europeans in Australia, Price has found that the affinitive ties that bind immigrant social groups occur at several levels, but the most basic level—occurring within all the others—is that of kinship and locality (Price 1963). The migration-linked communities discussed here may be less than representative of the overall result of the nineteenth-century Swedish migrations, but they are representative of the basic processes.

It is certainly true that the last couple of decades have seen exhaustive efforts to research the Swedish emigration to America. In many ways, it is also true that these efforts have reached the point of diminishing returns. Many have said as much. This essay, however, suggests that more can be done and that the research frontier is still, as it was in 1960, the development of a systematic understanding of the *entire* transatlantic migration experience. While considerable progress has been made toward that aim by scholars on both sides of the Atlantic, there is still some distance between them based on differing objectives and data incompatibilities. Perhaps renewed effort at longitudinal studies that are transatlantic in scope will close the distance.

Notes

1. A recent example is J. D. Gould, "European Inter-continental Emigration, 1815–1914: Patterns and Causes," *Journal of European Economic History* 8 (1979), p. 597.

2. For a more complete statement of the organization and aims of the Uppsala group, see Hans Runblom, "A Brief History of a Research Project," in Runblom and Norman (eds.), *From Sweden to America* (1976).

3. For a discussion of the roles of these disparate ideas, see Sune Åkerman, "Theories and Methods of Migration Research" in Runblom and Norman.

4. Notable exceptions are the monographs by Janson (1931) and Lindberg (1930), both of which viewed the American experience in the context of the Swedish background of the emigration.

5. For a useful discussion of the techniques for measuring persistence see D. Aidan McQuillan, "The Mobility of Immigrants and Americans: A Comparison of Farmers on the Kansas Frontier," *Agricultural History* 53 (1979), pp. 581–82.

Selected Bibliography

Åkerman, Sune. 1972a. "The Psychology of Migration." *American Studies in Scandinavia* 8.

———. 1972b. "Rural and Urban Immigration". *Scandinavian Economic History Review* 20.

———. 1975. "From Stockholm to San Francisco: The Development of the Historical Study of External Migrations." *Annales Academiae Scientarium Upsaliensis* 19.

———. 1977. "Swedish migration and social mobility: the tale of three cities". *Social Science History* 1.

————. 1978a. "International Migration and its relation to emigration." In Nils Hasselmo, ed., *Perspectives on Swedish Immigration: Proceedings of an International Conference on the Swedish Heritage in the Upper Midwest, University of Minnesota–Duluth, April 1–3.*

————. 1978b. "Towards an understanding of Emigrational processes." *Scandinavian Journal of History* 3.

Åkerman, Sune, Per Gunnar Cassel, and Egil Johansson. 1974. "Background variables of population mobility: an attempt at automatic interaction detector analysis: a preliminary research report." *Scandinavian Economic History Review* 22.

Åkerman, Sune, Bo Kronberg, and Thomas Nilsson. 1977. "Emigration, Family, and Kinship." *American Studies in Scandinavia* 9. *University of Illinois Bulletin*, 12, no 7.

Ander, O. Fritiof. 1933. "Some Factors in the Americanization of Swedish Immigrants, 1850–1890." *Journal of the Illinois State Historical Society.*

Babcock, Kendric C. 1914. *The Scandinavian Element in the United States.*

Barton, H. Arnold. 1975. *Letters from the Promised Land: Swedes in America, 1840–1914.* Minneapolis.

————. 1978a. "Clio and Swedish America: Historians, Organizations, Publications." In Nils Hasselmo, ed., *Perspectives on Swedish Immigration: Proceedings of the International Conference on the Swedish Heritage in the Upper Midwest, April 1–3, 1976, University of Minnesota–Duluth.*

————. 1978b. "Where do we stand now?" *Swedish Pioneer Historical Quarterly* 29.

Beijbom, Ulf. 1971. *Swedes in Chicago: A Demographic and Social Study of the 1846–1880 Immigration.* Studia Historica Upsaliensia 38. Växjö.

Benson, Adolph B. 1956. "The Assimilation of Swedes in America." *Swedish Pioneer Historical Quarterly.*

Benson, Adolph B., and Naboth Hedin, eds. 1938. *Swedes in America.* New Haven.

Bergendoff, Conrad. 1968. "The Swedish Immigrant and the American Way." *Swedish Pioneer Historical Quarterly.*

Bogue, Allan G. 1963. *From Prairie to Corn Belt: Farming on the Illinois and Iowa Prairies in the Nineteenth Century.* Chicago.

Brattne, Berit. 1973. *Bröderna Larsson: En Studie i svensk emigrantagent-verksamhet under 1880-talet.* Studia Historica Upsaliensia 50. Uppsala.

Capps, Finis Herbert. 1966. *From Isolationism to Involvement: The Swedish Immigrant Press in America, 1914–1945.* Chicago.

Carlsson, Sten. 1968. "Fran familheutvandring till ensamutvandring. En utvecklingslinje i den svenska emigrationens historia." In *Emigrationer: En bok till Wilhelm Moberg 20.8.1968.* Stockholm.

————. 1970. *Skandinaviska politiker in Minnesota 1882–1900: En Studie rörande den etniska faktorns roll vid politiska val i en immigrantstat.* Acta Universitatis Upsaliensia 1. Uppsala.

————. 1974. "From Mid-Sweden to the Midwest." *Swedish Pioneer Historical Quarterly.*

Conzen, Kathleen. 1980. "Historical Approaches to the Study of Rural Ethnic Communities." In Frederick C. Luebke, ed., *Ethnicity on the Great Plains.* Omaha.

Curti, Merle. 1964. *The Making of an American Community: A Case Study of Democracy in a Frontier County.* Stanford.

Dowie, J. Iverne, and Ernest M. Espelie, eds. 1963. *The Swedish Immigrant Community in Transition: Essays in honor of Dr. Conrad Bergendoff.* Augustana Historical Society.

Dunlevy, James A., and Henry A. Gemery. 1976. "Some additional evidence on settlement patterns of Scandinavian migrants to the United States: Dynamics and the Role of Family and Friends." *Scandinavian Economic History Review* 24.

Ellemers, J. E. 1964. "The Determinants of Emigration: An Analysis of Dutch Studies in Migration." *Sociologica Neerlandica* 2:1.

Erickson, Charlotte. 1980. "Explanatory Models in Immigration and Migration Research." In Ingrid Semmingsen and Per Seyerstad, eds., *Scando-Americana Papers of Scandinavian Emigration to the United States.*

Emigrationsutredningen (1908–1913) *Betänkande och bilagor* (1–20).

Fjellstrom, Phebe. 1970. *Swedish-American Colonization in the San Joaquin Valley in California: A Study of the Acculturation and Assimilation of an Immigrant Group.* Studia Ethnographica Upsaliensia 33. Uppsala.

Gjerde, Jon. 1979. "The Effect of Community on Migration: Three Minnesota Townships, 1885–1905." *Journal of Historical Geography* 5.

Gould, J. D. 1979. "European Inter-Continental Emigration, 1815–1914: Patterns and Causes." *Journal of European Economic History* 8.

———. 1980. "European Inter-continental Emigration: The Role of 'Diffusion' and 'Feedback'. *Journal of European Economic History* 9.

Gullberg, Bo, and Birgitta Oden. 1976. "AID Analysis and migration history." *Scandinavian Economic History Review* 24.

Hägerstrand, Torsten. 1947. "En landsbygdsbefolknings flyttningsrörelser. Studier over migrationen på grundval av Asby sockens flyttningsrörelser, 1840–1944." *Svensk Geografisk Årsbok* 23.

Hamberg, Eva. 1976. *Studier i internationell migration.* Stockholm Studies in Economic History 2. Stockholm.

Handlin, Oscar. 1951. *The Uprooted: The Epic Story of the Great Migrations that Made the American People.* Boston.

Hansen, Marcus Lee. 1940. *The Immigrant in American History.* Cambridge, Mass.

Hasselmo, Nils. 1974. *Amerikasvenska: En bok om språkutvecklingen i Svensk-Amerika.* Lund.

Hekanson, Nels. 1942. *Swedish Immigrants in Lincoln's Time.* New York.

Janson, Florence. 1931. *The Background of Swedish Immigration, 1840–1930.* Chicago.

Jerome, Harry. 1926. *Migration and Business Cycles.* New York.

Kälvemark, Ann-Sofie. 1972. *Reaktionen mot utvandringen: Emigrationsfrågan i svensk debatt och politik, 1901–1904.* Studia Historica Upsaliensia 41. Uppsala.

———, ed. 1973. *Utvandring: Den svenska emigrationen till Amerika i historiskt perspektiv: En antologi.* Stockholm.

———. 1977. "The Country that Kept Track of Its Population: Methodological Aspects of Swedish Population Records." *Scandinavian Journal of History* 2.

Kastrup, Allan. 1975. *The Swedish Heritage in America: The Swedish Elements in*

America in Their Historical Perspective. (St. Paul, MN: Swedish Council of America).

Katz, Michael. 1975. *The People of Hamilton, Ontario West.* Cambridge, Mass.

Kronberg, Bo, and Thomas Nilsson. 1975. *Stadsflyttare. Industrialisering, migration och social mobilitet med utgångspunkt från Halmstad, 1870–1910.* Studia Historica Upsaliensia 65. Uppsala.

Lindberg, John S. 1930. *The Background of Swedish Emigration to the United States.* Minneapolis.

Lindgren, Raymond E. 1979. "Emigration and Migration: Studies in Demography." *Swedish Pioneer Historical Quarterly* 30.

Lindmark, Sture. 1971. *Swedish-America, 1914–1932: Studies in Ethnicity with Emphasis on Illinois and Minnesota.* Studia Historica Upsaliensia 37. Uppsala.

Ljungmark, Lars. 1971. *For Sale—Minnesota: Organized Promotion of Scandinavian Immigration, 1866–1873.* Goteborg.

Malin, James C. 1935. "The Turnover of Farm Population in Kansas." *Kansas Historical Quarterly* 4.

McQuillan, D. Aidan. 1979. "The Mobility of Immigrants and Americans: A Comparison of Farmers on the Kansas Frontier." *Agricultural History* 53.

Nelson, Helge. 1943. *Swedes and Swedish Settlements in North America.* 2 vols. Lund.

Nilsson, Fred. 1970. *Emigrationen fran Stockholm till Nordamerika 1880–1893: En Studie i urban Utvandring.* Studia Historica Upsaliensia 31. Uppsala.

Norberg, Anders, and Sune Åkerman. 1973. "Migration and the building of Families." In *Aristocrats, Farmers and Proletarians: Essays in Swedish Demographic History.* Studia Historica Upsaliensia 47. Uppsala.

Norman, Hans. 1974. *Från Bergslagen till Nordamerika: Studier i migrationsmönster, social rörlighet och demografisk struktur med utgångspunkt fran Örebro lan, 1851–1915.* Studia Historica Upsaliensia 62. Uppsala.

Odén, Birgitta. 1963. "Emigrationen från Norden till Nordamerika." *Historisk tidskrift* 83.

Ostergren, Robert C. 1973. "Cultural Homogeneity and Population Stability Among Swedish Immigrants in Chisago County." *Minnesota History* 43.

———. 1979. "A Community Transplanted: The Formative Experience of a Swedish Immigrant Community in the Upper Middle West." *Journal of Historical Geography* 5.

———. 1980. "Prairie Bound: Migration Patterns to a Swedish Settlement on the Dakota Frontier." In Frederick C. Luebke, ed., *Ethnicity on the Great Plains.* Omaha.

———. 1981a. "Geographic Perspectives on The History of Settlement in the Upper Midwest." *Upper Midwest History* 1.

———. 1981b. "The Immigrant Church as a Symbol of Community and Place in the Upper Midwest." *Great Plains Quarterly* 1.

———. 1981c. "Land and Family in Rural Immigrant Communities." *Annals of the Association of American Geographers* 71.

Ottey, Abram C. F. 1940. *The Swedish Race in America.* Philadelphia.

Price, Charles A. 1963. *Southern Europeans in Australia.* Melbourne.

Quigley, John M. 1972. "An Economic Model of Swedish Migration." *Quarterly Journal of Economics* 86.

Rice, John G. 1973. Patterns of Ethnicity in a Minnesota County, 1880–1905. Geographical Report No. 4, Dept. of Geography, University of Umeå.

———. 1977. "The Role of culture and community in frontier Prairie farming." *Journal of Historical Geography* 3.

———. 1978a. "The Effect of Land Alienation on Settlement." *Annals of the Association of American Geographers* 68.

———. 1978b. "Marriage behavior and the persistence of Swedish settlements in Minnesota." In Nils Hasselmo, ed., *Perspectives on Swedish Immigration: The Swedish Heritage in the Upper Midwest.*

Rice, John G., and Robert C. Ostergren. 1978. "The Decision to Emigrate: A Study in Diffusion." *Geografiska Annaler* 60.

Rondahl, Bjorn. 1972. *Emigration, folkomflyttning och säsonarbete i ett sågverksdistrikt i södra Halsingland, 1865–1910.* Studia Historica Upsaliensia 49. Uppsala.

Runblom, H., and H. Norman, eds. 1976. *From Sweden to America: A History of the Migration.* Minneapolis.

Runblom, Harald, and Lars-Göran Tedebrand. 1979. "Future Research in Swedish-American History: Some Perspectives." *The Swedish Pioneer Historical Quarterly* 30.

Runeby, Nils. 1969. *Den nya världen och den gamla. Amerikabild och emigrationsuppfattning i Sverige, 1820–1860.* Studia Historica Upsaliensia 30. Uppsala.

Salisbury, Robert S. 1978. "Swedish-American Historiography and the Question of Americanization." *Swedish Pioneer Historical Quarterly* 29.

Semmingsen, Ingrid. 1978. "Nordic Research into Migration." *Scandinavian Journal of History* 3.

Soderberg, Kjell. 1977. "Personal Characteristics and Selective Migration." *American Studies in Scandinavia* 9.

Stephenson, George M. 1932. *The Religious Aspects of Swedish Immigration.* Minneapolis.

Sundin, Jan. 1979. "The Demographic Data Base at the University of Umeå." In *Time, Space and Man: Essays on Microdemography.* Stockholm.

Tedebrand, Lars-Goran. 1972. *Västernorrland och Nordamerika, 1875–1913: Utvandring och aterinvandring.* Studia Historcia Upsaliensis 42. Uppsala.

Thernstrom, Stephan. 1969. *Poverty and Progress: Social Mobility in a Nineteenth Century City.* Cambridge, Mass.

———. 1973. *The Other Bostonians: Poverty and Progress in the American Metropolis, 1880–1970.* Cambridge, Mass.

Thistlethwaite, Frank. 1960. "Migration from Europe Overseas in the Nineteenth and Twentieth Centuries." *Rapports Vol. V XIe Congres International des Sciences Historiques.*

Thomas, Brinley. 1954. *Migration and Economic Growth: A Study of Great Britain and the Atlantic Economy.* Cambridge.

Thomas, Dorothy Swaine. 1941. *Social and Economic Aspects of Swedish Population Movements, 1750–1933.* New York.

Throne, Mildred. 1959. "A population study of an Iowa County in 1950." *Iowa Journal of History* 57.

Vedder, R. K., and L. E. Galloway. 1970. "The Settlement preferences of Scandinavian Emigrants to the United States, 1850–1960." *Scandinavian Economic History Review* 18.

Wilkinson, M. 1967. "Evidences of Long Swings in the growth of Swedish Population and Related Variables, 1860–1965." *Journal of Economic History* 27.

Wiren, Agnes. 1975. *Uppbrott fran Örtagård: Utvandring från Blekinge till och med ar 1870*. Bibliotheca Historica Lübensis 34. Lund.

7

Aspects of Italian Emigration, 1881–1915

Luigi Di Comité

The outstanding characteristics of Italian migration in the period from Unification of the Kingdom to the present can be briefly summarized in the following manner:

- Until 1880, migration is only of moderate importance, and concerns primarily the regions of northern Italy.
- From 1881 to World War I there is a boom in overseas emigration, but within the total flow, transoceanic emigration is of greater importance than emigration to European countries, especially emigration to the United States.
- In the period between the two world wars, emigration diminishes as restrictive emigration policies predominate.
- From 1945 until the early 1970s, emigration to economically developed European countries and internal migration, which flows from south to north, predominates, with the aim of internal redistribution of population.

• During the 1970s we observe a new kind of migratory movement, and Italy becomes a country of immigration for the first time in her history.[1]

Taking these facts into account, we should pause for a moment to consider more carefully the first two of the five phases and focus in particular on the second; that is, on the growth of transoceanic emigration.[2]

Population Growth and the Regional Migration Balances in the Period 1861–1911

The basic data available for the study are taken from the five population censuses between 1861 and 1911. Tables 7.1–7.3 have been constructed from census data on births and deaths and show, for each region and for the country as a whole, population size (i.e., population present at time of census), and average annual growth rates of the population between census periods calculated according to the formula

$$r - \left(\frac{P_{t+h}}{P_t}\right)^{1/h} - 1 \qquad (1)$$

where the meaning of the symbols are evident, and data on intercensal migration movements, according to the formula

$$S_{(t, t+h)} = P_{t+h} - \left[P_t + (N_{t, t+h} - D_{t, t+h})\right] \qquad (2)$$

where symbols are again evident.[3]

From the point of view of demographic dynamics, if we disregard data for the period 1861–1870 because of territorial changes, table 7.1 shows that Italy's population increased from 26,801,105 in 1871 to 34,671,377 in 1911, with a mean annual growth rate of 6.55%. This represents an average of the growth rates for the three periods as follows: 1871–1881 (r = 6.02%), 1881–1901 (r = 6.93%), and 1901–1911 (r = 6.35%).

Over this period the annual rate of variation of the population did not undergo significant modification, and this despite the fact that, by 1870, the demographic transition had begun.[4] The transition involved, as demographers know, a fall in gross mortality rates in its first phase and a diminution in the expansionary force of the population.

From the data reported in table 7.2 we find that there are marked

Table 7.1

CENSUS POPULATIONS AT YEAR END FOR THE PERIOD
1861–1911

	Population				
Regions	1861 (31-XII)	1871 (31-XII)	1881 (31-XII)	1901 (10-II)	1911 (10-VI)
Piemonte	2.764.263	2.899.564	3.070.250	3.317.401	3.424.450
Liguria	771.473	843.812	892.373	1.077.473	1.197.231
Lombardia	3.104.838	3.460.824	3.680.615	4.282.728	4.790.473
Veneto	—	2.642.807	2.814.173	3.134.467	3.527.360
Emilia-Romagna	2.005.834	2.113.828	2.183.391	2.445.035	2.681.201
Toscana	1.967.067	2.142.476	2.208.869	2.549.142	2.694.706
Marche	883.073	915.419	939.279	1.060.755	1.093.253
Umbria	513.019	549.601	572.060	667.210	686.596
Lazio	—	836.704	903.472	1.196.909	1.302.423
Abruzzi e Molise	1.212.835	1.282.982	1.317.215	1.441.551	1.430.706
Campania	2.625.830	2.754.592	2.896.577	3.160.448	3.311.990
Puglia	1.315.269	1.420.892	1.589.064	1.959.668	2.130.151
Basilicata	493.049	510.543	524.504	490.705	474.021
Calabria	1.139.796	1.206.302	1.257.883	1.370.208	1.402.151
Sicilia	2.392.414	2.584.099	2.927.901	3.529.799	3.672.258
Sardegna	588.064	636.660	682.002	791.754	852.407
ITALIA	21.776.824	26.801.105	23.459.628	32.475.253	34.671.377

Source: Commissariato Generale Dell'Emigrazione, *Annuàrio statistico dell'emigrazione italiana dal 1876 al 1925*, Rome, 1926.

regional disparities in the rate of variation of the population both as regards annual growth rates and their evolution over time: I will not deal with these problems in the present study, however, only point out that there is a marked dualism between the north and south, where we find rising rates over time in the north, and the opposite trend in the south.

Two factors help us to understand these differences:

1. the fact that the demographic transition and the beginning of the decline in crude death rates had different starting dates in the north and the south,
2. the different propensities to migrate in the various regions of Italy.[5]

For what concerns migratory phenomena, the intercensal balances in table 7.3 show that, nationwide, the decades between 1861 and 1911 can be divided into two periods; 1861–1881, the pretransition period; and 1881–1911, the first phase of the demographic transition period. These periods show the differences in migration phenomena at the regional level during the fifty years in question and provide interesting data for an analysis of migration.

During the interval 1861–1881, all central-northern regions of Italy seem to participate in the migratory deficit. In the first decade (1861–1871), there is a global migratory deficit of about 150,000 persons. This must be considered partial, however, as it does not take into account regions that were not part of the Kingdom of Italy in 1861. The deficit involved only the regions of central and nort ern Italy; the migratory balance is positive in the south. In the second decade (1871–1881), there is a negative migratory balance, even in the south, of 42,000 persons.

The negative balance, however, is relatively small (in the Kingdom of the Two Sicilies and in Sardinia, in fact, the balance is positive), while the major part of the deficit, 330,000 people, is concentrated in the central-northern regions.

Bearing in mind the fact that between 1871 and 1911, the southern regions accounted for 40 percent of Italy's resident population while the central-northern regions accounted for slightly more than 60 percent, we

Table 7.2

MEAN ANNUAL GROWTH RATES OF THE POPULATION,
1861–1911

Regions	1,000 r			
	1861–1871	1871–1881	1881–1901	1901–1911
Piemonte	4.79	5.74	4.06	3.08
Liguria	9.00	5.61	9.91	10.25
Lombardia	—	6.18	7.96	10.90
Veneto	—	6.30	5.66	11.49
Emilia-Romagna	5.26	3.24	5.94	8.96
Toscana	8.58	3.06	7.53	5.39
Marche	3.60	2.58	6.38	2.92
Umbria	6.91	4.01	8.08	2.78
Lazio	—	7.71	14.83	8.21
Abruzzi e Molise	5.64	2.64	4.73	−0.73
Campania	4.80	5.04	4.57	4.54
Puglia	7.75	11.25	11.03	8.11
Basilicata	3.49	2.70	−3.48	−3.34
Calabria	5.69	4.20	4.49	2.23
Sicilia	7.74	12.57	9.83	3.84
Sardegna	7.97	6.90	7.84	7.17
ITALIA	—	6.02	6.93	6.35

Source: Commissariato Generale Dell'Emigrazione, *Annuàrio statistico dell'emigrazione italiana dal 1876 al 1925*, Rome, 1926.

Table 7.3

STABILITY OF THE MIGRATORY MOVEMENT BETWEEN CENSUSES, 1861–1911

Regions	Intercensus intervals			
	1861–1871	1871–1881	1881–1901	1901–1911
Piemonte	− 76.770	− 94.988	− 286.469	− 155.991
Liguria	− 3.782	− 12.712	35.379	32.153
Lombardia	*	− 64.739	− 214.733	− 40.160
Veneto	—	− 70.497	− 462.266	− 202.040
Emilia-Romagna	− 30.154	− 47.036	− 174.252	− 94.487
Toscana	− 12.030	− 57.009	− 113.690	− 128.414
Marche	− 30.937	− 25.644	− 88.055	− 98.007
Umbria	-- 4.403	− 7.949	− 34.013	− 54.408
Lazio	—	61.003	94.631	− 20.196
Abruzzi e Molise	− 12.251	− 38.854	− 161.709	− 168.472
Campania	− 22.137	− 12.431	− 299.127	− 166.651
Puglia	25.698	15.021	− 16.360	− 76.387
Basilicata	− 3.025	− 20.724	− 114.446	− 64.381
Calabria	− 14.729	− 28.042	− 176.550	− 138.815
Sicilia	19.865	39.441	− 169.208	− 207.894
Sardegna	14.207	2.894	− 9.869	− 35.720
ITALIA	*	− 362.266	− 2.190.737	− 1.619.870

*Rate not calculated because of territorial variations

Source: Commissariato Generale Dell'Emigrazione, *Annuario statistics dell'emigrazione italiana dal 1876 al 1925*, Rome, 1926.

turn to an analysis of the period 1881–1911, the first phase of the national demographic transition.

Table 7.3 shows that the migratory hemorrhage intensified over time; it rose at the national level from an annual deficit of about 36,000 between 1871 and 1881, to 219,000 between 1881 and 1901, and to 160,000 between 1901 and 1911.

At the national level, beginning in 1881, the demographic equilibrium was broken by a progressive decline in mortality rates while birthrates remained high so that balance was restored through migratory deficits. The southern regions now became increasingly important contributors to these deficits because of the delayed decline in the birthrate in the period of demographic transition.

Regional disparities in the natural movements of the population, however, can only partially explain the "major" migratory deficits in the southern regions: exodus movements in these regions of the dimensions observed between 1881 and 1911 were more the result of socioeconomic factors than of demographic factors—a fact that is evident from the very low values—even negative values—observed in the annual rate of variation of the population in these regions during the period under consideration (excluding Puglia and Sardinia).

Italian Emigration, 1881–1915

For a more profound analysis of Italian migration, we must examine the statistics on immigration and emigration, since the population balances provide only a partial view of the phenomenon.

Unfortunately, the nature of the available statistical material does not lend itself to this kind of analysis as the basic data provide only a picture— in the present case in summary form for the whole country—"of Italian citizens who expatriated under conditions of great economic hardship."

Taking this into account, and also the fact that we lack aggregate data on the number of repatriates, tables 7.4–7.6 present the relevant data now available on emigration. Analysis of these statistics reveals some interesting facts. In the thirty-year period 1881–1911, the migratory deficit of over 3,800,000 persons stands in direct contrast to the growth of the emigrant population, who number over 13,400,000, indicating a considerable increase in the number of repatriates who returned to their homeland on either a temporary or a permanent basis.

Furthermore, from the data in tables 7.4 and 7.5, it is clear that there were many more repatriates between 1900 and 1915 than in the preceding twenty-year period (1880–1900), as over the entire interval, 80 percent of the emigrants were males.

Tables 7.4 and 7.5 show that the emigrants went to a limited number of destinations: between 1881 and 1915, the preferred destinations were the United States (30.73% of the total), Argentina (13.00%), France (11.36%), Switzerland (9.45%), Brazil (8.95%), and Germany (8.82%). The data on destinations, however, do not offer a clear picture of the modifications that occurred in these flows, unless one considers separately the data relating to the separate decades between 1881 and 1910.

Analysis of these data show that the original equilibrium between emigration to European and Mediterranean-basin countries and emigration to overseas countries breaks down so that between 1881–1890 and 1901–1910 the migration to overseas destinations increases from 50.55 percent to 58.32 percent.

Notable changes also occur over time in the internal distribution of these flows. Among the European countries, Germany and Switzerland acquire greater importance as countries of destination at the expense of France; among the overseas countries, the United States gains at the expense of Argentina, but most of all of Brazil.

The United States received the greatest share of Italian emigrants. Table 7.6 and figures 7.1 and 7.2 show that, with notable variations, the

Table 7.4

TOTAL NUMBER OF EMIGRANTS FOR SELECTED DESTINATIONS, 1881–1915
(thousands)

Countries	Time Periods				Total
	1881–1890	1891–1900	1901–1910	1911–1915	
France	374.071	259.283	572.616	325.317	1.531.287
Germany	86.392	230.931	591.044	280.906	1.189.273
Switzerland	71.175	189.062	655.668	357.977	1.273.882
European & Mediterranean countries	929.201	1.288.001	2.512.008	1.217.677	5.946.887
Argentina	391.503	366.820	734.597	259.957	1.752.877
Brazil	215.552	580.224	303.361	107.422	1.206.559
Canada	6.272	5.915	65.105	71.134	148.426
United States	245.230	514.327	2.329.451	1.054.701	4.143.709
Transoceanic countries	950.000	1.546.725	3.514.682	1.525.382	7.536.789
TOTAL	1.879.201	2.834.726	6.026.690	2.743.059	13.483.676
Number of males*	1.523.899	2.229.148	4.945.475	2.197.626	10.896.148

Source: Commissariato Generale Dell'Emigrazione, *Annuario statistico dell'emigrazione italiana dal 1876 al 1925*, Rome, 1926 (my elaborations).

Table 7.5

TOTAL NUMBER OF EMIGRANTS FOR SELECTED DESTINATION, 1881–1915
(percentages)

Countries	1881–1890	1891–1900	1901–1910	1911–1915	1881–1915
France	19.91	9.15	9.50	11.86	11.36
Germany	4.60	8.15	9.81	10.24	8.82
Switzerland	3.79	6.67	10.88	13.05	9.45
European & Mediterranean countries	49.45	45.44	41.68	44.39	44.10
Argentina	20.83	12.95	12.19	9.48	13.00
Brazil	11.47	20.47	5.03	3.92	8.95
Canada	0.33	0.21	1.08	2.59	1.10
United States	13.03	18.14	38.65	38.45	30.73
Transoceanic countries	50.55	54.56	58.32	55.61	55.90
TOTAL	100.00	100.00	100.00	100.00	100.00
Percentage of males*	81.09	78.64	82.06	80.12	80.81

Source: Commissariato Generale Dell'Emigrazione, *Annuario statistico dell'emigrazione italiana dal 1876 al 1925*, Rome, 1926 (my elaborations).

Table 7.6
EMIGRANTS FOR SELECTED DESTINATIONS, 1881–1915.
(thousands)

Years	Total (a)	European & Mediterranean basic countries (b)	Trans- oceanic countries (c)	United States (d)	$\frac{(d)}{(a)}100$	$\frac{(d)}{(c)}100$
1881	135.832	94.768	41.064	11.482	8.45	27.96
1882	161.562	101.736	59.826	18.593	11.51	31.08
1883	169.101	104.818	64.283	21.256	12.58	33.07
1884	147.017	90.698	56.319	10.582	7.20	18.79
1885	157.193	83.712	73.481	12.485	7.94	16.99
1886	167.829	84.952	82.877	26.920	16.04	32.48
1887	215.665	85.363	130.302	37.221	17.26	28.56
1888	290.736	86.036	204.700	32.945	11.33	16.09
1889	218.412	94.823	123.589	25.434	11.64	20.58
1890	215.854	102.295	113.559	47.952	22.21	42.23
1891	293.631	106.056	187.575	44.359	15.11	23.65
1892	223.667	109.421	114.246	42.953	19.20	37.60
1893	246.751	107.769	138.982	49.765	20.17	35.81
1894	225.323	113.425	111.898	31.668	14.05	28.30
1895	293.181	108.664	184.517	37.851	12.91	20.51
1896	307.482	113.235	194.247	53.486	17.40	27.53
1897	299.855	127.777	172.078	47.000	15.67	27.31
1898	283.715	147.803	135.912	56.375	19.87	41.48
1899	308.339	167.572	140.767	63.156	20.48	44.86
1900	352.782	186.279	166.503	87.714	24.86	52.68
1901	533.245	253.571	279.674	121.139	22.72	43.31
1902	531.509	246.855	284.654	193.772	36.46	68.07
1903	507.976	225.541	282.435	197.855	38.95	70.05
1904	471.191	218.825	252.366	168.789	35.82	66.88
1905	726.331	279.248	447.083	316.797	43.62	70.86
1906	787.977	276.042	511.935	358.569	45.50	70.04
1907	704.675	288.774	415.901	298.124	42.31	71.68
1908	486.674	248.101	238.573	131.501	37.02	55.12
1909	625.637	226.355	399.282	280.351	44.81	70.21
1910	651.475	248.696	402.779	262.554	40.30	65.18
1911	533.844	271.065	262.779	191.087	35.79	72.72
1912	711.446	308.140	403.306	267.637	37.62	66.36
1913	872.598	313.032	559.566	376.776	43.18	67.33
1914	479.152	245.938	233.214	167.481	34.95	71.31
1915	146.019	79.502	66.517	51.720	35.42	77.75

Source: Commissariato Generale Dell'Emigrazione *Annuario statistics dell'emigrazione italiana dal 1876 al 1925*, Rome, 1926.

Figure 7.1: Emigrants for Selected Destinations, 1881–1915

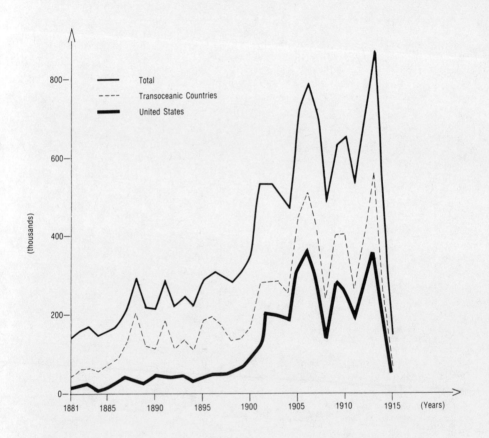

Figure 7.2: Incidence of Expatriates for the United States Compared to the Total Number and to the Transoceanic Emigrants, 1881–1915

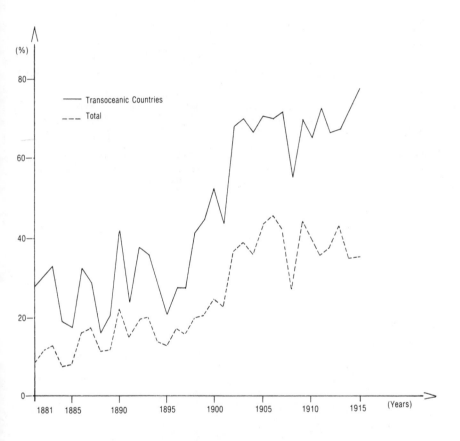

migratory flow from Italy to the States increased until 1913—that is, until the outbreak of World War I. In the final five-year period (1911–1915), emigrants to the United States comprised roughly 40 percent of the total number of emigrants, and slightly under 70 percent of the emigrants to overseas destinations.

Conclusions

The data reported in the preceding pages provide a very concise picture of Italian emigration from 1881 to World War I. The brevity of the exposition does not allow me to give a detailed picture of the socioeconomic characteristics of the migrants or of the contributions of the migratory flows from the various regions of the country.

I defer in these matters because of limitations of space, to the recent study of socioeconomic characteristics of emigrants from Italy to the United States by Glazier, which reports preliminary findings on the qualitative and quantitative characteristics of Italian emigration to the United States.[6] I hope in the near future, however, to undertake an analysis of the contribution of the various regions to Italian emigration between 1880 and World War I.

Notes

1. For the standard criteria of classification, refer to L. Di Comite, *"Problemi Statistici delle migrazioni,"* Annali di Statistica, Series IX. Volume I, Rome, 1981.

2. For an analytic view of the problems connected with Italian emigration, refer to D. De Marco, *Per una storia economica dell'emigrazione italiana*, in "Tendenze dell' emigrazione italiana: ieri, oggi" (edited by A. Dell' Orefice), Librairie Droz, Geneva, 1978; E. Sori, *"L'emigrazione italiana dall' unità alla seconda guerra mondiale,"* Bologna, 1979.

3. For the nineteenth century, the values of (2) have been drawn from L. Di Comite, *Su talune caratteristiche strutturali ed evolutive della popolazione italiana nella seconda metà del XIX secolo,* "Rassegna Economica," 1976, n.1.

4. For the way in which the demographic transition in Italy and in Europe has occurred, see L. Di Comite, *Teoria e prassi della transizione demografica*, in "Studi in onore di Paolo Fortunati," CLUEB, Bologna, 1980; J. Bourgeois Pichat, *La transition demographique en Europe*, Relazione presentata alla "Conférence Démographique Européenne de 1982," Conseil de L'Europe, Strasbourg, September 21–24, 1982.

5. With regard to the factors determining migratory phenomena and principal characteristics, past and present, of such phenomena, refer to N. Federici, *Migrazioni fisiologiche e migrazioni patologiche: la realtà italiana*, in "Studi in onore di Guglielmo Tagliacarne," "Istituto di Statistica ecnomica della Facoltà di Scienze statistiche, demografiche ed attuariali dell'Università di Roma," Rome, 1974; A.

Golini, *Gli stadi migratori in Italia e l'attuale fase delle migrazioni interne*, "Rassegna Economica," 1979, n.2.

6. On this problem, see Ira A. Glazier, *Ships and passengers in emigration from Italy to the U.S., 1880–1900*, in "Le genti del mare meditteraneo," edited by Rosalba Ragosta, volume 2, pages 1097–1125, Naples, 1981; L. Di Comite and I. A. Glazier, *Socio-Demographic Characteristics of Italian Emigration to the United States from Ship Passenger Lists: 1880–1914*, in "Ethnic Forum," Volume 4, Numbers 1–2, 1984.

8

Social and Psychological Factors in Migration from Italy to Argentina: From the Waldensian Valleys to San Gustavo

Kristin Ruggiero

From the nineteenth century to today, from official reports to the popular medium of films such as *Bread and Chocolate*, one of Italy's main concerns has been emigration. Italians then (as now) lived in an emigrant culture. Growing interest in the social and psychological factors of this phenomenon is bringing us closer to an understanding of the various dimensions of this culture. Students of the subject have often portrayed the typical emigrant as an indigent moved by economic forces, and the decision to emigrate as the choice of a desperate man. Even today many scholars and Italians involved with contemporary emigration have been reluctant to relinquish this vision of migrating man.

In recent years scholars have composed elaborate models, usually economic, to explain emigrant behavior. A careful review of this literature by J. D. Gould in the *Journal of European Economic History* in 1979, however, stresses the need for a still more vigilant examination of commonly used concepts like push and pull factors as well as for more localized studies. In addition, several contributors to the work *Human Migration* edited by William McNeill and published in 1978 emphasize the need for more local material.[1] Through my own investigation of two local migratory movements, I hope to "rehabilitate" or elevate migrating man to a somewhat more positive stature than that in which he has often been placed.[2] The first movement follows nineteenth-century Italians from Piedmont to the province of Entre Ríos in Argentina. The second, which I refer to only occasionally for purposes of comparison with the twentieth century, involves the contemporary emigration of the Bellunese from the Veneto.

Such village-oriented studies offer a chance to view the culture of migration on the micro level. While some aspects are relatively apparent from this perspective, others are more difficult to reconstruct. For example, overpopulation and underproduction, insufficient land and agricultural crises, agents and promises of a better future are more self-evident than social and psychological factors. But emigration seems to transcend economic trends, labor markets, commodity prices, greater social mobility, technological innovations, and the presence abroad of relatives and friends. Though these conditions do influence behavior, concentration on them alone makes emigration seem too concrete and formulaic, and thus somehow a phenomenon out of the hands of the people themselves, that is, something that happens to people. There must be something else going on, though, because, with all the fine work produced on emigration, we are still left with the question of why, if all that is needed is the correct combination of stimuli, does not every situation meeting such criteria produce emigration. Questions of how an individual decides to emigrate; of what distinguishes an emigrant from a nonemigrant; of what emigrants are basically, quite aside from subjects of external factors like labor demands and so on continue to perplex us.

Emerging from the cloud of fog of the Po River valley about fifty miles southwest of Turin, one comes upon the small pre-Alpine town of Torre Pellice. The village itself occupies part of the Pellice Valley while many of its hamlets and farms hug the steep of the front range of the Cottian Alps. The town is best known as the center of the Waldenses, now Protestants, who have occupied the valleys of the Pellice, the Chisone, and the Germanasca since the twelfth century. In the nineteenth century, as local lore has it, a depressed economy prompted the dispersal of much of Torre Pellice's population. Among the emigrants figured some Waldenses who settled in San Gustavo in Argentina between about 1895 and 1910.

The character of the town has not changed greatly since the nineteenth century: the inhabitants still number around 4,000; depopulation of the mountain areas continues toward the industrial centers of Italy and abroad; agencies, like today's Comunità Montana, continue to make recommendations similar to those of the nineteenth century to reinvigorate the area. More importantly, the rhetoric of emigration remains the same—

of desperate, impoverished men and women having to migrate in order just to live.

Poor economic conditions could be easily verified, though. Characteristic of the higher elevations of the Pellice Valley is their lack of arable land.[3] A visitor in 1854 commented on the difficulty of cultivation in the valley "where neither vehicles nor animals with a load [could] manage and where the farmer himself had to carry hay on his head from the valley floor to the top of the mountain"; where one had to "reconstitute the fields [each year] by collecting the soil of the foothills and carrying it up on one's shoulders. . . ."[4]

Small and dispersed landholdings, averaging less than two and a half acres, contributed to the problems of farming.[5] An intense desire for land meant that farmers hoarded each piece they could obtain regardless of its size and location. These scattered holdings wasted farmers' time and energy both in transporting tools, animals, and produce between plots and in limiting the kinds of implements and production techniques that could be used.[6]

The need for land was legitimate. In the eighteenth century the population of Torre Pellice numbered about 1,500 persons, 80 percent of whom were involved in agriculture. This meant that approximately five acres of arable land supported ten people. By 1864 when the population had increased to 3,500—2,500 of them in agriculture—the same amount of land had to suffice for twice as many people.[7] It is no wonder that such a scarcity roused what government investigators termed an "invincible passion" for land and that some families reportedly had to feed their children grass.[8]

The years of the 1850s further contributed to the situation with poor harvests and crop diseases, increased food prices, high mortgage payments, contraction of agricultural prices, and increased taxes.[9] Nascent industry failed either to absorb or to interest the agricultural sector. Nor were other alternatives found.

These economic conditions together with the greater mobility of the Waldenses after Charles Albert's decree of 1848 have been held to be the most important agents in emigration from Torre Pellice.[10] However accurately they represent the economic picture, though, they still leave us to account for such facts as the following: that at the same time as this strong emigration movement there was also considerable immigration *into* Torre Pellice; that Waldenses did not follow up on alternatives to emigration; and that it was not the most destitute who left the valley.[11] Correspondingly in contemporary Belluno, Southern Italian migrants, who now compose nearly a third of the population, have moved into many public office jobs.

Local analysis of this strange immigration movement into what is popularly called the "North's South" and "Italy's Cinderella" rests on the explanation that Southerners know better how to compete for public positions and pursue them more energetically than the Bellunese. Meanwhile, seemingly quite illogically, we find the Bellunese on building sites in North and South America, in ice cream parlors in Germany, and at construction works in Libya. While some of these emigrants adopt the rhetoric that pictures Belluno as a depressed area and the emigrant as Italy's stepchild, many openly explain that they do not leave because of economic need. A similar set of circumstances in both Torre Pellice in the nineteenth century and in Belluno today demands that we ask what mentality lies behind emigration.

Going beyond economic need brings us to an examination of some alternative characteristics that identified emigrants and in fact went on to influence their relations with native Argentines.[12] To begin with, an analysis of the decision-making process discloses something of the nature of the social and psychological factors of migration. Important human and individualistic elements affected the Torre Pellice migration as people became involved in the debate on the local level. Within this episode, repeated in different versions in villages throughout Italy, lies at least part of the answer to the other factors involved in emigration.

Villagers were exposed to a multiplicity of issues and personalities preceding their decision to emigrate. The Waldensian church, financiers, entrepreneurs, immigration agents, and newspaper editors controlled many information sources and introduced suggestions and colonization schemes from outside the actual community of prospective emigrants. Several of these influential people originated, moreover, from outside the valleys and even from outside Italy, such as fellow Protestants, some of whom were at the same time personally interested in the business end of emigration. In fact, it is hard to separate these people by occupation or by type of interest they took in emigration because, in a small town especially, churchman, businessman, landowner, and editor often overlapped.

Local debate on the advisability of emigrating at all and if so, on its destination, was heated. The motive of community forces was to control the movement if at all possible. One might expect that the villagers became pawns in the process. Emigration agents moved effectively among the inhabitants as is evidenced by the number who appeared in Torre Pellice requesting licenses and by the interest the prefect of Pinerolo and the mayors took in them.[13] Waldensian newspapers, with frequent articles on emigration, circulated widely among the population. The church, basically opposed to emigration, eventually succumbed to the times to the extent that in the 1870s it even initiated its own colonization plans. Fellow Protestants, sympathizers, and businessmen held public meetings to spread information on the topic.

In 1856 the first public meeting on emigration that villagers attended took place, sponsored by the church and chaired by the pastor of Torre Pellice. More than 600 persons participated with delegates present from all the churches of the Pellice Valley. Some representatives stubbornly continued to oppose emigration, advocating instead the promotion of mountain industry. Many, however, favored emigration and nominated a commission of five to search for a suitable destination.

At the higher level of participants, support wavered between migrating to Argentina or Sardinia. The church administration basically objected to long-distance migration, especially to Argentina, which it described as the gloomiest choice of all. One of the pastors, though, who had corresponded with an agent of the Argentine government stationed in Europe, assured the assembly that Argentina was not an unknown, backward land and was in any case preferable to Sardinia. Someone else agreed with church administrators because he remembered (not too well it would seem) that some Swiss colonists who had gone to the Argentine capital of Rio de Janeiro (sic) had later found themselves penniless. Appropriate to the nature of committees, this one too came to no definite conclusion but did request that the church administration investigate possible destinations. The church declined to head such a group since the issue represented special interests, but it did agree to solicit information on colonies.[14]

A month later the church called another meeting at which it presented information gathered on North and South America, North Africa, and Sardinia. The report judged Argentina and the United States unsuitable and continued to promote Sardinia because of its good soil, its relative proximity to the valleys, and Piedmont's interest in developing the region, as Sardinia formed part of Piedmont at this time. A land reclamation project in Piedmont and a colonization project in Aleria also drew some attention, while the same pastor as before continued to favor Argentina.[15]

Villagers were pressed hard to choose Sardinia. The sympathies of the church administration and most of the pastors lay there, undoubtedly to a great degree because a local banker, for many years one of the two lay members of the administration, had been at the same time one of the members of the financial commission of the state and a friend of Camillo Cavour, who wanted to develop the agricultural potential of Sardinia. More pro-Sardinian propaganda began to appear at subsequent meetings, but still a number of families favored Argentina. In fact, many had sold their property to raise money for the move. But local counsel continued against long-distance migration.[16]

Quite suddenly, though the debate had centered all along on the merits of Argentina and Sardinia, eleven Waldenses from Villar Pellice, on the advice of a relative in South America, ignored all attempts to control the movement and emigrated to Uruguay. This represented the first movement to South America; soon Argentina also became a preferred destination, and today these two countries hold the major Waldensian centers outside Italy.

Though the vanguard movement had resisted control, community groups continued trying to assert their influence over villagers considering emigration. A local newspaper published the letters of a colonization agent from Turin who knew conditions in Argentina and Uruguay and advised that Sardinia was preferable. The church asked him to speak in favor of Sardinia at the annual synod in 1871. At this time the church, too, embraced colonization more actively by considering forming its own company to promote settlement in Tuscany.

A disastrous colonization venture in Argentina lent fodder to the attempts to discredit America in the eyes of prospective emigrants. In the 1870s an Anglican pastor-turned-agent of a British colonization company engaged a group of Waldenses to accompany him to the province of Santa Fe. The project failed almost completely and the pro-Italian colonization group in Torre Pellice used reports of its demise to buttress their arguments. The colony's administrators were accused of moral corruption; what government there was served mainly to protect the landed magnates; and agents of the colony had forged letters as if from satisfied clients emphasizing the beauty of the colony. Apparently their so-called Eldorado was located near quicksand and beset by wild animals and Indians.[17]

Regardless of reports on the sinking fortune of the settlement, the betrayal of Waldensian trust by the Anglican pastor, and negative information on Argentina in general, emigration to the republic continued in force. By the 1870s villagers had established chains and major Waldensian colonies emerged in the countryside of Entre Ríos, Santa Fe, and Buenos Aires provinces. An observer could not have predicted with any accuracy the destination of Waldenses since in the end emigrants made their decision independently of community pressure.

This episode does not describe, then, a desperate, ignorant, totally impoverished peasantry, as the masses of emigrants have sometimes been portrayed. Rather it describes independent thinkers and decision makers. The groups who opposed them used persuasive logic and rhetoric. They charged that emigration disrupted the home and depleted the agricultural labor force, thus ruining the social fabric of the valley for those who stayed behind.[18] Moral arguments had been used on the populace since the time temporary migrations to France and Switzerland began. The church based its objections on religious, moral, and even hygienic grounds.[19] Emigrants faced complaints that they were drunken, morally loose, and religiously undisciplined, which resulted in a number of expulsions and readmissions to the church. Officials leveled further accusations of frivolity, worldliness, and materialism against emigrants. Commentators claimed that villagers emigrated in order to get ahead and to have an easier time of it making a living. Materialism supposedly made farmers "coldly formal, arrogant, and sterile in their religion."[20] It was contact with the working classes in resort areas and with urban, industrial centers that supposedly led to corrupt morals. Emigrants working in a cotton mill in France were described as "penetrated by doubt, incredulity, and materialism" that led to "moral laxity."[21] Moreover, when youths returned home after being abroad for some time they bore questionable ideas and bad habits.[22] Furthermore, the church worriedly noted that as Waldenses departed the valleys, Catholics moved in to replace them, following the movement of industries into the Pellice, threatening traditional Waldensian territory and changing their providential role.

Villagers were asked why, in fact, they did not consider this industry, for an example, as an alternative to emigration.[23] Outsiders, usually Catholic, began coming into the valley in the 1870s, 1880s, and 1890s, mainly as industrial workers. Interestingly, they began to appear in the passport application records ten to twenty years later as prospective emigrants, most likely reflecting their improved economic situation or the collapse of a particular factory.[24] Waldenses, however, do not seem to have figured in industry. By tradition farmers, perhaps they were reluctant to change occupation and life-style or to integrate with the more Catholic population of the lower valley. Or perhaps it was because industry often hired mainly women and children. Far from being helped by industry, the Waldensian economic situation might even have been hurt by the rise in prices occasioned by the increasing available wealth.

Frustrated by Waldenses' seeming lack of attraction to alternatives to emigration, a local newspaper queried in the 1890s: "If foreigners can get jobs in Torre Pellice, why can't Waldenses?"[25] It was a pertinent question especially as some of the factory owners seem almost certainly to have been of Waldensian or foreign Protestant origin, suggesting that they would have been receptive to hiring their coreligionists.[26] More puzzling still was the fact that Waldenses had been accustomed to emigrating temporarily to work abroad in factories. Perhaps though when it came to a permanent occupation they preferred to go several thousand miles to

Argentina than several miles to local factories. Just as seasonal emigration to France allowed farmers to maintain their agricultural life in the valleys, so, too, did emigration to Argentina appear more natural than industry in Torre Pellice in order to preserve a certain way of life.

Local opposition also demanded to know why, since Alpine farmers remained inactive during the winters, they did not engage in light industry that would occupy spare time and benefit them financially. An editorial suggested that "idle emigrants, dissipating in French resorts, [would do better to be doing] artisan work at home."[27] Because tourists began enjoying Torre Pellice as early as 1870, the promoters of Alpine industries for the valley speculated that the market for souvenir items existed if only the farmers would take advantage of it.[28] A church-sponsored organization called the Waldensian Artisans, had tried in fact as early as the 1850s to promote craft industries.[29] To test its effectiveness a Torre Pellice newspaper drew up a list of the first graduates. When it found them all established in shops in the town rather than invigorating the mountain economy, the paper was outraged. It speculated that the ungrateful graduates either had found that they could succeed better elsewhere; had got a taste for town life and freedom; or had thought they would have to work too hard to find a job in the mountains.[30] Even cash doles contributed by Protestants abroad to stimulate artisan industry did not produce the desired results.[31]

Arguments against emigration received wide publicity. Newspaper articles tried to shame villagers into staying put by appealing to them "not to abandon the valleys where their forefathers had weathered hard times."[32] Papers published monthly emigration figures and reprinted articles from other sources, both national and local, for the benefit of the Pellice audience. One such article reprinted from a Pinerolo paper presented a wrenching scene of the departure for America of a group of ninety farmers at the railroad station, emphasizing that it seemed a shame when the South lacked agricultural workers.[33] The year before, the same paper had published a long poem on emigration to America—a dialogue between a father and his children. The children appeal to their father to emigrate while the father, symbol of authority, expresses faith in Italy's future and reaffirms the values of his forefathers. To his children's pleas, he replies that Italy is good and beautiful and that they must remain in their fatherland where God would watch over them.[34]

Confronted on all sides with moral opposition in particular, villagers who persisted in their ideas had already distinguished themselves from nonemigrants. Their society, that is Waldensian society, accused them of being faithless, materialistic, and uncaring about the family. They had to face the complaints of landowners worried that emigration might raise the cost of labor. They were confronted with journalists' discouraging and tearful reports. Finally they had to dodge the parries of businessmen and agents seeking to promote their own interests. By taking part in open meetings, considering and debating the alternatives, and in the end making their own decision, they established their identity as self-reliant and independent individuals.

The fact that in general these people came from a migrating culture further helps to identify potential emigrants. From Torre Pellice, they first emigrated abroad as refugees. Later they went to France and Switzerland to work in industrial and resort centers. To grow sufficient food, they had to buy up several small plots of land often situated far from each other, and work them as peripatetic farmers. In April or May when the snows began to melt they migrated to higher elevations to graze their animals. Left alone until October, their families continued farming and gathering chestnuts.[35] In the winter, if they did not remain at home, the men might be off again to Nice or Marseilles.

Constant migration cast its participants in the role of provincial cosmopolitans with all the ambiguity that implies. It provided them with a broader perspective: they adapted to foreign social and work environments; they became accustomed to defining their lives in terms of future goals; and they learned the art of self-imposed deprivation in order to survive in the present and to progress in the future without giving up rural life.

Though applicable only to the Waldensian situation, the church contributed, too, to defining emigrant character. In its position as the most influential institution in society, it accustomed its members to a certain structure and mode of operation. Most levels of society imitated the careful organization of the central administration that had been so successful in regulating valley life. The generally felt need to organize because of its minority position and the limited size of the population made Waldensian small-scale bureaucracy especially effective and sensitive to members. By the time Waldenses began to emigrate, they had directly participated in organized groups, which yielded them valuable experience when they needed to organize in Argentina. The religious community's bureaucratic, rational organization transferred to Argentina gave Waldenses the advantage of a community structure in a relatively unstructured environment.

At the close of the analysis of this episode, what can I say in general about the social and psychological environment of Torre Pellice that helps explain, along with the economic situation, the town's emigration movement? I have documentation and indications of several distinctive characteristics of these emigrants.

Those who left had participated in public debates along with the most organized and influential sectors of society. They had resisted persuasion, condemnation, and outside pressures; had broken traditional restraints; and had made independent decisions. These characteristics do not describe sheeplike masses of impoverished peasants. This self-reliant and resourceful nature is often identified with mountain border areas, but I suspect it is just as often true of plains emigrants. The Bellunese express this sentiment today when they say, for example, "If we want something done up here in the mountains we have to do it ourselves."

Basically dissatisfied, some villagers in Torre Pellice began living for the future and eventually emigration became a tradition. Although we do not know the number of times a person emigrated before he finally went to Argentina, we do know that emigration was the general culture. Already in the nineteenth century Friulani youth were reportedly growing up with the knowledge they would work abroad. In Belluno, constant emigration has meant that people now find themselves in a rut of change for the sake of change, in an inescapable spiral—inescapable less for economic reasons than for reasons of certain values and mentality. In their work it is almost as if they feel secure only in the familiar temporariness of emigration.

In fact, the whole attitude toward work differs among emigrants. In Torre Pellice, farm life meant extended periods of overwork and inactivity. Oftentimes the periods of overwork took place abroad and those of inactivity at home. An important psychological fact, it is often expressed today as "I work in France, but I live in Italy." Work in this situation truly does become *massacrante* (exhausting) as Italians describe it. "Work" in this context means that one's time is fully consumed with working, and "live" means periods of vacation at home in Italy. It expresses a different way of looking at time, or of dividing one's time. It differs especially from the rhythm of Italy's life today, which integrates "living" time into a long workday and six-day workweek. Emigrants express the desire to work but maintain that even so they cannot get ahead in Italy. As one of the Waldensian emigrants to San Gustavo said, "We worked like asses in Argentina. Of course we worked like this in Italy, too, but in Italy we never got anyplace."[36] Preoccupied with work, emigrants were and are fiercely proud of their industriousness. To this day their idea of a frontier consists of a new place to conquer in terms of work. The perception that it is primarily through their work that they gain respect and build self-esteem perhaps keeps them renewing that by emigrating. Expectations can sometimes be found to determine work habits. Hence one hears people today say of an industrious emigrant: "If he had stayed in Italy, he would have just slept all day."

Perhaps such a person seeks liberation from his environment, often restricted as much socially and psychologically as economically. Certainly in Torre Pellice emigrants, especially youths, brought down accusations on themselves of seeking a change in their environment. All over in areas of emigration the nineteenth century documents an environment full of petty and narrow-minded concerns; the authoritarianism and conservatism of local *padroni* and church; and the almost machinelike expanded agricultural family in which the individual played only an insignificant part. Today the Bellunese speak of the monotony of mountain agricultural life and the narrowness of an Italian society measuring itself by "bella-" and "bruta figura." As a result, one of Argentina's attractions, both in the nineteenth century and today, is what the emigrant perceives as its more open, egalitarian society.

Yet at the same time evidence seems to indicate that emigration from Torre Pellice signified not so much a break with Italy as a continuation of family and farm life. And it is the same with contemporary Bellunese emigration, much of which is motivated by the desire to return and build a house in the province. Emigrating when not economically pressed to do so and with the intention of maintaining a part of their life in the homeland leads one to speculate how emigrants view their act. Do they see it as a way of sustaining their preemigrant life or as a complete change, a stage in a linear progression to something better? Emigrants themselves seem to want it both ways and thus are ambivalent about reentering Italy, for example, which is one of emigration's present concerns.

We can speculate perhaps, in sum, that emigrants and nonemigrants are corollaries of one cohesive cultural ethos. That is, they need each other, in social, psychological, and economic terms. We remember, for example, that within the family distinctions are made between members in that one child may be designated to look after the family business, another to care for the parents, another to go into the church, and so on. Perhaps there is also specialization in the case of emigration where it is in the nature of village society that some people go and others stay. In many ways Belluno society divides up this way. Nonemigrants note the lack of sensibility and understanding of emigrants, and returned emigrants remark about the town's stagnant society and find they prefer the company of other returned emigrants.

Emigration appears to be a product of a certain culture and mentality, then, as much as and in some cases more than an economic measure. If we look at the phenomenon this way, migrating man appears in a somewhat more positive light than scholars, emigration officials, and even he himself might imagine. It is interesting how rhetoric and obvious economic problems have colored the way we look at this man and have made him perhaps unrecognizable even to himself. Impressed with the rhetoric and the description of himself as victimized by impersonal forces that his province had the misfortune to attract, he has acquired the feeling of a *figliastro* (a "second citizen"). (The politics necessary to promote the interests of emigrants, legitimate interests granted, can be held partly responsible for clouding the nature of emigration.) Perhaps a greater awareness of such social and psychological factors raised by the examples of Torre Pellice and Belluno will emerge from this study.

Notes

1. J. D. Gould, "European Inter-Continental Emigration 1815–1914: Patterns and Causes," *Journal of European Economic History* 8(3)1979, pp. 593–679. William H. McNeill and Ruth S. Adams, eds., *Human Migration, Patterns and Policies* (1978, Indiana University Press in association with the American Academy of Arts and Sciences): see articles by Charles Tilly and Sune Åkerman as examples.

2. John W. Briggs in his *An Italian Passage, Immigrants to Three American Cities, 1890–1930* (New Haven: Yale University Press, 1978) has also tried to improve the image of the emigrant.

3. Mountain towns represented 66 percent of the total Pinerolo territory; plains, 21 percent; and hill towns, 13 percent. F. Adamo, "Introduzione," in *Ricerche sulla regione metropolitana di Torino: Il Pinerolese*, F. Adamo et alia, eds. (Università degli Studi di Torino, Facoltà di Economia e Commercio, Laboratorio di Geografia Economica "Piero e Dino Gribaudi," publication no. 7 [Turin: Università degli Studi di Torino, 1971]), vol. 1, p. 5.

4. Teofilo Pons, *Cento anni fa* (Torre Pellice, 1958?), p. 3.

5. Giunta per l'inchiesta agraria e sulle condizioni della classe agricola, *Atti della Giunta . . .* (Rome: Forzani, 1883), vol. 8, tomo 1, fasc. 1, p. 218.

6. Ibid., p. 269.

7. Augusto Armand-Hugon, *Torre Pellice, dieci secoli di storia e di vicende* (Torre Pellice: Subalpina, 1958), p. 156. The total amount of arable land for Torre Pellice was 1,920 hectares. Pierluigi Jalla, *Le Valli Valdesi, problemi economici e di emigrazione* (Torre Pellice, 1966?), p. 23, also states that the average size of a mountain plot was 2 to 3 hectares. The *Inchiesta agraria*, p. 218, reports mountain properties as averaging less than 1 hectare.

8. Ibid., p. 61; and Pons, p. 3.

9. Poor harvests and diseases affecting vines and silk worms affected Torre Pellice especially in the 1850s.

10. Not until King of Sardinia Charles Albert's decree of emancipation in 1848 did Waldenses have the freedom of physical mobility to emerge for any length of time from their traditional mountain habitats where they had been confined for religious reasons since the twelfth century. The decree did not alter their social and economic situation though, and they continued to reside primarily in the hill and mountain areas.

11. Prospective emigrants were usually solvent. See Torre Pellice, Municipal Archives, Busta-Archivio, Categoria 13ª, Esteri, Classe 1–2–3, Cartella 1, Scaffale 4, Casella 1; Folder 7–Registro–Certificati spediti dal sindaco dal 1865 al 1893; the

remainder of this volume contains the *nulla-osta* for 1889 through 1900. Busta-Archivio, Categoria 13ᵃ, Esteri, Classe 3, Cartella 1, Scaffale 4-Registri delle domande di nulla osta per ottenere passaporti per l'estero dal 1901 al 1922; 1935–1947. This one source shows the immigration into Torre Pellice and the solvency of the emigrants.

12. Kristin Ruggiero, "Gringo and Creole, Foreign and Native Values in a Rural Argentine Community," *Journal of Inter-American Studies and World Affairs*, 24(2)1982, pp. 163–82. This article deals with the relation between immigrants and the Argentine population in San Gustavo.

13. Torre Pellice, Municipal Archives, Busta-Archivio, Categoria 13ᵃ, Esteri, Classe 1-2-3, Cartella 1, Scaffale 4, Casella 1; Folder 5–Agenti d'Emigrazione, 1897–1900, Categoria IV, Classe 3ᵃ, fasc. no. 2.

14. Pons, pp. 7–8.

15. Ibid., p. 9.

16. Ibid., pp. 10–11.

17. Torre Pellice, Municipal Archives, Busta . . . ; Folder 3, Emigrazione, Anno 1832–1900, Categoria IV, Classe 3ᵃ, fasc. 1; item: copy of a note from the Prefettura of Torino, dated August 10, 1872.

Ibid.; item: extract of a note to the Sottopreffetura of Pinerolo from the Ministero dei Affari Esteri on Colonia Alejandra in Argentina, 187?.

L'Echo des Vallees, January 12, 1872; February 9, 1872; February 28, 1873; March 14, 1873.

Archivio Tavola Valdese, *Rapport* . . . , 1874.

18. ATV, *Rapport* . . . , 1892, from report on Villasecca.

19. Ibid., 1883, from report on Villar Pellice.

20. See Tavola reports for 1870, 1872, 1885, 1886, 1889, 1890, 1897, 1898, 1904, 1908, 1909.

21. ATV, *Rapport* . . . , 1889, p. 17.

22. Ibid., 1909, from report on Massello.

23. In the early nineteenth century, Torre Pellice could boast of a wool clothing factory that employed 100 people. About 1840 the cotton industry moved into the Pinerolo area and employed more people. German, Swiss, or British capital often financed such establishments. Foreign industrialists from Protestant areas often located in the Pellice because they had become familiar with the conditions through the Waldenses. A combination of Swiss and local interests built a large cotton plant in Pralafera, on the boundary between Torre Pellice and Luserna San Giovanni in 1833. By 1852, when a fire destroyed it, it employed more than 500 people. Only a few miles to the east, the Bibiana cotton-spinning mill employed about 250 people in 1854. By the 1850s the area between Torre Pellice and Bibiana had become the most important Pinerolese industrial district. In addition, tourism had developed into an "industry" in the Pellice in the nineteenth century. The majority of the valley's industry, however, was based on the larger textile manufacturers and on a printing house. See Armand-Hugon on section entitled "Industria e Commercio" and Giuseppe Dematteis' "L'eredita storica nella formazione della regione" in F. Adamo et alia, p. 48.

24. Kristin Ruggiero, "Italians in Argentina: The Waldenses at Colonia San Gustavo, 1850–1910," PhD dissertation, Indiana University, 1979.

25. *Avvisatore Alpino*, January 20, 1895, and March 9, 1894.

26. Armand-Hugon from section entitled "Industria e Commercio" where the following factory owners of probable Waldensian connections are mentioned: Peyrot, Malan, Long, Pasquet, Geymonat; and the foreigners Gaddum, Gruber, and Theiler, who possibly were English and German Protestants, were listed.

27. *Avvisatore Alpino*, November 8, 1883, and December 17, 1885.

28. Ibid., September 10, 1886.

29. Ibid., October 4, 1883.

30. Ibid.

31. Pons, p. 5.

32. *L'Echo des Vallees*, August 25, 1871.

33. *Avvisatore Alpino*, October 23, 1885.

34. Ibid., May 2, 1884.

35. *Inchiesta agraria*, p. 451.

36. Interview with Carlos Baret, La Paz (Argentina), September 20, 1976.

9

At the Crossroads of Economic Development: Background Factors Affecting Emigration from Nineteenth-Century Germany

Walter D. Kamphoefner

The dividing of lands and fields undoubtedly increases the population, . . .
but it increases only the number of consumers, but not, to the same extent,
that of the producers . . . and then what is left over for times of need, or for
the state? . . .
. . . The division even of individual fields should be allowed near towns
and in factory and artisan districts; let it run its course undisturbed, for
example, in Ravensberg, Mark, Tecklenburg, and Berg; but take care to
prevent it in the rural areas around Paderborn, Münster, Julich, and Cologne. These lands are the graineries, when those of the factory districts give
out.[1]

These recommendations, drawn from a description of agriculture
in Westphalia by Johann Nepomuk v. Schwerz, an early nineteenth-
century German agronomy expert, provide a good illustration of the
population dynamics in Europe on the eve of industrialization. Attitudes
such as this, sometimes formally set down in population policies at the
state or province level, but more often simply practiced at the village level

174

in the decision for an open or a restrictive settlement policy, were among the most important background factors influencing the level of emigration from Germany in the nineteenth century. Regions of rural industry reached a crossroads during this period. Some made the transition to modern machine industry, as did Berg and Mark and neighboring areas along Ruhr. Those that did not, such as Tecklenburg and Ravensberg, saw a large proportion of their artisan population made redundant by the competition of industrializing regions. Where such displaced groups, rural but only marginally agricultural, made up a large share of the population, heavy overseas emigration was usually the result. In purely agricultural regions such as the Münsterland or Paderborn, population pressure seldom reached such extremes.

Accounts of German emigration as far back as Friedrich List have ascribed to inheritance systems the primary role in influencing regional variations in emigration. While in the greater part of Germany *Anerbenrecht* (impartible inheritance) prevailed, in Southwest Germany and, after the Napoleonic occupation, in Rhineland Prussia and most of Hesse, *Realteilung* (partible, equal division among heirs) was the rule. The latter system, it is argued, encouraged population growth and led to progressive splintering of peasant holdings, a "dwarf economy" in which many marginal operators were driven to emigration.[2]

This view is not entirely wrong but is misleading unless further qualified. Although eighteenth-century emigration was largely restricted to areas of Southwest Germany such as the Palatinate, Baden, and Württemberg, pietistic religion and the depredations of French invaders were probably more important causes than Realteilung. This region was the source of the earliest and heaviest exodus in the nineteenth century (see figure 9.1). But Realteilung was neither a necessary nor a sufficient condition for heavy emigration. Rates from the industrial areas of the Rhineland were among the lowest in Germany. Moreover, there were districts in Northwest Germany such as Osnabrück and Minden, areas of Anerbenrecht, with emigration rates comparable to Baden and Württemberg.[3] Because of the emphasis on Southwest Germany, these heavy rates of emigration from parts of the Northwest have gone largely ignored. The Osnabrück District had an annual emigration rate of over 1 percent for the thirty years before the American Civil War. In the years 1860 to 1866 (assuming equal accuracy of record keeping in Hanover and Prussia) Osnabrück had a higher rate of emigration than any Prussian district. The emigration rate in the neighboring District of Minden also ranked consistently near the top in all of Prussia.[4]

A feature common to all these areas of heavy emigration was a well-developed cottage linen industry carried on by the rural lower class on a

Figure 9.1: Index of Relative Intensity of Emigration by District: Persons in America per 1,000 Inhabitants of District of Origin

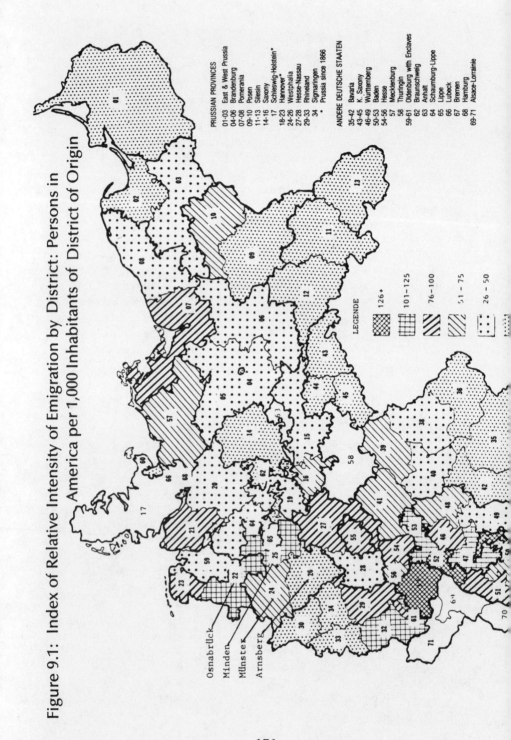

PRUSSIAN PROVINCES
01-03 East & West Prussia
04-06 Brandenburg
07-08 Pomerania
09-10 Posen
11-13 Silesin
14-16 Saxony
17 Schleswig-Holstein*
18-23 Hannover*
24-26 Westphalia
27-28 Hesse-Nassau
29-33 Rhineland
34 Sigmaringen
* Prussia since 1866

ANDERE DEUTSCHE STAATEN
35-42 Bavaria
43-45 K. Saxony
46-49 Wurttemberg
50-53 Baden
54-56 Hesse
57 Mecklenburg
58 Thuringin
59-61 Oldenburg with Enclaves
62 Braunschweig
63 Anhalt
64 Schaumburg-Lippe
65 Lippe
66 Lubeck
67 Bremen
68 Hamburg
69-71 Alsace-Lorrainie

LEGENDE

126+
101-125
76-100
51-75
26-50

176

part-time basis but rapidly succumbing to machine competition in the nineteenth century. This downfall of cottage industry is the predominant factor that must be superimposed upon inheritance systems to understand patterns of emigration. Though its effects were perhaps most dramatic in the Northwest, it was also important in Central and Southwest Germany. What is significant for America is that, at least until the Civil War, expulsive forces in Europe were the main factors behind emigration, and the displaced rural lower class constituted the majority of emigrants. Thus any success that German immigrants achieved in America requires a better explanation than that they were middle class before they left.

Flight to America was not necessarily the only alternative. A second, related factor affecting emigration was the development of—or failure to develop—centers of modern machine industry, which could absorb surplus population. Both of these factors will be examined with special reference to the region of Northwest Germany, especially Hanover and northern Westphalia.[5] This region is unified linguistically by its Low German dialect and culturally by traditions of independent peasantry *(Grundherrschaft)* and impartible inheritance. These characteristics set the Northwest apart from the districts of great estates (Gutsherrschaft) east of the Elbe, and on the south from Hesse and the Rhineland, the approximate northern extent of High German dialects and customs of partible inheritance.

The influence of rural industry on population growth, though already noted by contemporary observers, was first examined in detail for the Zürcher Oberland in Rudolf Braun's anthropologically oriented *Industrie und Volksleben* (Industry and People). Franklin Mendels then provided a more rigorous economic formulation and testing of this thesis for the area of Flanders and also coined the term *protoindustry*. As it will be used here, protoindustry refers to the decentralized, rural, labor-intensive production of goods for a distant market, usually supplemented by marginal agriculture.[6]

Although Mendels made an important contribution by illuminating the interrelationship between economic and demographic processes, other aspects of his model are less convincing. He calls protoindustrialization, quoting the subtitle of his dissertation, "the first phase of industrialization," but subsequent studies suggest that he was overly optimistic. One might argue that it was a necessary precondition for industrialization, but by no means a sufficient one. Examples of *deindustrialization*, regions that failed to make the transition to modern, mechanized industry, were every bit as common as "success stories." It is precisely such regions where modern industrialization took place, belatedly or not at all, that will constitute the chief focus of this essay.

The handloom linen industry prevalent in Northwest Germany differed in minor details from that in other regions, but protoindustry everywhere brought with it similar demographic consequences. It contrasted sharply with a system of near-subsistence peasant agriculture that, especially in areas of impartible inheritance, was practically self-regulating. Since an heir had to wait until his father's death or retirement before he could marry and take over the farm, late marriages and small families were the rule. These built-in restrictions on population growth were eliminated almost completely in a system of rural industry. A loom and a rented cottage were the only prerequisites for marriage and the establishment of an independent existence. With early marriage came also large families, especially since children were now an economic asset, ready to be put to work spinning at the age of five. This process created an expanding rural lower class, which could find employment only through the expansion of rural industry. The end result was concentrations of population too large even to be fed, much less adequately employed by local agriculture alone.[7]

During the first half of the nineteenth century, the handloom linen industry in Germany suffered a series of shocks that reduced it from a major supplier for export to economic insignificance. The Napoleonic Wars and the continental blockade denied Germany access to its main markets in the Western Hemisphere, especially Latin America. The exclusion of British competition from the Continent temporarily compensated for this loss, but the end of the war found the South American colonies on the road to independence and their markets firmly in the hands of the British, accompanied by an enormous expansion of handloom weaving in Ireland. Second, linen production was being mechanized, first the spinning and then the weaving, with Ulster taking the lead and German production centers making the transition only belatedly and incompletely. Third, linen itself was increasingly being replaced on the market by cotton, which was better adapted to mechanized production. Thus a once-blooming rural industry faded into insignificance, and many of the areas where it had flourished reverted to simple agriculture.[8] For the landless or land-poor classes dependent on linen weaving for supplementary or even primary income, the decline of the industry had serious consequences that reached catastrophic proportions in times of agricultural crisis such as the mid-1840s. These crises produced waves of emigration, which appear upon cursory observation to have been especially heavy in areas with a concentration of rural industry.

The three Districts of Westphalia present in microcosm three contrasting patterns of economic and demographic development (see table 9.1). In the east, Minden-Ravensberg, a center of protoindustry in the form of linen weaving and spinning, was the most densely populated area in all Prussia at the beginning of the nineteenth century. But its patterns of high birthrates and rapid population growth were reversed before midcentury by the collapse of the linen industry, leaving in its wake widespread misery and massive emigration that subsided only when parts of the region made a successful, if belated, transition to modern textile and other industries.[9]

The rugged District of Arnsberg in the south, traditionally a center of small-scale charcoal iron industry, witnessed during the nineteenth century the booming growth of Germany's largest concentration of heavy industry, the *Ruhrgebiet* (Ruhr Area). Here emigration was the lowest, and birthrates and population growth the highest in Westphalia, although the shifting economic center of gravity from southeast to northwest did require some internal migration.

To the west, the sandy plain of the Münsterland, level and easily worked if not especially fertile, had traditionally been the home of a prosperous, independent peasantry engaged in comparatively large-scale agriculture. Patterns of late marriage and low birthrates brought only a low rate of emigration and slow growth of population into the period of industrialization. These characteristics are clearly reflected in District statistics even though the economic regions generally correspond more to geography than to administrative boundaries.

Table 9.1

CHARACTERISTIC ECONOMIC AND DEMOGRAPHIC
PATTERNS

Typical district	*Münster*	*Minden*	*Arnsberg*
Economic type	Agricultural	Protoindustry	Modern Industry
Birthrate to 1850	low	high	high
Crude rate 1841–55[a]	123	164	160
Tendency thereafter	steady	lower	higher
Crude rate 1862–67[a]	127	156	181
Emigration rate	moderate	high	low
Recorded yearly rate 1844–59[b]	17.8	32.8	6.7
Net migration loss, 1843–52[c]	26.0	56.3	0.5
Population trend	slow, stable growth	fast growth then stagnation	continued fast growth
Annual growth rate 1818–43	.70%	1.24%	1.77%
Annual growth rate 1843–58	.27%	.12%	1.46%

[a] Live and still births per 1,000 women age 14–44.
[b] Officially recorded emigration per 10,000 population.
[c] Difference in population gain between censuses and surplus of births over deaths during the same time span, annual net migration loss per 10,000 population.

Table 9.2

CORRELATION BETWEEN EMIGRATION RATE AND PROTOINDUSTRY FOR SELECTED AREAS OF WESTPHALIA

Unit of Observation	Independent Variable	Dependent Variable	Correlation Coefficient	N of Cases
District Münster by *Kreis*	Looms per capita, 1816	Emigration rate, 1832–50	.87	10
District Münster by *Kreis*	Looms per capita, 1831	Emigration rate, 1832–50	.88	10
District Münster by *Kreis*	Looms per capita, 1849	Emigration rate, 1832–50	.86	10
District Minden by *Kreis*	Spinner families + looms per capita, 1838–49	Emigration rate, 1851–60	.63	10
Kreis Tecklenburg by *Gemeinde*	Looms per capita, 1827	Emigration rate, 1832–50	.59	17

While the broad regional outlines of the extent of protoindustry are easily sketched, a more differentiated measure of its intensity at the local level is not so easily obtained. Where weaving was the primary activity, as in Districts Münster and Osnabrück, the number of looms is a good indicator; but where large proportions of the population were engaged in spinning, as in Minden, statistical information is harder to find. The existing information suggests, however, that over half the population in all these areas was directly involved in the linen industry. Another indication of the importance of rural industry is the volume of linen sales, which amounted to nearly 10 Thalers per capita annually in some areas.[10] These areas were no longer agriculturally self-sufficient, another reflection of the dependence on protoindustry.

The widely varying intensity of rural industry in the early nineteenth century is reflected in several inventories of linen looms at the local level in the Münster and Minden districts. The number of looms per capita in 1816, 1831, and 1849 were correlated with the per capita rates of emigration for the years 1832 through 1850 from each rural *Kreis* of District Münster (table 9.2). The results in all cases are very similar: an *r* value approaching .90 for the association between rural industry and emigration. For the Minden District, credible emigration statistics are not available until the 1850s, and spinners as well as weavers have to be taken into account to approximate the extent of rural industry. Here too the correlation with emigration rates is rather close, though not so high as in

Münster. Even at the *Gemeinde* level, where social-psychological factors would have the greatest impact, rural industry proved to be a good predictor of emigration rate in Kreis Tecklenburg.[11]

At least for these areas of Westphalia, the association between rural industry and emigration is very strong. To learn more about patterns of regional variation in intensity of emigration, a more diverse area, the Kingdom of Hanover, was subjected to a statistical analysis of the relationship between rates of emigration and various measures of population density and economic specialization. In a way this investigation resembles a drama in which the two leading characters never actually appear on stage: no suitable figures exist on handloom weaving in Hanover, and statewide emigration figures are only available from 1859 on, after the peak years of emigration. Nonetheless, areas with high emigration rates in earlier years generally continued these patterns throughout the period studied, and protoindustry shows itself clearly if indirectly through its effects on other "characters."[12]

Despite these limitations, a multiple regression with six variables explained over one-third of the variation in emigration rates at the Kreis level and over 80 percent at a higher level of aggregation. The variables in table 9.3 were selected from a larger list for the most combined explanatory power, with one exception. Fertility rates, included for illustrative purposes, were apparently inconsequential as a factor in emigration. But just because this was true in 1860 does not mean that it was so thirty years earlier. By midcentury, emigration had begun to affect population structure and birthrates. In fact, another variable, the crude birthrate uncontrolled for age and sex, showed greater explanatory power, but in the "wrong" direction: high birthrates corresponded with low emigration.

Table 9.3

MULTIPLE REGRESSION OF ECONOMIC AND DEMOGRAPHIC VARIABLES WITH EMIGRATION RATE, 1859–61: KINGDOM OF HANNOVER, BY KREIS

	Simple r	Beta
Persons/Dwelling	−.39	−.32
Persons/Unit land area	−.15	.35
% Pop. agricultural dependents	.50	.55
Children < age 1/Women age 20–45	.02	.04
Livestock/Person in agriculture	−.18	−.02
Livestock/Unit land area	.004	−.32

R² for all variables = .35
N of cases = 101

This merely reflects the fact that, because of the selectivity of migration, there were fewer women of childbearing age in areas of heavy emigration, and a skewed sex ratio besides.

The negative bivariate correlations with residential and population density convincingly refute any crude *Lebensraum* (living space) interpretations and suggest that urban industry presented an alternative to emigration. But once urbanization is controlled for, the beta coefficient shows that emigration increased with population density. In fact, the relationship when plotted appears slightly curvilinear. The purely agricultural regions, with the lowest population densities, fall in the middle range of emigration rates. At one pole stand the industrializing areas, with the highest density and the lowest emigration; at the other, the protoindustrial regions, with statistically moderate levels of crowding (in reality more severe because of their rural character), the sources of heaviest emigration.

Further confirmation of these patterns is provided by occupational statistics. The strongest predictor of emigration proved to be the proportion of the population who were dependents of the agriculturally employed. The number of agricultural dependents was of course closely correlated with the total agricultural population, and the latter variable was nearly as good a predictor, but the difference suggests that emigration was heaviest where families of tenant farmers rather than unmarried farmhands constituted the main source of agricultural labor. Since rural industry was practiced almost entirely on a part-time basis, most linen weavers also fell under the agricultural rubric in the occupational census. This is supported by the fact that emigration was highest where there were many agriculturists but little agriculture: the more livestock per farmer or unit of land area, the less emigration. Above all, what is reflected in these figures is the precarious economic situation of those engaged in rural industry. Taken together, these patterns of association further underscore the tripartite division into regions of protoindustry, modern industry, and full-time agriculture.

To guard against the ecological fallacy, the occupational structure of the emigration was investigated at the individual level. This provided additional evidence that the rural lower classes were indeed being displaced by the decline of protoindustry. Although several scholars have argued that much of the German emigration was middle class in character through 1860, this generalization is not borne out by empirical evidence from emigrant lists. Instead, in all areas with substantial protoindustry, two-thirds or more of the emigrants were landless tenants or agricultural laborers, the classes most dependent on supplementary income from rural industry.

The preceding evidence has established the importance of protoindustry in influencing levels of emigration in Northwest Germany. What remains to be examined is how far this thesis can be extended to other areas of Germany. Its impact was mainly limited to the first two-thirds of the nineteenth century. In the new waves of emigration after the American Civil War and the founding of the German Empire, protoindustrial decline no longer played the predominant role. From that point on, East Elbian Prussia became increasingly prominent as a source of emigration, and factors other than rural industry come into play. Also, the flood tides of emigration peaking in the years 1846 and 1854 marked the last agricultural crises of the "old type." Thereafter, the problems of food production and distribution no longer plagued Germany, and the fluctuations of emigration rates correspond ever less with those of grain prices.[13]

For the earlier part of the nineteenth century, nevertheless, it is important to evaluate the role of protoindustry in other areas of heavy emigration, particularly those with inheritance systems of equal division of land among heirs (Realteilung). Two extreme hypotheses have been posed: (1) Inheritance systems made little difference. If there is no significant population growth, any system will work; if there is considerable growth, any system will run into trouble. (2) While Anerbenrecht is basically a self-regulating demographic system, except when subverted protoindustry, Realteilung is an inherently unstable system that encourages overpopulation and splintering of agricultural holdings. But the truth probably lies somewhere between the two extremes: while Realteilung held a greater latent tendency toward excessive population growth, this tendency could be realized under either inheritance system when it was encouraged by the existence of forms of Nebenerwerb (part-time employment outside agriculture).[14] It is important to remember that inheritance systems do not originate in an economic vacuum, nor is their operation in practice always what one might expect from the legal provisions. Inheritance customs often continued unabated after inheritance laws were altered with the rise of modern German states.

After we have seen the importance of the rural textile industry in Northwest Germany, it would appear profitable to reexamine Southwest Germany and explore the relationship between protoindustry and emigration. Württemberg, Baden, and Hesse all had a considerable amount of handloom weaving, suffered varying degrees of deindustrialization, and were states with some of the earliest and heaviest emigration in nineteenth-century Germany.[15] The exact dimensions of the textile industry in Southwest Germany are difficult to determine from existing statistics, for there, as in Westphalia, protoindustry was intertwined so closely with agriculture that it was often hard to distinguish the main occupation from the sideline. Several estimates from the midnineteenth century, including

Figure 9.2: Annual Emigration Rates from Osnabrück and Württemberg, 1830–1860

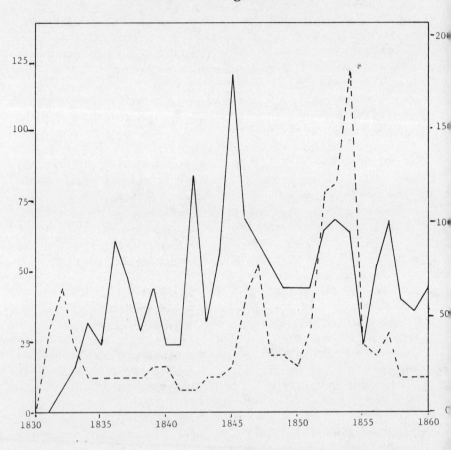

one by Gustav Schmoller, place the number of people engaged in manufacturing and commerce in Württemberg nearly equal to the agricultural population. But an occupational census in 1852, which found 44 percent of all enumerated artisans also engaged in agriculture, illustrates the impossibility of any precise delineation of the occupational structure. With reference specifically to textile workers, an 1861 statistic placed Baden second in the whole *Zollverein* (Customs union) in number of master linen weavers, with 54 per 10,000 inhabitants. When part-time weavers are taken into consideration, the figure is 110 for Württemberg, compared to roughly 170 for Westphalia. In Baden part-time weavers were apparently not enumerated. Besides linen weavers there were a considerable number of workers in protoindustrial woolen production. Though the figures on textile workers appear low in relation to total population, it must be remembered that since most flax was locally grown and most wool locally spun, each weaver was backed up by several spinners.[16]

One important contrast between the Northwest and the Southwest was the wine industry of the latter. Wine growers, like linen weavers, were not always self-sufficient in foodstuffs, and were dependent on a distant, uncertain market. Moreover, their product was very sensitive to weather. The fluctuating conditions in the wine industry explain most of the differences in the emigration curve between the two regions of Germany (figure 9.2). The great drop in linen prices came in the early 1840s, and in the Osnabrück District in the Northwest, emigration reached its peak in the 1840s rather than in the 1850s. A time-series analysis for the three decades before the Civil War showed that linen earnings had considerably more influence on emigration than did grain prices, though at best only about 20 percent of the variance could be explained. In the Southwest, the collapse of the linen industry was cushioned by bountiful wine harvests; the 1846 vintage was the most profitable for a decade before or after. However, 1850, 1851, and 1854 were among the four worst years in the century, and the intervening two years were also below average. This combined with high grain prices to drive the emigration curve to record heights. In time-series analysis from 1830 to 1860, grain prices are a much better predictor of emigration than wine income, and even the terms of trade between grain and wine does not do as well as grain alone. In cross-sectional analysis, however, it can be seen that emigration was highest in the 1850s in vineyard regions.[17]

Württemberg's early statistics and stable county boundaries provide an ideal data set with which to test the factors influencing emigration. The association patterns of the wine-growing variable are most striking: very influential in the 1850s, but negligible in the 1840s and even slightly negative in the 1860s, as industrialization in the Neckar region began to

Table 9.4

MULTIPLE REGRESSION OF ECONOMIC AND
DEMOGRAPHIC VARIABLES WITH NET EMIGRATION RATE,
1842–1870: KINGDOM OF WÜRTTEMBERG, BY *OBERAMT*

Simple r	*Net4252*	*Net5457*	*Net6570*
Linen Weavers/Capita	.35	.14	.23
Livestock/Unit improved land	.35	.39	.32
Births 1842–52/Women age 20–45	−.08	−.01	−.11
Vineyards as % of land area	.29	.56	.25
% of Cropland in potatoes, 1860	.61	.56	.61
% of Landholdings under 2 acres	.61	.57	.58
Beta	*Net4252*	*Net5457*	*Net6570*
Linen weavers/Capita	.32	.32	.17
Livestock/Unit improved land	−.06	.13	−.11
Births 1842–52/Women age 20–45	−.21	−.03	−.20
Vineyards as % of land area	.01	.48	−.06
% of Cropland in potatoes, 1860	.29	.17	.43
% of Landholdings under 2 acres	.50	.10	.40
R² for all variables	.64	.53	.51
N of Cases	63	63	63

gain momentum. But protoindustry was also important; the weaver variable was the second most influential in both the 1840s and the 1850s. With
less specification error, it may have been greater, for woolen workers are
not taken into account, nor are the famous Black Forest clockmakers who
were being squeezed out by factories. The proportion of dwarf landholdings had a strong influence in both the 1840s and the 1860s, but in the
1850s its influence was overshadowed by the overlapping vineyard variable. In fact, there was a greater affinity between the emigration patterns
of the 1840s and the 1860s than of either with those of the 1850s. Since the
statistics of potato acreage were from 1860, it is less surprising that this
variable was more influential in the 1860s than in the decade of the potato
famine. Bivariate correlations showed that there was a mild degree of
association between emigration and population density, but multi-
collinearity prevented the use of this variable in multiple regression. In any
case, viniculture rather than inheritance patterns explained most of the
population density and fragmented holdings, being correlated at +.73
with the former and +.51 with the latter as measured by the proportion of
farms under 2 acres. Outside the wine region of the Neckar, even where
partible inheritance prevailed, there were few areas with a population
density exceeding 100 per square kilometer. This further underscores the
point that inheritance systems grew out of local economic conditions, and

were not applied mechanistically or contrary to good economic sense by irrational peasants.[18]

The influence of livestock holdings on emigration rates was similar in both regions of Germany. The more livestock per person, and to a lesser extent the more per unit of land, the lower the emigration rate. Although all stock was combined into cow equivalents in the multiple regression, bivariate correlations were also carried out for each type of livestock separately. Most consistent was the negative relationship between emigration and horse holdings, whether in relation to man or land. This was an unambiguous reflection of full-time, prosperous peasant agriculture. Regions of high emigration also had fewer cattle per person, but more intensive agriculture in such regions tended to even out the cow-land ratio. In contrast to other livestock, swine seemed to encourage emigration, but they were relatively few in number, and probably played the same role for the German poor as for the Irish. Sheep showed a strong negative relationship with emigration in Northwest Germany that is lacking in the Southwest. In the North, sheepherding was concentrated in sandy, infertile, sparsely populated heaths. Intensification of agriculture with the spread of root crops brought such areas increasingly under cultivation and absorbed surplus population. In the Southwest, by contrast, most sheep grazing was done in rough terrain not much good for anything else. Moreover, the woolen textile industry was also declining in these areas. In general, however, the similarities between the Northwest and the Southwest stand out more than the differences.

To take yet another example, the District of Trier in the Eifel region of Rhineland Prussia might appear to be a classic illustration of the ills of Realteilung. It had the highest emigration rate in all of Prussia from 1844 to 1859. But here too the decline of a traditional industry, if not strictly protoindustry, played a decisive role. The charcoal iron industry in nineteenth-century Germany suffered a fate similar to that of handloom weaving, with similar results in terms of emigration, as the case of the Eifel demonstrates. While iron manufacturing could scarcely be called a cottage industry though it was located in rural areas, it nevertheless shared with the linen industry the characteristics of Nebenerwerb (local industry) and dependence on nonlocal markets. Though the persons at the furnace may have worked full time, the numerically much larger contingent of woodchoppers, charcoal burners, teamsters, and ore loaders consisted almost exclusively of peasants working part-time. Ore digging was almost entirely seasonal labor confined to the winter. Like the linen industry, the iron industry was a prime factor in producing heavy concentrations of rural population. As a German scholar who has conducted a thorough case study of migration patterns from the Eifel has concluded, "without a doubt the relative population density of the greatest part of the Eifel at the beginning of the nineteenth century was to a large degree influenced by the iron industry."[19]

With the development of modern ironmaking processes using coke from coal and relying on steam instead of water power to run hammers and rolling mills, a modern iron industry sprang up near the coal fields, and the charcoal iron industry could no longer compete. As with textiles, the changes took place first in England and were imitated in Germany. The Eifel iron industry received a staggering blow in 1839, when English and Belgian iron began flooding the German market. Compounded by several years of bad harvests, the crisis lasted well into the 1840s and set off a wave of emigration that brought population growth in the District of Trier almost to a standstill. Nearly half of the emigration during the decade came from two *Kreise*, Adenau and Daun, areas of "restricted agricultural opportunities and strong dependence on industry of a large proportion of the population."[20] But Kreis Schleiden, the center of the iron industry, was the source of relatively few overseas emigrants despite an absolute decline in population after 1840. Instead, Schleiden's proximity to Aachen allowed most of its surplus population to find employment in the rapidly developing modern industries there. For most of the Trier region, however, German industrialization did not offer this alternative and the consequence of deindustrialization was, as a German scholar points out, an exodus overseas:

> Even examples of well-to-do persons emigrating cannot negate the *bitter necessity* of the Eifeler migration in general; . . . Much more decisive than the only modest development of agriculture in this context is the absolute decline of industry in the Eifel . . . The industrial districts of the Rhineland on the Inde, Ruhr, and Saar were strong enough from 1840 to 1870 to slowly eliminate the industry of the Eifel, but not yet strong enough to take up the majority of those Eifeler lacking bread and prevent them from leaving the Fatherland.[21]

A related issue needing consideration is the influence of urbanization and industrialization and the extent to which internal migration posed an alternative to overseas emigration. Some of the most extensive work in this area has been done by the Uppsala Group, thanks to the detailed system of parish registry in Sweden. An important outgrowth of this research is the concept of "urban influence fields," the observation that "expanding larger towns and cities attracted the population in the surrounding rural areas and thereby curbed the amount of emigration to America." This effect was naturally most widespread from a large city such as Stockholm but often extended as far as twenty kilometers from a town as small as 20,000.[22] The same phenomenon is observable in other countries as well, for instance, in the Netherlands and in Denmark. But while cities tended to retard overseas emigration from the surrounding regions, the cities themselves in some cases had higher than average emigration rates. The city of Copenhagen and especially the Danish provincial towns are good examples of this. In Sweden overseas emigration was highest from rural areas, though when continental migration is included, cities were more heavily affected than the countryside. Even where cities were the source of a disproportionate amount of emigration, much of it consisted of short-time residents of rural origin, as has been documented in both Scandinavia and Switzerland.[23]

Emigration from nineteenth-century Germany shows evidence of urban influence fields similar to other areas of Europe. The influence of urbanization and, perhaps more important, industrialization has already been seen in the low rates of emigration from the Ruhr district, Silesia, the Kingdom of Saxony, and Berlin. Further evidence is presented in table 9.5, which compares emigration rates from a number of cities with those from the surrounding and administratively separate rural *Landkreis* and then with the whole District in which both were located.[24] In contrast to Scandinavia, most of these cities not only reduced emigration from the adjoining rural areas but also showed a low or lower rate of emigration themselves. The difference may be that major Scandinavian cities were mostly ports, while the German cities considered here are all inland. Münster, Trier, Freiburg, and Carlsruhe fit the model especially well, showing a regular upward progression in emigration rates as one moves

Table 9.5

EMIGRATION RATES FROM SELECTED GERMAN CITIES
AND THEIR HINTERLANDS

	City	Landkreis	District
Münster, 1832–50	4	8	16
Osnabrück, 1832–66	25	95	92
Hannover, 1859–61	6	1	14
Braunschweig, 1853–60	17	17	24
Trier, 1855–63	14	21	27
Stuttgart, 1854–55	17	92	101
Karlsruhe, 1850–55	10	53	91
Freiburg i.B., 1850–55	17	27	64
Berlin, 1844–59	3		7
Berlin, 1860–66	5		13
Berlin, 1867–71	3		12

Figure 9.3: Contributions of Each Kreis to Total Westphalian Migration to the City of Bochum[1] and Overseas[2] Respectively

Kreis with 4 % or more of total Westphalian migration overseas

Kreis with 4 % of more of total Westphalian migration to Bochum

1. Figure above Kreis name, where over 2.5%. Source: David Crew, "Industry and Community," p. 50.

2. Figure below Kreis name. Calculated from statistics for the years 1862–1871. Source: T. Bödicker, "Einwanderung und Auswanderung," pp. 304–18.

away from the city. Osnabrück and Stuttgart both had relatively low emigration rates, but apparently were not growing fast enough to absorb much population from the surrounding countryside. With Braunschweig, too, the contrast with the rural surroundings is less than spectacular. But emigration rates from Berlin regularly ranged from one-third to less than one-half that of its hinterland, the district of Postdam. All these figures underscore further the point that German emigration was disproportionately rural in origin.

The choice between the alternatives of internal versus overseas migration was not, however, governed entirely by proximity to urban areas, as figure 9.3 indicates. The protoindustrial regions of northern and northeastern Westphalia stand out on the map of emigration. But the most striking feature of the map is the negative correlation between overseas emigration and internal migration to the city of Bochum in the booming coal fields of the Ruhr. Though much of the city's population was recruited from the neighboring countryside, there was also a considerable longer distance migration from Eastern Westphalia. Distance alone or difficulties of transportation hardly differentiates these areas from Minden-Ravensberg, especially after 1850, when the Cologne-Minden Railroad gave the latter direct connections to the heart of the Ruhr. It would, of course, be dangerous to draw sweeping conclusions from the experience of Bochum alone, but it does appear that protoindustrial workers largely rejected the alternative of internal migration to centers of heavy industry in favor of overseas migration. Perhaps coal mining was simply too foreign to their work experiences, though many agricultural laborers made this transition. But Scandinavian research suggests that the most important factor was probably the preexisting tradition of emigration to America. Inhabitants of two Swedish towns reacted very differently to economic crisis at the turn of the century, depending on their previous migratory traditions. In both cases the response was a surge of out-migration, from one town directed overseas, from the other to other parts of Sweden, each following the path of earlier migrants. In the protoindustrial regions of Westphalia, emigration overseas had set in well before the Ruhr began its great expansion in the 1850s and was able to offer an alternative. Later migrants continued to follow these accustomed paths, while people from other rural areas without this migratory tradition were more likely to move to the Ruhr.[25]

Although it has been argued that protoindustry was the predominant factor in heavy rates of emigration from parts of Northwest Germany, this is not to say that other factors were entirely without influence. Perhaps the most important of these was the *Hollandgängerei*, seasonal labor in the fields, dikes, and peat bogs of Holland. Like the linen industry, this practice was an important source of income for the rural lower class and also experienced its downfall in the early nineteenth century, so the influences of the two are difficult to separate. But from the few statistics that are available, it appears that migratory labor was considerably less important than protoindustry in inducing population pressure and emigration. The former was a less convenient side-occupation than linen weaving and had a built-in safety factor that usually prevented such heavy concentrations of rural population as produced by protoindustry: seasonal migration was often the first stage of permanent emigration. According to an estimate from the late eighteenth century, one Hollandgänger in ten from the Osnabrück region failed to return each year.[26]

Another factor that is often cited as a cause of emigration is the *Markenteilung* or division of common lands that took place in many communities around the beginning of the nineteenth century. There is no doubt that this worked to the disadvantage of the tenant farmer, who was not consulted in the process and who usually lost the privilege of grazing his cows on the common pasture without gaining anything in return. But common lands were divided all over Germany, though not always with the consequence of heavy emigration as happened in areas with concentrations of rural industry. In fact, one of the forces behind the decision to divide the commons was that population growth often led to overuse and deterioration of the community pasture and forests, which could only be halted by turning them into private property. Thus, areas with heavy rural industry were frequently among the first to begin to divide their commons.[27]

At first glance there appears to have been a close association between protoindustry and Protestantism, suggesting that a propensity toward either cottage industry or migration might simply be manifestations of greater enterprise in a Weberian sense. Indeed, the migration intensity in Protestant Minden-Ravensberg does stand in stark contrast to that in Catholic Paderborn. Likewise, Tecklenburg with the heaviest emigration in the Münsterland, was one of the few Protestant areas there. But upon closer examination, one sees that Catholic weavers in Kreis Ahaus showed emigration rates rivaling those of the Tecklenburgers. Other examples can be found in the Osnabrück region, where the arch-Calvinistic county of Bentheim had the lowest migration rates in the entire District. The protoindustrial areas of the former Bishopric, a mixture of Catholics and Lutherans, showed consistently heavy emigration rates that had no correspondence to confession. If any more proof is needed, it is provided by *Amt* Damme in adjoining Oldenburg, heavily Catholic, but with probably the highest emigration rates in the whole region.[28]

Though specific economic forces played a predominant role in influencing rates of emigration from the areas considered, the general economic health of different German states was probably not entirely inconsequential. Only part of the differences in emigration rates between the states of Oldenburg and Hanover on the one hand, Prussian Westphalia on the other, can be explained in terms of thoroughness of record keeping. The level of population decline in Oldenburg suggests that emigration was in fact highest there, and the difference in rate between Hanover and Westphalia continued even after 1866, when both were under Prussian administration. A certain hierarchy suggests itself here. Oldenburg was a small state in a backwater region with little potential for industrialization. Hanover was a medium-sized state with some beginnings of industry but was cut off from the potential markets of the Zollverein until 1854. Restrictions on internal migration and obstacles in the way of factory production further hindered the mobilization of an industrial labor force. More important than any direct inducements that Prussia offered the machine textile industry or any obstacles that it placed in the way of overseas emigration was the general economic climate within the state. Internal migration was completely unrestricted in an area comprising over half of Germany, and the already large potential market was further extended by the Zollverein. So within Prussia the alternatives to emigration were much more numerous and attractive than in smaller states, but the liberal Prussian freedom of trade and domicile applied only to her own citizens. As in Hanover, so also in Southwest Germany restrictions on the right of marriage and domicile greatly hindered population mobility and probably retarded industrialization, but succeeded less in lowering birthrates than in raising illegitimacy rates. This doubtless figured in the decision of many people to emigrate as well, although lack of such restrictions in the Bavarian Palatinate did little to retard emigration there.[29]

Although emigration from Eastern Germany resulted primarily from the crass inequalities in land distribution in this region of Junkers and great estates, there were a few areas east of the Elbe where rural industry also played an important role. In Prussian Saxony, for instance, protoindustry was widespread, particularly in the Eichsfeld area, and the District of Erfurt ranked fifth in all of Prussia, right between Minden and Münster, in rate of emigration for the years 1844 through 1859. Silesia presents an exception to the general association between protoindustrial decline and emigration. Although many of the Old Lutheran emigrants from Silesia in the 1840s had been weavers, the emigration rate for the Liegnitz District was less than half that of Saxony. Several factors may account for this. Whereas the Elbe provided Saxons with a natural highway to the emigrant harbor of Hamburg, migration from Silesia was channeled down the Oder in the direction of Berlin. Silesians constituted that city's largest group of distant migrants in 1871. Because of the language barrier, potential emigrants were generally restricted to the German half of the population. The development of heavy industry within Silesia may have taken up some of the slack left by declining protoindustry, for the province generally showed a positive balance of internal migration during the 1850s.[30]

Looking beyond the borders of Germany, we find the spread and subsequent demise of the potato has often been regarded as sufficient cause for Ireland's unequaled emigration rates. But a recent study concluded that "the regional variations in the incidence of emigration over much of the northern half of Ireland were related to the rise and demise of the linen industry." By midcentury, modern industrial growth in Ulster was sufficient to keep emigration low by Irish standards. In the rest of the island, a certain correspondence can be detected even at the province level between protoindustry, population pressure, and proletarization, particularly in Connaught, the poorest of the four provinces. A quantitative investigation using county-level data from 1841, the eve of the potato famine, has confirmed these suspicions and demonstrated that a high level of employment in the rural textile industry was closely associated with growing population pressure—low age at marriage and high nuptuality rates leading to high crude birthrates—and with indicators of pauperization such as poor housing and fragmented and infertile landholdings. This was not, however, much reflected in emigration rates of the famine decade, which were relatively uniform outside industrialized Ulster. The throes of deindustrialization were indeed felt most severely in Connaught; a decline of population that was the highest in all Ireland bears witness to that. However, this was less the result of heavier emigration than of higher death rates during the famine.[31]

A few other areas should be briefly mentioned. A recent issue of the *Scandinavian Economic History Review* devoted to protoindustry was quite critical of the concept as it applied to northern Europe. But perhaps this is because these scholars were looking for a "happy-ending story," the first stage of modern industrialization. Their efforts might have been more fruitful if they had focused their attention on the issue of population pressure. Swedish emigration research, at any rate, has discovered higher emigration in districts of rural industry (not always strictly protoindustry) than in purely agricultural districts where a greater proportion of the land was arable. Moreover, the fishing industry and especially its support branches such as boatbuilding, sailmaking, and net braiding have much in common with protoindustry: seasonality and part-time employment, dependence on a distant and uncertain market, and concentration in regions of low agricultural potential.

The Swiss Canton of Zurich is another area where a wave of emigration in the 1840s was directly associated with the decline of handloom cotton weaving. The Scottish lowland district with the most domestic textile production was also the one with the highest emigration rate, and a recent study has shown that the great majority of textile workers among British immigrants to the United States were poorly qualified hand workers rather than heralds of the machine age. Protoindustry may also be part of the reason why there were more Bohemians than immigrants from Austria proper in the United States in 1870. In rural Flanders, however, redundant linen weavers were apparently more attracted by industrializing areas of Belgium and northern France than by overseas migration.[32] But taken together, all the evidence presented here strongly suggests that protoindustrialization and subsequent deindustrialization were much more important factors in European emigration during the first half of the nineteenth century than has been previously realized.

This study also has important implications for students of American immigration and ethnicity. It is apparent that expulsive forces in Europe were the predominating factors in emigration before 1860 and that the people departing Germany were considerably less prosperous than has previously been assumed. This becomes even more evident when the occupational structure and personal characteristics of emigrants are examined. Thus the degree of socioeconomic mobility that German immigrants achieved in America can only be understood adequately if one begins in Europe and investigates the occupational and social composition of the emigrating group.

Notes

1. Johann Nepomuk v. Schwerz, *Beschreibung der Landwirtschaft in Westfalen* (Stuttgart, 1836; facsimile reprint, Münster, 1979), pp. 12–13, 21.

2. The best source on German emigration is still Mack Walker, *Germany and the Emigration, 1816–1885* (Cambridge: Harvard University Press, 1964), here especially pp. 1–69, 153–94. On distribution of emigration within Prussia, see also T. Bödicker, "Die Einwanderung und Auswanderung des preussischen Staates," *Preussische Statistik* 26 (1874), pp. i–viii. On inheritance systems see Walker, pp. 47–48; Wolfgang Köllmann and Peter Marschalck, "German Emigration to the United States," *Perspectives in American History* 7 (1973), 513, 524–28; Marcus Lee Hansen, *The Atlantic Migration, 1607–1860* (Cambridge: Harvard University Press, 1940), pp. 211–14.

3. Since the definition of emigration and the thoroughness with which it was recorded varied widely from state to state in Germany before national unification, I used the United States Census of 1870 to determine the cumulative amount of emigration from the various German states, Prussia, Baden, Bavaria, etc. Then I used German state statistics to "allocate" this emigration, so to speak, to the various

Districts within each state and calculate the per capita emigration rates. For information on sources and the exact values of index figures for each District, see Walter Kamphoefner, *Westfalen in der Neuen Welt: Eine Sozialgeschichte der Auswanderung im 19 Jahrhundert* (Münster: 1982), Appendix C.

4. When capitalized, the word *District* will be used here to refer to Prussian *Regierungsbezirke*, Hanoverian *Landdrosteibezirke*, or *Kreise* of Württemberg, administrative areas averaging about 300,000 in population. On emigration from Northwest Germany, see Karl Kiel, "Gründe und Folgen der Auswanderung aus dem Osnabrücker Regierungsbezirk (1823–1866)," *Mitteilungen des Vereins für Geschichte und Landeskunde von Osnabrück*, 61 (1941), 85–176; Adolf Wransmann," "Das Heuerlingswesen im Fürstentum Osnabrück," 2 parts, *Mitteilungen des Vereins für Geschichte und Landeskunde von Osnabrück*, 42 (1919), 52–171 and 44 (1921), 1–154; Albin Gladen, *Der Kreis Tecklenburg an der Schwelle des Zeitalters der Industrialisierung* (Münster, 1970); Johannes Ostendorf, "Zur Geschichte der Auswanderung aus dem alten Amt Damme (Oldenburg)," *Oldenburger Jahrbuch*, 46/47 (1942–1943), 164–297; Herbert Hitzemann, "Die Auswanderung aus dem Fürstenum Lippe" (Ph.D. diss., University of Münster, 1953). For figures on emigration from Prussia, see Bödicker, "Einwanderung und Ausanderung," pp. i–viii. On Osnabrück see Kiel, pp. 165–76; Wransmann, II, p. 85.

5. Those who would object to my dividing of Province Westphalia should note that "Northwest Germany," as I have defined it, corresponds exactly to the adjacent regions "Lower Saxony" and "Northern Westphalia" as defined by Frank B. Tipton, Jr., *Regional Variation in the Economic Development of Germany During the Nineteenth Century* (Middletown, Conn.: Wesleyan University Press, 1976), pp. 8–9. As late as 1880 the Northwest remained disproportionately rural (pp. 61, 182–83, 189). Treating Westphalia as a unit masks important differences between the industrializing Ruhr and the rest of the province. Tipton combines Districts Arnsberg and Düsseldorf as an economic unit spanning province boundaries.

6. Rudolf Braun, *Industrialization und Volksleben: Die Veränderung der Lebensformen in einem ländlichen Industriegebiet vor 1800 (Zürcher Oberland)* (Zurich, 1960); Franklin F. Mendels, "Industrialization and Population Pressure in Eighteenth-Century Flanders" (Ph.D. diss., University of Wisconsin, 1970). Mendels (p. 7) defines protoindustry as "any type of market activity involved in the transformation of natural raw materials into commodities of a higher type of elaboration, as long as the overwhelming majority of the labor force involved in that activity is doing it at home and/or on a part-time basis." See also Charles Tilly and Richard Tilly, "Agenda for European Economic History in the 1970s," *Journal of Economic History*, 31 (1971), 184–98; Wolfram Fischer, "Rural Industrialization and Population Change," *Comparative Studies in Society and History*, 15 (March 1973), 158–70.

7. I have been better able to document the end result of protoindustry, i.e., population pressure, than the process by which it occurred. Census data for the area of study are not available until the midnineteenth century, when protoindustry was already in decline, emigration was heavy, and fertility patterns could be expected to change. Nevertheless, the early marriage and large families of protoindustrial workers were the subject of frequent comment in the literature. Furthermore, a growing body of research, based primarily on parish reconstruction, attests to the differential fertility of protoindustrial and agricultural populations. An exhaustive review of the literature, including an extensive theoretical discus-

sion, on protoindustry in general and its impact on family structures and strategies in particular has recently been provided by Peter Kriedte, Hans Medick, and Jürgen Schlumbohm, *Industrialisierung vor der Industrialisierung: Gewerbliche Warenproduktion auf dem Land in der Formationsperiode des Kapitalismus* (Göttingen, 1977), especially pp. 171–86. English version under the title, *Industrialization before Industrialization: Rural Industry in the Genesis of Capitalism* (Cambridge University Press, 1981). To the extent that one can generalize from this literature, the prime component of population growth under protoindustry was earlier marriage and to some extent higher nuptuality rates and gains through internal migration. These brought a net increase in growth rates despite higher infant mortality and perhaps lower age-specific intramarital fertility as well among protoindustrial populations.

Berkner, "Peasant Household Organization and Demographic Change in Lower Saxony (1689–1766)," in Ronald Demos Lee, ed., *Population Patterns in the Past* (New York: Academic Press, 1977).

8. For accounts of the linen industry in Northwest Germany and its decline see Karl Biller, *Der Rückgang der Handleinwandindustrie des Münsterland* (Leipzig, 1906); Heinz Schierenberg, *Blüte and Verfall der lippischen Leinenindustrie* (Münster, 1914); Edith Schmitz, *Leinengewerbe und Leinenhandel in Nordwestdeutschland (1650–1850)* (Cologne, 1967); Hermann v. Laer, "Protoindustrialisierung und Industrialisierung in Ostwestfalen," *Diplomarbeit*, University of Münster, 1971; Gerhard Adelmann, "Strukturelle Krisen im ländlichen Textilgewerbe Nordwestdeutschlands zu Beginn der Industrialisierung," in Hermann Kellenbenz, ed., *Wirtschaftspolitik und Arbeitsmarkt* (Munich, 1974) pp. 110–28; Walter Achilles, "Die Bedeutung des Flachsanbaus im südlichen Niedersachsen für Bauern und Angehörige der unterbäuerlichen Schicht im 18. und 19. Jahrhundert," in Hermann Kellenbenz, ed., *Agrarisches Nebengewerbe und Formen der Reagrarisierung im Spätmittelalter und 19./20. Jahrhundert* (Stuttgart, 1975) pp. 109–24. An excellent source that includes far more than the title implies is a series of articles by Stephanie Reekers, "Beiträge zur statistischen Darstellung der gewerblichen Wirtschaft Westfalens um 1800," in *Westfälische Forschungen:* "Teil 1: Paderborn und Münster," vol. 17 (1964), pp. 83–176; "Teil 2: Minden-Ravensberg," vol. 18 (1965), pp. 75–130; "Teil 3: Tecklenburg-Lingen, Reckenberg, Reitberg und Rheda," vol. 19 (1966), pp. 28–78; "Teil 9: Lippe und Stadt Lippstadt," vol. 29 (1978/79), pp. 24–116.

Of all the areas considered here, only in and around Bielefeld did a successful if "crisis-filled transformation to industrialization . . . with temporary and partial de-industrialization" take place (Kriedte, Medick, and Schlumbohm, *Industrialisierung*, pp. 307–8). Tecklenburg, Osnabrück, Lippe, and much of District Minden can be classified without qualification as areas of "de-industrialization," reverting, at least for a time, to agriculture (Adelmann, "Strukturelle Krisen," pp. 127–28). A machine textile district did develop in the western Münsterland, but outside the former areas of heavy protoindustry. Here see the maps in Reekers, "Statistische Darstellung, Teil 3," pp. 29–50. The consequences would, of course, be different where a trouble-free transition to machine industry took place, but such successes were as much the exception as the rule in the German textile industry.

9. Minden-Ravensberg consists of the old Prussian parts of District Minden: *Kreise* Lübbecke, Herford, Minden, Halle in Westfalia, and Bielefeld. The more recently Prussianized parts of the District were not nearly so heavily protoindustrial. From the figures in Bödicker, "Einwanderung und Auswanderung," p. iv, it appears that District Minden had a lower emigration rate than Münster in the

1840s. However, this is purely the result of underenumeration, as statistics on net migration balance show: Alexis Markow, *Entwicklung der Aus-und Einwanderung, Ab- und Zuzüge in Preussen* (Tübingen, 1889), pp. 174–75, 189–91, 214–17.

10. Reekers, "Statistische Darstellung, Teil 3," pp. 34 ff., "Statistische Darstellung, Teil 1," p. 128; Adelmann, "Strukturelle Krisen," p. 118.

11. Figures on looms for District Münster were obtained from Biller, *Rückgang der Handleeinwandindustrie;* emigration figures from emigrant lists, see Kamphoefner, *Westfalen in der Neuen Welt*, Appendix A. The figures on looms by *Gemeinde* were taken from Gladen, *Kreis Tecklenburg*, p. 197, and Reekers, "Statistische Darstellung, Teil 1," p. 174. Emigration figures for Minden in Staatsarchiv Detmold, M1 IA 95, 101, 111; weavers and spinners in 1838 from Staatsarchiv Münster, OP 1042, vol. 1, pp. 161 ff.; weavers in 1949 from *Tabellen und amtliche Nachrichten über den Preussischen Staat für das Jahr 1849*, vol 4 (Berlin 1855), pp. 678 ff.

12. Raw data for this section were obtained from *Zur Statistik des Königreichs Hannover* (Hanover, 1850–1867), vols. 2, 6, 9, 11. Population figures were derived from the 1864 census, occupational figures and livestock from 1861. Various types of livestock were combined into cattle equivalents according to the formula of the Prussian Census: 1 cow = $\frac{2}{3}$ horse = 10 sheep. Swine were not included in the variables because their numbers were so small, and a test at a higher level of aggregation indicated that their effect was negligible. Except for cities of over 10,000 population, administratively independent towns were added to the *Kreis* in which they were located, since their economies were closely tied to their rural hinterlands. A regression using the same variables at the level of 17 *Historische Landesteile* of Hanover produced R^2 exceeding .80. A statistic on the number of looms by *Landesteil* was available from 1861 and was correlated at .44 with emigration rates, but figures from this late date hardly reflect earlier patterns of protoindustry, as a comparison with production figures from 1838 shows. See Fritz v. Reden, *Das Königreich Hannover, statistisch beschrieben* (Hanover, 1839), pp. 362–63. For more information on variables and for bivariate correlations with emigration rates see Kamphoefner, *Westfalen in der Neuen Welt*, pp. 34–50.

13. Friedhelm Gehrmann, "Regionale Wachstumsdifferenzierung in Deutschland, 1850–1961." Forschungsbericht, Projekt Ho 81/42 der Deutschen Forschungsgemeinschaft (Walter G. Hoffmann, Projektleiter), n.d., pp. 25–39. Gehrmann shows that before 1860 the fluctuations of emigration rates were higher in agricultural than in industrial states, but thereafter industrialized states showed greater extremes. Moreover, the correlation between wheat prices and emigration rates became progressively weaker after 1855.

14. See the discussion of inheritance systems in Berkner, "Peasant Household Organization," pp. 53–57, which compares peasant holdings in districts of partible and impartible inheritance in southeastern Hanover. Of the two districts compared in this study, Calenberg, with impartible inheritance, had an emigration rate only half that of Göttingen, with partible, according to Hanoverian statistics from 1859 to 1864. But as Berkner points out, the main question is whether there were intervening variables such as protoindustry involved.

Statistics on the *Kreis* or equivalent level for the whole of the German Empire showed that among those areas with the largest proportion of extremely small landholdings (under 2 hectars), three of the first five and six of the first twenty were in Württemberg. But those in first and third place, Zellerfeld in the Harz and Siegen in southern Westphalia, both traditionally centers of mining and metal working, had rather low emigration rates, again showing the importance of local economic factors. Hans Lang, *Die Entwicklung der Bevölkerung in Württemberg* (Tübingen, 1903), p. 19.

15. Kriedte, Medick, and Schlumbohm, *Industrialisierung*, pp. 293, 306.

16. Figures on Baden from Georg v. Viehbahn, *Statistik des zollvereinten und nördlichen Deutschlands*, part 3 (Berlin, 1868), p. 902 ff. Lippe-Detmold was in first place. When part-time weavers are taken into consideration, the index for Lippe is nearly 220 looms per thousand inhabitants, for Westphalia roughly 170, for Württemberg 110. In Baden part-time weavers were apparently not enumerated. See also Wolfgang von Hippel, "Bevölkerungsentwicklung and Wirtschaftsstruktur im Königreich Württemberg 1815/65: Überlegungen zum Pauperismusproblem in Südwestdeutschland," in Ulrich Engelhardt, V. Sellin, H. Stuke, eds., *Soziale Bewegung und politische Verfassung: Beiträge zur Geschichte der modernen Welt* (Stuttgart, 1976), pp. 303–306; Peter Borscheid, *Textilarbeiterschaft in der Industrialisierung: Soziale Lage und Mobilität in Württemberg (19. Jahrhundert)* (Stuttgart, 1978). Statistics on the balance of trade of Württemberg for the years 1811 to 1821 give further indication of the significance of the textile industry before much mechanization had taken place. The largest item among around 8.5 million *fl.* worth of exported manufactured goods was woolen goods worth around 2 million *fl.* Next in importance were linen wares, bringing in nearly 1.5 million, while in fourth place, surpassed only by leather wares, was cotton yarn worth over 800,000 *fl.* Together these three textile goods made up around half of Württemberg's exported manufacture, according to Gerhard Seybold, *Württembergs Industrie und Aussenhandel vom Ende der Napoleonischen Kriege bis zum Deutschen Zollverein* (Stuttgart, 1974), pp. 133–45.

17. Data on wine vintages from 1827 to 1890 are contained in *Württembergisches Jahrbuch*, 1890, vol. 1, pp. 55–57. Data on grain yields and population were obtained from the 1900 volume of the same source. Data from Hannover were taken from *Zur Statistik des Königreichs Hannover*, vols. 6, 9, 12.

18. The data set used in the multiple regressions was constructed from data published in various volumes of Württembergisches Jahrbuch, except for emigration figures for the 1850s and 1860s, which were taken in part from archival sources in Haupstaatsarchiv Stuttgart, E Inm. 143, 146. The ideal emigration statistic would be total overseas emigration, but since this was not generally available, net migration balance, that is to say, all migration crossing the boundaries of Württemberg, was used instead. Overseas migration for the years 1854–55 was correlated more closely with net than with gross migration for the years 1854–57. The livestock equivalencies were those used by the Prussian Census: 2/3 horse = 1 cow = 4 swine = 10 sheep = 12 goats.

19. Richard Graafen, *Die Aus- und Abwanderung aus der Eifel in den Jahren 1815 bis 1955* (Bonn-Bad Godesberg, 1961), pp. 22, 27. It is true, however, that *Kreis* Prüm, which until the nineteenth century had a form of indivisible inheritance (p. 34), had the lowest population density in the Eifel and a low emigration rate, but industry was also not as heavy there.

20. Ibid., p. 45.

21. Ibid., p. 52. On the decline of the Eifel see also Tipton, *Regional Variations*, pp. 79–80, 131–132.

22. Harald Runblom and Hans Norman, eds., *From Sweden to America: A History of the Migration* (New York: Academic Press, 1975), pp. 134–36, 158–59.

23. Robert P. Swierenga and Harry S. Stout, "Dutch Immigration in the Nineteenth Century, 1820–1877: A Quantitative Overview," *Indiana Social Studies Quarterly*, 28 (Autumn 1975), pp. 17–23; Kristian Hvidt, *Flight to America: The Social Background of 300,000 Danish Emigrants* (New York: Academic Press, 1975), pp. 40–63; Runblom and Norman, *From Sweden to America*, p. 137; Leo Schelbert, *Einführung in die schweizerische Auswanderungs-geschichte der Neuzeit* (Zurich, 1976), pp. 28–32, 191.

24. Sources of Table: Münster emigrant lists, see Kamphoefner, *Westfalen in der Neuen Welt*, Appendix A; Karl Kiel, "Gründe and Folgen," p. 176; *Beiträge zur Statistik des Herzogthums Braunschweig*, 1 (Braunschweig, 1874); Josef Mergen, *Die Amerika-Auswanderung aus dem Stadtkreis Trier im 19. Jahrhundert* (Trier, 1962), p. 74; *Zur Statistik des Königreichs Hannover*, vol. 9, pp. 2–12, 134–59; T. Bödicker, "Auswanderung und Eiwanderung," p. vii; *Beiträge zur Statistik der inneren Verwaltung des Grossherzogtums Baden/Wr.*, vol. 5, pp. 1–35; for Stuttgart, archival sources cited in note 18. For a confirmation of this pattern in another region see Kai Detlev Sievers, "Schleswig-Holstein im Rahmen der deutschen Überseewanderung des 19. Jahrhunderts," *Zeitschrift für Schleswig-Holsteinische Geschichte*, 101 (1976), pp. 285–307, here especially p. 301.

25. Runblom and Norman, *From Sweden to America*, pp. 161–63. Sources of figure 9.2: Internal migration from David Crew, "Industry and Community: The Social History of a German Town, 1860–1914" (Ph.D. diss., Cornell University, 1975), p. 50; Emigration from *Preussische Statistik*, vol. 26, (1874), pp. 304–18. On migration to the Ruhr see Klaus Tenfelde, *Sozialgeschichte der Bergarbeiterschaft an der Ruhr im 19. Jahrhundert* (Bonn, 1977), pp. 230–38. There was, of course, some migration from Minden-Ravensberg to the Ruhr; the point is that it was small in comparison with overseas migration or with internal migration from other areas.

26. Statistics on *Wanderarbeiter* from Wilhelm Kleeberg, "Hollandgänger und Herringsfänger," *Neues Archiv für Landes- und Volkskunde von Niedersachsen*, vol. 2, no. 5 (1948), 200–201; Reekers, "Statistische Darstellung Teil 3," p. 37; "Statistische Darstellung, Teil 9," pp. 79–80. Emigration rates for Osnabrück from Karl Kiel, "Gründe und Folgen," p. 176; Meyer, *Teilungsverbot*, p. 59, citing Justus Möser.

27. Hermann v. Laer, "Protoindustrialisierung," p. 30; Hitzemann, "Auswanderung aus Lippe," pp. 25–26; Christa v. Graf, "Johann Bertram Stüve und die Befreiung des hannoverischen Bauerntums," *Mitteilungen des Vereins für Geschichte und Landeskunde von Osnabrück*, 79 (1972), 33; Gladen, *Kreis Tecklenburg*, pp. 29–31; Linde, "Das Königreich Hannover," p. 443. *Markenteilung* is largely discounted as a factor behind emigration in District Lüneburg by Theodor Penners, "Entstehung und Ursachen der uberseeischen Auswanderungsbewegung im Lande Lüneburg vor 100 Jahren," *Lüneburger Blätter*, 4 (1953), 101–121.

28. Reekers, "Statistische Darstellung, Teil 3," p. 40.

29. Hans Linde, "Das Königreich Hannover an der Schwelle des Industriezeitalters," *Neues Archiv für Niedersachsen*, vol. 5, no. 24 (1951), p. 434; Walker, *Germany and the Emigration*, p. 183 ff.; Adelmann, "Strukturelle Krise," pp. 126–28; Klaus-Jürgen Matz, *Pauperismus und Bevölkerung: Die gesetzliche Ehebeschränkungen in den Süddeutschen Staaten während des 19. Jahrhunderts* (Stuttgart, 1980).

30. Helmut Godehardt, "Die Auswanderung von Bewohnern der

Eichsfeldischen Gemeinden des Kreises Mühlhausen," *Eichsfelder Heimatshefte*, 9 (1969), 8–24. Although the Eichsfeld was an island of *Realteilung* in a sea of *Anerbenrecht*, Godehardt argues that the fragmentation of holdings was encouraged more by protoindustry than by the inheritance system, and caused problems only when the textile industry declined. Bödicker, "Die Auswanderung des preussischen Staates," p. vii; Marcus Hansen, *The Atlantic Migration* (Cambridge: Harvard University Press, 1940), p. 139; Tipton, *Regional Variations*, p. 103.

31. Brenda Collins, "Proto-industrialization and pre-Famine emigration," *Social History* 7 (1982), pp. 127–46; Eric L. Almquist, "Pre-Famine Ireland and the Theory of European Protoindustrialization: Evidence from the 1841 Census," in: *Journal of Economic History* 39 (September 1979), S. 699–718; ibid, "The Growth of the Linen Industry in Northern and Northwestern Ireland, 1750–1820," paper presented at the Eleutherian Mills-Hagley Conference on Economic History, Wilmington, Delaware, 9–10 December 1977; Oliver MacDonagh, "The Irish Famine Emigration to the United States," *Perspectives in American History*, 10 (1976), 419–27. For economic and demographic statistics see Arnold Schrier, *Ireland and the American Emigration, 1850–1900* (Minneapolis: University of Minnesota Press, 1958), pp. 158–66; K. H. Connell, *The Population of Ireland, 1750–1845* (London: Oxford University Press, 1950).

32. *Scandinavian Economic History Review*, vol. 30 (1982), esp. Edgar Hovland, Helge Nordvik, and Stein Tveite, "Proto-Industrialization in Norway, 1750–1850: Fact or Fiction?" pp. 45–56.

33. Runblom and Norman, *From Sweden to America*, pp. 156–59, 163–64; Leo Schelbert, "On Becoming an Emigrant: A Structural View of Eighteenth and Nineteenth-Century Swiss Data," *Perspectives in American History*, 7 (1973), 453–56; Malcolm Gray, "Scottish Emigration: The Social Impact of Agrarian Change in the Rural Lowlands, 1775–1875," *Perspectives in American History*, 7 (1973), 102–6, 150–53; David J. Jeremy, *Transatlantic Industrial Revolution: The Diffusion of Textile Technologies Between Britain and America, 1790–1830s* (Cambridge: MIT Press, 1981), pp. 144–49. For a more general discussion see the section on "De-Industrialisierung" in Kriedte, Medick, and Schlumbohm, *Industrialisierung*, pp. 292–321.

10

German-Jewish Migration in the Nineteenth Century, 1830–1910

Avraham Barkai

Mobility is the most outstanding feature of German-Jewish history in the nineteenth and early twentieth centuries. From the end of the Napoleonic war German Jewry was "on the move." But while its social and political development have been subject to quite extensive research, migration remains somewhat neglected. No generally accepted estimates of its real extent and directions, both inside Germany and abroad, are available. The interrelation of geographic with demographic and social change has hardly been investigated. If, as one recent researcher claims, the overwhelming majority of Jewish families in Germany changed their domicile inside the country or migrated from or to other countries between 1852 and 1933, migration must have been a major factor in the social development of German Jewry as a minority group.[1] This essay is therefore a study in minority-group migration under conditions of a changing environment. It tries to investigate some main aspects of Jewish *Binnenwanderung* (internal migration) and emigration as compared with the general German population movements, and its social and economic impact on German Jewry—those who emigrated and those who stayed behind.

Binnenwanderung was the quantitatively more extensive process, reflecting the general trend toward an industrial society and the specific mobility of the Jewish minority connected with it. Urbanization has been regarded as the most important trait of internal migration, linked with economic and social ascent and an adjustment of Jewish occupational structures to changing environmental conditions. Though this picture is valid in broad lines for the whole nineteenth century, recent research is increasingly inclined to question some of its basic allegations and development stages. Factual and quantitative analysis have by now persuasively established that the process was by far slower and more complex than has hitherto been recognized. The urbanization, or more specifically metropolitanization, of the German Jews was mainly a phenomenon of the late nineteenth and early twentieth centuries. Its connection with economic improvement and social ascent is by no means direct and unequivocal.[2]

In 1882 56,000 (17 percent) of all German Jews lived in the forty-five big cities of 100,000 and more inhabitants, in which two-thirds of them were to live in 1925.[3] Close to 27 percent were still living in villages of less than 2,000, and in some regions this percentage was considerably higher: 50.8 percent in the Hessian Großherzogtum, 45.5 percent in Bavaria, 43.6 percent in Baden, and 35.8 percent in Wurttemberg. Prussia already had the most urbanized of all German Jews: only 23.7 percent of Prussian Jews lived in villages, compared with 64.4 percent of the general population. But this was caused by exceptional conditions in Poznán where the Jews had been banned from settling on the land, and in Berlin-Brandenburg with its rapidly growing Jewish population. In the Prussian provinces of oldest Jewish settlement the picture was different: in the Rheinprovinz 44.3 percent and in Westphalia 30.9 percent of the Jews were in 1880 still living in villages.[4] Even more indicative of belated urbanization is the fact that the great majority of the Jewish population in these industrially most advanced regions lived in places of under 20,000 inhabitants: 71 percent in Westphalia and 62.7 percent in the Rhineland. Thirty years later the proportions had radically changed. In 1910 only 45.6 percent in Westphalia and 34.6 percent in the Rhineland lived in places of this category, while almost one-half of all Jews of the Rheinprovinz were concentrated in cities of over 100,000 inhabitants.[5]

If the massive Jewish *Landflucht* (flight from the land) occurred only toward the end of the century at an advanced stage of German industrialization, another generally accepted assumption becomes open to reconsideration. Historians regard the rush into the cities to be caused by previous economic improvement of the village-Jews and as a means to further advance, via better education and new economic opportunities. However, a close study of preserved tax records discloses that in many villages actually the oldest and best situated Jewish families, paying the highest taxes, were those who remained until the end of the century while the poorer left earlier—either to towns or to emigrate abroad.[6] The depression following the economic crisis of 1873 was a time of severe agrarian recession, promoting structural reassessment and the installation of public or cooperative trade and credit corporations in the countryside.[7] Traditional Jewish occupations like cattle dealing and rural trade were obviously affected by these developments. Besides this the rising waves of anti-Semitism in the 1870s and 1880s clearly disadvantaged the Jews in relation to their non-Jewish competitors. Accordingly the move into the cities appears in a new light: as the uprooting of many Jewish families from their generation-long homes, probably more often than not connected with economic losses.

Geographically Jewish internal migration followed in broad lines the general trend from the agrarian eastern parts of Germany to the industrializing west and southwest.[8] But this general observation remains rather inconclusive without a more detailed analysis of regional population gains and losses and of the demographic and social composition of the migrants. Important divergences from the general movement come to the fore by a closer look at data that have been quoted to prove that Jewish migration differed only in pace, not in direction, from that of the non-Jews.[9] In Prussia again only Berlin-Brandenburg shows positive migration balances up to 1895. All other provinces, most markedly the industrializing Westphalia, show relative and sometimes even absolute losses of their Jewish population during this time.[10] The Rhineland registered Jewish population gains from migration only at the end of the century, when at least a part of the newcomers were Eastern European Jews.

I have elsewhere dealt with Jewish internal migration during the first stages of German industrialization and examined some of its specific aspects, as compared with the general movement.[11] The most important fact is probably that in the course of emancipation, economic rather than political or legal considerations became decisive in the Jews' choice of residence. The search for better educational facilities can in this context also be regarded as a means for further economic and social advance on the intergenerational level. Beside this, Jewish internal migration took place mainly *en famille*, in contrast to the non-Jews, whose young and mostly unmarried farmhands moved to the factories and mines of the newly opening industrial areas. This was certainly not the destination of Jewish migrants who preferred centers of trade and services. This is however only part of a more complex story that has still to be investigated. Fortunately such investigation is presently under way, and we may look forward to its forthcoming publication for more insight.[12] Here I attempt to deal in some more detail with German-Jewish emigration abroad, mainly to the United States, in the context of the general German movement and of the Jewish mass emigration from Europe during the nineteenth century.

Jewish emigration from Europe has been estimated at about 4 million people among the approximately 50 million who left Europe between 1825 and 1925.[13] Of these, German Jews were even by maximalist estimates no more than a tiny minority of less than 5 percent. Nonetheless they are regarded as "the pioneers of Jewish expansion over the earth and of Jewish immigration to a great number of European states . . . In the first half of the 19th century they have sent emigrants to England and France. The greater part of the so-called English Jews, i.e., the English-Jewish bourgeoisie . . . descends from German Jews whose ancestors lived . . . in the villages and small towns of Bavaria and Prussia. Likewise the forefathers of many French Jews came from Poznán and Bavaria."[14] But the vast majority of German-Jewish emigrants crossed the ocean to the United States of America, to become "the pioneers of a migration overseas that knows no parallel in Jewish history . . . and was basically to transform the Jewry not only of Germany but of the whole world."[15]

If the German Jews were only a small part of the Jewish exodus, their part in the general German emigration of that time was evidently even smaller. But the quantitative aspect of our problem is not what part of German emigration was Jewish, but what part of the German-Jewish population left to go abroad. More qualitative comparison is to provide us with some insight as to the differences of Jewish emigration in its demographic and social composition, its adaptation to the new country, and finally its impact on those German Jews who remained behind.

The German Jews were at the time a very distinctive group, different from their Gentile environment in almost every legal, demographic, and social sense. They diverged from the majority in rights of settlement and occupation as in their family life, their rates of propagation, and their economic conduct. The ways and motivations of their emigration must therefore also have been different, to be explained as a phenomenon per se and not just as a part of general German population movements. Beside this, the German Jews—nicknamed "the Jeckes" by Yiddish-speaking Jews, in a blend of admiration, envy, and reciprocal contempt—were also a distinctive group inside European Jewry, owing to peculiar and original characteristics that they preserved long after leaving Germany. Even today Jews of German origin show a remarkable adherence to their earlier traditions and an impressive group cohesion.[16] Their ways of

migration and adaptation to new conditions may well serve as an exem-
plary case study of minority-group inertia and the perseverance of group-
characteristic behavior in a new environment.

German Jews had already appeared in North America in small
groups in the early eighteenth century.[17] In 1733 one of the first groups
arrived in Georgia, where they had been involuntarily sent off by the
Sephardic congregation of London.[18] However, these and other early
immigrants had little to do with the later waves of German or German-
Jewish immigration. The general mass movement[19] started with the "emigration fever" of 1816 in Baden and Wurttemberg,[20] gained momentum
during the 1840s and 1850s to reach its first peak in 1854 with close to a
quarter million emigrants (0.7 percent of total German population) in one
single year.[21] Fluctuating between annual numbers of 40,000 to 140,000
the emigration curve reached a new apex of 221,000 in 1881 and of 204,000
in the following year and remained relatively high until 1893. After this,
emigration gradually declined to an annual average around 25,000 up to
1914.[22] In this way five million Germans left their homes in the course of a
century, the vast majority to the New World. Until midcentury they came
mainly from the southwest. Later emigration spread slowly to the west
and north of Germany. "German emigration reached its first crest in the
Southwest and West in the middle of the fifties, its second in central
Germany towards the end of the fifties and its third in the East in the
seventies and eighties."[23]

Unfortunately all the scholarly investigations quoted here entirely
neglect Jewish emigration, and their sometimes very detailed statistics
totally omit the confession of the emigrants. We, therefore, have far less
reliable quantitative estimates of the extent and nature of Jewish emigration, its development over time, and regional origins. To this day estimated
figures of Jewish emigrants, derived from both German and American
sources, differ very widely. To cite only some extremes: Hersch (1946)
estimated 50,000 German-Jewish immigrants to the United States between 1830 and 1870 and 10,000 more to western Europe, allotting almost
none to the time after 1870.[24] Lestschinsky (1960) spoke of 150,000 for the
whole nineteenth century[25] and Bruno Blau (1950) of 250,000 between
1830 and 1930.[26] Estimates based on American records tend generally to
be higher and sometimes highly exaggerated, like the Deutsch-Amer-
ikanisches Conservations Lexicon of 1869/71, which counted no less than
600,000 German Jews then living in America.[27] In Glanz's (1943) opinion
most of the 190,000 Jews living in the United States in 1877 were of
German descent,[28] an estimate roughly corroborated by the cautious
estimate presented in 1914 by Joseph Jacob on behalf of American Bureau
of Jewish Statistics, concluding that nearly 200,000 of the "original

quarter million" of American Jews in 1881 were of German descent.[29] This is in my opinion a balanced and plausible estimate, in line with the negative migration balance of close to 140,000 for the 1845–1871 period that I calculated from German sources.[30]

The assumption that German-Jewish emigration practically ended or at least sharply declined after 1880 does not stand up to the statistical evidence,[31] which clearly proves that the Jews played a prominent part in the later emigration waves. Alone from Prussia, according to Silbergleit's data, close to 17,000 Jews must have left between 1880 and 1885 and 13,000 more in the following five years.[32] These figures accord more or less to an American investigation of the registers of three main ports of entry between 1881 and 1910, counting over 20,000 German-Jewish immigrants.[33] Not all emigrants went to the United States and some must have entered at other ports or over the Canadian border. Together all this justifies the assumption that between 1871 and 1910 more than 50,000 to 60,000 Jews emigrated from Germany.[34]

An accurate calculation is unattainable given the present status of quantitative sources. Still in the light of all the above evidence an "emigration deficit" of over 200,000, including the emigrants and their offspring, between 1810 to 1910 appears as a cautious and very probably underrated estimate. Its importance has to be evaluated in relation to the development of the Jewish population that remained in Germany. In 1910 their number amounted—in the boundaries of 1871—to 615,000.[35] Accordingly I seem to be on safe ground in the assertion that German Jewry lost by emigration in the hundred years up to 1910 at least a quarter of the population that it would have counted had no emigration occurred. The impact of this drain on the further demographic and economic development of the Jewish minority group must have been considerable, the more so if, as every evidence indicates, most of the emigrants were younger, poorer, but also probably better trained and more enterprising than the average. But before we turn to the demographic and social structure of Jewish emigration, a short survey of its time stages and regional origins, as compared with the general German movement, is appropriate.

Here again significant divergences come to the fore. Jewish, like non-Jewish, German emigration started in the South but somewhat later: in the 1820s and mostly 1830s. And while the first non-Jewish emigrants came from Baden and Wurttemberg, the first Jewish wave started mostly from Bavaria. Here it "introduced a new development in modern Jewish history . . . a transplantation of a young generation of German Jews to a new soil while at the same time the life of the Jewish community in Bavaria continued as before."[36] Glanz is here evidently wrong: Jewish community life in Bavaria all but continued as before. According to statistical evi-

dence, Bavarian Jewry lost between 1818 and 1871, not only its entire
natural growth by the emigration, but declined even in absolute terms
from 53,200 to 50,600.[37]

Jewish emigration gained impetus in the 1840s and 1850s and seems to
have anticipated the move to the North and East of Germany. Poznán lost
between 1834 and 1871 over 50,000 Jews. Roughly one-half of those went
to Berlin, the rest evidently emigrated abroad.[38] Moreover, of the general
negative migration balance in Poznán between 1856 and 1871 63.2 percent
were Jews: 26,500 out of 42,000.[39] In other words, at the time the Jewish
component made up the greater part of German emigration from
Poznán.[40] The same seems to be true for West Prussia, where Jewish
migration also started in the 1840s, causing an absolute decline of the
Jewish population from 25,000 in 1855 to 14,000 in 1871, that is, by 56
percent. Although we lack information on how many of them left for other
German regions a good part must have emigrated overseas.[41]

Turning now to the demographic and social composition of the emigration, we find the differences between Jews and non-Jews even more
outstanding. By all existing evidence, non-Jewish emigration was predominantly a middle-class phenomenon. Its greater part was small freeholders or their sons and to a much lesser extent craftmasters, and most of
them were married.[42] In many cases the returns of sold property served to
cover travel expenses and the first steps in the new country. There were, of
course, also cases of poor emigrants. Aristocratic landlords made use of
the distress of small freeholders to buy off their land, handing out the
money only before embarkation—to make sure that the old owners really
left. During the notorious potato famine of the late 1840s local authorities
sometimes went out of their way to dispatch paupers and criminals by
sending them in groups overseas.[43] But all these were clearly exceptional
cases that started protest and indignation among the German settlers in
America.[44] The bulk of German emigrants were peasants or their second-
or laterborn sons who intended to settle in the United States—at least up
to 1895—on free land provided by the Homestead Act of 1862. Only 20
percent to 30 percent of the emigrants were small craftsmen and of other
occupations. Until the midcentury, 70 percent to 80 percent emigrated
with their families, and even later, when emigration moved east and
included more unpropertied farmhands and "unterbäuerliche Schichten"
(lower classes of peasants), married emigrants were the majority. In 1901–
1910 they still made up over 40 percent.[45]

Though we have far less quantitative evidence on Jewish emigration,
descriptive sources and contemporary publications clearly indicate that, in

contrast to the non-Jewish emigration, Jewish emigration was mainly a movement of the young, the unmarried, and the poor. Many of them had their fare paid by charity, taking advantage of the eagerness of communities to get rid of transcending migrants. Youngsters set out in their teens as journeymen after concluding their apprenticeship and earned their transport in stages, working their way to port. Many of them traveled by the cheaper sailers long after steamships had started to cross the ocean.[46]

Here also were, of course, exceptions. Sons of bankers and merchants went abroad to gain experience or to establish branches of the home firm. The "Märzpogrome" (March massacres) of 1848 called into existence the "On to America" propaganda that found some response in Germany. But originating in Vienna, the movement seems to have attracted its main support in the Hapsburg empire. Its followers were mainly disillusioned young intellectuals from Bohemia and elsewhere, among them Adolf Brandeis, the father of the later High Court judge.[47] We also know of a few cases where whole communities, or their greater part, emigrated together in families, as in Ichenhausen in Swabia, accounted for in a newspaper correspondence from 1840.[48] From Meiningen in Prussian Saxony we are told that over 100 persons gathered to emigrate together. Intending to establish a community in America, they took the necessary functionaries and their paraphernalia with them on their way.[49]

Still most of the emigrating families already belonged to the second wave, following sons and brothers who had crossed over before. Usually the family and community allegiance of German-Jewish emigrants remained very strong. Soon after those young people had settled and gained some foothold they made arrangements for brothers and sisters to follow them, while older parents were usually supported at home. Connections with the old home place were cultivated with the explicit purpose to transplant, not only whole families in the broadest sense, but also neighbors and relatives from other villages in order to create in America "a larger informal family-society at the core of the local Jewish population. In many cases such a comprehensive family-society became the nucleus of the first Jewish community."[50] Indeed Glanz considers "this 'pulling after' of brothers, sisters and other relatives to be the most significant feature of German-Jewish immigration to America."[51]

Another important difference between non-Jewish and Jewish emigration was that the Jews, at least until the 1870s, were not primarily motivated by economic consideration. Legal and social discrimination played at first a much more important role. First among those stood the Matrikel (Registration) laws, which denied many young Jews the right to remain at their birthplace and found a family.[52] In a letter from New York dated 1841 we are told of the consecration of a new synagogue whose congregation were "German immigrants driven from Bavaria, the duchy of Baden etc. by oppressive laws. One of these laws forbade Jews to marry; and among the immigrants were many betrothed couples, who married as soon as they landed at our shores trusting their future support to the God of Jacob."[53] Observers at the German places of departure also pointed out that a comparison of non-Jewish with Jewish emigrants shows "many more single persons than families (among the Jews) who are motivated not by greed, but by the conviction that (here) they will not be able to settle and found a family."[54]

Legal discrimination had, of course, also economic aspects, like the limitation of freedom of movement, settlement, and occupation. Learned craftsmen could not establish business because Matrikel laws and the "Zünfteordnung" (Guild Regulations) made their admission dependent on approval by the guilds, or at least on the condition that their craft was not "overfilled."[55] "Young men who have absolved their apprenticeship and journeymen-term as well as any man of other confession who can show considerable means . . . can not obtain right of settlement. What is left for them to do, than search for another fatherland?"[56] In one documented group of emigrants no less than two-thirds were learned craftsmen. "The 'educational policy' of the Bavarian kingdom had miserably backfired, presenting the United States with a generally fit and active influx of newcomers."[57] Today we know that most of these artisans did not perform their trade in America and preferred to go back to peddling. In Bavaria they had followed the benevolent advice of liberal emancipators and Jewish organizations to become "productive." The fact that they were ultimately compelled to leave illustrates the futility of this whole attitude and was significant for the further economic and occupational development of the German Jews. Beside the above, another reason for emigration, understandably not often mentioned, was the wish to escape military service. But this was by no means an exclusively Jewish motive.[58]

Most of the emigration came from villages and small towns, at least before the more urban Jewish population of Poznán joined in it. Jewish public opinion was much concerned about the drain of so many young people from the dwindling village communities. In 1839 a correspondent from Würzburg complained that "many a small community might be . . . unable to maintain religious services and school" after so many "mostly young and industrious people" have left, and the same is heard from many other parts.[59] Notwithstanding these concerns, Jewish opinion as articulated in published sources was by no means unanimous, as can be seen in the "On to America" controversy. Whatever misgivings may have been vented, their impact was evidently negligible as proven by the figures. There was also no lack of published encouragement of a more commercial nature: in one single issue of the *Allgemeine Zeitung des Judentums* from May 1850, no less than four different guidebooks, dictionaries, etc. for emigrants to America were advertised. One of them deserves attention for noting "special consideration of Texas and California."[60] From the 1850s on, more and more advertisements offered open jobs in American communities for teachers, cantors and *shohets* (kosher slaughterers).

This brings us to a short review of the German-Jewish immigrant's adaptation to his new country, the United States. Here the differences between Jews and non-Jews become so evident that further comparison seems out of context. For some time the former compatriots remained together in the choice of their places of settlement. "These familiar German surroundings translated to the New World, in part with identical economic functions, provided the Jew with a solid footing in the early years."[61] In the 1830s and 1840s they joined German settlers in Pennsylvania, in the 1850s in Wisconsin and Ohio. "The German-American Athens, Milwaukee . . . like the whole state of Wisconsin, resembles with its climate, its agricultural products and inhabitants a piece of South-Germany . . . so German that one could for years live there comfortably and attend to business without speaking anything but German . . . (among the) 250 to 300 Jewish families one finds no, or only a few poor. The majority is well-to-do, some are rich. In the commercial sphere some Jewish houses are outstanding."[62]

For a short while it seemed that the Jews had indeed succeeded to "transplant Bavaria to America." Settling all over the land, preferably in regions of strong German settlement, they almost immediately went back to "carry a pack" and peddle their wares among the newly upgrowing farms like their fathers in the old homeland.[63] Even learned artisans who initially started work in their skilled trade found it more profitable to return to peddling. Not, of course, as a permanent station, but as a favorable transitional way to earn a living and gain some capital during the early period of economic adjustment.[64] But in most areas the "German-Jewish symbiosis" came to an end before long. The Jews proved again to be the more mobile element: their next stage was moving on to open a store in the expanding West or the Pacific Coast.[65] The South also was attractive and held for some time the most prosperous Jewish population. Whites were welcome in pre-Civil War Georgia or Carolina, and the Jews were unquestionably accepted as such and adjusted to the prevailing mores.[66] With the growing economic adjustment and the geographic separation, their relations with the Germans ceased to be a problem for the Jewish immigrants. Instead they were increasingly faced with the issue of their place inside American Jewry.

The economic success of the German Jews was to become the main cause for the preeminence of the group inside American Jewry, from the start of the Jewish mass immigration and in many respects to this very day. American-Jewish "high society" was recruited not only from those scions of the rich families from Frankfurt or Hamburg who went back to eighteenth-century Court-Jews like the Schiffs or the Warburgs. Many more ascended from the early Bavarian immigrants who had come to America "for the most part poor, soiled-looking and underfed." The celebrated "Our Crowd" of the Seligmanns, Kuhns, Loebs, and others were a close-knit group with strong family cohesion. They passed all stations from Pennsylvania to Cincinnati to finally become the established German-Jewish financial aristocracy of New York.[67]

Economic success was the cause of the Germans' eminence in American Jewry long after Eastern European mass immigration reduced them to a small minority. True, this spectacular rise was the success story of "a handful that ascended to the top rung of the ladder." But this does not imply that all the rest "reached up, lost their grip and perished at the bottom."[68] In between we find the multitude of a prosperous middle class. Already in 1856 we learn of the Jewish community in Cincinnati counting some 6,000 souls, that "only 150 are in need of aid," while the rest "enjoys unusual prosperity and practically all the Jews belong to the well-to-do middle class."[69] Fifteen years later we have similar reports from Detroit[70] and Albany[71] in the same German newspaper from Cincinatti, all written by its editor J. M.Wise, and from many other communities that he untiringly toured. All over the United States German-Jewish entrepreneurs had established prosperous industrial and commercial firms. Probably the most innovating and also the most "typically Jewish" were in the branch of garments production and trade, which was to become one of the leading industries in the United States. After 1880 when Jewish mass immigration started from Eastern Europe many new immigrants found employment with these German-Jewish enterprises.[72]

The Eastern European Jews who until 1910 were to increase the Jewish population of the United States to almost ten times the number of 1881,[73] were all but enthusiastically welcomed by their German-Jewish precursors. Contempt for the "Ostjuden" was openly vented by those as early as the 1840s, when only a trickle of them arrived on American shores, mostly from Prussian Poznán and West Prussia, and therefore no lesser "German nationals" than their Bavarian coreligionists. Nevertheless, they were abused as "the Pollack . . . the filthiest creature of all classes . . .

because of him they begin even here to use the word 'Jew' as an insulting epithet."[74] The argument was very much the same that was used forty or fifty years later by Jews in Germany against the immigrating Galician and Russian Jews. In America many of the German "old-timers" viewed the later immigrants as "a threat to American Jewry . . . that would imperil Jewish status, create anti-Semitism, and ultimately wreck all that had been created by the older immigrants." Though assistance for the newcomers was generously organized, there is also evidence of efforts and interventions to stop, or at least to reduce, the flood of immigration.[75] The former marginally strained relations between the "Bayers" and their Poznánian and Silesian compatriots, snobbishly refered to as the "Wasserpollacken," grew with growing immigration into a genuine antagonism, so much so that "finally all conflicts among Jewish groups in America were viewed in terms of the Bayer versus the Pollack."[76]

There can be little doubt that the antagonism was mainly and first initiated by the German old-timers. In fact, the isolationist group cohesion of German-born or -descendant Jews is a phenomenon that can be observed in almost every country to which they emigrated in greater numbers at any time. This may in itself be an understandable trait in a migrating minority group, but unfortunately it also includes a remarkable constancy of group-oriented conceit and prejudice. There seems to exist no equivalent trait among Eastern European Jews in America, who can no longer be distinguished by their places of origin, while "differences and antagonisms persist and can be readily observed even when Germans and East Europeans are no longer separated by wide class and cultural gulfs." The former cultural or educational advantage of the Germans has indeed long eroded, and some evidence even indicates superior educational and academic attainments of the Eastern Europeans. On the other hand, the German descendants have apparently retained their economic superiority.[77] This remarkable persistence of group identity and cohesive isolation is certainly worth more profound investigation, but would transcend the scope of this essay. But some final remarks on the religious aspect of the phenomenon may be in place. German influence is generally accepted to have been constitutive in the field of institutionalized religion of American Jewry.[78] Even here the antagonism between the "Bayer" and the "Pollack" came to the fore. Isaac M. Wise of Cincinnati, whose influence was substantial in this field, reported on many cases where Polish and German Jews were unable to unite in religious service and two or more synagogues had to be maintained even in places with relatively small Jewish populations.[79] Generally German congregations were more and earlier open to religious reform that may rightfully be regarded as "imported" from Germany, to become the leading version of practiced Judaism in the

United States. Temple "Emanu-El" in New York served from its foundation in 1874 as model and mentor of reformed service, ultimately to be
followed also by Eastern European congregations.[80] But even then, and to
a wide extent to these days, congregations remained separated on lines of
descent—not to speak of the ultraorthodox sectarian communities of Wil-
liamsburg and the Bronx or their like.[81]

To conclude this essay we must turn back to Germany for a tentative
evaluation of the influence of the emigration on those Jews who remained
there and who were after all the majority. As I have dealt elsewhere at some
length with this problem for the time of the first emigration waves some
short remarks may suffice.[82] If there is still some argument about the exact
numbers of emigrants, opinions hardly differ about the age of most: young
people in their twenties or early thirties, in many cases younger. We are,
therefore, on safe ground with the conclusion that it was first of all the
emigration of this age group that caused the remarkable decline of natural
growth rates among the German Jews in the second half of the nineteenth
century. Up to 1864 the birth surplus of the Prussian Jews was more or less
constant at an annual average of 16–17 per thousand. From then on the rate
rapidly and consistently fell to no more than 1.7 percent in 1905–1910.
Jewish death rates were all the time lower than overall averages of the
general population, and they continued to decline. The descending
growth rates were, therefore, the result of declining births, from 33
percent annually in 1861–1863 to only 16.5 percent in the 1905–1910
interval.[83]

   On the influence of emigration in the economic sphere we have much
less clear-cut evidence, but it can be assumed with a high degree of
plausibility. It was an exodus of younger, vocationally better trained, and
by reasonable guess also more industrious, daring, and enterprising elements of Jewish society, as proven by the success of most of them in
America. Their departure must obviously have reduced internal competition for old and new economic opportunities to the benefit of those who
stayed in Germany.[84] A contemporary report well illustrates this; writing
a family history it tells us of the decline of the Jewish community of
Walldorf in Prussian Saxony by emigration and its changed economic
situation: "Before a great number of poor Jews received alms of money,
flour etc. . . . . This changed slowly for the better. The emigration of many
to North-America and the greater freedom of movement significantly
improved the situation. By the end of the 1860s almost no more paupers
remained in the community."[85]

   During the first stages of German industrialization, emigration very
probably was the single most important cause for the decline of Jewish

lower classes.[86] In 1860 the German Jews were not only a wealthier but also a more homogeneous group, in terms of income and property, than the previous generation. It was surely no coincidence that the same period was also one of a large emigration—whatever the exact figures. Emigration was partly caused by the shortage of economic opportunities. Incidentally it also proved to be a major cause, together with industrialization and progressive emancipation, for economic improvement for the Jews who stayed in Germany. But emigration did not stop and was quite considerable up to 1895. The question that remains open to further research, therefore, is the possible relationship of later emigration to the economic development of German Jewry and to the deterioration of Jewish economic positions toward the end of the nineteenth century.

Notes

1. The statement is from Professor Usiel O. Schmelz of the Hebrew University in Jerusalem in a preliminary report on his extensive research of the demography of German Jewry in the nineteenth century up to 1933. I wish to thank Prof. Schmelz for letting me use this material and for many useful suggestions.

2. See Steven M. Lowenstein, "The Rural Community and the Urbanization of German Jewry," in *Central European History*, vol. 13 (1980), pp. 218–36; also by the same author, "The Pace of Modernisation of German Jewry in the 19th Century," in *Yearbook of the Leo Baeck Institute* (YLBI), vol. 21 (1976), p. 41ff.; Avraham Barkai, "Jews at the Start of Industrialisation," in *Revolution and Evolution: 1848 in German-Jewish History*, Schriftenreihewissenschaftlicher Abhandlungen des Leo Baeck Instituts Mr. 39, Tübingen 1981, p. 126 f.; the same, "Die sozio-ökonomische Situation der Juden in *Rheinland—Westfalen zur Zeit der Industrialisierung, 1850–1918*," in *Konferenzband des Historikertags Nordrhein-Westfalen*, Essen Juni 1982.

3. Jakob Lestschinsky, *Das wirtschaftliche Schicksal des deutschen Judentums, Aufstieg, Wandlung, Krise, Ausblick, Schriften der Zentralwohlfahrtsstelle der deutschen Juden und der Hauptstelle für Jüdische Wanderfürsorge* Nr. 7, Berlin 1932 (Lestschinksy /32), p. 60; Schmelz report.

4. All data calculated from official statistics in Friedrich Bosse, *Die Verbreitung der Juden im Deutschen Reich, Auf Grundlage der Volkszählung*, vom 1. Dezember 1880, Berlin 1885, p. 132.

5. Barkai, *Rheinland-Westfalen*, deals in detail with the economic and social implications of this surprising situation.

6. Ibid., and also in Klaus H. S. Schulte, *Dokumentation zur Geschichte der Juden am linken Nieder'hein seit dem 17. Jahrhundert*, Düsseldorf 1972; p. 256; unpublished archival sources substantiate similar developments in the Siegland area (Hauptstaatsarchiv Düsseldorf, Landratsamt Siegburg, Nr's 196, 513, 277).

7. Hans Rosenberg, *Große Depression und Bismarckzeit, Wirtschaftsablauf,*

Gesellschaft und Politik in Mitteleuropa, Berlin 1976[2], p. 38f.; Knut Borchardt, *Die industrielle Revolution in Deutschland*, München 1972, p. 73f.

8. Frank B. Tipton, Jr., *Regional Variations in the Economic Development of Germany during the Nineteenth Century*, Middletown, Conn., 1976, p. 45ff. Jakob Segall, *Die beruflichen und sozialen Verhältnisse der Juden in Deutschland*, Berlin 1925, p. 7.

9. Lestschinsky/32, p. 53.

10. Bruno Blau, "Judenwanderungen in Preußen, 1870–1905," in *Zeitschrift für Demographie und Statistik der Juden* (ZDSJ) *Herausgegeben vom Bureau für Statistik der Juden, Berlin*, vol. 6 (1910), p. 145ff. Detailed for Rhineland and Westphalia, Barkai, *Sozio-ökonomische Situation*.

11. Barkai, "Start of Industrialisation," p. 126ff.

12. By Schmelz, see note 1.

13. Jakob Lestschinsky, "Jüdische Wanderungen im letzten Jahrhundert" in Welt-wirtschafts Archiv (WWA), Kiel, vol. 25/I (1927), p. 69 (Lestschinksy/27).

14. Ibid., p. 74.

15. Lestschinsky/32, p. 42.

16. Marshall Sklare, *America's Jews*, New York 1971, p. 7ff.

17. Max J. Kohler, "The German Migration to America," in *Publications of the American Jewish Historical Society* (PAHJS), vol. 9, New York 1901, p. 88f.

18. Leon Hühner, "Jews in Georgia in the Colonial Period," quoted by Kohler, ibid.

19. See Mack Walker, *Germany and the Emigration 1816–1885*, Cambridge, Mass., 1964; Friedrich Burgdörfer, "Migration across the Frontiers of Germany," in Walter F. Wilcox (ed.), *International Migrations* (Demographic Monographs vol. 8) vol. 2, pp. 313–89; Wolfgang Köllmann, "Bevölkerungsgeschichte 1800–1970," in Hermann Aubin u. Wolfgang Zorn, *Handbuch der deutschen Wirtschafts-und Sozialgeschichte*, vol. 2, Stuttgart 1976, pp. 9ff.

20. Walker, p. 7ff.

21. Burgdörfer, p. 333.

22. Gerd Hohorst, Jürgen Kocka, and Gerhard A. Ritter, *Sozialgeschichtliches Arbeitsbuch, Materialen zur Statistik des Kaiserreichs 1870–1914*, Munich 1978, p. 38.

23. Burgdörfer, pp. 316, 330, 346; Köllmann, p. 31, Walker, p. 7f.

24. Leon Hersch, "Jewish Migration during the last Hundred Years," in *The Jewish People, Past and Present*, vol. 1, New York, 1946, p. 40.

25. Lestschinsky, "Jewish Migrations, 1840–1956," in I. Finkelstein (ed.), *The Jews, Their History, Culture and Religion*, vol. 2, New York 1960[3], p. 1559 (Lestschinsky/60).

26. Bruno Blau, *Das Ende der Juden in Deutschland, Congregation Beth-Hillel, New-York, 1950*, quoted by C. C. Aronsfeld, "German Jews in Victorian England," in YLBI, vol. 7 (1962), p. 312.

27. Quoted by Rudolf Glanz, "The Emigration of German Jews up to 1880," in YIVO—*Annual of Jewish Social Sciences*, vol. 2–3 (1947/48) p. 81fn. (Glanz/43).

28. Ibid., p. 85.

29. Joseph Jacobs, "Jewish population of the United States, Memoir of the Bureau of Jewish Statistics of the American Jewish Committee," in H. Bernstein

(ed.), *The American Jewish Yearbook*, *5675*, Philadelphia 1914, p. 345. Jacobs' figures seemingly include all German-speaking Jews.

30. See the statistical appendix of Barkai, "Start of Industrialisation," pp. 146f.

31. As Jacob Toury *Soziale und politische Geschichte der Juden in Deutschland 1847–1871*, Zwischen Revolution, Reaktion und Emanzipation, Schriftenreihe des Instituts für Deutsche Geschichte, Universität Tel-Aviv, vol. 2., Düsseldorf 1977 (Toury/Gesch.), p. 43.

32. Heinrich Silbergleit, *Die Bevölkerungs- und Berufsverhältnisse der Juden in Deutschland*, Bd. 1: *Freistaat Preußen*, Berlin 1930, p. 15.

33. Samuel Joseph, *Jewish Immigration to the United States from 1881 to 1910*, New York 1914, p. 162.

34. As claimed by Schmelz in his report.

35. *Statistik des Deutschen Reichs, Herausgegeben vom kaiserlichen Statistischen Amt*, vol. 240 (1910), Berlin 1913, p. 210.

36. Rudolf Glanz, "The 'Bayer' and the 'Pollack' in America," in *Jewish Social Studies* (JSS), vol. 17 (1955) (Glanz/55) p. 28.

37. H. Engelbert, *Statistik des Judentums im Deutschen Reich, ausschließlich Preußens, und in der Schweiz*, p. 10.; *Encyclopaedia Judaica*, vol. 3, Berlin 1929, p. 1182.

38. Salomon Neumann, *Die Fabel von der jüdischen Masseneinwanderung, Ein Kapitel aus der preußischen Statistik*, Berlin 1880, p. 10; Tab. C.

39. Ibid., p. 7; Lestschinsky/32, p. 43.

40. Walker, p. 78. Though he ignores Jewish emigration entirely through the whole book, this becomes nonetheless evident.

41. Max Aschkewitz, *Zur Geschichte der Juden in Westpreußen*, Marburg/Lahn 1967, p. 129.

42. Walker, p. 110.

43. Ibid., p. 86f.

44. Ibid., p. 76f.

45. Köllmann, p. 30ff.; Burgdörfer, p. 341f., 357ff.; also: Hauptstaat archiv Düsseldorf, Landratsamt Bonn, Nr. 62, emigration records 1860–1892, stating occupation, marital status, and destination.

46. See f.i. the memoirs of Walter Frank in Jacob Rader Marcus (ed.), *Memoirs of American Jews, 1775–1865*, vol. 1, Philadelphia 1955, p. 303f.; Monika Richarz, *Jüdisches Leben in Deutschland, Selbstzeugnisse zur Sozialgeschicht, 1780–1871*, Stuttgart 1976, p. 189f.; Toury/Gesch., p. 49f.

47. J. Toury, *Turmoil and Confusion in the Revolution of 1848, The Anti-Jewish Groups in the "Year of Freedom" and Their Influence on Modern Antisemitism* (in Hebrew), Merhavia, Israel, 1968, p. 73 (Toury/Turmoil); Guido Kisch, "The Revolution of 1848 and the 'On to America' Movement," in PAHJS, vol. 38, New York 1948/49, p. 196; R. Glanz, "Source Material on the History of Jewish Immigration to the United States," in YIVO Annual etc., vol. 6 (1951) (Glanz/51), p. 78.

48. Israelitische Annalen, Frankft.a.M. 1840, p. 73ff., quoted by Lestschinsky/32, p. 47.

49. Allgemeine Zeitung des Judentums (AZJ), vol. 3 (1839), p. 256.

50. Glanz/55, p. 31ff.

51. R. Glanz, "The German-Jewish Mass Emigration, 1820–1880," in American Jewish Archives, vol. 22 (April 1970), (Glanz/70), p. 52.

52. AZJ, vol. 3 (1839), p. 215.

53. Kohler, p. 96.

54. AZJ, ibid.

55. J. Toury, "Jewish Manual Labour and Emigration, Records from some Bavarian Districts (1813–1857)," in YLBI vol. 16 (1971), (Toury/71), p. 55; AZJ vol. 1 (1837) p. 264.

56. AZJ, ibid.

57. Toury/71, p. 55.

58. Ibid., p. 56; Walker, p. 159.

59. AZJ, vol. 3 (1839), p. 155, 347.

60. Ibid., vol. 14 (1850), p. 275f.

61. Glanz/43, p. 86.

62. Isaac M. Wise in *Die Deborah, Allgemeine Zeitung des Amerikanischen Judentums,* Cincinnati, vol. 16 (1870), Nr. 8; Stephen Birmingham, *"Our Crowd," The Great Jewish Families of New-York,* New York 1967, p. 53f.

63. Sklare, p. 7; Richarz, p. 158, 466ff.

64. Richarz, ibid., p. 476; see also the introduction of J. R. Marcus, p. 6f. and Franks memoirs there, p. 307.

65. Glanz/43, p. 93; Marcus, ibid., p. 11.

66. Israel J. Benjamin, *Three Years in America, 1859–1862,* New York 1975 (Hannover 1862), p. 76.

67. Birmingham, p. 81 and pass.; Sklare, p. 7.

68. Marcus, p. 8.

69. Die Deborah, 1856, p. 302.

70. Ibid., vol. 16, p. 10.

71. Ibid., p. 31.

72. L. Levine, *Women's Garment Workers, A History of the International Ladies Garment Worker Union,* New York 1924, p. 9, 15; Lestschinsky/32, op.cit., p. 43.

73. Jacobs, p. 342.

74. AZJ, 1846, p. 448; Glanz/43, p. 97.

75. Sklare, p. 9.

76. Glanz/55, p. 33 and pass.

77. Sklare, p. 11ff.

78. Marcus, p. 13.

79. Die Deborah, 1871, p. 31.

80. Benjamin, p. 78; Kohler, p. 97f., Glanz/55, p. 37.

81. Sklare, p. 24.

82. Barkai, "Start of Industrialisation," p. 135ff.

83. Silbergleit op.cit., p. 14f.; No full data for all Germany are available but as one-half to two-thirds of German Jews lived in Prussia and also taking into account the existing data from a few other German Länder, the Prussian data may well serve as representative for the whole Jewish population in Germany.

84. Arcadius Kahan in: Nachum Gross (ed.), Economic History of the Jews, New York 1975, p. 94ff.; Simon Kuznets, Economic Structure and Life of the Jews (Preliminary Draft at the Kaplan Library, The Hebrew University, Jerusalem 1956), p. 56ff.

85. Richarz, op.cit., p. 271.

86. Bernard S. Weinryb, "Deutsch-Judische Wanderungen in 19. Jahrhundert" in: Der Morgen, vol. 10, Berlin 1934, p. 4ff.

11

The Geographic Background of East European Jewish Migration to the United States before World War I

Shaul Stampfer

Migration is one of the central themes in the history of the Jewish people. When one deals with the history of the Jews in the last 150 years, a good case can be made for presenting migration as the central issue, at least in terms of its universality. One measure of its centrality is apparent from a very simple fact. Were one to ask how many sixteen-year-old Jews of today could carry on a conversation with their great-great-grandparents, one would find that only a small minority, perhaps 10 percent, could understand their ancestors' vernacular well enough to speak it. This startling fact is a direct result of migration. Three of the five major centers of Jewish population today, the United States, Israel, and Argentina, have Jewish communities descended almost entirely from immigrants who came in the last century. Their descendents now speak the local languages almost exclusively. In France, the center of gravity of the Jewish community has shifted from Alsace Lorraine to Paris, and a majority of the Jewish population is of relatively recent origin. In the Soviet Union, the Jews have moved in large numbers out of the former Pale of Settlement so that the largest Jewish communities in the Soviet Union today, those of

Moscow and Leningrad, are located in cities that had sharply limited Jewish population before the revolution. The linguistic shift from Yiddish to Russian is in part, then, a product of large-scale internal migration in the Soviet Union. The Jewish communities of Germany and Poland are almost nonexistent as a result of the Nazis. The Jewish populations of Islamic countries such as Morocco, Iraq, and Yemen are shadows of their former size as a result of emigration to Israel and France.

Migration has understandably affected not only the distribution of Jewish population and its economic makeup but has also been a central issue of Jewish thought and consciousness. The most obvious example of this is the rise of Zionism, which posited mass migration as the only means of a solution to the "Jewish problem." Perhaps less attention is given to the fact that for groups such as the Bund, the Jewish socialist labor movement active in Eastern Europe and in the United States, or for liberal religious groups, a denial of migration as a means for solving key problems of Jewish life was a central element of their self-definition. Utopian movements that sought to combine migration with establishment of an ideal society captured the imaginations of many and led to attempts by fewer to put them into practice. Much of the large-scale Jewish philanthropy in the nineteenth and twentieth centuries was devoted to aiding one aspect or another of migration. Funds were raised to aid resettlement and transportation. The impact of migration on the cultural and social aspects of Jewish life goes without saying.

The importance of migration has not gone unnoticed and has attracted the attention of many scholars. While it was going on in full force, many of the studies devoted to Jewish migration were concerned with the practical implications of the research.[1] It was thought that the analysis of the scope of the migration as well as of the factors affecting it could give guidelines for social planners and serve as well as an aid in forecasting future migration trends. With the decline in migration and the potential of migration, both as a result of governmental policies and the disappearance of reservoirs of potential migrants, these studies began to acquire a more historical cast and emphasized analysis and a study of basic causal factors.[2] The rapid assimilation of Jews in their own countries of residence and their adaptability to new environments have added interest to the questions of the background of migration because the answers may provide clues as to the mechanisms of adaptation and social transformation.

The most obvious cause for migration of Jews was in many cases acts of anti-Semitism. That was certainly the case with regard to migration of Jews from Eastern Europe to the West, and it is this migration that will be the central topic of this essay. The emphasis on anti-Semitism as a key

factor in Jewish history is a common one. The contrast between America
as the land of freedom and the enshackled lands of Europe is just as
traditional a theme. There are, indeed, a number of reasons to take anti-
Semitism seriously as a factor in emigration. The bulk of Jewish migration
from Eastern Europe to the West came in the years after 1881. This
coincided with the reigns of Alexander II and Nicholas II and major
changes in Russian policy toward the Jews. The reign of Alexander II
(1855–1881) was marked by far-reaching changes in the legal status of Jews
and the beginnings of large-scale industrialization in the czarist empire.
While relatively few Jews were able to take advantage of the liberalization
in their legal status, there were major changes in the expectations of many.
These hopes were rudely dashed after the assassination of Alexander II.
Not only was the policy changed, but in the same year there was a series of
pogroms. They not only caused many casualties but also shocked many
Jews who had faith in the future of Jews in the czarist empire. The
"temporary laws" of 1881 led to the expulsion of many Jews from their
homes, for many cities and towns were declared by these laws as off limits
for Jews—and with the expulsion came loss of livelihood. The attitude of
the regime to the Jews was most vividly expressed by the epigram attributed to Pobedonotsev, an influential member of the government.
Asked what would become of the Jews he was supposed to have said that
one-third would convert, one-third emigrate, and one-third die.[3] Indeed,
this period marked more significant changes in the governmental attitude
toward Jewish emigration. In theory, emigration was against the law.
While given the irregular enforcement of the law in Russia, this did not
necessarily mean that there were major hindrances to Jewish individuals
leaving Russia—for palms could always be greased; this did mean that the
organization of emigration and even the selling of tickets or the commercial
representation of steamship companies were not necessarily legal and
could even be subject to prosecution. However, in consequence of the
regime's dislike and fear of the Jews, ambivalent as it, indeed, sometimes
was, permission was eventually given for the Jewish Colonization Association to aid emigration. Its activities were limited by restrictions that varied
from time to time, but its very activity is a testimony to the desire of the
regime to be rid of the Jews.[4]

The question of the factors affecting Jewish emigration from Russia
has most recently been dealt with by Simon Kuznets in his study on the
immigration of Russian Jews to the United States.[5] He points out that
members of national groups besides Jews also emigrated from the czarist
empire at the turn of the century in significant numbers. This was clearly
not related to anti-Semitism. Moreover, among the Jewish immigrants to
the United States were many Jews from Galicia and Hungary, and this

was apparently not tied to a significant upsurge of anti-Semitism in these lands. The same appears to have been the case with regard to Jewish immigration to Great Britain[6] and Argentina.[7] In both cases the timing of immigration did not appear to be tied solely to outbreaks of anti-Semitic violence, and in both cases significant numbers of Jews came from outside the czarist empire. Indeed, pointing to pressures of a hostile government does not suffice to explain the migration of Jews from Russia. The regime of Nicholas I in the early nineteenth century was very harsh in the treatment of Jews. His policy of press-ganging twelve-year-old Jewish boys for thirty-year terms of service in the army led to widespread despair and bitterness but not to any significant degree of migration. Hence it is important to consider other factors that could have affected Jewish migration.

Kuznets points to two interrelated factors, demographic growth and economic pressures, as being crucial for understanding the patterns of migration of Russian Jewry. In the course of the nineteenth century, the Jewish population of the czarist empire increased dramatically. From 1,600,000 in 1825, the number of Jews is supposed to have reached 5,175,000 in 1900.[8] It is generally accepted that the relatively rapid rate of increase of the Jewish population as compared to the non-Jewish population can be attributed to a lower rate of child mortality, though it is difficult to explain why the Jewish population grew so rapidly precisely at this time and not earlier. Such a growth inevitably causes strains unless one of three conditions prevails. The first is that excess population can gravitate to areas that provide new opportunities. The second is that new occupations become available on the spot. The third is that occupational patterns do not change but there is a growing market or increased demand for the services and occupations hither to be performed. The Jews in czarist Russia were for the most part required by law to live within the confines of the old Polish-Lithuanian Commonwealth with the addition of the newly annexed lands in the south. This area was known as the Pale of Settlement. The geographic limitations on Jewish residence was not lifted by the czars so that Jews could not try their luck as traders or artisans in the Russian hinterland. The rate of industrialization in the areas where Jews were allowed to live was outpaced by the rate of Jewish population growth. Moreover, for a variety of reasons Jews tended to be excluded from working in the new factories that were founded. In the absence of an increased demand for their services, there was a significant degree of pauperization among the Jewish masses. It is clear that under these conditions there was pressure to migrate even without outbreaks of open violence.

It is almost a truism that every migration is selective and the migration of Jews from Eastern Europe is no exception. It has been convincingly demonstrated that:

> the Jewish immigrants reflect the same selectivity from the base population as many other long-distance immigration flows: a greater proportion of men than women and a greater concentration in working ages . . . this selectivity among Russian Jewish immigrants was far less marked than among non-Jewish immigration in that the proportion of women and children was much higher among Jewish immigrants. Thus the latter approximated more closely the structure of families and "normal" population than the non-Jewish immigration.[9]

It would appear that for men, the factors affecting migration were mainly the product of economic and demographic pressure while the phenomonon of significant female and child migration, which reflected a desire to make a permanent home in the United States, was the product of anti-Semitic pressures. The Jewish migration was selective in another respect, and this was with regard to the occupational breakdown of the migrants. As Kuznets puts it:

> Granted the limitations of the data, the differences between the structure of gainfully occupied Jewish immigrants and that of Jews in Russia in 1897 (and in Austria in 1900) are wide and indicate significant selectivity. The sector that is markedly overrepresented among the Jewish immigrants is that of the skilled workers . . . On the other hand, the commerce and professional groups are underrepresented.[10]

It is harder to apply commercial or professional skills in a new land than to apply an artisan's skills there, and it is clear that those who had better chances of absorption tended to migrate in greater numbers.

Selectivity as to age, sex, and occupational background can be determined from the immigration bureau and census data. However, these sources do not contain information on the geographical background of the immigrants. The data collected at ports of entry were broken down according to the country of origin and not by regions within a given country. Knowing precisely where the immigrants came from is important both for assessing the reasons for their migration as well as the pattern of their absorption in the United States. The ideal would be a full analysis of the data from the ships' passenger lists. However, such studies are only beginning, and it will take time to get results. The question of the geographic background of the immigrants remains, and it is an important one. Kuznets puts it this way:

If the Northwestern region was the dominant source of Russian Jewish immigration to the United States, the finding would be of a particular interest because of the associated cultural differences. The region was characterized by more advanced learning and a more rationalist movement in religion, in contrast to the greater role of pietistic and Hassidic movements in the South and in Poland.

But firm data to test the hypothesis of differential propensity toward emigration among the regions of the Pale are lacking. Moreover, it is easy to find conflicting statements in the literature.[11]

There is, however, a way to get an indication of the breakdown of the regions of migrant origin by analysis of the membership of landsman-shaften.

Landsmanshaften were organizations of immigrants formed on the basis of common origin from a specific town or city in Eastern Europe, and they were a common phenomenon among the East European Jewish immigrants in the United States. Varied functions were filled by these organizations. They provided a framework for social life and often served as mutual aid societies as well. Landsmanshaften raised funds to send aid to the town or city that they represented. Among the immigrants there was a strong sense of responsibility to family and friends overseas. It was common for immigrants to save all they earned in order to send money to bring over relatives. Landsmanshaften provided the framework for supporting the community at large in the city of origin. While it was usual for people to be more interested in supporting the town that they came from than other ones, not all members of a given landsmanshaften were necessarily from the same location. People often joined landsmanshaften out of convenience or on the basis of personal friendship. The different landsmanshaften varied as well in the degree to which they emphasized their ties with the city of origin and organized support for the Jews of that city. Therefore, a majority but not necessarily all of the members of landsmanshaften chose their organization on geographic grounds.

During the Great Depression of the 1930s, the Works Progress Administration sponsored a study of the landsmanshaften organizations in New York.[12] This study concentrated on the social, historical, and organizational aspects of the landsmanshaften. Over two thousand landsmanshaften responded to a questionnaire appended to the study. In addition to information on activities and leadership, the questionnaire asked about the number and the percentage of members in the landsmanshaften who were not from the home community. With this information we were able to test the theory that most Jews who came to the United States from Eastern Europe were from the northwestern part of the Pale Settlement. As New

York had by far the most extensive immigrant community of East European Jews, we are dealing with the largest body of landsmanshaften in North America. There is no reason to believe that immigrants from the northwestern part of the Pale were more likely to participate in landsmanshaften than the immigrants from any other areas. It is possible, however, that immigrants from smaller towns in Polish or South Russian areas might have had greater difficulty in organizing landsmanshaften as their populations were more fragmented. According to the census of 1897, Jews in the northwestern part of the Pale tended to be somewhat more urban than Jews in the southwestern portion, but the difference was less than 20 percent (85 percent urban in the northwest as opposed to 69 percent in the southwest). Jews in Congress Poland had undergone about the same degree of urbanization as in the northwest. Therefore, an analysis of landsmanshaften membership should give considerable information on the geographical origins of Eastern European Jews.

In analyzing the membership lists I have adopted the following criteria: the percentage of non-hometown members was deducted when reported from the total membership; the entire membership of the landsmanshaften were treated as coming from the hometown when the background details of the membership were not given. When more than one organization of the immigrants from a town was recorded, I took the sum of the members of organizations as the membership for that town. I have no doubt that in reality there was a fair degree of overlap and that many individuals belonged to more than one organization. However, since I was interested in relative weights and not in absolute numbers, I have assumed that errors of dual membership as well as of nonreported nonlocals will cancel each other out.

The main difficulty in dealing with the landsmanshaften lists was in the identification of the locations. Since most of the immigration occurred at the turn of the century, I relied on the *Evreiskaia Entsiklopedia*, the Russian-language Jewish encyclopedia published in 1915, to check locations. As the encyclopedia was published in Russian with an eye to a Russian reading public, it was reasonable to assume that its coverage of localities in the czarist empire was fairly complete. I was able to identify about 75 percent of the home communities of the landsmanshaften. My guess is that many of the towns that I could not identify were too small to be included. When, as often happened, a home community was claimed by several cities or towns I simply chose the locality that had the largest Jewish community at the turn of the century as the correct one. An analysis of the origins of the landsmanshaften membership identified as coming from the Pale is presented in table 11.1.

In table 11.2 we compare the geographical origins of membership in landsmanshaften to the regional breakdown of the Jewish population in the Pale of Settlement in 1897.

The data in table 11.2 show that there was a very strong overrepresentation of immigrants from the northwestern part of the Pale and a correspondingly low level of migration from the south and southwest. This is particularly interesting because most of the anti-Semitic violence took

Table 11.1

GEOGRAPHIC ORIGINS OF IMMIGRANTS IN LANDSMANSHAFTEN ORGANIZATIONS

Gubernia (Province) of the Pale (Region in parentheses)	Membership of the Landsmanshaften from Gubernia
Bessarabia (South)	4,284
Cherson (South)	787
Chernigov (Southwest)	593
Ekaterinoslav (South)	1,054
Grodno (Northwest)	20,246
Kiev (Southwest)	5,222
Kovno (Northwest)	4,559
Minsk (Northwest)	16,065
Mohilev (Northwest)	3,618
Podolia (Southwest)	8,124
Poltava (Southwest)	1,169
Vilna (Northwest)	6,478
Vitebsk (Northwest)	2,095
Volyna (Southwest)	6,081
Congress Poland	26,368

Table 11.2

JEWISH POPULATION AND LANDSMANSHAFT MEMBERSHIP (Percentages)

Region	Jewish population as percentage of total Jewish population of Pale of Settlement	Landsmanshaft membership from region as percentage of total landsmanshaft membership from Pale
Northwest	29.0	50.0
South	14.9	06.0
Southwest	29.1	20.0
Congress Poland	26.9	24.0

Table 11.3
TOTAL JEWISH IMMIGRATION TO THE U.S. AND LANDSMANSHAFT MEMBERSHIP 1851–1914

Country (1)	Total Jewish immigration to U.S. by country (2)	Percentage of immigrants by country (3)	Total membership in Landsmanshaft by country (4)	Percentage of membership in Landsmanshaft of total (5)
	No.	%	No.	%
Austria-Hungary	380,600	18.9	25,722	18.9
Rumania	80,600	4.0	3,648	2.6
Czarist empire (Pale)	1,557,100	77.0	106,743	78.4
Total	2,018,300	99.9	136,113	99.9

place in the south while the economic crisis was greatest in the northwest. Thus my data shed light not only on the "human capital" aspect of immigration but also on the relative significance of the causes of migration.

Is there a way to test the accuracy of our conclusions and, in particular, of the assumption that the landsmanshaften membership is a reliable indicator of the relative size of immigrant flow from a given region? Short of a check of the ship passenger lists, there is no perfect test. One method that offers some help is presented in table 11.3. It is based on the fact that, while we do not have reliable data on the region of origin, we do have data on the number of Jews who immigrated from Eastern European countries to the United States between 1851 and 1914.

Columns 3 and 5 in table 11.3 show the landsmanshaften membership is a good indicator of the relative size of the migrant population from a particular region. The fact that this finding is supported by comments of contemporary Jewish observers is reassuring.

When studying the background of the migrants and especially the question of their "mental baggage," one additional factor should be kept in mind.

The move to America might well have been motivated by economic considerations, but it was opposed not only by sentimental attachments to the home but by religious ones as well. It was generally felt that it was impossible to observe Jewish religious commandments in the United States, and this was, indeed, not far from the truth. Laws of sexual purity, the sabbath, and even kosher food laws were often hard to keep. Therefore, rabbinic and Hassidic leaders were said to have opposed immigration to

America, though little of this opposition has been preserved in writing. Those who did immigrate were then, ipso facto, those who were least likely to heed the words of the rabbis and who thus had a decided bent toward rationalism and an openness to change.[13] It is interesting to note in this context an interesting difference between Hassidic and non-Hassidic rabbinic opposition to emigration to America. Gartner cites aptly the advice of the famous Rabbi Israel Meir Hakohen of Rabin, known as the "Hofets Haim," who advised those who went abroad to return to Eastern Europe as soon as possible.[14] What is significant for us is that this statement was written in a summary of Jewish law that Rabbi Hakohen wrote for immigrants from Eastern Europe. His opposition to moving abroad was tempered, then, by a realistic understanding of the fact that it could not be stopped and had to be taken seriously. I know of no similar response by an important Hassidic figure.

It is hoped that this study of the geographic origins of East European immigration will be enriched in the near future by more detailed information from the ship passenger lists. A study based on the personal characteristics of immigrants from the passenger lists will provide an opportunity to study not only the origins but also the changing profile of Jewish immigration over time. This will be useful for studies of changing conditions in the Pale as well as for studies of immigrant adjustment in America. Where they got to is directly related to where they came from.

Notes

1. See, for example, Charles Bernheim, *The Russian Jews in the United States* (Philadelphia, 1903), or Samuel Joseph, *Jewish Immigration to the United States, 1881–1910* (New York, 1914).

2. For more important recent studies see notes 5–7 as well as Salo Baron, *Steeled by Adversity* (Philadelphia, 1971), chapter 10; M. Wischnitzer, *To Dwell in Safety* (Philadelphia, 1948), L. Gartner, "Immigration and the Formation of American Jewry," *Journal of World History* 11 (1968): 297–312; L. Hersch, "International Migrations of the Jews," *International Migrations II* Willcox, ed. (New York, 1931), pp. 471–520 and, of course, the sources they cite. An interesting study in Hebrew is that of Shimshon Kirshenbaum, *The Immigration of the Jews of Russia and Poland into Germany, France and England in the Last Quarter of the Nineteenth Century and Their Settlements in These Countries* (Jerusalem, 1950). Many studies in many languages on Jewish migration were written by Jacob Lestschinsky. For a bibliography of his works see the jubilee volume in his honor (Jerusalem, 1961). Another useful work in Hebrew is A. Tartakower's *Hedudei Hayehudim Daol* (Jerusalem, 1947). An important corrective to popular misconception is J. Sarna's "The Myth of No Return," *American Jewish History* 71 (2 December 1908).

3. On Pobedonotsev and his relations to the Jews see *Encyclopedia Judaica*

(Jerusalem, 1971) 13: 664. On the crisis following the assassination of Alexander II see chapter 2 of J. Frankel's *Prophecy and Politics* (Cambridge, 1981).

4. On the whole issue of official attitudes in Russia to Jewish emigration see the very important article by Hans Rogger, "Tsarist Policy on Jewish Emigration," *Soviet Jewish Affairs* 3:1 (1973), 26–36.

5. Simon Kuznets, "Immigration of Russian Jews to the United States: Background and Structure," *Perspectives in American History* 9 (1975): 35–124.

6. On the immigration to England see Lloyd Gartner, *The Jewish Immigrant in England 1870–1950* (London, 1960).

7. On the immigration to Argentina see Laim Avni, *The History of Jewish Immigration to Argentina, 1810–1950* (Jerusalem, 1982). Hebrew.

8. Lestschinsky cited in Kuznets, p. 63. The discussion in this paragraph and the next is based on the Kuznets article. The tables presented here rely on the data Kuznets transmits there.

9. Ibid., p. 94.

10. Ibid., pp. 104–5.

11. Ibid., pp. 116–17. On the question of the "human capital" of the Jewish immigrants see the fascinating book of Thomas Kessner, *The Golden Door: Italian and Jewish Immigrant Mobility in New York City, 1880–1915* (New York, 1977).

12. *The Jewish Landsmanschaften of New York* (New York, 1938). Yiddish.

13. On this topic see the interesting article of Charles Liebman, "Orthodoxy in American Jewish Life," *American Jewish Yearbook* 66 (1965): 21–98.

14. Gartner, ibid. p. 30. An interesting study that touches on orthodox attitudes to settlement in America is Rod Glogower's "The Impact of America Upon Responsa Literature," *American Jewish History* 69 (2 December 1979): pp. 257–69.

12
Hungarian Migration Patterns, 1880–1930: From Macroanalysis to Microanalysis

Julianna Puskás

The issue of mass migration from Hungary in the first decade of the twentieth century was extraordinarily well suited to serve as ammunition in the war of words between the various different political groupings, for it was a phenomenon amenable to the most antithetical interpretations. In fact, emigration was a problem multifariously related to the social and political and economic problems that had accumulated by the first decade of the twentieth century: the social tensions resulting from the extreme inequalities in land distribution, the national conflicts resulting from the multinational composition of the population, the difficulties with industrialization and modernization resulting from a backward social structure, and the problem of national independence from Austria. These problems decisively colored the ways contemporaries saw the scope of emigration, and colored also the reasons given for it, as well as the evaluations of its economic and social repercussions.

All this hindered the contemporary commentators in their ability to gain an overview of the migration process. While they give a great deal of useful information, they necessarily lack historical perspective, and their views are tainted with the spirit of nationalism dominating most people's thinking at the time.[1]

The migration issue was, thus, a valuable bone of contention to contemporaries; but as soon as the big wave of emigration abated, interest in it ceased almost overnight, and nobody seemed to care for the social phenomenon that earlier had caused such excitement.[2]

The 1960s marked the start of a new period in the investigation of international migration.

Recently, the history of mass migration to the United States from the former territories of the Austro-Hungarian Monarchy and Tsarist Russia has been the subject of studies in a number of countries (Austria, Czechoslovakia, Finland, Hungary, Poland, Romania, Yugoslavia). Social scientists have concentrated on the scope of emigration and its causes, on the population loss that it entailed, on the attitudes of the ruling classes (landowners and industrialists) to the migration movement, and on the governments' emigration policies.[3] There has been a great deal of discrepancy in the accounts given of the scope of the movement, of the number of people involved, no less than there has been disagreement on the causes, and demographic and economic consequences of the emigration process.

We can account for these differences partly in terms of the shortcomings of the statistical data available. Researchers dealing with emigration from East Central Europe face special difficulties: the emigrants were often mistakenly registered in the statistics, and not with the ethnic group to which they really belonged; furthermore, the national boundaries kept changing.[4] Most researchers deal only with the migration movement of their own ethnic group, and thus concentrate primarily on making up for the deficiencies and ideological repercussions of the earlier interpretations of the phenomenon of emigration. However, such one-sided emphasis on the losses suffered by one's own ethnic group without consideration of the movements of other peoples leaves one wide open to the danger of making one-sided evaluations, and is unlikely to lead to an understanding of the mechanism of the social process of emigration.

On the basis of these considerations, I have relied mainly on comparative studies in my research on the history of overseas migration from Hungary. They promise a more realistic delineation of the evolution, dimensions, and characteristics of overseas emigration. The comparative method gives a better picture of the international context of the process, makes it easier to collect control data and to work out more convincing evidence.

The Migration Pattern on the Basis of Macroanalysis

Large-scale overseas emigration from Hungary began in the 1880s (see figure 12-1). Sporadic cases had occurred before, but these may also be regarded as precursors of the later mass movement; in short, emigration was not a characteristic demographic feature in Hungary prior to the 1880s. Through the use of quantification and the mathematical-statistical analysis of time series, it was possible to reconstruct the trends of mass overseas migration, to discover its phases and cycles (see figure 12.2). The distribution of the number of emigrants indicates that the process had three phases: the initial phase until the year 1890, the growth phase to the years 1905–7, and the saturation phase from 1908 to World War I. Emigration from Hungary was cut off in full swing by the outbreak of the war.[5]

The examination of the methods of compilation of the various statistical sources and their comparative analysis has shed light on a circumstance generally neglected by most researchers so far: the data for the Austro-Hungarian Monarchy, and within it, for Hungary, show significant differences between the migration traffic, i.e., the number of people actually moving about, and the number we find for the migration balance. To give just one example: between 1890 and 1910, the migration traffic for Hungary was 1,433,172 (seaport statistics) while the net migration balance was 813,280.

One reason for the difference was the high ratio of remigrants. On a conservative estimate, 35–40 percent of all the emigrants returned to Hungary after spending some years in the United States.[6] Another reason for the difference was that quite a few people made the trip to America and back a number of times. The fact that the shipping companies naturally registered them every time led to cumulations in the emigration data.

This tendency of the emigrants to go back and forth is confirmed by a great many contemporary accounts and by the oral testimonies, all of which indicate that emigrants from Hungary did not leave for America with the intention of settling there for good. This was the most typical feature of the economic migrations of the time. The emigrants regarded their stay abroad as temporary, and only wanted to improve their economic position at home with the money earned abroad. The hopes and plans of the emigrating agrarian population centered around an independent existence in Hungary, to be realized after their return with the money earned in America. The intention to return and set up on their own gave them the strength to accept a standard of living in their new surroundings that was often far below the domestic standard, all in order to save as much money as possible for the realization of their objectives.

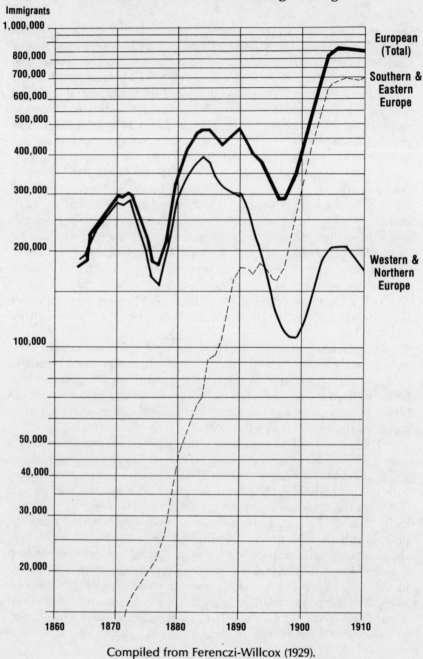

Figure 12.1: Trends of Immigration to the United States, 1860–1910: Seven-Year Moving Averages

Immigrants

European (Total)

Southern & Eastern Europe

Western & Northern Europe

Compiled from Ferenczi-Willcox (1929).

Figure 12.2: Trends of Immigration to the United States from Austria-Hungary, Italy, Russia: Seven-Year Moving Averages, 1860–1910

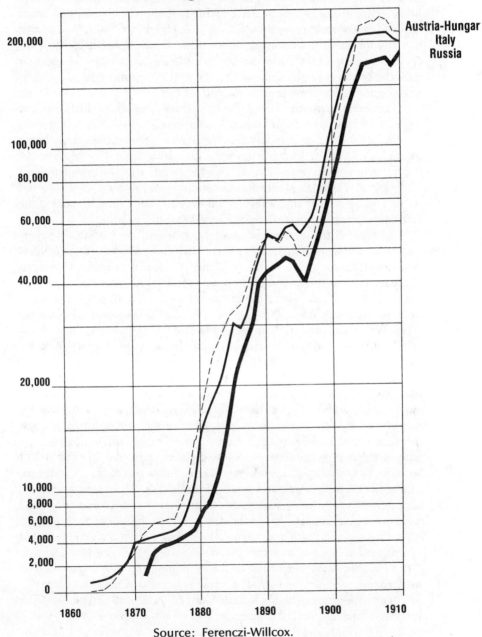

Austria-Hungary
Italy
Russia

Source: Ferenczi-Willcox.

As time went by, the influence of the new environment or their failure to achieve their initial goals gradually undermined their plans to return home, pushed the decision to do so further into the future, and made hopes of it more and more illusory. For most emigrants, then, the decision to settle for good was not made at the time of their departure. At times, they returned to Hungary before finally settling in the United States, for it took the conflicts of readjustment to the old environment for these emigrants to decide to leave their homeland for ever.

Comparative studies have permitted a more realistic evaluation of the *frequency of emigration* from Hungary, and have exploded the myth that, next to Ireland, it was Hungary that suffered the greatest population losses through emigration. Comparison with European figures has shown that the frequency-index of emigration in proportion to the total population for Hungary as a whole fell short of the indexes for Sweden, Norway, and Italy. The figures for the peak years, however, place Hungary among the European countries most severely affected by emigration.

As regards the *occupational structure*, it would be a mistake to over-emphasize the social homogeneity of the emigrants, although mass emigration from Hungary was without a doubt a rural movement. The social characteristics of the migrants, however, varied somewhat from phase to phase. In the initial phase, the emigrants' social composition was more differentiated in Hungary, too: as in Western Europe, the main pioneer types were craftsmen, tradesmen, and persons with broken careers. They sailed overseas, taking their families with them in the majority of cases, with the intention of creating a new life for themselves.

The second phase, that is, the phase of growth, was characterized by the large number of peasants among the emigrants. The number of independent landowning peasants was relatively small, most of them being agricultural day laborers. In the saturation phase, the occupational distribution of the emigrants again became more highly differentiated. The ratio of the nonagricultural emigrants grew as compared to what it had been in the growth phase, and there was a higher percentage of independent artisans, tradesmen, and even of intellectuals. However, their numbers were not so great as to alter the basically agrarian character of mass emigration. Among the peasants, the ratio of the propertied peasant emigrants was higher than in the previous phase, a trend clearly reflected by Hungarian emigration statistics for the years 1906–7 and 1911–13.[7]

The *demographic composition* of the immigrants from Hungary underwent changes too. In the period of growth the ratio of males was remarkably high. Young men predominated. Many of them were married and had left wives and families at home. In the saturation phase, there was a remarkable increase in the ratio of emigrating females and children. This was partly due to the nuclear families' being reunited in the United States, but also to the family ties in the broad sense which appear to have had a major part in recruiting emigrants: according to data from 1910, 80 percent of the immigrants from Hungary when questioned by the Immigration Officers stated that they were coming to join relatives already in the USA.[8]

Before 1914, the multinational composition of the overseas emigrants from Hungary did not reflect the ratio of the various ethnic groups in the population of the delivering country.

The two largest groups arriving in the United States from Hungary were the Slovaks and the Magyars; they made up more than one-half of all the newcomers from Hungary. The Croats and Slovenes were less significant, accounting for 15 percent (most Slovenes started out from Austria); the Germans, we find, left Hungary in almost equal numbers (see tables 12.1 and 12.2).

If the emigrants from Hungary to the United States are divided into two groups, Magyars and non-Magyars, it becomes obvious that more than two-thirds of the emigrants were non-Magyars. However, the ethnic composition of the emigrants from the Monarchy—and from Hungary as well—varied considerably during the period under discussion. In 1899, the Slovaks made up 25.2 percent of all the emigrants from the Monarchy. They started mass overseas migration earlier than the Poles, who at this time comprised 18.7 percent of those who were leaving Austria-Hungary.

These peculiarities of the multiethnic composition of emigration have

Table 12.1

THE ETHNIC DISTRIBUTION OF THE IMMIGRANTS TO AMERICA IN PERCENTAGE, 1899–1913[9]

Ethnic group	From Austria-Hungary	From Hungary
Polish	18.7	—
Slovak	15.4	26.8
Magyar	14.2	26.3
Croat-Slovene	14.0	16.6
German	11.4	15.0
Czech-Moravian	4.3	—
Jewish	7.5	5.7
Ruthenian	7.3	2.1
Bosnian	2.7 Serbian-Bulgarian	2.3
Romanian	3.1	6.9
Italian	0.8	—
Others	0.6	2.3

Table 12.2

DISTRIBUTION OF IMMIGRANTS FROM EAST-CENTRAL
EUROPE BY NATIONALITIES (1899–1924)

Percentage	Nationality
27.1	Hebrew
22.1	Polish
8.5	German
8.5	Slovak
8.3	Hungarian
7.1	South Slavs
4.0	Ruthenian
4.0	Russian (Ukrainian)
3.9	Litvanian
3.3	Finnish
2.3	Bohamian-Moravian
2.3	Romanian

Total Number of Immigrants = 6,502,109

Source: Compiled from Ferenczi-Willcox (1929).

impelled certain historians to find political reasons for the movement, to explain it in terms of discrimination against the national minorities.[10] It is comparative study that discloses the oversimplification in these interpretations.

The Hungarian emigration statistics for 1899 or 1913 offer information about the regions from which the emigrants came.[11] These show that emigration overseas was very intensive in some parts of Hungary and almost nonexistent in others. (See figure 12.3) Emigration was most frequent from the northeastern region of the country. There were some other emigration regions as well, geographically far apart. The question arises as to why emigration centers developed in these particular areas. Although the economic and social conditions of these regions showed some similarities, they were not so clear-cut as to adequately explain the increased readiness to migrate. Neither the demographic, nor the economic conditions within the country varied so greatly as to account for the substantial differences which appeared in the spread of emigration.

The most notable characteristic of the geographical position of the emigration centers is that they fell more or less outside the pull of Budapest, the major industrial center. Generally, but only generally, these regions were not in the flatlands, but in mountainous districts where nature was less benign. They were mostly districts where agriculture on

Figure 12.3: Emigrants from Hungary to the Overseas, 1899–1913

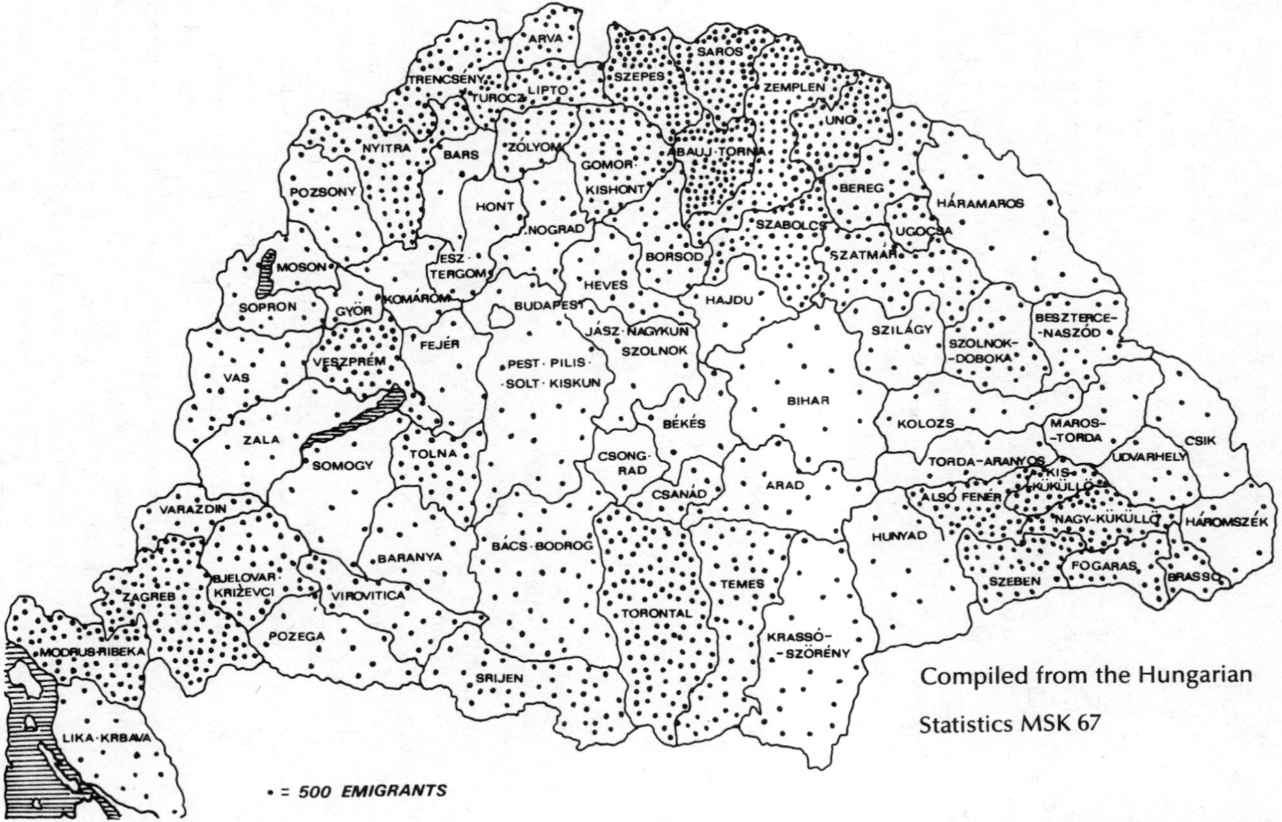

Compiled from the Hungarian Statistics MSK 67

• = 500 EMIGRANTS

peasant farms had to be supplemented by other kinds of labor. The ethnic composition of the migration regions differed from region to region.

Mass migration started among the Slovaks and the Germans in the districts bordering Galicia. It, was they who transmitted the migration wave to other parts of the country: it spread first in their immediate neighborhood, and later among other ethnic groups living in the vicinity. While personal relationships played an important role in the spread of emigration, the center of migration of the Magyars developed in the counties of the north and the east, in the vicinity of the Slovaks.[12]

In Hungary, among the Slovaks and Carpatho-Ukrainians, a way of life based on migration had been established long before overseas migration began. For at least a century, they had been migrating to the lowlands in the center of the country in search of agricultural jobs.[13] The Germans were also mobile, and not only the craftsmen but also the German peasant families who grew up aware of the need for geographic mobility owing to their special system of inheritance based on the indivisibility of the estate. The Germans were pioneers in making a region a migration region, although their economic and social status hardly impelled them to migrate.[14] The regional differences in emigration from Hungary derive from the characteristics of the migratory mechanism, from the necessary combination of push and pull factors. Emigration spread in the form of similar chains or centers of emigration in the ethnically more homogeneous countries of Europe too, such as the Scandinavian countries, or Italy, or Germany.[15] Everywhere, mass emigration began in the regions far from the industrial centers, in those lacking in natural resources and in regions in some way more open to areas and peoples already familiar with emigration. Since these regions in Hungary were inhabited mostly by non-Magyar ethnic groups, and since the Magyars lived mostly in the country's central, more enclosed plains, it was geographic location, the proximity of areas where migration had previously occurred, which primarily accounted for the difference in the non-Magyar population's inclination to emigrate. It is not clear, however, that the ethnic problem can be considered a determining factor. The geographic location of a given country's emigration regions cannot be explained in terms only of domestic causes. The wave of European migration also exerted its influence. Just as the links can be found between the regions within a country, so the links can be found between countries and ethnic groups as well, especially as some regions crossed over state borders (figure 12.4).

It is not easy to see this very complex social movement in its historical context. The research I have done on emigration from Hungary indicates that the most important factors in explaining emigration were overpopulation in the agricultural sector, and the differences between the Hungarian

Figure 12.4: Political Map of Ethnic Frontiers of Austro-Hungarian Empire

and the American standards of living. However, there was also undoubtedly a general increase in mobility brought about by industrialization.
This led to new ways of life, broke the old ties that previously linked
individuals to their old communities. All this made them open to new
experiences and new ideas, which in turn fostered new wants and demands.

In the early 1920s, that is, by the time the unrest due to the war, the
revolutions, and the territorial changes had abated and emigration from
Hungary could have resumed, the United States shut its gates to the
"undesirable" peoples of East Central Europe. The "push" factors of
emigration, however, continued to operate in Hungary. In the 1920s, the
emigrants headed for previously less popular places: Canada and South
America, and those who stayed in Europe, to France and Belgium. Those
hoping to find a way to enter the United States also headed for Canada.[16]
    The Depression effectively put an end to all opportunities for mass
emigration. Between 1930 and 1940, overseas migration (but migration
generally, too) was to be counted in the hundreds, not the thousands.[17]
    In the limited number of cases of overseas migration between 1920
and 1940, we find an amalgam of economic and political motives among
the incentives to move. The series of political events that shook Hungary
after World War I and in the 1930s made Hungarians, too, join the ranks of
that special type of emigrant, the political exile, and saw a rise in the
number of intellectuals and tradesmen among the emigrants.

Some Characteristics of the Hungarian Immigrants' Settlement Pattern in the United States

In keeping with a broader interpretation of the phenomenon of migration,
I have not confined my studies to the donor country, Hungary, but have
followed the emigrants to their new environment, and studied their settlements, the formation of their communities.
    For a delineation of their settlement patterns, I have relied mostly on
United States census data. These indicate that almost all the immigrants
coming from Hungary found jobs in Pennsylvania, Ohio, New York,
New Jersey, West Virginia, and Illinois, mostly in the mines and in
various branches of heavy industry, in the iron foundries and the steel
mills. It was here that American industry proved practically insatiable in
its demand for unskilled labor.
    Within these states, the Hungarian settlements were scattered. Pitts-
burgh, New York, Cleveland and their environs were cities in a chain of

larger and smaller settlements. They were to be found, moreover, in hundreds of mining camps far from any town. Comparative examination of the patterns of movement and settlement of the ethnic groups coming from Hungary shows that these were, for the most part, similar. It seems, therefore, that those coming from the same region tended to settle near one another; we cannot speak of lines of demarcation separating the various ethnic groups of new immigrants, especially those coming from the Austro-Hungarian Monarchy. If we examine the regional distribution of the immigrants coming from just Hungary, however, we find a number of differences as well. The non-Magyar immigrants were much more likely to concentrate in Pennsylvania, Ohio, and Illinois than the Magyars, who went rather to New York and New Jersey.[18] This was probably because the Magyar immigrants formed the most differentiated group socially of the nationalities coming from Hungary: there was a higher ratio of skilled workers, artisans, and intellectuals among them[19] (see figure 12.5).

I have had opportunity to study the church registers of a number of Hungarian-American parishes.[20] The data indicate that the parishioners hailed from geographically widely scattered places. There were some who had come from the same village, but this was not typical. They were, however, likely to have come from various communities in the same county, or from various counties in the same emigration region. But all the church registers I have looked at list parishioners from counties that fell outside these regions as well; for instance, the members of the Hungarian Reformed Church of Chicago had come from twenty-two different counties.

The personal accounts of those who had lived through the period, as well as the Hungarian-American newspapers, call attention to the high degree of geographical mobility among the immigrants, who were as prone to keep on moving from place to place within the United States as to return to the Old Country and then back again.

Research into local history is what is needed if we are to come to understand the development of the settlements that they did establish, and the changes in the communities that they formed.

New Research on the Basis of Microanalysis

The macrolevel research I have described has, along with the results yielded, brought to light a whole series of questions that I had little hope of answering satisfactorily on the basis of the more traditional sources.

Neither the emigration statistics nor the bulk of other contemporary sources show us the migration phenomenon in all its complexity.

The effort to find answers to such questions had led many researchers

Figure 12.5: Distribution of Immigrants by Occupation and Ethnic Groups, 1899–1924

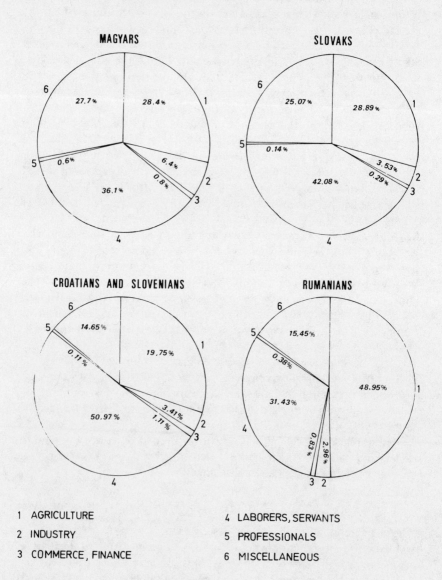

1 AGRICULTURE

2 INDUSTRY

3 COMMERCE, FINANCE

4 LABORERS, SERVANTS

5 PROFESSIONALS

6 MISCELLANEOUS

to turn to local investigations, to do microanalyses of small groups and communities.[21] Just what groups and communities are likely to yield representative evidence from microanalysis we can gather on the basis of the macroinvestigations conducted to date.

For my own in-depth study, I have chosen a village (Sz.) in the emigration region of northeastern Hungary, a community that promises to provide data representative of the Magyar Protestant peasant emigrants.[22]

Emigration fever reached this village relatively late, after the turn of the century. Thus, the older generation still has vivid memories of the emigrants. My first task, therefore, was to gather as much information as possible through oral testimony. I started by seeking out in the village the man reputed to have kept the closest track of the events related to the village and its population. My informant, a man of seventy-seven, recalled those who had left for overseas, proceeding street by street. Altogether he gave me information on 228 people. With a few exceptions, he also remembered the year they had left and had information on the emigrants' marital status and economic position. In the village I got advice from the emigrants still living on who to look up in the United States and in Canada, and where to find them.

I was able to spend the first half of the year 1982 in the United States and Canada and to look up those emigrants and their descendants. From those I met I recorded all information they had on their families, relatives, and their fellow emigrants. I showed them the data sheet I had prepared on the 228 persons my first informant had spoken of, and supplemented and corrected the data on the basis of their observations.[23]

The reliability of my first informant was confirmed by most of what they said; corrections were needed for the most part only in respect to the years of departure from Hungary.

I was able to draw up the data sheet on the basis of all who had left the village between 1904 and 1960. There were, of course, some missing data. My informants could tell me only the names of some of the emigrants, and that they had gone to, or had been to, America, but nothing more concrete as to the date of their departure. And since there was no one who could remember back that far, there is no clear evidence as to who or what group it was that started the entire overseas emigration movement by being the first from the village to sail overseas.

On talking to my informants, I wanted more than just a list of names. In the course of the interviews I was able to trace a number of life histories, to get information on the motivations behind a number of individual decisions to leave. I was able to gather data on the family's demographic and economic background, on the members of the family who were left behind, on the kind of jobs the new immigrant worked on in America, on the places they moved to, on the economic position they achieved, and on the fate of their children.

Large quantities of data are still to be collected, and their analysis is largely yet to be done. But what we already have at hand is enough material to answer questions on which the national data yields no information.

I could get information, for example, on the following questions: Which kinship ties were most influential in causing others to emigrate? How far did emigration break up the nuclear family? Who did the married men leave behind, and how were these families reunited?

Kinship ties operated in the spread of the emigration wave throughout the community. Not, however, in the way they did among the peasant emigrants of Western Europe, where the nuclear family was likely to leave together for the United States, or was soon reunited there.

Couples and families among the emigrants from Sz. were an exception; of a large family (eight or ten), three, four, or five of the siblings were likely to emigrate one after the other at intervals of a year or more. There were married men, bachelors, and unmarried girls among the emigrants. Most of the single men and girls got married in the United States. These were the ones who were likely to settle there permanently, whether they married a fellow villager or someone else. The emigrant heads of families tended, for the most part, to return to the families left behind. Occasionally, a husband would send for his wife and children, or only his wife, entrusting the children to the grandparents' care. Couples thus reunited tended also to return to Hungary, taking with them the children born in America. These children, when they grew up, could, as American citizens, return to the United States even in the 1930s after immigration had already been restricted. This was the group "born in America and brought up in the Old Country." (They were not listed in the immigration statistics!)

I should like to present the most important details of the migration and remigration of one particular family that I have been able to trace (see figure 12.6). Lajos P. was born in 1883 into a farming family, the youngest of seven children. He was still a bachelor when he sailed for North America in 1903. (Some informants thought that he had been there once before.) In any case, he already had a sister living in the United States in 1903. Lajos P. went to West Virginia to a mining area; he and a few of his fellow villagers got jobs in the mine. Among the people of his native village that Lajos P. was associated with during his time in the United States was Lea L. An illegitimate daughter Julianna L. was born to them, probably in 1905. Lajos P. returned to his village in 1908, and soon married Hermina A. The young couple lived with Lajos P.'s parents, and worked the family

Figure 12.6: An Example of One Type of Migration

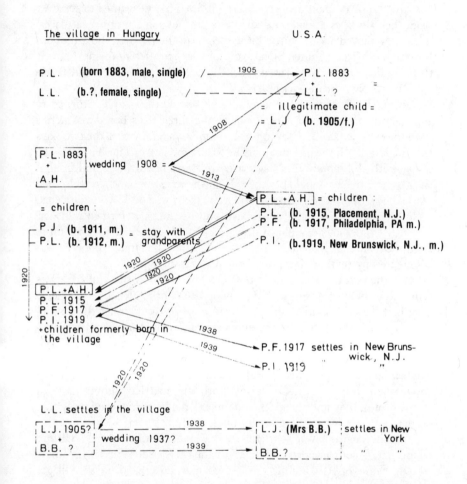

The village in Hungary   U.S.A.

P.L.   (born 1883, male, single)   / ———— 1905 ————→ P.L. 1883
L.L.   (b.?, female, single)   / — — — — — — → L.L. ?
                                              = illegitimate child =
                                              = L.J   (b. 1905/f.)

P.L. 1883
  +   wedding 1908 =
A.H.

= children :   P.L.+A.H. = children :
                                    P.L. (b. 1915, Placement, N.J.)
P.J   (b. 1911, m.) = stay with   P.F. (b. 1917, Philadelphia, PA m.)
P.L. (b. 1912, m.)   grandparents P.I. (b.1919, New Brunswick, N.J., m.)

P.L.+A.H.
P.L. 1915
P.F. 1917
P.I. 1919
+children formerly born in   P.F. 1917 settles in New Bruns-
  the village   wick, N.J.
                                    P.I. 1919   "   "

L.L. settles in the village

L.J. 1905? ——————— 1938 ———→ L.J. (Mrs B.B.) settles in New
    +   wedding 1937?   York
B.B. ?   —————————— 1939 ——→ B.B.?   "   "

247

plot. Two sons were born to them: József P. in 1911, and László P. in 1912. In 1913, Lajos P. returned to the United States, taking his wife with him. The two little boys they left in the village in the care of their grandparents. Initially, Lajos P. again made for West Virginia, but he wanted to get away from the mines, and took on a variety of odd jobs in a number of places. That they moved about quite a bit we see from the fact that the three sons born to them in the United States were all born in different towns: Lajos P. (1915) in Placement, N.J.; Ferenc P. (1917) in Philadelphia, Pa.; and István P. (1919) in New Brunswick, N.J.

Immediately after the end of World War I, the couple returned to Hungary to their native village, taking the three boys born in America with them. The family of seven was reunited when they took the two boys they had left with the grandparents into their own care. The couple built a house with the money they had saved in the United States and bought twenty-two holds (1 hold = 1.42 English acres) of land, which they worked for themselves. One of their five sons, Lajos P. (1915) finished secondary school, attended university, and became a Reformed minister. The other four boys completed only elementary school, and stayed on to farm their parents' land. In the 1920s and 1930s, the family property was augmented by further land purchases to about forty holds.

At the end of the 1930s, two of the boys born in the United States returned to New Brunswick, N.J. Having been born in the United States, they had American citizenship too, and did not come under the restrictions put on immigration by the quota system. They traveled with American passports, Ferenc P. in 1938, István P. in 1939. The latter had been only two years old when his parents took him to Hungary, and knew no English on his return; when World War II broke out, he, too, was drafted, and learned English in the U.S. army. Both boys married within their own ethnic group; they and their descendants are the branch of the family that permanently settled in the United States.

At the beginning of the 1920s, Lea L. also returned to her village, taking her American-born daughter Julianna with her. The village knew who the father of her daughter was. Lea L. married a man from the village, and had four more children. Julianna L.'s first marriage was not a success: in 1937 or 1938, she married B.B.; soon afterwards, she took advantage of her American citizenship to move to the United States; her husband was able to join her there before the war broke out.

Lajos P.'s family represents one type of back and forth transatlantic migration. A look at the data calls attention to a number of factors that researchers will do well to keep in mind. The size of an immigrant family, for instance, can easily be mistakenly reconstructed on the basis of the records of just any one Hungarian-American parish. For in what one parish register are the births of all six of Lajos P.'s children recorded? Another aspect to pay attention to is the incidence of families who returned to their native village taking the children born in America with them. In this one village, at least eighteen more of the children "born in America but brought up in the Old Country" went back and forth during the interwar years, traveling with their American passports. This is one source of the discrepancy between the migration statistics and the number of people who actually left the country for good in these years, for neither the Hungarian emigration nor the American immigration statistics captured this group.

In trying to map the family background, the demographic, economic, and social parameters of a given emigrant, I again started out from the recollections of my informants. To check what I had learned and for purposes of obtaining control data, I studied the church registers in the village. The collation of the two sets of data helped to identify and to trace the kinship ties among the emigrants, and provided written documentation to back up my investigations. The land registers were my written sources for data and controls on the economic position of the emigrants, on the size of their property and land. When I tested the reliability of these data, however, the limits of their usefulness also became clear. For I found that the land registers did not, for the most part, offer a true picture of the de facto property relations. The house and land were often in the parents' name even when members of the younger generation were already farming it quite on their own. For this reason, it might well be that the percentage of "agricultural laborers" and "day laborers" in the emigration statistics is higher than was actually the case.

The Sz. emigrants were usually agricultural laborers with many children and small plots. Their children, though they stood to inherit some land, were unlikely to get a share large enough on which to base an independent existence. At the same time there was considerable land to be had around the village. About half of the arable land there, around 3,000 holds, consisted of small estates owned by the nobility, and this type of nonpeasant holding was much more likely to be put up for sale than the less mobile big estates. The inhabitants of Sz. set about buying up these small noble holdings with great energy from the 1870s on. In a little over 60 years they had bought up practically all the estates of this type, nearly 3,000 holds.

Among the peasants who bought land we find the "Americans." Some of them acquired as much as 35–40 holds, thus attaining rich peasant status. The majority of the "Americans," however, bought only small parcels of land of a few holds. My informants also recollect remigrants who resettled in the village without acquiring any land at all; very definite ratings were given to those who had "made good," and those who had "nothing" to show for their years in America.

I found that more than 50 percent of those who had gone to the United States returned within three to five years. A few returned after as many as fifteen to twenty years abroad. But I must also point out that even of those who ended up staying in America for good, the majority kept on buying bits of land in the village back home. The interviews with the emigrants and their descendants all indicate that they spent years as industrial workers in the United States dreaming of a better future as farmers back in the village in Hungary. It often took decades for them to finally make up their minds never to return. As one of them put it: "When I bought the first acre of land, I said to my wife: 'Now we have three acres of land,' for back home our lease said we had to cultivate three acres of land to get the produce of one. We bought the second acre of land, and said we now had six. 'We'll only stay in America and work so hard until we have twenty acres, and then we'll go home,' I used to say to my wife when she'd worry about my working seventy-two hours a week as a longshoreman." (They, for instance, never returned to Hungary.)

The people I managed to talk to had very different reasons for deciding at last to settle for good in the United States or, conversely, to return to their native village. All of them, even those who ended up staying, mentioned that the thought of returning preoccupied them for years. They would gladly have turned their backs on the hardships of the new life especially in the early years, had they had the money to return, and had they not been ashamed of doing so.

On the basis of my informants' recollections, the following settlement pattern emerges for the immigrants from Sz. Since we have not been able to track down the names of the first villagers to leave, we do not know how they came to hear of the two West Virginia mining areas which most informants specify as the locations that consecutive groups from the village went to upon first landing in the United States. No permanent settlement of villagers from Sz. was formed in these two mining locations, however. From here, they either returned home, or went somewhere else in the United States. In the course of their travels, a villager or two stayed behind in Cleveland, Detroit, or McKeesport.

A more permanent and rather large colony was set up in New Brunswick, N.J. They were attracted by the town's growing industries, the cigar factory, and especially the Johnson & Johnson company. A migration route grew up between the two mining communities and New Brunswick, with the families of Sz. moving back and forth between the two as job opportunities offered themselves now here, now there. The mines provided the men with harder jobs, but also with higher wages. On the other hand, there were fewer job opportunities for the women in the mining places than in the towns. The main source of income, and that available only to married women, was the keeping of boarders. In New Brunswick jobs were at hand mostly for the girls and the women; the cigar factories employed mostly female workers.

We do not yet know who were the first Hungarians to settle in New Brunswick. But there is no doubt that those who stayed behind in the village were most influenced by New Brunswick settlers; to this day, the village has the closest ties to New Brunswick.

During the interwar years, with immigration to the United States restricted, people from Sz. started making their way to Canada: first they tried their luck in agriculture in the prairies, and then moved east toward the Great Lakes, to settle in and around Hamilton, Ontario. Although much weaker than that between the village and New Brunswick, a sort of magnet developed between Hamilton and the village as well.

In the case of all those who settled in Canada, we find either kinship ties (sibling, cousin) to those from the village who had settled in America, or a tradition of migration in the family: a father or father-in-law who had been in the United States earlier, in the years preceding World War I.

My informants were good sources for an examination of how geographic and occupational mobility tied in with social mobility. What was the most that they hoped to achieve? Who had managed to achieve it, and how? I have already mentioned that for those who ended up returning, the highest possible status was that of a well-off peasant—the purchase of forty to fifty holds of land with the money saved in America. Of those who stayed in America, two had managed to rise from the rank of wage laborers to become independent businessmen, the owners of a saloon and a butcher shop, respectively, and to become relatively wealthy men. These success stories were as familiar to the villagers back home as to the immigrant community, and were occasions of interesting embellishments.

On the basis of oral testimony available, we can delineate the salient features of the lives of the immigrants' children as well, that is, the second generation. My informants have given me answers as to how many children there usually were in a family, what language was spoken at home, what kind of education the children got, what kinds of jobs and social strata they ended up in. Were they likely to stay in the same community as their parents, or to disperse? How frequent was marriage within the community? And if someone married outside it, what ethnic group was he or she likely to choose?

I have yet to process all the responses given to the above questions. However, even at this point I can safely say that the peasant background, the peasant value system influenced the children's chances of social mobility. It was easier for children to make money or add to what they had made than to receive a university education. There was considerable continuity of settlement between the first and second generation, at least where the immigrants lived as a community. Most of the second generation married within the ethnic group, at least in New Brunswick. Mixed marriages were likely to be made by those whose parents already had broken away from the group in the course of moving about. It is this same group that is least influenced by the norms and expectations of the native village.

I have tried to give a more concrete presentation of the complexity of migration through analyzing the most diverse types of information available on a village of transatlantic migrants, gathering my data in both the donor village and in the host communities. Oral testimonies form the very backbone of my research. The information obtained in this way I intend to collate with whatever written information is available on both sides of the Atlantic. In Hungary, for instance, these will include the church registers and land registers already mentioned, as well as passport lists; in the United States, passenger lists, census manuscripts, church records, and property lists will need to be studied. A comparison of the data available from the two sources—oral and written—will, hopefully, give a good indication of how far these immigrants' itinerant laborer status affected their figuring in the above types of American records.

The effectiveness of the approach would be greatly enhanced through more systematic cooperation among researchers of the topic on both sides of the Atlantic, if, for instance, coordinated studies were to be conducted seeking answers to analogous questions. Although we are in the eleventh hour, there is still time to tap the sources of oral history available on the issue of migration. They are hardly sources that we can afford to waste.

Notes

1. See Imre Barcza: A magyarországi kivándorlások irodalma (A bibliography of emigration from Hungary), Budapest, 1908.

2. The subject of the emigration from Hungary is barely touched on in a page and a half of volume 5 of Hóman B.-Szegfü Gy.: Magyar történet (Hungarian history) in a chapter entitled "Népi erők pusztulása" (Decay of the people).

3. See Frantisek Bielik, ed.: Slováci Vo Svete, Bratislava, 1980; Frantisek Bielik-Elo Rákos: Slovenske Vystahovalectvo, Dokumentary I. Bratislava, 1969; Celina Bobinska-Andrzej Pilch, eds.: Employment-Seeking Emigrations of the Poles World Wide in the 19th and 20th Centuries, Krakow, 1975; Andrzej Brozek: Polonia Amerykanska, 1854–1938, Warszawa, 1977; Hans Chmelar: Hóhepunkte der österreichischen Auswanderung: Die Auswanderung aus den im Reichsrat vertretenen Königsreichen und Ländern in den Jahren, 1905–1914, Wien, 1974;

Ivan Cizmic: Jugoslavenski Iseljenicki Pokret u SAD i Stravanje Jugoslavenske Drzavo 1918, Zagreb, 1974; Julianna Puskás: Emigration from Hungary to the United States before 1914, Studia Historica Academiae Scientiarum Hungaricae, Bp. 1975; Julianna Puskás: Kivándorló magyarok az Egyesült Államokban, 1880–1940 (Emigrant Hungarians in the United States 1880–1940), Budapest, 1982; Julianna Puskás: From Hungary to the United States (1880–1914), Budapest, 1982; István Rácz: A paraszti emigráció és politikai megítélése Magyarországon 1849–1914 (Peasant migration and its political assessment in Hungary, 1849–1914), Budapest 1980; István Rácz: A parasztok elvándorlása a faluról (The migration of the peasants away from the villages), in, István Szabó, ed., A parasztság Magyarországon a kapitalizmus korában, 1848–1914 (The peasantry in Hungary during the age of capitalism, 1848–1914), vols. 1–2, Budapest, 1965.

4. The United States immigration offices listed the arrivals by ethnic groups only from 1899 on. For criticisms of the shortcomings of statistical sources, see the works listed in note 3.

Official registration of the emigrants in Hungary started in 1899. The Central Statistical Office data for 1899–1913 provide source material impressive by any standard. See: A magyar szent korona országainak kivándorlása és visszavándorlása 1899–1913 (Emigration and remigration in the countries of the Hungarian Sacred Crown) (Magyar Statisztikai Központi Hivatal, Magyar Statisztikai Közlemények, New series 67 = MSK vol. 67).

5. For details of the trends see: Julianna Puskás: From Hungary to the United States (1880–1914), Budapest, 1982, pp. 20–25.

6. American immigration authorities started to register remigrants in 1908. These sources show 584,344 immigrants from Hungary for the period between 1908 and 1913, and 221,596 remigrants, i.e., 37.9% of the immigrants returned to their homeland. Hungarian sources, less exact, show a 32.9% rate of return for the same period.

7. See the statistical sources in Julianna Puskás: Kivándorló magyarok az Egyesült Államokban, 1880–1940, Budapest, 1982, p. 77.

8. Of that number, 17.8% said they were going to join "friends"; only 2.2% said they had "neither family nor friends" in the United States. For the data, see MSK vol. 67: table 48, p. 57.

9. Annual Report, 1899–1913, in Ferenczi-Willcox: International Migrations, I, New York, 1929, Table 13, pp. 460–70; and MSK vol. 67, table 46, p. 56.

10. Cf. the works in note 3.

11. MSK vol. 67 contains a county-by-county breakdown of the emigrants by nationality, age, and sex, thus providing data for regional analysis.

12. For details, see the chapter: "The emigration regions" in J. Puskás: From Hungary to the United States (1880–1914), Budapest, 1982, pp. 56–63.

13. See Imre Katona: Atmeneti bérformák (Transitional wage forms) and Zoltán Sárközi: A summások (Seasonal workers) In: I. Szabó (1965), vol. 2, pp. 382–406 and 321–71.

14. In MSK vol. 67, p. 26, we read the following: "The Germans belong among the more educated and most prosperous inhabitants of the country, and are usually tied to their settlements by long-standing traditions; their propensity for urban life, their employment in trade and industry, and, where they farm, their more highly developed farm technology all would be reasons for them to be least

affected by the swelling waves of emigration." See J. Puskás: From Hungary to the United States (1982), p. 32.

15. See the maps in H. Runblom-H. Norman, eds.: From Sweden to America: A History of Emigration, Minneapolis-Uppsala, 1976; Reno Kerö: Migration from Finland to North America in the Years between the United States Civil War and the First World War, Turku, 1974; and Celina Bobinska (1975).

16. For the Hungarian immigrants to Canada, see: N. F. Dreisziger, ed.: Struggle and Hope: The Hungarian-Canadian Experience. Toronto, 1982.

17. See J. Puskás: Kivándorló magyarok az Egyesült Államokban, 1880–1940 (1982), pp. 164–81.

18. See the state-by-state distribution of Magyars, Croats, Slovaks, and Romanians in the 1910 census.

19. Compiled from the American statistical data in Ferenczi–Willcox (1929).

20. The Protestant parishes in Pittsburgh, Pa., East Chicago, Ill., Cleveland, Ohio, Bridgeport, Conn., and New Brunswick, N.J.

21. See, e.g., Bo Kronborg, Thomas Nilsson, and Andres A. Svalestuen, Nordic Population Mobility: Comparative Studies of Selected Parishes in the Nordic Countries, 1850–1900. American Studies on Scandinavia, vol. 9, nos. 1–2, Oslo-Bergen-Tromso, 1977.

22. The village Sz. had a population of 2,625 in 1900; it is more than 50 km from the nearest industrial center.

23. J. Puskás: Magyarok az Egyesült Államokban és Kanadában—interjuk (Hungarians in the United States and Canada—interviews). Tapes are in the manuscript archives of the Institute of Historical Research of the Hungarian Academy of Sciences.

13

Emigration from Yugoslavia prior to World War II

Ivan Čizmić

It is commonly said that the United States is a nation of immigrants. However, speaking of the Yugoslavs one can say that they are the nation of emigrants. Their emigration had already begun in the fifteenth century and, with smaller or greater intensity, depending on the period of time, continues to this day. That emigration achieved mass proportions with the Turkish occupation of the Slavic lands. And as a result thousands upon thousands of people saved their lives by settling in the neighboring lands and thus avoided the Turkish oppression. This emigration from the Turkish-held territories lasted from the fifteenth to the eighteenth centuries.

While this first mass emigration was caused by the Turkish wars, the latter emigration was mostly due to the new economic, political, and social conditions in their Slavic homeland. Because of those social and economic changes, especially the abolishment of serfdom during the first half of the nineteenth century, the peasant ceased to be bound to his land and could freely dispose of his private property. The decline of the village communes *(zadruga)*, the former commonly occupied estates, was responsible for the dwindling of land into small plots. Thus, farms with small or scattered land increased, but the structure of agriculture remained unchanged. In addition, capitalistic forms of production increased as well, stimulating the sales and purchase cycle as a result of which some people became rich at the expense of others. Although the acreage of the farms grew smaller, social differences grew larger, and life became more difficult. The penetration of modern capital into the village structure overburdened the peasants with loans, pauperizing them and turning many of them into proletarians. Under such conditions, working one's own land became the safest occupation. However, the process of further subdividing land into small parcels continued. The father's estate was being divided among all his sons and, as a rule, his unmarried daughters. Such a system of inheritance produced the extremely unprofitable diminution and parceling of the land so that it could no longer feed the entire household. Moreover, the backward and underdeveloped cities with their weak industries were unable to provide employment on any large scale. The rapid average growth of population was not accompanied by adequate industrial growth, and because of this the forces of production remained idle. This created a surplus of agricultural population that inevitably forced them to leave their crowded land. The uncertain political conditions existing in the South Slavic lands in the second half of the nineteenth and beginning of the twentieth centuries also contributed to the creation of greater economic difficulties. Thus, the unsolved economic, social, and political problems represented the general reasons for the mass emigration during the period of modern colonialization.

Poor economic conditions in the second half of the nineteenth century were the main reason for emigration. The years of poor harvest with their food shortages, overdue loans of the population, and in the maritime provinces the decline of sailing ships, fishing, and wine-making industries in addition to the economic and political negligence of that region triggered mass emigration.

In spite of its economic nature, that emigration was also political. The Croatian politician S. Radić, in his book *Moderna Kolonizacja i Slaveni* (Modern Colonization and the Slavs) points out that the reason for emigration is "that somewhere in the world there is more good and justice."[1] Politicians from the ranks of Social Democrats insisted on giving the reasons for emigration in political and class terms and maintained that the emigration of workers cannot be divorced from the essence of capitalism in the same vein as worker's unemployment, overproduction, and consumption below human needs.[2]

Among the reasons for emigration one should also add the efforts of young men to avoid military duty as well as the tradition of "emigration for the sake of emigration," even when there were not any particular personal reasons. There were also reasons for emigration that acted independently, outside the Yugoslav territory. The rapid industrial growth of certain countries, especially the United States, constantly attracted a new working force from the underdeveloped countries. In connection with that I must single out the activity of countless agents of steam companies and industrial companies who convinced many people to emigrate.

The large number of emigrants (about 700,000) who left the South Slavic lands prior to World War II and the alarming consequences that followed forced almost all the important social and political circles to reflect upon emigration.[3] Since the end of the past century the press has continuously warned against the reasons and results of emigration. The journal *Dom* (The Home), published in Zagreb, wrote in 1902: "What is happening to the Croatian nation today is not just emigration; this is its decay, its disembarkment. Almost everyone runs away from here . . ."[4] The Zadar-based *Narodni List* (The National Gazette) commented: "From the economic and political point of view emigration presents a loss for the future development of Croatian life and should it continue in its present direction and numbers it will bring about the suicide of our nation."[5] In addition, the newspapers of South Slavic emigrants in the respective countries of their residence whose editors had experienced in person the misery of immigration, pointed out the negative outcomes of immigration for the Croatian national interests. Thus, the weekly *Zajedničar* (The Fraternalist), published in Pittsburgh, remarked in 1911 that "The emigration from Croatian lands to America during the last ten years was of such great proportions that it could become the chief danger for the survival of our nation."[6]

Our civic leaders began even more often to express their concern for the excessive emigration. Accordingly, in 1903, Tadija Smičiklas, president of the Yugoslav Academy in Zagreb, stated: "Croatia has been so economically neglected because the best part of our nation emigrated, chiefly to America. If we continue in the same direction Croatia will have to perish. Labor force goes overseas, and at home only old men, women, and children are left."[7] The poet Antun C. Matoš warned in 1911 that "the emigration to America is our most acute problem today. It is our social, political and even moral problem. Our folk, the local people, blindly rush to America, and their empty native homeland is slowly but surely being taken over by the foreigners. This is a terrible fact, the most timely and tragic issue which our sociologists, politicians, and moralists powerlessly face today."[8] The parson of the Croatian church in Kansas City, Fr. M. D. Krmpotić, addressed a letter in 1907 to the Sabor (Diet) in Zagreb in which he described in detail the condition of the Croats in the United

States. He demanded the prohibition of emigration. He also quoted certain Americans who said: "We are depopulating some countries of Southern Europe, it is not right."[9]

Politicians, most of all those from the opposition, have frequently singled out the question of emigration as one of the most important problems in the life of the South Slavs. They have done so in the Croatian Sabor, in the Diet in Budapest, and in the Imperial Council in Vienna.

Nevertheless, it is necessary to stress that in spite of those negative reactions on emigration, there were also those that expressed the positive side of emigration. Fran Milobar, the Croatian economist of the beginning of this century, saw profits coming from emigration. In his book *Izabrana poslavlja iz narodnog gospodarstava* (Selected Chapters from National Economy) he said: "This is from the standpoint of national economy the most desirable kind of emigration, because it balances the relationship between the number of population and the means of obtaining a living. The population surplus not only can feed itself in the foreign world, but it also brings a portion of its wages home and raises incomes in their native region. This way the people can live without social difficulties even in those lands which are overcrowded. And in the regions where overpopulation does not exist the people can accumulate enough capital to manage their economy." Milobar had also seen the negative aspects of emigration, especially as far as the South Slavic nations were concerned, and he said in the same source: "However, the small nations, no matter how crowded in their land, should make efforts so that their emigrants are not lost at least in the national or ethnical sense. The small nations, particularly areas which are not overpopulated, would commit suicide by allowing their people to emigrate on such a scale. Cautious and patriotic governments will make every effort that such emigration never takes place."[10]

Emigration from the South Slavic lands prior to World War I possessed certain specific features. Thus, there was a very small percent of returning emigrants in comparison with those who emigrated. At that time in Croatia only about five thousand emigrants a year came back, but about forty thousand left their country.[11]

According to the existing statistics, over 86 percent of all emigrants were rural people. Of the urban population only occasional requests for emigration were made by a merchant or artisan apprentice.

It follows from the information available on the age profile of emigrants that they came from the best age and employment groups. Their absence had a very negative effect on the local economy.[12]

The emigrants were mostly males. Initially there was very little female emigration. Emigration of entire families was even more rare. This confirms that emigration was temporary, for the sake of employment. In the years preceding World War I the number of women applying for emigration to join their husbands or to marry increased. The number of emigrating females in 1901 was 10 percent, but in 1912 it reached 30 percent.

The division of families had strong sociological repercussions. Many years of absence of the male members of the family, and especially that of the father, meant a significant change for the rural household, causing a difficult and irreparable situation. To illustrate this point I will quote just one report of the administration of the Karlovac County to the government in Zagreb; it states:

> The negative side of emigration indicates that the husbands who settle in America forget their family left at home and leave them at the mercy of other people. The husband leaves his wife and a number of children and frequently they do not maintain any ties for several years. Subsequently, they lose their households, the wife becomes unfaithful and has love affairs with other men. The husband, having returned after a long time spent in America, finds his farm in miserable condition and develops a bad relationship with his wife.[13]

Public opinion of the South Slavic countries of that period was dissatisfied with mass emigration and demanded a means to prevent it. Hence there was talk about the necessity of a wide campaign that would explain to the people the advantages of working in their own country. This turned attention to the vast spaces of uncultivated land that could be settled by our Slavic people, instead of going to foreign countries. There was also a project to establish a patriotic association that would purchase agricultural land and sell it to the peasant at the cheapest prices and most convenient rates. The endurance and diligence shown by our emigrants in American mines, factories, and on railroad construction was stressed, and comments were made that, if our people worked like that in their own native country, in a few years they would get equally as rich as in America. This work would increase the quality and value of the peasant's land, and he could work for himself instead of enriching the already rich foreign world.

But in spite of all this, and with some exceptions, the emigration steadily increased. The factors that could limit the emigration were out of the reach of the South Slavic countries. These were the restrictive regulations that the United States government periodically adopted as well as the economic crises that from time to time occurred in America. The Austro-Hungarian authorities did not prevent emigration, and they only wanted to keep it under control. Before World War I the military draftees were not allowed to emigrate.

If there were no restrictive immigration laws and temporary crises in the United States, and if Austria-Hungary did not prevent emigration before World War I, emigration would continue to progress. What would be the consequence of that? Until that time about half a million people had emigrated from Croatia and in 1910 Croatia had a population of 3,500,000.

Even after World War I the emigration from Yugoslavia did not stop completely. This process continued although with a lower average of 18,000 people annually, because at that time the countries of immigration began most energetically, one after another, to limit the flow of emigration. Because of this and because of the economic depression and unemployment in the countries accepting immigrants, the number of emigrants from Yugoslavia declined so that in the 1930s there were only a few persons emigrating and those were going to join their families or relatives. Between the two wars, according to official statistics, 190,000 people left Yugoslavia, while 87,000 came back.[14]

Because of these reasons the emigrant question in Yugoslavia between the two wars was qualitatively different from that of Austria-Hungary. For the new government the emigrant question was not as important as the problem of straightening out its relations with the emigrants. Therefore, already in the first postwar years the issue of the return of the emigrants was raised. However, at that time the prevailing opinion was that the emigrants should not be encouraged to return. Obviously, in the unstable conditions of this early postwar period no one wanted to risk employing the emigrants. But besides that, the problem of the return of the emigrants was becoming increasingly acute for Yugoslavia's emigration policy. The world economic depression, especially in the overseas countries, was beginning to be felt. It was evident that unemployment would first affect the foreign workers and this would be reflected in spending and savings patterns. As a result the emigrants began to express a spontaneous desire to return to their native land with their remaining savings.

The inability of Yugoslav industry to employ large numbers of returning emigrants, the rapidly spreading economic depression, and the fact that emigrants quickly spent their savings, so that they did not have money to pay travel expenses home was partly responsible for the fact that the greatest part of Yugoslav emigrants never returned. Besides the economic reasons I should mention also those of a political nature that discouraged them from returning, such as national and class oppression that occurred in Yugoslavia between the two world wars.

We have always treated the decision of our people to stay in their new homeland as a tragedy because we were convinced that they were so-called temporary emigrants. The fact is that South Slavic emigration was not the same as emigration in Western European and in the Scandinavian countries. The people who emigrated from those countries represented surplus population, mostly working class, who could not be employed by domestic industry. They also emigrated with the idea that they would never return and would have to build their future in the adopted homeland. Peasants also emigrated from those countries with the same idea after having sold all their possessions and settled in large groups in preselected areas.

For nations in Northern and Western Europe the emigration question was very simple; the emigrants solved their biggest problem, finding a home in the new lands, and by choice or by birth, they became the citizens of their new homeland.

South Slavic emigrants, however, Slavic emigrants in general, as well as a small number of Czechs, Italians and Iberian emigrants, belong to another category of emigrants. Emigration here consists mostly of peasants from areas that are not overly-populated, who emigrate for the reasons that only in a small number of cases, force people to become permanent emigrants.

Only a small number of the South Slavic emigrants left their homes with the intention of remaining abroad. As we have seen, however, conditions beyond their control forced them to stay there permanently. And this was one of the reasons why public opinion reacted so unfavorably against mass emigration. Another reason was the fact that with the passage of time it had become more evident that the emigrant children were forgetting their native language and undergoing the unavoidable process of assimilation. This, as the final consequence, led to the loss of their national identity.

The journal *Dom* as early as 1902 wrote the following:

> Each of us leaves home as a Croat and in a distant foreign land thinks of the old home and family, and many wish to return. But aren't you wrong? When the man feels well in the foreign land, when he makes acquaintances and finds friends there, especially when he is married and builds his new home he asks about the old home no more. There are many Croats Slovenians in America, even rich ones, who don't care about their old home. They are already lost, "fallen into the melting pot"—but they do not see or feel it. They used to be our people but they are no more. We are the only ones who feel it: it hurts us, but they are fine. It is like when one cuts off his finger; it hurts the man but that cut-off finger is only a dead piece of flesh. It does not feel any pain . . .[15]

The publicist and politician A. Tresić-Pavičić, who in 1906 had visited the Croatian settlements in the United States, called the Croatian-Americans his lost brothers.[16] The writer M. Krleža wrote:

Emigration to America is ever-increasing and everyday it is more like a
threatening nightmare . . . Tens of thousands travel over the ocean, where in
a second generation they will become alienated and cease to be members of
our nation . . .[17]

The fact that hundreds of thousands of Yugoslav emigrants did not
come back home but stayed permanently in their new homeland convinced many individuals in Yugoslavia, during the time between the two
wars, of the need to take a broader and more flexible attitude toward the
phenomenon of assimilation. Assimilation was then discussed as the principle question. Should the emigrants assimilate or the conditions for their
return be created? Those who were against assimilation maintained that
the emigrants must lead a "double life," and frequently an example of the
Francophone Canadians was used. A more tolerant stand was taken toward naturalization. The Savez organizacija isljenika (The League of Emigrant Organizations), the institution that operated in Zagreb,
recommended the greatest possible number of emigrants take the citizenship of the country of their residence, because citizenship is only a
legal question. Through it the emigrants will achieve the same legal
equality of position and treatment as the rest of the citizens of a given
country. The president of that organization, M. Marjanović, was convinced that the emigrants, or it is better to say immigrants, should grow
accustomed to their new environment, but their old homeland should
maintain such ties with them that they and their descendants would
remain attached to their mother nation and work for the benefit of their old
fatherland.[18]

Proposals were made, such as the so-called rotating emigration, to
slow down the process of assimilation. According to this method, when
some people leave, others must come back. This would stop the process of
assimilation in the emigrant settlements. Meanwhile, there were also
individuals in Yugoslavia who were in favor of total assimilation. Why
should the emigrants, for reasons of false pride or fiction, make their life
more difficult in their new homeland? If they cannot maintain their
nationality, let them assimilate as fast as they can.[19]

Of course, all those debates that were conducted in Yugoslavia in the
1930s had more academic than practical significance and did not exercise
any influence on the real effects of assimilation in the countries of residence of the Yugoslav emigrants. Public opinion was informed of this
matter quite successfully in the article by I. Lupis-Vukić entitled "Sto
utječe na odnarodjivanje Hrvata u Americi? (What Influences the Denationalization of the Croats in America?). He immediately pointed out that
the term that we use—*denationalization*—is used in the United States as

Americanization or assimilation. This only concerns those immigrants who want to stay permanently in America. Those who wish to return home are as much ours as we who stayed in our native land. Immigrants' children, according to Lupis, are Americans. However, he literally says: "But there is another relationship which we should maintain and preserve even in the distant future among us and our descendants in America, the relationship which is called an intelligent conscience about the stem from which our American descendants arrived."[20]

Economic issues occupy an important place in our emigration policy. I have already mentioned which economic factors caused the emigration from the South Slavic lands. The question arises as to how much economic profit we have derived from our emigrants. H. Sirovatka in 1907 calculated that on the average every Yugoslav immigrant in the United States saves about five hundred dollars after three years of work. Sirovatka's conclusion was: "Don't think of America all you who are needed for work at your farm. Only if you have a surplus of workers will it pay for one or two to seek employment there."[21] Nevertheless, I would like to point out that the purchasing power of the U.S. dollar was at that time two and one-half times greater in Austria-Hungary than in the United States. Even later the situation in Yugoslavia was similar. And Benko-Grado calculated that the real daily wage in the Anglo-Saxon nations was 44 percent higher than in Yugoslavia.[22]

The positive influence of emigration on the economic development of the South Slavic lands was observed from the beginning. This was because of emigrant earnings which were sent home. Until the First World War the South Slavic emigrants sent $334 million. The importance of this sum can best be understood in relation to Yugoslavia's foreign loans.[23] The total amount of those loans was $32 million less than the inflow of the emigrant money. It is well known how the foreign loans covered the steadily growing passive balance of payments in Yugoslavia which amounted to $114,200,000.[24] For that reason alone it is necessary to underline the important role of the emigrant remittances in keeping up the value of the dinar. Even after the expiration of the loans emigrant remittances were an important source of foreign currency in the country.

The remittances used to come into Yugoslavia in the form of American bank checks or in postal savings accounts or they were carried by the Yugoslavs returning from abroad. Although we do not have reliable information about how this money was spent, it is quite certain that most of it was invested in private estates. It has been noted that the price of land and of houses rose because of the increased demand from the emigrants. Unfortunately, there was no organized influx of emigrant capital or investment in larger enterprises despite the existence of such possibilities at the time. It is a pity that such opportunities were missed. The money was not even invested in the regions from which the emigrants came, and this was one of the reasons why it was difficult to transfer immigrant capital to the Old Country.

From the previous discussion we have seen that emigrant remittances helped to maintain the value of the Yugoslav currency and increased and strengthened the country's capital. The remittances helped to offset the balance of payments deficit. Even the war reparations, after World War I, lagged behind them. Naturally, the influx of emigrant money, especially as far as the capital investments and savings of those emigrants who stayed abroad are concerned, could have been much greater. This would have benefited not only the emigrants themselves but also the Yugoslav economy. However, no adequate measures were undertaken to that end in our country.

Emigrants also had an indirect influence on the economic development of Yugoslavia. After their return they raised the living standards of their fellow countrymen, and had an impact on the improvement of domestic production. The government was also relieved of some of its obligations as the depressed areas were supported by money sent back by the emigrants. Thus, the government was able to use these funds for other purposes.

Thus the emigrant contribution to the economic growth of Yugoslavia can be summarized under three headings: (1) the influence of the emigrant remittances on the balance of payments, (2) the role of emigrant savings in the growth of national capital and wealth, and (3) the role of emigrants in the rise in the standard of living throughout the entire nation as well as their economic aid to the depressed areas.

It is very likely that hundreds of thousands of emigrants, had they stayed on their land, would have contributed to the growth of the economy. However, given the economic and political conditions of the time in Austria-Hungary and later in Yugoslavia, they made an even greater contribution by emigrating. From the human capital point of view, however, it was a loss. It was precisely this factor that began to worry our people during the period between the two wars. It became clear that emigration could not be looked upon only from an economic point of view, but demanded a more comprehensive perspective. The issue had a wider significance, especially in view of the fact that a large number of Yugoslav emigrants and their descendants lived outside Yugoslavia. In addition, there was a continuous tendency to emigrate from our poorest regions. Some people proposed at the time to establish a Ministry of Emigration, dedicated to the solution of this difficult problem. It would put to an end the flow of emigration. M. Bartulica believed that this could be best achieved in the following manner: emigration was to be regulated and files were to be maintained in the home country, especially in the poorer regions. It was important to understand why people wanted to settle in unknown foreign countries. It was the responsibility of the state to initiate a program of economic development for the depressed areas, which otherwise would become completely deserted due to emigration. Even if emigration from some area was unavoidable internal colonization measures should be tried, as in Yugoslavia in the 1930s there was plenty of land to accommodate surplus population. Internal colonization could prevent further emigration. A better industrial policy could also stop emigration and, thus, suitable industries should be built in the densely populated regions. Emigration could be accepted as a lesser evil only when it was impossible to find a solution within the existing economic framework. In such a case, however, emigration policy should take care of each emigrant.[25]

It is obvious that the relationship between the emigrant and his native country involves many complex questions of an administrative, economic, and cultural nature. In Austria-Hungary the state administration was forced to create a special emigration service. In Croatia this service began in 1883, when it was decided that emigration was to be controlled by the police. The government in Zagreb adopted a rule in 1901 that regulated "the shipping of persons of working and peasant status to the overseas countries." At the end of 1905 the Emigrant Fund was established in Zagreb. In 1909 the laws regulating a number of problems connected with emigration from Croatia were enacted.[26]

In 1910 the Sabor passed an emigration law. For the first time a definition of an emigrant was offered. According to this law "an emigrant is one who goes abroad for an unspecific period of time and finds a steady occupation."[27]

Yugoslavia between the two wars also had its emigrant service. A law concerning emigration was passed in 1921. The law gave a detailed description of the state organs responsible for the emigration problems and the administration of all emigration and immigration units. The law defined the word *emigrant* as follows: "According to this law the emigrant is that citizen of the Kingdom of Serbia, Croatia, and Slovenia who emigrates for the sake of manual employment or who emigrates to his relatives who emigrated earlier under the same conditions."[28]

This brief summary of emigration service in Yugoslavia concludes this essay. I would be most gratified if this presentation leaves you with an understanding of how deeply the problem of emigration penetrated the fabric of our society. Finally, I would like to emphasize that, no matter how complex and real the problem of immigration has been for the United States, this problem also was and is important for the Yugoslav nation, especially in view of the fact that emigration from Yugoslavia did not stop even after World War II and continues up to this day.

Notes

1. Radić, Stjepan, *Moderna kolonizacija i Slaveni* (Modern Colonization and the Slavs), Zagreb, 1904, p. 337.

2. *Slobodna riječ* (The Free Word), Zagreb, August 30, 1907, No. 38.

3. For the number of those who emigrated see Josip Lakatoš, *Narodna statistika* (National Statistics), Zagreb, 1914, p. 64, Milan Jevetič, *Za čast američkog Srpstva* (For the Honor of American Serbdom), New York, 1918, p. 5, and Ferdo Gastrin and Vasilij Melik, *Slovernačka isterija*, 1813–1914 (Slovenian History: 1813–1914), Belgrade, 1951, p. 131.

4. *Dom* (The Home), March 27, 1902, No. 6.

5. *Narodni list* (The National Gazette), July 16, 1904, No. 57.

6. *Zajedničar* (The Fraternalist), Pittsburgh, Pa., February 9, 1910, No. 5.

7. *Dom*, May 28, 1903, No. 10.

8. *Hrvatski glas* (The Croatian Voice), Winnipeg, Christmas issue of 1960.

9. *Archiv Hrvatske, Spisi Sabora* (Archives of Croatia, the Sabor Reports), No. 1069/1906–1911.

10. Milibar, Fran, *Izabrana poglavlja iz narodnog gospodarstva* (Selected Chapters from National Economy), Zagreb, 1902–1903, p. 238.

11. Naše iseljeničko pitanje (Our Emigration Question), Split, 1913, p. 21.

12. According to the age profile for 1900–1902 period, the emigrants under twenty years of age represented 25.8% of the total; those twenty to twenty-nine, 33.6%; thirty to thirty-nine, 24.3%; forty to forty-nine, 13.3%; and over fifty years of age, 3.0%. (Cf. Lakatoš, quotation 62.)

13. *Archiv grada Karlovca, Fond gradskog poglavarstva* (Archives of the City of Karlovac, Fund of the City Administration), Report of February 13, 1912.

14. Holjeva, Veceslav, *Hrvati izven domovine* (Croatians Outside Their Homeland), Zagreb, 1967, pp. 36–48.

15. *Dom*, March 27, 1902.

16. Tresić-Pavičić, A., *Preko Atlantika do Pacifika, Život Hrvata u Sjevernoj Americi* (Over the Atlantic to the Pacific: The Life of the Croatians in North America), Zagreb, 1907.

17. Krleža, Miroslav, "Odlomci romansirane biografije Frana Supila, o petogodišnjici smrti 1917–1967" (Fragments of the Fictionalized Biography of Fran Supil; On the Fiftieth Anniversary of His Death: 1917–1967), *Forum*, Zagreb, Nos. 5–6, 1967, p. 566.

18. *Iseljenička nedelja* (The Emigrant Week), Zagreb, 1933, p. 213.

19. Benko-Grado, Artur, "Naš migracioni problem u semi pro i contra" (Our Migration Question in a Pro and Contra Scheme), *Jutarnji List* (The Morning Gazette), October 10, 1933.

20. Lupis-Vukić, Ivan, "Sto utječe na odnarodivanje Hrvata u Americi (What Influences the Denationalization of the Croats in America)," *Kalendar "Hrvatski Radisa*, 1941, p. 51.

21. Sirovtka, Hinko, *"Kako je u Americi i komu se isplati onamo putovati?"* (How Is It in America and For Whom It Makes Sense to Travel?), Zagreb, 1907.

22. Dunda, J. N., *"Izgledi naših iseljeničkih uštednji* (Possibilities for Our Emigrants' Money Savings)," *Ekonomist* (The Economist), Zagreb, Nos. 11–12, 1904, p. 429.

23. ———, "Znacenje iseljenickih uctednji za našu placévnu bilansu" (The Significance of Emigrant Savings for Our Balance of Payments), *Ekonomist*, Nos. 4–5, 1940, p. 143.

24. Ibid., cf. quotation no. 149.

25. Bartulica, Milastislav, *Iseljenicka politica* (Emigration Policy), Zagreb, 1929.

26. For more on the emigration service in Yugoslavia, see A. Benko-Grado's "Razvitak naše državne iseljeničke službe" (The Development of Our State Emigration Service) in *Jutarnji list*, October 1939.

27. *Stenografski zapisnik Sabora* (Stenographic Records of the Croatian Diet), 1910–1915, Appendix 7.

28. *Iseljenički propisi* (Emigration Regulations), Zagreb, 1922, p. 37.

INSIDE THE TOWNS

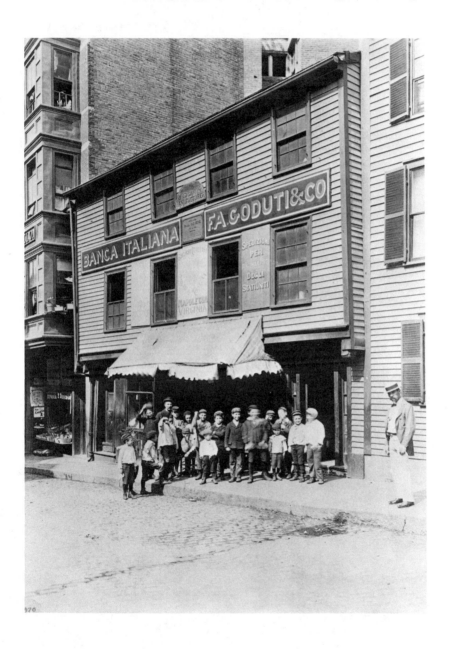

14

The Effects of Migration on the Demarcation of Industrial Areas

Jana Englová

The directions of the territorial movement of manpower resulting from economic developments at the end of the nineteenth century can be correctly determined by making a comparison of where members of the population were born and where they actually lived, provided these data came to light in censuses. In Austria this was the case beginning with the census of the year 1890. However, only a part of these results were published in *Oesterreichische Statistik*. Data on birthplace and place of residence gained from the census of the population of Austria carried out on 31 December 1900 were processed in greater detail as far as Bohemia was concerned by the Provincial Statistical Office of the Kingdom of Bohemia and published in the Reports of the Provincial Statistical Office of the Kingdom of Bohemia, volume 7, section 1, in 1905. These data are exceptionally interesting and provide a concrete picture of the movement of manpower that makes it possible to determine the direction of such movements and the main areas of their concentration.

In the census of 1900 only 51.3 percent of the inhabitants born in Bohemia (thus also in Austria) were counted in their native parishes. That

271

means that nearly half the population had moved from the parishes in which they were born. A further 19 percent of those born in Bohemia had moved from their native parish but remained in their native political district. Much more serious is the fact that nearly 30 percent had moved out of the district in which they were born (23 percent were in another district of Bohemia, 6.7 percent in parts of Austria other than Bohemia). The intensity of the internal movement of the population of Bohemia was greater than in Austria as a whole, where considerably more of the population, that is, 64.4 percent lived in their native parishes and only about one-fifth lived outside the political district in which they were born, that is, only 14.8 percent in another district of the same province and 6.1 percent in another province of Austria than their native one.

If we look a little more closely at the balance of movement within Bohemia, we can divide political districts into two basic groups. In the first are districts where outflow exceeds inflow of population and which thus have a passive migratory balance. (There are altogether 69 of these.) The second group consists of districts with an active migratory balance, where more inhabitants have moved in than have moved out (these number 26). Within these groups there is further differentiation according to the intensity of migration (see figure 14.1).

While there were various reasons for this internal movement of the population, the most prevalent were economic reasons. This fact comes to the fore when making comparisons as to the proportion of the agricultural population in districts with a passive and an active migration balance (see figure 14.2). It can be clearly seen that districts with a high rate of influx of population for the most part have a low proportion of people engaged in agriculture and vice versa. (Only two districts with an active balance of migration of the lowest category, that is, of up to 5 percent—have a more than 40 percent proportion of agricultural workers).

The highest balance of influx of population is possessed by two areas of Bohemia. Apart from *Prague and its surroundings*, these are *the districts of the North Bohemian brown coal basin:* Ústí nad Labem (Aussig), Teplice (Teplitz), Luchcov (Lux), Most (Brüx), and Chomutov (Komotau), which are important areas of population inflow. Four of these districts belong to the highest category of districts with an active migratory balance. At the same time they are districts that had only a small proportion of agricultural inhabitants (e.g., Teplice had only 7.5 percent, Most 12.9 percent, Ústí nad Labem 14.4 percent, Duchcov 15.6 percent and Chomutov 23 percent). The appeal of the Prague area and that of the North Bohemian brown coal basin can be judged on the basis of their balance of migration compared with other districts of Bohemia. In this way it is possible to reconstruct the main migratory currents toward these

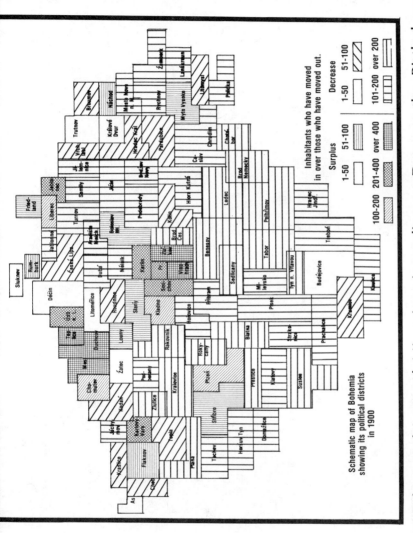

Figure 14.1: Balance of Internal Migration According to Data on the Birthplaces of the Population on 31 December 1900

273

Figure 14.2: Proportion of Agricultural Population in Individual Districts (on 31 December 1900)

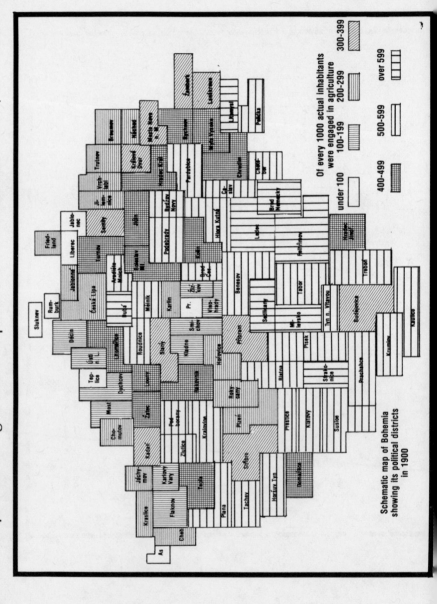

274

two areas, while the districts of the North Bohemian coal basin show a greater force of attraction, drawing the population of more distant districts toward the interior of Bohemia.

It is worth noting that the flow of population into this area from neighboring Saxony was only insignificant. In general, it can be said that more than one-third of the population of the five political districts of the North Bohemian brown coal fields had moved there from other districts (altogether 37.62 percent). There were nearly five times more of those who had moved into this industrial area from elsewhere than of those who were born there and then moved out.

For estimating the dynamism of internal movements of the population in certain periods of time, it is advantageous to compare data from two successive censuses and then work out the numerical differentiation. When comparing places of birth and places of residence between the years 1890 and 1900, internal migration is very evident. The increase in the power of attraction of the districts of the North Bohemian brown coal basin was greater than that of Prague and its surroundings even though this, too, had increased.

By combining the results of the active internal migration balance (on the basis of a comparison of data on where people were born and where they lived) with the falling proportion of the agricultural population, it is possible to achieve a standardization of the industrial areas of territory under investigation. Intensive internal migration currents in the period between the two censuses of the population make it possible to record the dynamic speed of the development of these principal industrial areas. On the territory of Bohemia and, if necessary, of other provinces of Austria, it is possible to do this for the closing decade of the nineteenth century.

15

Ulster Emigration to Philadelphia, 1847–1865: A Preliminary Analysis Using Passenger Lists

Deirdre Mageean

> With my bundle on my shoulder,
> Faith: there's no man could be bolder;
> I'm leavin' dear old Ireland without warnin',
> For I lately took the notion,
> For to cross the briny ocean,
> And I start for Philadelphia in the mornin'.

The port of Philadelphia featured prominently as a destination for eighteenth- and nineteenth-century emigrants from Ireland, particularly those departing through Ulster ports. Links between this part of Ireland and Philadelphia go back to the early eighteenth century when, after a lull at the beginning of the century, emigration from the north of Ireland resumed on a considerable scale about 1724, the destination being the Delaware River ports of Newcastle and Philadelphia and not the New England ports that had dominated hitherto. Dickson, in *The History of Ulster Emigration to Colonial America*, notes that in 1729 1,155 of the 1,708 immigrants who landed at Philadelphia were Irish, most of them being from the north.

The increasing popularity of Philadelphia was encouraged and strengthened by the trade links between the port and north of Ireland. Flax seed from America was imported for the linen trade, and in the early spring flax seed fleets from Philadelphia and New York arrived in the north Irish ports. Instead of returning empty the ships provided transport for those who desired to go to America, a pattern that continued into the early nineteenth century. Hence, an ironic link between emigration and the linen trade was formed—the flax seed ships provided the means of emigration. Conversely, the fluctuations in the linen trade were partly responsible for emigration from the north of Ireland. There were other reasons for the popularity of Philadelphia, the main two being (a) the availability of good land after all suitable land in New England had been occupied or granted; and (b) all Irish immigrants, regardless of religion, enjoyed the broad toleration granted by the 1701 Pennsylvania charter of privileges. The preeminence of Philadelphia over other American ports as the destination of north Irish emigrants is seen in table 15.1, which compares the number of emigrant vessels that were advertised to sail between 1750 and 1775.

Note the particularly strong connection with the port of Londonderry, one that was to continue well into the nineteenth century, establishing a "beaten path" with people emigrating to the same place as those who had gone before. "Philadelphia was the American port best known to Londonderry emigrants and so to Philadelphia the bulk of them went" (Dickson, 1976, p. 151).

Firmly established as one of the urban centers to which the Irish steadily came, Philadelphia had over 5,000 Irish-born living in the county by 1800.[1] The city was a growing industrial center and in the 1840s began a period of remarkable growth. The combined population of the county and city of Philadelphia rose from 258,037 in 1840 to 408,762 in 1850 and then to 565,529 in 1860.[2] With availability of jobs and cheap housing the city had comfortably accommodated a steady influx of immigrants. However, even in such an expanding city the arrival of the "famine Irish" had a considerable impact, introducing a ghetto system and increasing religious tensions. By 1850 there were 72,312 Irish-born in the county of Philadelphia, 18 percent of its total population, by 1860 there were 95,458 (17 percent) and in the city the Irish remained the largest foreign-born group until 1910.[3] The famine Irish, like their predecessors, were mainly from the north of Ireland. "The representation of Ulster names in Philadelphia was notable, as can be seen in McElroy's Philadelphia Directory for 1850–

Table 15.1
NORTH AMERICAN DESTINATION OF VESSELS SAILING FROM IRELAND 1750–1775

Port of Departure	N.S. & P.E.I.	Mass.	N.Y.	Pa.	Del.	Md.	Va.	N.C.	S.C.	Ga.
				Destination						
Belfast	2⅓	⅓	23¾	64¾	½	13	2½	6½	20⅚	6
Londonderry	9½	0	2½	99	0	2½	0	3½	10	½
Newry	¾	¾	23¼	42¾	1	6	0	2½	6½	⅓
Larne	1	0	20	18¼	2¾	3½	0	0	12	0
Portrush	0	3½	12¼	11½	2¼	0	0	½	0	0
Totals	13⁷⁄₁₂	4⁷⁄₁₂	81¾	236¼	6½	25	2½	13	49⅓	7
Percentage of whole	3.1	1.1	18.5	53.5	1.5	5.7	0.6	3.0	11.2	1.7

Note: Fractions indicate voyage shared with other ports in the table
Source: Dickson (1976), p. 225

65 . . . The immigrants came from both the north and the west of Ireland and were mostly young and single" (Clark, 1973, p. 34).

But what direct evidence do we have about these Ulster emigrants to Philadelphia? Who were they and how did they travel—alone or in groups? How were their passages arranged—by a prepayment system or in Ireland itself? Were there any changes in these features of migration between the peak famine years and the lower intensity migration of the 1850s and 60s?

The manifests of ships entering Philadelphia, although recorded from 1820 onward, do not give details on the area of origin within Ireland until the later half of the century. As with the other urban centers of Irish immigration, analysis of the immigrants has so far relied on data pertaining to the area of destination. Some sources that have survived permit considerable analysis of migrants from the northwest of Ireland, namely the papers of two major Londonderry shipping firms specializing in the passenger trade—J. & J. Cooke and W. McCorkell & Co. Their registers list some 40,000 passengers leaving the port of Londonderry for various destinations in America and Canada from 1847 to 1867. These lists give names, ages, and place of residence in Ireland, the name of the vessel and the date of sailing. Details are also given on how the passage money was paid—for instance, prepaid by agents or relatives in America, paid by poor-law union, estate owner, or by the individual himself—usually in installments to a local agent of the firm.

Londonderry was the major port for Irish emigration to America and Canada until the end of 1830, and continued as a major port for the passenger service until the end of the 1870s, serving the entire north-western region of Ireland. The firms of Cooke and McCorkell had strong connections, not only with the port of Philadelphia, but also with the Canadian ports of Quebec and St. John, New Brunswick, the latter borne out of the timber trade.

Figure 15.1 shows the total number of ships sailing in each year of the period 1847–1867 covered by the register. The hiatus in sailings to Philadelphia in the 1860s was mainly due to the disruption of the Civil War. In all, 46 of the 137 sailings (33.6 percent) were to Philadelphia and, as can be seen in figure 15.1, the temporal pattern of these sailings closely parallels that of total sailings. The number of ships going to Philadelphia thus paralleled the general trend in the migration flow that is characterized by two main features: the famine peak of 1847 and the large exodus it set in motion until the mid-1850s; and the gradual decline in numbers until the late 1860s. The critical years were 1846 and 1848. In both years the potato crop failed completely. The 1847 bookings were the largest ever made out of the port of Londonderry. After this immediate peak of 1847, the years following witnessed an unparalleled exodus: "people were departing, others were preparing to depart, and thousands more contemplating a similar move as soon as the opportunity presented itself" (Johnson, 1966, p. 52).

Figure 15.1: Ships from Londonderry to North America (shaded = to Philadelphia)

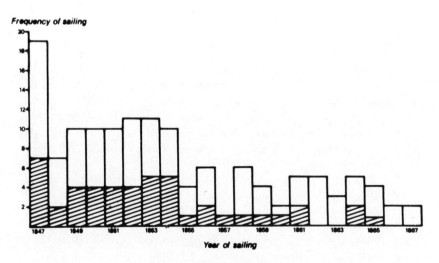

Source: Cooke Registers

From 1853 onward a certain measure of prosperity returned to the country, and both agriculture and commerce became more settled; consequently the migration flow gradually grew less. By the mid-1860s the sailing ships of the 'Derry firms were facing severe competition from the steamers operating from Liverpool. These faster and more efficient packets eventually killed the sailing ship trade by the end of the nineteenth century.

The present analysis examines a subset of these sailings, namely,

- the period 1847 to 1849—the immediate famine period; and
- the period 1858 to 1865 when the sailings had stabilized into a post-exodus pattern.

The Cooke registers provide information on thirteen ships in the first period and seven in the second, as summarized in table 15.2. There is some variation in the type of information available in the register; for instance, the early registers provide details on the ages of children under fourteen only, whereas from the mid-1850s onward all passenger ages are recorded. Only the later period provides information on the occupations of the passengers and this somewhat sporadically.

Information on age and occupation can be supplemented by that on the American manifests against which the ships' registers were checked. So the present analysis concentrates on information that is constant across both periods and directly extractable from the registers. Therefore, analysis of age and occupation shall not be dealt with in this essay.

Prepayment of Fares

Bookings with the 'Derry firms were made in two ways, either locally, or through agents in America. For their local bookings, the firms depended on their city offices and agents who were distributed widely through the surrounding districts and who were paid a commission on the number of passages they sold. Additionally, the firms relied considerably on passenger bookings from America and Canada made by Irish people who wished to bring out their friends and relatives. In 1827 McCorkell wrote to a friend in New York:

> The emigration from here to the States appears to be steady, we think with your assistance in New York that a number of passengers might be engaged to be sent out from here . . . The fact is that if fifty passengers are engaged in New York it is the means of ensuring whatever ship they are engaged for her complement of passengers. [Cooke, p. 115.]

The importance of prepaid bookings and American remittances as a factor in Irish emigration was very considerable. Several sources have quoted the large sums of money sent across the Atlantic to Ireland: Folde-Adams draws particular attention to the importance of prepaid passages for Ulster emigrants:

> At Londonderry, where the practice was oldest and most deeply rooted, ships were chartered for the sole purpose of taking out those whose passages had been pre-paid . . . This system was largely confined to the districts of extensive emigration. The evidence from the Poor Inquiry Commissioners is

Table 15.2

LONDONDERRY SHIPS TO PHILADELPHIA, 1847–49, 1858–65

Name of Ship	Number of Passengers	Date of Sailing
Superior	202	18.2.47
Herschell	101	8.3.47
Hartford	204	16.3.47
Montpellier	105	21.4.47
Alleghany	159	26.4.47
Mary Stewart	86	1.5.47
Barbara	128	10.5.47
Mary Campbell	154	1.3.48
Hannah Kerr	227	18.3.48
Envoy	186	23.2.49
Garland	119	28.3.49
Superior	219	5.5.49
Garland	93	27.7.49
Total 1847–49	1,983	
Elizabeth	190	Spring 58
Elizabeth	276	Spring 59
Elizabeth	299	Fall 60
Elizabeth	239	Spring 61
Elizabeth	323	Spring 64
Nubia	202	Fall 64
Huron	129	Spring 65
Total 1858–65	1,658	

Source: Registers of J. J. Cooke, Public Record Office of Northern Ireland, D 2893 (1)

far from complete, but it is at least suggestive that of the fifty-seven parishes reported as receiving aid for emigration from America, all but ten were in Ulster and the adjacent counties of Sligo and Longford, and in Cork. [Folde-Adams, 1932, p. 182.]

The 'Derry firms had at least three agents in Philadelphia, of whom details are known. All three were born in Ulster counties and, having emigrated to America, became successful merchants. They were all members of the Friendly Sons of St. Patrick of Philadelphia for the Relief of Emigrants from Ireland and over many years handled the American bookings for Cooke and McCorkell, responsible for bringing out passengers ranging from individuals to groups as large as ten or twelve.

Individual or Group Travel?

The methods of paying the passage across the Atlantic has implications for the form of migration, the numbers who could go and how they traveled, e.g., individually or in groups, particularly during times of crisis in the sending society. The general view expressed in the literature is that the postfamine migration was dominated by the movement of individuals, often in "chain migration." Less is written on the immediate famine period and even less on the prefamine period. Folde-Adams, referring to the period 1815–45, states that "the Irish preferred to emigrate in families when they could," but recent work has shown that the prefamine movement contained a surprisingly large number of young single people.[4]

Table 15.3 shows how, for the 'Derry samples, the number of individual bookings increased significantly between 1847 and 1865 whilst the number of group bookings decreased significantly in the same period. The term *bookings* applies to the sum of money payed to the firm or its agents for a ticket or tickets. These were classified according to whether the sum was for an individual, a family, nonkin traveling together, and so forth. Table 15.4 examines in more detail the number of people traveling on each booking. As expected from table 15.3, table 15.4 shows a significant increase in the number of individuals and a correspondingly significant decrease in the numbers traveling in groups. Interestingly, not only are there relatively more individuals traveling, but those who do travel together do so in smaller groups.

Mass migration in group units is a common feature of flight from disasters, and the data in table 15.4 support the view that

the famine movement swept away a whole section of society, rather than a mere aggregation of individuals; in fact . . . its basic unit was the family

. . .it was the family as a whole which was going, not the "surplus members." [McDonagh, 1956, pp. 328–29]

For the famine-Irish the question was not one of whether to go but how to find the means to go.

Paying for the Passage

One means of raising the passage money which was unique to Ulster was the practice whereby, as old leases expired, the tenants left the proceeds of the sale of their tenant-right. There was considerable evidence of sales of tenant-right during the famine period (McDonagh, 1956, p. 325). Another form that reached its height during the famine period was landlord-assisted migration and assisted pauper migration from the workhouses. Invariably, this form of migration was directed to the British colonies in Canada. It is noteworthy that the Cooke registers record this form of migration to Quebec and St. John, New Brunswick, only. Under the Poor Law Relief Acts of 1838 and 1847 the Poor Law Commissioners were empowered to levy an emigration rate in order to raise the funds to assist

Table 15.3

FORM OF BOOKINGS FROM DERRY

	Frequency of Individual Bookings	Frequency of Group Bookings	Total
1847–49	512 (56.4%)	395 (43.6%)	907
1858–65	867 (78.0%)	244 (22.0%)	1,111
	$\chi^2 = 106.6$	$P < 0.001$	

Source: Cooke Registers

Table 15.4

FREQUENCY OF PASSENGER TRAVEL—INDIVIDUAL AND GROUP

	Frequency of Passengers Traveling			Average Size of Group
	As Individuals	In Groups	Total	
1847–49	512 (25.8%)	1,471 (74.2%)	1,983	2.2
1858–65	867 (52.3%)	791 (47.7%)	1,658	1.5
	$\chi^2 = 266.84$	$P < 0.001$		

Source: Cooke Registers

the emigration of the destitute of the union. The 1847 act also gave facilities for assisting landlords who encouraged their destitute tenants to emigrate. Until 1849 the provisions of the act required that the destination of the emigrants should be to the Queen's Dominions. Even when this provision was waived the bulk of assisted migration was directed to Canada. Finally, there was assistance from those who had previously emigrated, either through prepaid passages or through remittances sent back. There is no form of evidence about the scale or extent of the postal remittances to Ulster, but there is information about the frequency of prepaid passages, and it was a well-established practice in this part of Ireland. Doubtless this is largely attributable to the duration and extent of previous emigration from Ulster. When disaster struck in 1846 the fruits of the previous emigration were the efforts made to help friends and relatives in Ireland to flee starvation and disease.

The effects of the famine on emigration lasted until 1854, after which the pattern settled down. Assisted pauper emigration decreased dramatically, and the form of migration changed from a flight by families to a more regular pattern of "betterment emigration" by individuals. One possible explanation for the shift in the form of migration is a change in the pattern of prepayment.

Table 15.5

FREQUENCY OF FARE TYPES

	Prepaid	Self-Paying	Total
1847–49	681 (34.3%)	1,302 (65.7%)	1,983
1858–65	499 (30.1%)	1,159 (69.9%)	1,658

$$\chi^2 = 7.24 \qquad P < 0.01$$

Source: Cooke Registers

Significantly more people paid their own passage in the later period 1858–65, and this is consistent with the idea that a great effort was made by those Irish in America to pull families out of Ireland during the famine crisis. Although the proportion of prepaid bookings remained remarkably similar over the two periods (31.9 percent compared to 31.77 percent) the number of people traveling as prepaid decreased significantly. This change in the number of people traveling as prepaid could be due either to a decrease in the prepayment for groups or individuals, or both. In fact, there was a distinct decrease in the average size of prepaid groups (figure 15.2). Theoretically such a decrease could arise because the size of groups/families available in the population "at risk" in Ireland had decreased through mortality or previous emigration. But this cannot be the case

Figure 15.2: Average Size of Prepaid Groups on Board
Ships Sailing from Ulster to Philadelphia Between 1847
and 1849 (top) and Between 1858 and 1865 (bottom).
The Two Distributions are Statistically Distinct
(Mann-Whitney U = 19, p 0.05)

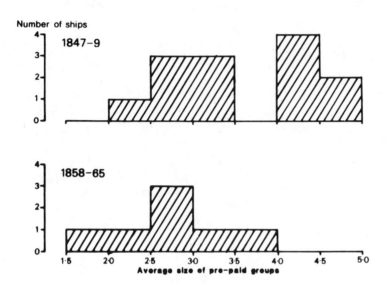

Source: Cooke Registers.

because the size of the self-paying groups remained constant over the
period, being an average of 3.7 in the early years, and an average of 3.5 in
the later years. Hence, the change depicted in figure 15.2 is uniquely
associated with the use of prepayment.

In the famine period significantly more nuclear families than expected
had their fares prepaid whilst in the 1858–1865 period many fewer nuclear
families than expected had their fares paid.

Conversely, couples (married couples without children and sibling
pairs) were significantly more frequent in the postfamine era. Thus, whilst
prepayment of passages was an important factor in both periods, the
mechanism responded according to the nature of the emigration causes.
Hence whole families were pulled out in the cataclysm of 1847–49 whereas
the post-exodus period of the late 1850s and 1860s witnessed the betterment migration of individuals and couples.

Table 15.6
PREPAID GROUPS

	Couples	One-parent Families	Nuclear Families	Total
1847–49	49	40	37	126
1858–65	53	23	8	84
Total	102	63	45	210

$\chi^2 = 15.66$ df $= 2$ P < 0.001

Source: Cooke Registers

Notes

1. Clark, D. (1973), *The Irish in Philadelphia*, Temple University Press, Philadelphia, p. 161.

2. Ibid., p. 31.

3. Ibid., p. 29.

4. Ó Grada, Cormac (1981) "Across the Briny Ocean: Irish Emigration to America 1800–1850." Paper presented to the Second Conference of Scottish and Irish Social and Economic Historians, Strathclyde.

Mageean, D. M. (1981) "Pre- and Post-Famine Migrant Families: Patterns and change." Paper presented at the Annual Meeting of the Social Science History Association, Nashville, Tennessee, 22–25 October.

References

Cooke, Sholto. 1961. *The Maiden City and the Western Ocean*, Morris & Co., Dublin.

Clark, Dennis. 1973. *The Irish in Philadelphia*, Temple University Press, Philadelphia.

Dickson, R. J. 1976. *Ulster Emigration to Colonial America, 1718–1775*. Ulster Historical Foundation, Belfast.

Folde-Adams, William. 1932. *Ireland and Irish Emigration to the New World from 1815 to the Famine*. Oxford University Press, Oxford.

McDonagh, Oliver. 1956. "Irish overseas emigration during the famine" in R. Dudley-Edwards and T. Desmond Williams. 1956. *The Great Famine*, Dublin.

16

The Formation of Chicago's
"Little Italies"
Rudolph J. Vecoli

Two decades ago Frank Thistlethwaite admonished us not to think of immigrants as "an undifferentiated, mass movement of 'peasants' or indeed 'artisans' thronging towards immigrant ports from vaguely conceived 'countries of origin' like 'Italy,' 'Germany,' or even 'Poland' or 'Ireland'." "Seen through a magnifying glass," he observed, "this undifferentiated mass surface breaks down into a honeycomb of innumerable particular cells, districts, villages, towns, each with an individual reaction or lack of it to the pull of migration."[1] Thistlethwaite's advice has been taken to heart and fruitfully applied in microstudies of immigrant origins. However, once the immigrants are safely transported across the Atlantic they appear to assume the uniform national identity that they lacked at the movement of embarkation. Our literature on ethnic groups is replete with generalizations about Irish Americans, Polish Americans, and Italian Americans as if these were homogeneous entities. In fact such labels often disguise at least as much as they reveal. To assume that a Swabian becomes a German, a Gorali a Pole, or a Calabrian an Italian through a sea change is as unjustified as to assume that they instantaneously become Americans upon landing.

If we are to advance the study of immigration beyond the level of facile generalizations, we need a series of microstudies that trace particular contingents of immigrants from their specific origins to their specific destinations. And we need to ask what bearing those specific origins and the characteristics associated with them had upon outcomes in terms of settlement, employment, politics, mobility, ethnicity, and assimilation. This study seeks to analyze the process of formation of Chicago's "Little Italies" in terms of such specific origins. Seen from this perspective the history of the Italians in Chicago becomes the sum of the collective histories of the dozens of village groups that comprised this migration.[2]

When the Italians arrived in Chicago in the 1880s they found a tough and raw, but fluid, urban environment. In the formation of their neighborhoods, the Italians did not conform to the neat model of the Chicago school of urban sociology. According to Robert E. Park and Ernest W. Burgess, the city could be conceived of as being divided by concentric rings in which land use was determined by the competition of business, industrial, and residential needs.[3] By analogy to natural ecology, this theory portrayed the city as an organic whole consisting of natural areas that existed in symbiotic relationship with each other. In the Parkian model, arriving immigrants established their area of first settlement in the central ring, adjacent to the downtown business district. As they assimilated socially and economically, they migrated outward to areas of second and third settlement. This intra-urban migration became a yardstick for measuring the rapidity and degree of assimilation. Such a deterministic model, however, does not allow for the influence of human agency, cultural preferences, and chance. All of these in my analysis had a great deal to do with the particular pattern of Italian settlement in Chicago.

Contrary to the concentric ring theory, the most important factor in shaping Chicago's cultural and industrial geography was the lakeshore and the Chicago River with its north and south branches. Providing means of water transport and waste disposal, the river banks became choice industrial locations. Consequently the river wards became the districts housing the immigrant workers who manned the city's factories, mills, and packinghouses. Meanwhile, the Loop emerged as the central business district at the mouth of the Chicago River. While the ethnic map of the city was shaped in part by this industrial ecology, it also reflected the distinctive histories and characters of the various immigrant groups.

Although the majority of the Italians did settle in the river wards, the imposition of the Parkian model ignores significant internal differences, such as time of arrival and Old World origins, that had a great deal to do with the siting of their neighborhoods. A large proportion of the Italians *initially* settled in outlying areas of the city and even the suburbs. For there was not *one* Little Italy in Chicago but at least sixteen discrete settlements, each with its own particular history, character, and reputation (fig. 16.1).

The Genoese (actually from the region of Liguria and not the city of Genoa) were the pioneers of the Italian immigration to Chicago. From the 1850s on they were conspicuous as fruit peddlers, confectioners, saloonkeepers, and restauranteurs. Living in rooms behind or above their stores, they clustered on the busy streets of the downtown district. A distinctive Genoese settlement developed on the Near North Side in the angle of the Chicago River and its north branch (A).[4] After the great fire of 1871, a general migration of Genoese to this area, which had escaped the conflagration, occurred. As they prospered, many built two- and three-story structures with business premises on the ground floor and living quarters above. By 1884, there were 455 Italians living in the district, and the number never increased much beyond a thousand. The neighborhood remained solidly Genoese, and was shunned by the southern Italians, who were not welcome. The first Italian church, the Church of the Assumption, was established here in 1881. Although frequented by Italians from other neighborhoods, it was always known as "*la chiesa degli Genovesi*" (the church of the Genoese).[5]

From the 1870s on, Chicago's role as the railroad labor market for the central and western United States drew increasing numbers of Italians, especially those from the southern regions. At any given time, the city's Italian population was composed to a large extent of these migrant laborers. Gradually permanent settlers ensconced themselves in emerging Italian neighborhoods. By 1900 practically all of Italy's regions were represented in Chicago, and the predominance of the *meridionali* was already pronounced. It would become increasingly so in the succeeding decades. Chicago's Italian-born population grew dramatically during a half century: from 552 in 1870 to 16,008 in 1900 to 59,215 in 1920. By the latter year, it was estimated that over 75 percent were from the *Mezzogiorno*.[6]

The province of Potenza in Basilicata sent a major contingent of its sons and daughters to Chicago. From the *paesi* of Trivigno, Corleto, and Calvello, but above all from Laurenzana, they began arriving in the 1870s. Settling south of the Loop in the midst of the city's vice district, they formed an early distinctive Italian settlement (B). Since the Dearborn Station, where the immigrant trains arrived, was nearby, the Italians called the area "Polk Depot." Others came from the province of Salerno in Campania, especially from the hilltowns of Senarchia, Oliveto Citra, Teggiano, and Ricigliano. This last paese was said to have lost half of its

Figure 16.1: Chicago's "Little Italies"

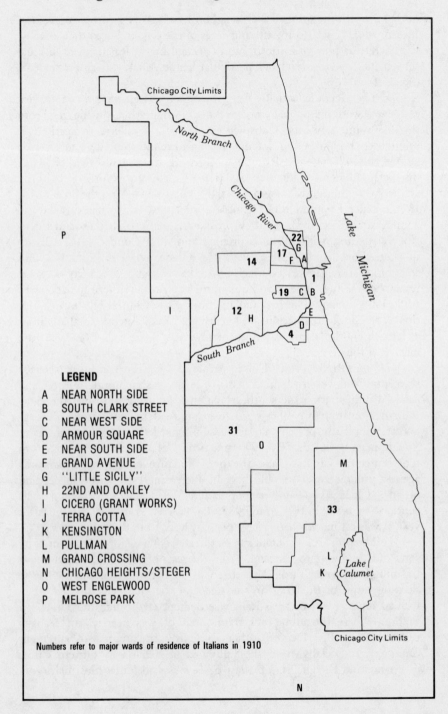

Chicago City Limits

North Branch

Chicago River

Lake Michigan

J

P

22

G

17

F

A

14

1

B

19

C

E

I

12

H

D

4

South Branch

LEGEND

A NEAR NORTH SIDE
B SOUTH CLARK STREET
C NEAR WEST SIDE
D ARMOUR SQUARE
E NEAR SOUTH SIDE
F GRAND AVENUE
G "LITTLE SICILY"
H 22ND AND OAKLEY
I CICERO (GRANT WORKS)
J TERRA COTTA
K KENSINGTON
L PULLMAN
M GRAND CROSSING
N CHICAGO HEIGHTS/STEGER
O WEST ENGLEWOOD
P MELROSE PARK

31

O

M

33

L

K

Lake Calumet

Chicago City Limits

Numbers refer to major wards of residence of Italians in 1910

N

population to emigration by 1890, the majority coming to Chicago. Meanwhile, from Calabria, immigrants from Cosenza and the nearby *paesi* of Rende, San Fili, and Fiumefreddo and from Nicastro and other villages in the province of Catanzaro augmented the growing colony. Others were arriving from Abruzzi-Molise, particularly from the provinces of Aquila and Campobasso. By the 1880s, the Polk Depot embodied the spectrum of the southern regions, but true to the spirit of *campanilismo*, the *paesani* clustered along the streets and alleys of the district. The Laurenzanesi preempted the more substantial buildings along South Clark Street, those from Ricigliano settled along Plymouth Court, those from Senarchia on Sherman, and so on. The Polk Depot settlement was a mother colony that spawned a number of other settlements. The conversion of the land to commercial purposes eventually drove the Italians elsewhere. However, this First Ward settlement, which became known as the "Dago district," was influential in shaping enduring prejudices against the Italians.[7]

As their numbers increased, the Italians expanded from the South Side westward across the Chicago River. Their coming, however, was violently opposed by the Irish, and it was only after many a bloody battle that they were able to establish a beachhead on the Near West Side. By the mid-1890s, however, they had advanced as far west as Halsted Street, which became the frontier between Irish and Italians for some years. In time this Near West Side settlement became by far the largest of the city's Italian colonies (C). In 1910, almost 25,000, approximately one-third of Chicago's Italians, resided in the Nineteenth Ward. This river ward contained some of the city's oldest and cheapest housing; it was also convenient to the Loop, where many Italians worked as peddlers and streetsweepers, and to the railroad depots, from which the labor gangs left the city.[8]

By 1900, this Little Italy extended from Polk Street on the north to Taylor Street on the south and Halsted and Canal Streets on the west and east. An Italian parish, the Church of the Guardian Angel, was established on Forquer Street in 1899, but by 1911 a new church, Our Lady of Pompeii, was built a mile further west for the Italians now living in the vicinity of Racine Avenue. The westward movement continued until by 1915 the more prosperous Italians had breached the exclusive neighborhood of Ashland Avenue. "Ascellando," as the Italians called it, became known as the Royal Italian Boulevard.[9]

This Near West Side colony was predominantly South Italian in character, drawing upon all the regions of the Mezzogiorno. As Father Edmund N. Dunne, the pastor of the Guardian Angel Church, commented: "The natives from Naples, Salerno, Bari, Basilicata, Abruzzi, Calabria, Catanzaro, le Marche, Lucca, Messina, and Palermo are as

plentiful as the English sparrow." Their neighbor Jane Addams observed
that the *contadini* sought to fill "an entire tenement house with people from
one village." It was said that if a few teams of oxen had been added to
Forquer Street the illusion of a *paese* in Campania would have been
complete.[10]

While the movement out of the Near South Side was primarily to
the west, the Riciglianesi particularly migrated southward into the Fourth
Ward. The removal of the segregated vice district to the Near South Side
diverted their march southwest along Archer Avenue and then south again
along Wentworth and Princeton streets. They settled thickly in the Armour Square district between Twenty-second and Twenty-fifth streets
with the New York Central Railroad tracks to the east and the Pennsylvania tracks to the west (D). The construction of the Church of Santa
Maria Incoronata on Alexander Street in 1904 attracted other paesani to
the neighborhood. Since many of the Riciglianesi plied the trades of
newsvendor, bootblack, and streetsweeper in the Loop, easy access to
downtown was an important consideration. This solid settlement of several hundred families exhibited the spirit of campanilismo par excellence.
Among the Riciglianesi it was considered a scandal for anyone to marry
out of the village group even unto the second generation of American
born.[11]

The Near South Side also attracted immigrants from Termini
Imerese in Sicily. While the Terminesi could be found in other parts of the
city, this settlement at the juncture of Archer Avenue, Clark and Twentieth streets in the First Ward became their most distinctive colony (E).
The only other Sicilians on the Near South Side hailed from Nicosia,
province of Catania. Although the Terminesi and the Nicosiani lived in
close proximity along South Clark Street, yet they retained their separate
identities, holding "tenaciously to their sacred, ancestral traditions."
Those from Termini were for the most part fruit peddlers while those from
Nicosia were mainly laborers. Although in time the Sicilians outnumbered the Riciglianesi, their neighborhoods remained quite distinct with
Twenty-second Street as the dividing line. While sharing the Church of
Santa Maria Incoronata, each group of paesani had its own religious
sodality and celebrated the feast of its patron saint. Together the Near
South Side and Armour Square districts by 1910 encompassed the city's
fourth largest concentration of Italians.[12]

Another major settlement took shape in the Seventeenth Ward in
an area bounded by the North Branch of the Chicago River on the east and
railroad tracks on the south (F). The earliest settlers, Genoese and
Tuscans, were soon outnumbered by southern Italians. Situated along
Grand Avenue and adjacent streets, the immigrants congregated by village

and regional groups: several hundred paesani from Calvello resided on Sangamon Street; other Potenzanesi were on Peoria Street; Luccesi along with Venetians and Romans located on Hubbard, Racine, and May streets, while those from Campania and Abruzzi were strung out along Grand Avenue and Ohio and Erie streets. After 1900, newcomers from Apulia and Sicily poured into the Seventeenth Ward; the former from Nola di Bari, Triggiano, and Modugno settled along Grand Street, while the latter from Termini Imerese and the province of Palermo established a "Little Sicily" in the southeastern corner of the ward. Their influx resulted in the withdrawal of the former residents, Norwegians, Germans, and Irish. In 1899 the Norwegian Church at Peoria and Grand was rededicated as the Church of Santa Maria Addolorata. Although the Seventeenth Ward was industrial in character, few Italians were employed in its factories. Rather they worked in the adjacent railroad yards or produce markets. The Grand Avenue colony in the Seventeenth and Fourteenth wards comprised the third largest agglomeration of Italians in the city, over 11,500, in 1910.[13]

The Near North Side had early sheltered a Genoese neighborhood; later Tuscans had fruit stores and saloons along Franklin, Wells, and Orleans streets between Grand Avenue and Chicago Avenue. To the north, plaster workers from Lucca employed in statuary shops centered about Division Street and Claybourne Avenue. In the first decade of the twentieth century a wave of immigration from Sicily swept over the Near North Side. By 1910, the Twenty-second Ward's Italians (now predominantly Sicilian) numbered almost 13,000, placing it second only to the Nineteenth Ward (G). The Terminesi were the earliest Sicilians in this part of the city as well. However, the major source became the villages in the hinterland of Palermo: Monreale, Bagheria, Alta Villa-Milica, Vicari, Ventimiglia, and Cimminna. Among these Palermitani were contadini who had worked on the sugar plantations in Louisiana and had subsequently migrated north. In 1904, the Church of St. Philip Benizi was built at the corner of Oak and Cambridge as *"la chiesa degli Siciliani"* (the church of the Sicilians). Described as a "mosaic of Sicilian villages," the colony extended from Chicago Avenue to Division Street and from Sedgwick Street to the river. In the heart of industrial Chicago, the paesani "retained their identity, living together as far as possible, intermarrying, and celebrating the traditional feasts." On Larabee Street were those from Alta Villa, on Townsend those from Bagheria, on Milton those from Sambuca-Zabat, and so on. This Little Sicily became notorious because of the frequency of murders and bombings. Such was its sinister reputation that its residents were often barred from employment and had difficulty moving into other neighborhoods.[14]

Table 16.1

ITALIAN POPULATION OF CHICAGO IN 1910 BY MAJOR
WARDS OF RESIDENCE

Ward	Born in Italy	Native of Italian Parentage	Total
1	3,045	1,853	4,898
4	1,892	1,242	3,134
12	813	348	1,161
14	1,652	1,402	3,054
17	4,910	3,593	8,503
19	14,649	8,757	23,406
22	8,216	4,564	12,780
31	638	637	1,275
33	2,963	1,091	4,054
Total for These Wards	38,778	23,487	62,265
Total for the City	45,169	27,737	72,906

Note: Of Chicago's 35 wards, these 9 reported a total of over 1,000 Italians, first and second generations combined.

Source: U.S. Bureau of the Census, *Thirteenth Census: 1910, Population*, II (Washington, D.C., 1913), 512–14. All references to population statistics for 1910 in the text are drawn from this source.

In 1910, two-thirds of the city's Italians resided in these five river wards (see table 16.1). Arranged in a semicircle around the downtown business district, a three-mile radius using the corner of State and Madison streets as a pivot would have included all of the settlements. Still a considerable and growing number of Italians lived in outlying districts and suburbs. Several thousand were scattered about the city, engaged in petty commerce for the most part. A number of settlements, however, emerged in response to localized employment opportunities. One of the few industries hiring Italians in the 1890s was the McCormick reaper works on Blue Island Avenue. A colony of Tuscans from Ponte Bugianese, Altopiano, San Gennaro, Ciesina, and Borgo Abuszarma took shape between Twenty-second Street and Blue Island Avenue running from Leavitt Street to Western Avenue. (H). Although most had been *ortolani* (truck farmers), the Tuscans worked at "McComio" (as they called it) or the nearby National Malleable and Casting Works. By 1910, the Italians in the Twelfth Ward totaled over a thousand. Having displaced the Swedes, the Lutheran Church on Twenty-fourth Place was converted to the Church of San Michele Arcangelo. The Tuscan colony, a stronghold of the Italian Socialist Federation, was known for its fierce anticlerical sentiment, and the church languished. When National Malleable opened its Grant Works in Cicero in 1910, many migrated from the 22nd and Oakley area to the new plant (I). Here they formed a small settlement of a few hundred persons between Laramie Avenue and Fiftieth Avenue and Twelfth and Fourteenth streets. Noted for its fiery radical spirit, the neighborhood had a cooperative store, recreation hall, and saloon, but no church.[15]

Another pocket of Tuscans, the Luccesi from Bagni di Lucca, Camaiore, and Barga, established themselves on the North Side between Fullerton and Diversey along the North Branch (J). Having a long tradition of working with ceramics, they found jobs with the Northwestern Terra Cotta Works, especially after a Luccese became a foreman. Known among themselves as "Terra Cotta," several hundred had settled in this part of the Twenty-fourth Ward by 1910.[16]

Work of a similar character attracted other Italians to Kensington on the west shore of Lake Calumet. As early as 1892 immigrants from Altipiano di Asiago, province of Vicenza (Veneto) worked here for the Illinois Terra Cotta and Lumber Company. Recruits from other provinces soon formed a substantial colony of Veneziani. After 1900 a large number of Calabresi and Piemontesi as well as smaller contingents from Lombardy, Tuscany, and Sicily also converged on Kensington. While many worked in the brick yards, an increasing percentage were hired by the nearby Pullman works and the Burnside shops of the Illinois Central Railroad. In 1902, the Kensington Italians numbered about a thousand persons, concentrated in an area east of Michigan Avenue to the Illinois Central tracks and from 115th to 120th streets (K). Reflecting an intense spirit of *regionalismo*, the various groups settled along certain blocks and formed their own mutual aid societies. Regional differences came out forcefully on the issue of religion. The Piemontesi tended to be strongly anticlerical while the Venetians and meridionali were more church-oriented. Immediately to the north of Kensington was the company town of Pullman. By 1912, some 900 Italians worked at the Pullman Palace Car Company and lived in the brick rowhouses (L). In the Thirty-third Ward, which included both Pullman and Kensington, the Italians, numbering over 4,000, made up one of the largest nationality groups by 1910.[17]

One other small neighborhood in the Thirty-third Ward in the district known as Grand Crossing was composed completely of Calabresi from the provinces of Cosenza, Catanzaro, and Reggio Calabria (M). The first settlers were laborers in section gangs who purchased lots and built houses. Later some worked in the Illinois Central shops at Burnside, others in a factory on Seventy-ninth Street, still others commuted to Pullman. The area had a semirural aspect with ample room for vegetable gardens. The only business establishments were a few groceries, a saloon, and a barber shop. Several hundred Calabresi settled compactly on Dobson and Greenwood avenues between Seventy-fifth and Seventy-ninth streets. They formed mutual aid societies, and in 1911 the Church of St. Francis de Paula was established. It was said of the Grand Crossing colony that "if one were to remove a single family with all its cousins, the whole neighborhood would be practically wiped out . . ."[18]

Meanwhile ten miles south of Kensington, other Italian immigrants were congregating in the industrial satellite city of Chicago Heights (N). The first were Marchegiani, particularly from the fishing village of San Benedetto del Tronto. Subsequently a large number of Abruzzesi from Castel di Sangro and Sulmona and smaller groups from Calabria, Sicily, and Lazio arrived. By 1910 numbering 3,224, the Italians were by far the largest nationality in the city. Initially employed on the railroads, the opening of the Inland Steel Plant in 1894 offered new opportunities, particularly after an Italian became foreman of the railcutting department. Some had worked in steel mills in France and Germany, but most of the Italians had been farmers or fishermen. Settling on Chicago Height's East Side between Fourteenth and Twenty-Sixth streets, each of the regional groups appropriated certain blocks: the Marchegiani on Hanover and Wentworth, the Abruzzesi on Twenty-third, the Calabresi on Sixteenth and Seventeenth streets. Mutual aid societies were formed along regional lines, and a section of the Italian Socialist Federation, in which the Abruzzesi and Marchegiani were especially active, was organized. The conflict between pro- and anticlerical elements was especially heated, but the Church of San Rocco was nonetheless dedicated in 1906.[19]

Three miles south of Chicago Heights, quite a number of Italians worked in the Steger Piano Company and lived in the company town of Steger. They were for the most part from Amaseno in the province of Frosinone (Lazio). A cabinetmaker from that *paese* had become foreman in the rubbing and finishing department, and whenever there was an opening he hired a *paesano*. In this fashion, the Amasenesi, most of whom had been day laborers on large estates, developed an occupational specialization in piano and furniture factories. So many of them settled in Chicago Heights that it became known as "Amaseno the Second."[20]

These outlying settlements were not created by immigrants seeking to escape from the inner city "ghetto." Rather they originated independently of the downtown Italian neighborhoods and grew through direct chain migration from specific *paesi* in Italy. Two major colonies, however, were initially formed by outmigrations from the river ward Little Italies. West Englewood, located about seven miles southwest of the Loop, attracted its first Italians from the South Clark Street settlement in the 1880s (O). Attracted by the low price of land, the early settlers from Oliveto Citra transformed the prairie into bountiful truck gardens. Because of their livestock, the area earned the nickname of Goatsville. The Olivetani formed a sodality in 1891 to celebrate the feast of *la Madonna del Carmine*. The widespread cult of this madonna and the rustic setting attracted thousands from the city to this annual *festa*. This in turn stimulated the growth of the settlement. Work was available on the railroad and streetcar lines and in building construction. The newcomers were also for the most part Salernitani from the paesi of Contursi, Campagna, and Senarchia. By 1910 the Italian population in the Thirty-first Ward, centering about Hermitage Avenue and Sixty-ninth Street, was over 1,200.[21]

A second garden community developed in Melrose Park, some eleven miles west of downtown Chicago (P). In 1890, the suburb was already the scene of real estate promotion among the Italians with excursions featuring balloon ascensions, fireworks, and Professore Ernesto Libonati's orchestra. Emilio de Stefano, leader of the Laurenzanesi in the South Clark Street quarter, was a promoter of this development. When he recovered from a serious illness, his wife in thanksgiving erected a chapel with a replica of the statue of the Madonna del Carmine, which stood in the church in Laurenzana. In 1894 the first *festa della Madonna* was held on the De Stefano farm in Melrose Park. This became the most popularly attended of the Italian feste, and many who came decided to settle here. As in West Englewood, the Italians built wooden shacks and established gardens on the virgin prairie. Because of the abundance of this crop, the settlement became known as Pepper Town. While the families engaged in subsistence farming, the men worked in nearby steel mills and foundaries, on section gangs, and in construction. By 1910, the Italian community numbered over a thousand and was rapidly growing. Two groups heavily represented in the colony were the Trivignesi and the Riciglianesi from Basilicata and Campagnia respectively. Sicilians, Calabresi, and Marchegiani were later arrivals. Regional lines appear to have been less sharply drawn in Melrose Park than in the other settlements. Such was the intermingling that it was said an outsider could not identify what part of Italy a Melrose Park Italian came from by his dialect.[22]

This panoramic view of the Italian neighborhoods of Chicago during the period of formation sketches their Old World origins, their economic base, something of their social and cultural character. Of course, each of these settlements had a history dense with life and deserving of study. If we had such histories of the Tuscans at Twenty-second Street and Oakley or of the Riciglianesi of Armour Square or of the Amasenesi of Chicago Heights, we would know much more about the Italian immigration than we do now. However, even this broad overview suggests the dangers of generalizing about the Italian experience in Chicago (or elsewhere for that matter). Unless we are willing to deal with the Italian immigration in all its complexity we run the risk of arriving at gross and erroneous conclusions. Certainly the crude North Italian-South Italian dichotomy that is employed by even recent studies is misleading as an interpretive scheme for understanding that immigration.[23]

In sum this analysis of Italian settlement in Chicago suggests several conclusions or better hypotheses to be tested in further research. First of all, the ecological model does not adequately explain the peculiarities of the spatial distribution of the Italian neighborhoods. Land use patterns, industrial location, labor market, and housing market did not in themselves *determine* where the Italians finally lighted. For example, one needs to explain the absence as well as the presence of the Italians. Why were they not to be found in significant numbers in the "Back-of-the-Yards" district or in South Chicago? Because they were not employed in the meatpacking plants or steel mills. But why were they not? Clearly the immigrants were not responding blindly to economic forces. They were able to exercise some choices in a "free labor" market, to express preferences for type of work and living environment. One must allow for the play of contingency, cultural preference, and human agency.

I have been particularly struck by the role of the pioneer who is the pathfinder, who chooses this rather than that fork in the road. For each of the paesani groups, one finds such a trailblazer at the beginning of the migration process. Francesco Lagorio served such a function for the Genoese. Arriving in the early 1850s, realizing a modest success, he sent for family and friends. It was about his restaurant on the Near North Side that the Genoese colony coalesced. In the case of the Laurenzanesi, Emilio de Stefano, who came to Chicago in 1873, became the acknowledged leader. It was De Stefano who was instrumental in bringing many from the province of Potenza first to the Polk Depot area and then to Melrose Park. A similar role was played among the Calabresi by Luigi Spizziri, who also arrived in the early 1870s and soon became an important padrone among his paesani. Lending money to would-be immigrants from Calabria, he was reputed to have brought more Italians than anyone else to Chicago and specifically to the South Clark Street settlement. For the immigration from Termini Imerese, Andrea Russo served as a guide and catalyst. Coming in 1882, he began as a peddler and ultimately became a large importer of Italian food products. Bringing relatives and paesani, he initiated a general immigration to the Grand Street colony of the Terminesi. Or one can cite the role of the anonymous foremen who secured jobs for their paesani with the Northwestern Terra Cotta works and the Steger Piano Company. These "founding fathers" had a great deal to do with directing the migrations from specific villages and provinces to particular destinations.[24]

Finally one cannot help but be impressed by the force of group solidarity in shaping the Italian neighborhoods of Chicago. Campanilismo and regionalismo expressed through the process of chain migration, mutual assistance, and cultural affinity exerted a profound influence upon the settlement patterns among and within the Little Italies. Of course, not all of the residents of a particular street or district came from specified villages, nor were all of the residents of these neighborhoods Italian. I am not arguing here the ethnic homogeneity of these settlements, but rather for a recognition of this powerful tendency to reconstitute community in accordance with Old World origins. Certainly the neighborhoods that were formed during the period of mass immigration remained intact for several decades. A map for 1930 plotting the Italian-born population of Chicago by census tracts reveals the persistence of these settlements over time. Although conversion of land to nonresidential uses and the influx of new migrant groups had resulted in certain population movements, yet the continuity of ethnic concentration over the period of two decades is remarkable. What this suggests is the enormous cohesive force of these neighborhoods.

While conducting research in Chicago during the late 1950s and early 1960s, I visited the sites of all of these settlements. By then some were in an advanced stage of disintegration, while others retained a remarkable vitality. Today some are gone altogether as in the case of the Near West Side neighborhood and the Little Sicily of the Near North Side. They were completely wiped off the face of the city by "urban renewal." But certain districts such as Melrose Park and Kensington remain even today strongholds of Italian American communities. As part of our agenda for the study of Little Italies and ethnic neighborhoods in general, we need analyses of those factors that make for the persistence of some and the disappearance of others. The history of particular communities from their genesis to their demise would contribute to our understanding of the role of ethnicity in shaping the cultural geography of our cities.

Notes

1. Frank Thistlethwaite, "Migration from Europe Overseas in the Nineteenth and Twentieth Centuries," in XIe Congrès International des Sciences Historiques, Stockholm, 1960, *Rapports*, 5: *Historiques Contemporaine* (Göteborg-Stockholm-Uppsala, 1960), 32–60.

2. For an effort to write the history of the Italians in Chicago from this perspective see my doctoral dissertation, "Chicago's Italians prior to World War I: A Study of Their Social and Economic Adjustment" (University of Wisconsin, 1963).

3. Robert E. Park, Ernest W. Burgess, and Roderick D. McKenzie, *The City* (Chicago, 1925), 1–62; Fred H. Matthews, *Quest for an American Society: Robert E. Park and the Chicago School* (Montreal, 1977), 121–56.

4. The letters refer to location symbols on Map of Chicago's Little Italies (figure 16.1).

5. Tanner, Halpin, and Co., comp., *D. B. Cooke & Co.'s Directory of Chicago for the Year 1858* (Chicago, 1858); Richard Edwards, comp., *Chicago Census Report; and Statistical Review Embracing a Complete Directory of the City* (Chicago, 1871); Local Community Research Committee, University of Chicago, "Documents: History of the Lower North Side" nos. 28, 29 (transcript in Chicago Historical Society); Chicago Board of Education, *School Census of the City of Chicago, 1884* (Chicago, 1884); and *School Census of 1898* (Chicago, 1899); *Diamond Jubilee of the Assumption Parish, 1881–1956* (Chicago, 1956). In addition, interviews conducted by the author in the various Italian neighborhoods of Chicago between 1957 and 1960 constitute one of the basic sources for this study.

6. U.S. Commissioner of Labor, *Ninth Special Report: The Italians in Chicago, A Social and Economic Study* (Washington, D.C., 1897), 21; Frank O. Beck, "The Italian in Chicago," *Bulletin of the Chicago Department of Public Welfare* (February 1919), II, 7.

7. Chicago Board of Education, *School Census, 1884;* Edith Abbott, *The Tenements of Chicago, 1908–1935* (Chicago, 1936), 110; *Golden Anniversary, 1904–1954, Santa Maria Incoronata Church* (Chicago, 1954); *L'Italia* (Chicago), Feb. 14, April 18, 1903; *Chicago Daily News,* July 15, 1887; *Chicago Tribune,* July 26, 1885, July 24, 1887, June 2, 1888, Feb. 23, 1890; *Chicago Record-Herald,* June 14, 1903; Agnes S. Holbrook, "Map Notes and Comments," in *Hull House Maps and Papers* (New York, 1895), 15–23.

8. Emilio Grandinetti, "50 anni di lotte e di aspirazioni fra gli Italiani di Chicago," *La Parola del Popolo* (Chicago), 9 (December 1958–January 1959), 87; U.S. Commissioner of Labor, *Seventh Special Report: The Slums of Baltimore, Chicago, New York and Philadelphia* (Washington, D.C., 1894), 38; Abbott, *Tenements of Chicago,* 77, 95. Table 16.1 reports on the Italian population of Chicago in 1910 by major wards of residence.

9. *Chicago Record-Herald,* June 14, 1903; *Diamond Jubilee of the Archdiocese of Chicago* (Des Plaines, Ill., 1920), 578, 645.

10. Edmund M. Dunne, *Memoirs of "Zi Pre"* (St. Louis, 1914), 2; Jane Addams, *Newer Ideals of Peace* (New York, 1911), 67.

11. *Golden Anniversary, 1904–1954, Santa Maria Incoronata Church;* Abbott, *Tenements of Chicago,* 113; Local Community Research Committee, "Documents: History of Armour Square," nos. 1, 2, 10; Evelyn B. Espey, "Old World Customs Continued in Chicago," *By Archer Road,* I (September 1907).

12. Evelyn B. Espey, "Archer Road," and "One of Our Neighbors," *By Archer Road,* I (May 1906), IV (May 1910); *L'Italia,* August 12, 1894, August 15–16, 22–23, 1896, March 16, 1901, March 21, 1903.

13. Chicago Department of Public Welfare, "Housing Survey in Italian Dis-

trict of the 17th Ward," *First Semi-Annual Report* (Chicago, 1915), 74; *Chicago Commons, 1894–1911* (n.p., n.d.); Abbott, *Tenements of Chicago*, 102; *L'Italia*, Feb. 24, 1894; G. Sofia, ed., *Missioni Scalabriniane in America* (Rome, 1939), 115.

14. Local Community Research Committee, "Documents: History of the Lower North Side," nos. 27, 30, 36, 61; Harvey W. Zorbaugh, *The Gold Coast and the Slum: A Sociological Study of Chicago's Near North Side* (Chicago, 1929), 165–73; *Chicago Daily News*, Nov. 11, 1922; *L'Italia*, Nov. 18, 25, Dec. 9, 1905.

15. Armando Pierini, "Provincia 'S. Giovanni Battista,' Canada," *Cinquantesimo: Numero Speciale de' L'Emigrato* (Monza, Italy), 49 (May–June 1953); 60; U.S. Immigration Commission, *Reports*, XXVI. *Immigrants in Cities* (Washington, D.C., 1911), 307–11; *Diamond Jubilee of the Archdiocese of Chicago*, 599; *La Parola dei Socialisti* (Chicago), Feb. 17, 1908; Anon., "The Development of Cicero" (typescript, Chicago Community Inventory, University of Chicago).

16. Interviews

17. Sofia, *Missioni Scalabriniane*, 103–6; *L'Italia*, Dec. 14–15, 1895, Oct. 4, 1902; Abbott, *Tenements of Chicago*, 151, 154; Alice Anderson, "Kensington" (ms., Chicago Community Inventory, 1924); Graham R. Taylor, "Satellite Cities: Pullman," *The Survey* 29 (Nov. 2, 1912), 121–26.

18. Abbott, *Tenements of Chicago*, 154–55; Local Community Research Committee, "Documents: History of Grand Crossing," nos. 1, 10; Frieda Bachmann, "Grand Crossing" (ms., Chicago Community Inventory, 1924); *Diamond Jubilee of the Archdiocese of Chicago*, 651.

19. *The New World* (Chicago), Dec. 15, 1906; *La Parola dei Socialisti*, March 5, 12, 1908.

20. *La Parola dei Socialisti*, March 5, 1908.

21. *Souvenir of the Golden Jubilee of the Parish of St. Mary of Mt. Carmel, 1892–1942;* Local Community Research Committee, "Documents: History of Englewood," nos. 1, 3, 4, 7; *L'Italia*, July 28–29, 1894; August 1–2, 1896; June 8, August 24, 31, 1901.

22. Melrose Park Village Board, *Souvenir, The Village of Melrose Park, Illinois* (Chicago, 1907); *Golden Jubilee of the Feast of Our Lady of Mt. Carmel, Melrose Park, Illinois, 1894–1944;* Sofia, *Missioni Scalabriniane*, 122; *L'Italia*, July 3, Sept. 13, 1890; August 4–5, 1894.

23. An oversimplified use of the North-South Italian dichotomy is Humbert Nelli, *The Italians in Chicago, 1880–1930* (New York, 1970).

24. Local Community Research Committee, "Documents: History of the Lower North Side," no. 28; *Chicago Tribune*, Feb. 28, March 4, 1886; Feb. 23, 1890; *L'Italia*, June 4, 11, 1892; June 30, 1894; Feb. 15–16, 1896; April 2, 1904; W. A. Goodspeed and D. D. Healy, eds., *History of Cook County, Illinois* (2 vols., Chicago, 1909), I; 812–13.

SOURCES AND METHODOLOGY

17

International Migration and Internal Migration: A Comprehensive Theoretical Approach

Robert J. Kleiner, Tom Sørensen, Odd Stefan Dalgard, Torbjørn Moum, and Dale Drews

The impetus for this essay was our growing awareness that the phenomenon of migration has often been approached with little theory or with simplistic theoretical formulations that fail to grasp or appreciate the complexities of the decision to migrate and the difficult problems experienced by those who seriously consider this act. In this essay, we will propose the essential elements of a theory of voluntaristic behavior that we believe captures these qualities of the decision. We will also suggest some of the methodological implications of the theory and provide data that illustrate the value of the approach being proposed. Finally, we will discuss the issue of whether migration from one country to another is a phenomenon that is the same as migration from one part of a country to another.

Before going into the specifics of this essay, it is important to make a number of observations about the "migration" literature. In the social sciences there appears to be a pervasive tendency to look at migration and its effects in negative terms. It is not uncommon to see concepts such as culture shock, role discontinuity, uprooting, isolation, vulnerability to disease, anomie, and anomia used to capture the qualities of the migration experience (e.g., Wirth, 1938; Malzberg and Lee, 1956; Fried, 1969; Sanua, 1969; Kleiner and Elazar, 1978). The sociological and psychological literature, in particular, contain studies that investigate the relationship of migration to mental illness, physical illnesses, violence, crime, alcoholism, drug addiction, and so forth (e.g., Wirth, 1938; Merton, 1964; Shannon and Morgan, 1966; Wax, 1971).

It is not our intention to evaluate these studies, but to show the pervasiveness of the assumption that migration is a problematic phenomenon with predominantly negative effects. Rarely is migration seen as desirable, and described in constructive, positive terms. Biographies, novels, and films, on the other hand, frequently portray migration in very positive terms. But these are usually success stories about particularly strong individuals and their families whose hard work and virtue enabled them to overcome "tremendous odds" to "make it" in the new environment (e.g., Semingsen, 1978). These materials extoll the virtues of success, striving, hard work, saving one's money, and so forth. They also fail to present a realistic picture of the migration experience.

There is also a large body of literature that has considered migration from a macrostructural perspective (e.g., Ernst, 1949; Kleiner and Parker, 1971; Morrison, 1982; DeAlbuquerque and McElroy, 1982). These studies focus on the socioeconomic characteristics of the society (or area) of origin *prior to* a mass migration and on the same characteristics *at the time of* migration. From such analyses, "causal" explanations or "pushes" are inferred to account for the migration (e.g., Fried, 1969; Kleiner, Parker, and Needelman, 1969; Kleiner and Parker, 1971). For example, the potato famine in Ireland in 1848 led to the mass migration of the Irish to the United States; pogroms in tsarist Russia in the 1880s and 1890s led to the mass migration of Jews to the United States; or the economic depression in the 1930s led to the migration of blacks from the southern to the northern or western parts of the United States.

Other studies focus on the socioeconomic characteristics of the country (or area) of destination, seeking to identify those conditions that existed at the time that apparently drew the migrant to the environment, that is, the "pulls." For example, the discovery of gold in California in 1848 led to the mass migration to that state; the rapid industrialization in the northeastern part of the United States in the 1880s and 1890s led to the migration of millions of European workers to the United States; or the existence of strong Norwegian enclaves in the United States (e.g., in Minnesota, Iowa, and Wisconsin) attracted Norwegian migrants to those states at the turn of the century.

The first set of macrostructural studies deals with the *pushes* to migration, and the latter set of studies deals with the *pulls* to migration.

But all of these studies, by and large, depend on aggregate statistics derived from official data gathering sources in the country (or area) of origin or on the data gathering sources in the country (or area) of destination. Such studies are critically necessary because they give us important ideas and insights about the dynamics of such population movements that we need to understand. It is important to recognize that causal inference and dependency on aggregate data may also lead to incorrect inferences as well, unless we develop more sensitive research methods.

We have drawn attention to the concepts of "pushes" and "pulls" to migration indigenous to the communities of origin and destination. These concepts and the notion of conflict that underlies their use are not new, but we want to draw out more fully the implications of this approach.

For convenience, we will focus on three points in the migration process, that is, the "community of origin," the "en route stage," and the "community of destination." If we consider the *community of origin* first, it is clear that, at *any given point in time*, there are many factors that could push an individual to leave. At the same time, there are many factors that could pull the individual back to remain in the community. Factors that push or pull can be found at many levels of analyses: (a) national and regional economic factors, (b) sociocultural factors, (c) neighborhood and/or community factors, (d) family relationships, and (e) personal and motivational characteristics of the migrants. These factors are indigenous to the situation and are objective characteristics of the situation. From the personal, or subjective, point of view, the more the migrants are aware of these pushes and pulls, the more they experience the conflicts that must be resolved. This situation may be referred to as a *multiple approach-avoidance conflict situation* (e.g., Lewin, 1935; Miller, 1944; Lewin, 1951), where "approach" is analogous to pulls to remain in the community of origin, and "avoidance" is analogous to pushes to leave the community. If the combined strength of the approach or pull factors is greater than the combined strength of the avoidance or push factors, the decision to remain will be made. Conversely, if the strength of the avoidance or push factors is greater than the approach or pull factors, the decision to leave will be made. (It should be kept in mind that remnants of the conflicts remain after the decision is made, and may become part of subsequent conflicts and decisions.)

At the same time that the migrants are evaluating the pushes and pulls associated with the community of origin, they must also evaluate the pushes and pulls associated with the community of destination. In the community of destination there are many indigenous factors pushing or discouraging the migrants from coming, and there are many factors pulling them to come. Just as with the community of origin, these factors can be found at different levels of analyses: (a) national and regional economic factors, (b) sociocultural factors, (c) neighborhood and/or community factors, (d) family relations, and (e) personal and motivational characteristics of the migrants. Again, from the subjective point of view, the more they are aware of these pushes and pulls, the more they experience multiple approach-avoidance conflicts associated with the community of destination. Thus, they (and their families, if involved) must deal with two sets of conflicts before the final decision is made.

The conflicts experienced in the community of origin are based on first-hand knowledge because the potential migrants live here, whereas the conflicts associated with the community of destination are based on second-hand knowledge gained from letters, books, newspapers, and verbal accounts from those who migrated at an earlier date.

Finally, when people consider migrating they must anticipate the conditions they may experience on the way to the new community of destination, that is, the "en route stage." For example, they must consider the costs, the comforts, the time of travel, the sanitation conditions, and the risk of sickness. If the en route situation involves heavily crowded conditions and high risk of illness, these will push the individual back to the community of origin. Low cost of fare and little travel time will pull the individual to travel to the new destination. Again, from the subjective point of view, if the individual is aware of all of these factors, he or she will experience a third set of approach-avoidance conflicts.

In this brief description, we have sought to define the parameters and complexities of the conflicts that underlie the decision to migrate or not to migrate. Clearly, the decision is not one that is made impulsively, or in a cavalier manner. It requires considerable thought and planning. This description also indicates the complexities of the data that one needs to collect to fully understand the migration process and the migration decision. An investigator who focuses only on the characteristics of the community of origin totally misses the influence of the community of destination and the en route stage on the decision. In a similar manner, an investigator who focuses only on the characteristics of the community of destination totally misses the influence of the community of origin and the en route stage on the decision. Some studies attempt to transcend these difficulties by looking at the aggregate characteristics of a given ethnic group in its community of origin, together with its aggregate characteristics in its community of destination, and infer a causal connection or interdependence between the two sets of characteristics even though there is no necessary connection between them. Once we have understood the decision-making process, we need to know what actually occurred with those who made the decision to migrate: to what extent their experience conformed to expectations, what problems occurred, and how adaptive they were to the new situation.

From our point of view, it is necessary to find the methods that will allow us to study the migration phenomenon in all its complexities. This means that we need social-structural, sociocultural, and social psychological data from a given time period with respect to the communities of origin, the communities of destination, and the en route stage.

In our own research, we have conducted surveys that gathered social psychological data from migrants about their communities of origin, their migration, their evaluation of their current community, and their relation to it (e.g., Parker and Kleiner, 1966; Dalgard, 1967; Kleiner, Parker, and Needelman, 1969; Kleiner and Dalgard, 1975). Our information from the several studies includes material on the economic factors that influenced the decision to migrate, the nature of the values that influenced the migrants' thinking, their relationship to their neighborhood and family, and information about their personal and motivational characteristics. Our data do not include all the material that our theoretical perspective demands. This is due to the fact that the perspective has evolved as our own experience and research on migration has progressed.

The perspective that we have presented imposes extremely difficult and complicated tasks on social scientists. They must collect wide-ranging types of data that require the use of research methods deriving from different disciplines. Is all this necessary or worth the effort? A few illustrations from the general empirical literature and from our own research in the United States and Norway will show why we believe that such efforts are necessary. In view of our particular interests, we will relate various aspects of the migration phenomenon to mental illness or psychiatric risk.

Is it important to know the values and norms of the original cultural context of the migrants to explain their mental health?

If we review the literature dealing with the migration of American Indian youth from the reservations in the United States to urban centers, a number of interesting results emerge (e.g., Cook, 1943; Price, 1968; D'Antonio and Samora, 1970; Hertzberg, 1971; Wax, 1971; Kleiner and Elazar, 1978). The Cherokee youth have been raised in a tribal milieu that had one of the most literate civilizations among the Indian tribes, that is, they had their own alphabet, printed materials, libraries, and so forth. In this context, they trained their youth to be ambitious and strivers for personal success. When many of the youth left to make their way in the urban centers, they went with these values, and they went with the support and encouragement of their elders.

The Iroquois youth, on the other hand, were raised to consider communal and family ties and identification to be of central importance. Personal ambition and striving were not considered important values. When these youth left for the urban centers, they did not go with the support of their elders. Their elders felt it was more important to stay on the reservation to help their people.

Thus, the youth from the two tribes went to the cities with somewhat different core value systems. When they came to the cities, all of them found racism and prejudice, and only the most menial jobs were available to them. Social mobility was difficult to realize. If we consider the migrants to be an aggregate of Indians, then we would predict the same response to these conditions. However, if we consider the tribes they came from, we would expect different responses. From the Cherokee point of view, their youth have been failures and the youth evaluate themselves in these terms as do their elders. The youth do, in fact, manifest neurotic symptoms and behavior problems in the community of destination, and in the community of origin if they return home. From the Iroquois point of view, ambition and success values aren't important to begin with. Therefore, the response to the conditions experienced in the city is not seen as reflecting on the individual. Such youth show a lower incidence of neurotic symptoms or behavioral problems than the Cherokee youth in the community of destination, and in their community of origin, if they should return. In fact, the youth are welcomed back to the reservation. If we were to look at these youth as Indians who migrated from a rural environment, we would observe these "contradictory" findings and would have difficulty interpreting them.

The empirical literature on migration and mental illness conveys the prevailing idea that mental illness is higher among migrants to an area than among those native to the area (e.g., Commons, 1920; Ødegaard, 1932; Weinberg, 1955; Astrup and Ødegaard, 1960; Murphy, 1965). This pattern is illustrated by the Cherokee and Iroquois. In our studies of in-migration, that is, migration from one part of a country to another, the opposite findings have been obtained, that is, mental illness rates were higher among natives than among migrants (e.g., Kleiner and Parker, 1959; Parker and Kleiner, 1966; Dalgard, 1967). We have also found that rates of mental illness were higher among migrants from one urban center to another than among migrants from rural areas to the urban center. These findings demonstrate the limited value of prevalent theories that explain high rates of mental illness among migrants in terms of culture shock, role discontinuities, anomie, and so forth.

We have found that migrants to an urban center who have strong social mobility strivings, high ambitions, and expectations of a more open opportunity structure than exists in the new environment have high rates of mental illness, that is, are high risk populations (e.g., Parker and Kleiner, 1966; Kleiner, Parker, and Needelman, 1969). Migrants with these characteristics come, in the main, from other urban (and high psychiatric risk) areas rather than from rural (and low risk) areas. If we had been concerned only with whether a person was a migrant from an urban or rural area, we would seem to have contradictory findings; but the structural, cultural, and social psychological data help to resolve away these apparent contradictions.

Are the nature of the communication between the migrants and their parents and the nature of the ties they have to their families important factors in their mental health?

In our research in Norway we found that, in general, higher levels of *communication* between individuals and their parents are associated with better mental health (Kleiner and Parker, 1973; Kleiner and Drews, 1983). Among the migrants, we found that those with higher levels of communication with their family and better mental health tended to come from rural areas. We found that the *nature of the family ties* was an important factor as well. In general, those migrants with better mental health were those who (a) felt it was important to do things with their parents, (b) enjoyed doing things with their parents, (c) were concerned about the problems of their parents, and (d) felt their parents respected them. These characteristics were more prevalent among the migrants from rural areas than among other migrants or those native to the community of destination. It is quite apparent that the migrants' ties to their parents contributed to their mental health.

Our research has also shown that migrant workers in the large city, who commuted home over long distances every night, had the same mental health risks as those migrant workers who commuted home on weekends. But the wives of those migrant workers who commuted on weekends had higher mental health risks than the wives of those workers who commuted daily. Such findings draw attention to the idea that migration, even for short periods, has implications for those who have important ties to the migrants.

Is it important to know with whom the migrant moved?

We have found that those migrating *alone* had the highest risk of mental illness, and those migrating *with their parents* were the second-highest risk population. On the other hand, those migrating with a *spouse* were the lowest risks. In addition, among those who migrated alone but had people precede or follow them within a short time, those migrants whose *parents* came during this period showed the highest psychiatric risks, whereas those whose *spouses* came during this period showed the lowest risks.

It is not our intention here to bring all of these findings together into an integrated pattern, although they lend themselves to such a task. We only want to illustrate that there are many aspects of the migration experience that contribute to the mental health status of the migrant. It is for this reason that we feel that a comprehensive perspective of the migration phenomenon is necessary.

Although surveys yield invaluable information and insights, they suffer from three problems: (1) they yield cross-sectional data, that is, they are collected at one point in time; (2) the data are social psychological, that is, they depend on the individual's memories and recollections of what occurred in the past; and (3) the data do not really allow us to construct the migrants' total experience from the decision-making phase in the community of origin, through the travel period, to their "integration" in the community of destination. In order to construct such a perspective, we have to develop longitudinal methods whereby we can follow a migrant through the process.

The Temple University National Immigration Archives provide the opportunity for developing such methods for following individuals from the community of origin to the community of destination. The Archives have all of the ships' manifests for an eighty-year period. These manifests include the names of all the people brought to this country during this period and information about each person. The information includes the particular town or city from which the migrant came, and the town or city to which he or she moved. This makes it possible to look back to the conditions that existed in the community of origin at the time of the individual's migration, and to look forward to the conditions that existed in the new community and how the migrant adapted to the new situation. The availability of names also allows us to link the individual's particular place in the Old World to his or her place in the New. This facility provides the opportunity for conducting more systematic longitudinal studies that will provide a deeper understanding of the migration phenomenon.

We mentioned, in the introduction, international migration and internal or in-migration, but have ignored the distinction between the two types of migrations. By international migration we mean the movement of individuals across their native country's boundaries with the intention of working and/or living in another country. Such movement will be referred to simply as "migration." By internal migration, we mean movement of individuals from one area of their native country to another within the same country with the intention of working and/or living in that new area. Such movements will be referred to as "in-migration."

It is tempting to treat the two types of movement together because both imply "uprooting" and "reintegration" demands on the individual and those who move with that person. We often find reviews of the research done on the effects of population movement including data from both types of migration, implicitly assuming that they can be treated as one phenomenon. At a given level of abstraction this may be justifiable, but at the concrete level we need to be aware of their similarities and differences. The differences may be of greater importance than the similarities in the ultimate decision on whether to move or not, and on the success or failure of the move. We would like to draw attention to at least five issues on which the two phenomena can differ considerably. Before enumerating them it is important to state that we believe the approach-avoidance conflict theory applies equally well in both types of movement, but the elements of the conflicts are similar in some respect and different in others. Also, the relative importance or weight of the differing elements makes the two types of migration different.

Physical Distance

It appears that migration implies the movement over longer distances than in-migration, although it doesn't necessarily have to mean this. If migration means crossing oceans, continents, or multiple national boundaries, the physical distances covered will usually be greater than moving from rural areas of a country to the urban centers, or from one urban center to another in the same country. On the other hand, if one merely moves across the border to a neighboring country, the physical distance may not be great. However, for us, the physical distance to be covered brings into the decision-making situation additional factors that need to be considered, for example, the economic resources needed to make the move, the economic resources that one can bring along, the conditions under which the movement occurs, and so forth. It is not necessary to go into great detail here, but simply to illustrate the implications of physical distance for the problem at hand.

Reversibility of the Decision and Act

Migration to another country is more irreversible than internal migration. This element is, in part, related to physical distance, because as the physical distance to be covered increases, the possibility of returning to the home country becomes more problematic. This is so because of (a) the economic demands such a return would make on the migrant and his or her family, (b) the conditions under which the move back to the homeland would be made, (c) the problems that may be associated with another major move, (d) the problems that members added to the family in the new country may have with the relocation, and so forth. We would expect or hope that potential migrants would consider the "reversibility of the decision" before undertaking the move. If they do not, and if the move to the new country is unsuccessful, reversibility or irreversibility of the move could take on the greatest significance for their well-being and quality of life in the new country.

Language Differences

Migration makes the chances for successful integration in the new country more problematic than in in-migration because the language of the migrants is often different from the language in the new country. If the migrants and their families do not know the new language, they will probably have much greater communication and interpersonal relations problems in the new environment than they would have experienced if they moved to another part of the home country. It would seem that differences in accent or dialect are less likely to be barriers than differences in language.

Cultural Differences

Migrants in international migration experience more problems than those in in-migration when the cultures of the countries of origin and destination differ. This will be a particularly potent factor in the migration experience if the migrants are not aware of differences beforehand, or if they have an inaccurate view of the differences. When the values, norms, role expectations, and ideologies of the countries differ, such differences can be most significant for the adaptation and health of the migrants in the new environment.

Assimilation and Cultural Pluralism

In migration, more than in in-migration, the migrants must sooner or later come to terms with the question of whether they and their families will continue to live according to the language and culture of their home country or change to the cultural demands and the language of the new country. With succeeding generations, assimilation to the new country becomes dominant, but the conflicts are most difficult for the first-generation migrants. They usually compromise and vacillate, which makes it difficult to relate to the new environment. If they are not aware of these conflicts prior to the migration, the effects of the problem may be quite potent, traumatic, and profound.

We have enumerated a number of factors that appear to be relatively more important in migration than in in-migration. Clearly, they suggest some qualitative differences between the two types of movement, but all of them must be considered in the migration and in-migration phenomena.

In summarizing this essay, our intention is to convey the complexities and intricacies of the international migration and internal migration phenomena by focusing on the many factors that enter into the decision to move or not to move. Our underlying theoretical perspective emphasizes "approach-avoidance conflict theory." This allows us to think in terms of the pushes and pulls intrinsic to the country or region of origin, to the country or region of destination, and in the en route stage. We have presented some selected findings to show why this comprehensive approach is necessary, and we have drawn attention to the methodological implications of this approach. We have also discussed the differences between international migration and internal migration that are seen more clearly from this perspective, and the implications of these differences for research to be carried out with each type of migration.

We have focused on the parameters of the factors that influence people to migrate from their community or region of origin, and the complexity of the conflicts that enter into the decision-making process. We now need to link the discussion again to the total perspective. At the outset, we drew attention to the following categories or levels of factors that come to influence migration: (a) national and regional economic factors, (b) sociocultural factors, (c) community and neighborhood factors, (d) family relationships, and (e) personal and motivational factors. We have shown that potential migrants who are aware of these factors and their possible effects face a more complex and difficult decision-making task, but this experience appears to give them better preparation for dealing with the implications of the decision that is ultimately made. (Of course, if *too many* factors are considered at the same time, the potential migrant may be overwhelmed by the task and choose to remain where he or she is.)

On the other hand, unawareness of the many factors that are active in one's particular situation simplifies decision-making and makes it a less onerous task. However, this simplified situation may also limit the migrant's capacity to deal with the demands emanating from the several sets of factors and may expose him or her to conditions in the new environment that are not understood. In such circumstances, the migrant would also experience frustration, anxiety, and feelings of being victimized by forces beyond his or her control.

From the point of view of social scientists, we cannot fully understand the migration phenomena by depending on the subjective realities of individual migrants because individuals are not fully cognizant of their situations. Similarly, social scientists cannot depend on the objective realities of the situation because many of these realities do not enter into the decision-making process at all, even though they may have effects on the migration experiences. A comprehensive approach that includes the subjective and objective realities provides us with a more perceptive understanding of migration. It also provides us with the opportunity to include in this strategy an evaluation of the effects of the interaction of these realities on the migration experience.

Bibliography

Astrup, C., and Ødegaard, Ø., "Internal Migration and Disease in Norway." *Psychiatric Quarterly, Supplement*, 34 (1960), pp. 116–30.

Commons, J. R., *Races and Immigrants in America*. New York: Macmillan, 1920.

Cook, S. F., *The Conflict Between the California Indians and White Civilization*. Berkeley: University of California Press, 1943.

Dalgard, O. S., *Migration and Functional Psychoses in Oslo*. Oslo: Universitetsforlaget, 1967.

D'Antonio, W. V., and Samora, J., "Occupational Stratification in Four Southwestern Communities." In J. H. Burma (ed.), *Mexican-Americans in the United States*. Cambridge: Schenkman Publishing Co., 1970, pp. 363–75.

DeAlbuquerque, K., and McElroy, J. L. "West Indian Migration to the United States Virgin Islands: Demographic Impacts and Socioeconomic Consequences." *International Migration Review* 16 (Spring 1982), pp. 61–101.

Ernst, R. *Immigrant Life in New York City, 1826–1863*. New York: King's Crown Press, 1949.

Frazier, E. F., *Black Bourgeoisie*. Glencoe: Free Press, 1957.

Fried, M., "Deprivation and Migration: Dilemmas of Causal Interpretation." In E. B. Brady (ed.), *Behavior in New Environments*. Beverly Hills: Sage Publications, 1969, pp. 23–72.

Hertzberg, H. W., *The Search for an American Indian Identity: Modern Pan-Indian Movements*. Syracuse: Syracuse University Press, 1971.

Kleiner, R. J., and Dalgard, O. S., "Social Mobility and Psychiatric Disorders." *American Journal of Psychotherapy*, 1975, pp. 150–64.

Kleiner, R. J., and Elazar, D. J., "Urban Heterogeneity, Ethnic Identity, Social Networks, and Social Integration," 1978.

Kleiner, R. J., and Parker S., "Migration and Mental Illness: A New Look." *American Sociological Review* 24 (1959), pp. 687–90.

———. "Current Status and New Directions for Mental Health Research." In M.

Levitt (ed.), *The Mental Health Field: A Critical Appraisal*. Detroit: Wayne State University Press, 1971, pp. 204–26.

———. "Network Participation and Psychosocial Impairment in an Urban Environment." In P. Meadows and E. H. Mizruchi (eds.), *Urbanism, Urbanization, and Change: A Comparative Perspective*. Reading: Addison-Wesley Publishing Company, 1976, pp. 322–37.

Kleiner, R. J., Parker, S., and Needelman, B., "Migration and Mental Illness: Some Reconsiderations and Suggestions for Further Analysis." *Social Science and Medicine*, 1969.

Lewin, K., *Dynamic Theory of Personality*. New York: McGraw-Hill Book Co., 1935.

———. *Field Theory in Social Science: Selected Theoretical Papers*. D. Cartwright (ed.), New York: Harper and Row, 1951.

Malzberg, B. J., and Lee, E., *Migration and Mental Disease: A Study of First Admissions to Hospitals for Mental Disease, New York, 1939–1941*. New York: Social Science Research Council, 1956.

Merton, R. K., "Anomie, Anomia, and Social Interaction: Contexts of Deviant Behavior." In M. B. Clinard (ed.), *Anomie and Deviant Behavior: A Discussion and Critique*. Glencoe: Free Press, 1964, pp. 213–42.

Miller, N. E. "Experimental Studies of Conflict." In J. McV. Hunt (ed.), *Personality and the Behavior Disorders: A Handbook Based on Experimental and Clinical Research*. Vol. 1. New York: Ronald Press, 1974, pp. 431–65.

Morrison, T. K. "The Relationship of U.S. Trade and Investment to Migration Pressures in Major Sending Countries." *International Migration Review* 16 (Spring 1982), pp. 4–26.

Murphy, H. B. M., "Migration and the Major Mental Disorders: A Reappraisal." In M. B. Kantor (ed.), *Mobility and Mental Health*. Springfield, Mass.: Charles Thomas, 1965, pp. 5–29.

Ødegaard, Ø., "Emigration and Insanity: A Study of Mental Disease among the Norwegian-Born Population of Minnesota." *Acta Psychiatrica et Neurologica*, 1932, Supplementum 1–4.

Parker, S., and Kleiner, R. J., *Mental Illness in the Urban Negro Community*. Glencoe: Free Press, 1966.

Price, J. A., "The Migration and Adaptation of American Indians to Los Angeles," *Human Organization* 27 (1968), pp. 168–75.

Sanua, V. D., "Immigration, Migration and Mental Illness." In E. B. Brady (ed.), *Behavior in New Environments*. Beverly Hills: Sage Publications, 1969, pp. 291–352.

Semingsen, I., *Norway to America*. Minneapolis: University of Minnesota Press, 1978.

Shannon, L., and Morgan, P., "The Prediction of Economic Absorptions and Cultural Integration Among Mexican Americans, Negroes and Anglos in a Northern Industrial Community." *Human Organization*, 25 (1966), pp. 154–62.

Wax, M. L., *Indian Americans: Unity and Diversity*. Englewood Cliffs: Prentice-Hall, 1971.

Weinberg, A. A., "Mental Health Aspects of Voluntary Migration." *Mental Hygiene* 39 (1955), 450–64.

Wirth, L., "Urbanism as a Way of Life." *American Journal of Sociology*, 44 (1938).

18

The Uses of Passenger Lists for the Study of British and Irish Emigration

Charlotte Erickson

The passenger lists of arrivals in United States ports constitute a remarkable first-hand documentation of a major part of the greatest movement of people in human history. The original lists, many of them in a very poor state of preservation, have been deposited by the National Archives in the National Immigration Archives at the Balch Institute in Philadelphia. Copies of the lists are available on microfilm. However, the project under way at the Balch Institute to place the information on the original lists in machine-readable form, beginning with the New York City lists of 1848, which have never been soundexed, holds the possibility of extending our knowledge by obtaining a more accurate picture of demographic, economic, and social aspects of the great migration.

The lists afford valuable information not provided in the compilations of statistics of migration made by either the New York Commissioners of Emigration or the federal authorities. In particular, they offer the opportunity to measure the degree to which movements consisted of family groups or single persons. It is already clear that a mature migrant stream may contain a relatively high proportion of females and even

318

children (as summarized in published figures) and still be in large part a movement of single males.[1] The use of the material on the passenger lists also makes possible cross tabulations, such as age by occupation or migrating units by occupation, not otherwise obtainable. The amplitude of seasonal fluctuations as well as numbers of deaths on typical voyages and length of voyages can be measured.

In addition to the contribution the lists can make to a fuller picture of the structure of migrating groups, they also present possibilities for record linkage of varying quality depending upon the records surviving in the emigrant-yielding parts of Europe. When indexed they can readily be used to trace particular emigrants or samples drawn from other sources.

Some writers are inclined to doubt the value of effort expended upon the lists that are not all complete, detailed, or accurate. Masters of vessels were required to sign an oath attesting to the accuracy of information submitted in accordance with the Passenger Acts regulating space or tonnage per migrant. Since masters were rarely, if ever, prosecuted for making false depositions and penalties were slight, M. A. Jones, for one, is unwilling to place any confidence in their submissions.[2] Moreover, anyone who has examined some of the lists is likely to be appalled when he comes across one in which the occupation column is filled in with ditto marks covering whole pages, or where national origin is returned merely as Great Britain and Ireland. If one rejects the lists as unreliable, how much more must we question the published figures compiled by often overworked clerks without the aid of calculating machines, much less computers? At the very least, a critical appraisal of the original sources may help us better to assess the statistics originally produced from them and used so extensively down through the years.

Thus some of us have been willing to take the plunge to use these documents. Professor Swierenga has studied the entire population of Dutch immigration to the United States from 1820 to 1880 as recorded in them, as part of his source material.[3] Basing his results in part on a sample of every tenth ship carrying Irish passengers to the port of New York, Joel Mokyr has employed them for his study of prefamine emigration from Ireland.[4] Nils Olsson has traced the Swedish immigrants listed before 1848 to provide a remarkable, though unanalyzed, prosopography.[5] And I have been examining them for the light they can throw upon English emigration, especially in comparison with other emigrants from the British Isles.[6]

That work began while I was searching the lists for another purpose with the discovery of a carefully compiled series of lists from the late 1880s. These lists, which documented the arrival of about 10,000 British immigrants, actually gave details of place of last residence as well as country of birth, information normally supplied on only an occasional list of British or Irish passengers. These good lists challenged some commonly accepted assumptions about the nature of British emigration to the United States during the decade when it reached its peak, both in numbers and in incidence in the population. Although the shrinking of population in the countryside, evident from the 1850s, continued during the 1880s, nearly four-fifths of the British people setting out for the States came from towns or cities of more than 20,000 inhabitants. While farmers were overrepresented, agricultural laborers were rarely to be found. Relying on indirect evidence, historians have tended to associate the emigration of that decade also with unemployment in some of the staple industries of the first industrial revolution—cotton textiles, iron and steel, and engineering. Such industrial workers tended to be underrepresented among emigrants, and preindustrial craftsmen still to be departing in excessive numbers at that late date. Among them, building trades workers and miners, whose work processes had been little changed by industrialization and who could take those skills virtually unchanged to the labor markets of a developing economy, were most conspicuous. Contrary to the usual depiction of the British emigration to the United States as predominantly one of skilled workers, at least 30 percent of the males were recorded as laborers during the years 1885–88.[7] Further evidence that this stream could be described as a labor migration, more akin in many respects to the incipient new immigration from southern and eastern Europe than to the classical model of old immigration, came from an analysis of traveling companions. Only one in eight of the adult males from England and Scotland traveled with other family members in spite of the relatively high ratio of females to males on these ships.[8]

The revisions suggested by these findings, as well as the check that they provided to both descriptive evidence and published official statistics, led me to wonder whether the ordinary passenger lists might be used to discover something more about the people who were leaving Britain earlier in the century. The period after the Napoleonic wars, when Britain's industrial strength was growing so astonishingly while sectors of her population experienced physical and social dislocation and relocation, and signs of serious social discontent erupted intermittently, is virtually a dark age so far as statistics of emigration are concerned. We have nothing on the sex, age, or occupations of emigrants. The six-month census of emigration that recorded the county of origin of emigrants during 1841 was never repeated.[9] Before the 1850s neither the British nor the American authorities distinguished the Irish from the British in a reasonably satisfactory way. Hence the history of emigration in this period has tended to focus on colonies and assisted migration for which some record exists in government documents. The larger unassisted movement was explained by the recitation of potential sources of emigrants, groups suffering from structural or technological change at various times—kelp gatherers, small-holders in the face of enclosure, handloomweavers, framework-knitters, for example. Or one called attention to the low wages of agricultural laborers.[10] The understandable want of precision and elements of specula-tion in such accounts seemed unavoidable.

At the outset I was not at all certain that the lists from this fascinating early period would be usable. While I had encountered some good lists from that period in the course of other research on individual migrants, there was no way of telling in advance whether or not most of them were carelessly compiled or whether it would be possible to separate the Irish passengers from the English, Scottish, and Welsh to a reliable degree. Thus some kind of pilot study was necessary. The uncertainties seemed to point to a sampling of a year or two. I chose 1831 and 1841 before examining the lists in any detail for any year, a formidable task in itself. These were both years of rising emigration that continued at a high rate relative to trend in the years 1832 and 1842. By choosing these dates I hoped to capture the groups contributing to an increased outflow while somewhat limiting the numbers to be counted or punched on cards. The coincidence of these years with census enumerations left the way open for comparing the emigrating population with the population from which they selected themselves. Moreover, these were both years in which the pushes to emigration of the kind so often cited in accounts of emigration from industrializing Britain were very much in evidence. Unlike the post-Civil War years, peaks of emigration in the 1820s, 1830s, and 1840s coincided more with periods of stress or depression in Britain, rather than with prosperity in the receiving country.[11] The year 1831 stands out as one of considerable agrarian hardship accompanied by machine-breaking riots in many places, and it was also one of the few years in which handloom-weavers were being displaced rapidly in cotton manufacture. The location of distress was more in the industrial sector in 1841, a year that followed several of poor harvests, high food prices, and heavy urban unemploy-ment.[12] The Chartist movement had just reached and passed its peak moment of challenge to social order, and many of the activists are known to have been seeking refuge or a new life in America.[13]

I want to discuss here some of the problems encountered in this substantial pilot project rather than to explore the findings in any detail. The research raised problems of sampling that I hope I have resolved in such a way that the mode of procedure for future work on passenger lists is now fairly clear, at least so far as a study of the British and Irish is concerned.

First of all, the existence of so many carelessly compiled lists, as
well as the very great numbers involved in British and Irish emigration,
seems to point to some sort of sampling. Any attempt to take all passengers on all ships will reduce the quality of the results in my view, by
including "garbage." Obviously sampling will also reduce the work for
those years for which no computerized databank is being compiled. But I
would advocate it in any case. The lists for any years to be studied must be
examined first and ranked for quality; those on which it is impossible to
distinguish the various nationalities of the British Isles, or for which
occupational data are provided only in general terms (e.g., mechanics and
artisans), or in which ditto marks are excessive, must be ranked as poor in
advance of drawing the sample, though obviously not excluded in advance.

Second, ships rather than individuals or migrating units should
form the sampling base. Methods commonly used for census and other
enumerations, of taking individuals or households, are not appropriate.
One reason for this is the poor quality of some lists. One would be
including faulty as well as accurate information. Furthermore, the study of
entire lists can improve the quality of the data. To give one example,
family members are not always listed in groups, and stray members can
often be consolidated with the rest of the family by examining an entire
list. If one wants to study intending migrants, persons stating an intention
to return to Britain or who had previously been in the United States,
returning U.S. citizens, and immigrants from other countries than those
being studied can be omitted, whereas they would flaw any attempt at
sampling individuals or households. Dealing in ships also provides an
economical means of including information about ships and their jour-
neys. Departure dates are not supplied on the manifests but can be found
for ships sailing from British ports.

An unsuspected problem encountered in the 1831 lists may appear
in others, namely that no lists survived for the entire months of April,
May, and August. Since these were clearly important months in the
emigration season, I selected intuitively a five-month sample that omitted
three of the winter months of low emigration and thus consisted of March,
June, July, September, and October. I resolved to test, if possible, the
quality of this sample when I tackled 1841.

A similar five-month sample did not work out very well in 1841. In
1831 the quality of lists had been such that only 13 had to be rejected
during these five months, whereas 222 were usable for the four leading
ports of immigration, New York City, Philadelphia, Boston, and New
Orleans.[14] The matching sample for 1841 required the omission of a much
larger percentage of lists because of poor quality, 116 out of a total of 252.

This outcome proved an additional reason for experimenting with a more scientific method of drawing a sample. To increase confidence limits I took a large sample of one in five ships, though, to maintain numbers, I did leave out ships arriving with fewer than six passengers. The incidence of poor lists made it necessary to modify the one-in-five sample, since I had decided not to feed the computer with poorly compiled data. I, therefore, adopted a one-in-five sample of ships and substituted plus or minus one ship if the sample ship list was poor. Sample ships and sample substitutes were coded separately. The desirability of finding substitutes for poor lists led me to reject the method of random numbers as a means of selecting the ships to be analyzed. The one-in-five method also made it possible to preserve quite well the chronological distribution of ship arrivals.

There is not space here to demonstrate all the results of my testing of various sampling methods. Fuller details may be found in my Final Report to the SSRC, a copy of which is lodged in the British Lending Library. I shall divide this discussion into three parts: (1) a comparison of my findings with published statistics for these years; (2) a comparison of a random number sample with a one-in-five sample in 1841; and (3) a comparison of a five-month sample with a one-in-five sample in 1841.

Comparison with Published Statistics

In general, the research establishes that the original passenger lists offer the chance of more accurate estimates of the numbers and nationalities of immigrants to the United States *via* American ports than are available in the British returns or in those published by the U.S. Department of State for the period. In addition, the estimates of occupation by nationality and of family composition of the migrating population are entirely new, as are details on age and sex.

The potential that the original passenger lists offer for more accurate statistics of immigration by nationality is suggested by tables 18.1 and 18.2. The U.K. figures refer, not to national origin at all, but to the location of the ports from which passengers embarked. The fact that the American figures, purportedly based on passenger lists, recorded exactly the same round percentage of Irish among the immigrants from the British Isles in 1831 and 1841 makes them look very suspect.

There are no British sources for the occupations of emigrants in this period. American figures are not broken down by nationality. (See tables 18.3 and 18.4.) Their crudeness as a profile of immigrants is suggested by the very large number of commercial occupations reported. This reflects not only the careless compilation that one now has greater reason to

Table 18.1

IMMIGRANTS TO THE UNITED STATES FROM THE BRITISH ISLES, 1831

	Ship lists (5 months only) %	U.K. returns of passengers to U.S.A. %	U.S. Immigration figures* %
English & Welsh	66.5	78.0	30.0
Scots	6.3	6.7	
Irish	27.2	15.3	70.0
	100.0	100.0	100.0
N =	8,441	23,418	8,247

*For fiscal year ending 30 September 1831

Table 18.2

IMMIGRANTS TO THE UNITED STATES FROM THE BRITISH ISLES, 1841

	Ship lists 1-in-5 sample %	U.K. returns of passengers to U.S.A. %	U.S. immigration figures %
English	37.5	86.8	30.0
Welsh	5.8		
Scots	7.5	4.6	
Irish	49.1	8.6	70.0
	100.0	100.0	100.0
N =	11,071	45,017	53,960

suspect but also the inclusion of passengers who were not intending to settle in the United States.

Comparison of One-in-Five with Random Numbers Sample

The systematic sample, whether adjusted for poor lists or not, represented the known ports of embarkation for the year 1841 rather better than did a random numbers sample. The latter (unadjusted for poor lists) contained only 27 ships from Liverpool—47 percent of the ships drawn by random numbers—whereas 63 percent of ships carrying British and Irish immigrants arriving that year in five U.S. ports originated in Liverpool. The overrepresentation of Liverpool in the systematic sample (66 percent or 68

Table 18.3

OCCUPATIONS OF MALES AGED 20 OR MORE ARRIVING IN
THE UNITED STATES, 1831

| Occupational Class | Ship lists (5 months only) | | | U.S. immigration figures |
	English %	Scots %	Irish %	All immigrants* %
Agriculture	24.6	15.3	20.2	31.1
Laborer	9.5	17.3	39.1	10.8
Preindustrial tertiary	2.1	0.5	1.8	6.7
Craftsmen	34.9	33.2	17.6	18.7
Industrial	16.5	15.8	12.6	2.3
Modern tertiary	12.4	17.8	8.7	30.4
	100.0	100.0	100.0	100.0
N =	1,794	202	959	8,617

*Other unspecified occupations (3.5%) omitted
Note: See Appendix B, pp. 3a–6, Final Report to Social Science Research Council, for details of occupational classes.

Table 18.4

OCCUPATIONS OF MALES AGED 20 OR MORE ARRIVING IN
THE UNITED STATES, 1841

| | Ship lists | | | U.S. immigration figures |
	English & Welsh %	Scots %	Irish %	All immigrants* %
Agriculture	20.9	16.9	14.8	30.5
Laborer	12.4	15.7	57.6	28.2
Preindustrial tertiary	2.3	1.5	2.0	2.2
Craftsmen	30.6	24.6	15.1	24.4
Industrial	22.8	25.8	5.7	.2
Modern tertiary	9.2	13.5	3.6	14.5
Gentlemen, students	1.8	1.8	1.2	—
	100.0	100.0	100.0	100.0
N =	1,848	325	1,943	40,540

*Omits other occupations not stated.

Table 18.5

MEAN NUMBER OF PASSENGERS PER SHIP ACCORDING TO VARIOUS SAMPLES, 1841

One-in-five sample unadjusted	145
usable lists	138
nonusable lists	156
sample substitutes	153
adjusted sample	144
Random numbers sample unadjusted	135
usable lists	127
nonusable lists	151
sample substitutes	145
adjusted sample	133

percent adjusted) is not serious. Thus there was no reason to reject the systematic sample on this basis.

I expected good lists to have been made more frequently for vessels carrying fewer passengers and a systematic sample, with substitutes, to underweight the more crowded or larger vessels. It is true that usable lists in both the systematic and random samples were on average slightly shorter than lists that were rejected. When substitutions had been made, however, the mean number of passengers per ship returned to that of the original unadjusted sample, 144 for the one-in-five sample (as compared with an initial mean of 145) and 133 by the random number method (from an original mean of 135). Thus the expected weakness of the systematic sample, adjusted with substitutes, did not emerge. (See table 18.5.)

The main reason for the larger mean in the case of the one-in-five sample is that it contained more of the larger ships coming from Liverpool.

The variance in passengers per vessel of the two sorts of sample unadjusted was almost identical. Substitutions raised that of the random numbers sample and reduced that of the systematic sample by approximately equal amounts, but in both the differences were slight.

The one-in-five sample unadjusted agreed almost perfectly with that sample adjusted on account of poor lists with respect to date of arrival. The adjusted sample contained one fewer June arrival and one more in July and one fewer in September. (One ship had to be omitted for want of a suitable adjacent arrival.) Furthermore, the one-in-five sample had a distinctly better chronological distribution when compared with all arrivals than did a sample drawn by random numbers when the latter had been adjusted for poor lists. That adjustment underweighted the busy summer months whereas the adjusted one-in-five sample did not.

Thus the tests suggest that the systematic sample is at least as good, even using substitutes, as the more awkward method, in this case, of random numbers. The total number of British arrivals in five ports in 1841 estimated by sampling one-in-five ships came to almost exactly the same number as were reported in State Department statistics of arrivals that year—53,560 as compared with 53,960. This further enhanced confidence in the method and also indicated that the published totals were not so deficient in 1841 as they had been in 1831.

Comparison of Five-month with One-in-Five Sample, 1841

The next step was to ascertain whether a five-month sample, such as was necessary to take in 1831, approximated the systematic one-in-five sample sufficiently to give confidence in the findings. I have taken nationality and occupation as the two most sensitive criteria by which to estimate the credibility of the five-month samples.[15]

It will be seen from table 18.6 that estimates by these two sample methods are remarkably close. The chief difference is that MONMAT (five-month sample) appears to underestimate the Irish arrivals by about 2 percent and to overestimate the Scots. This is explained when one looks at the proportion of the various groups in monthly arrivals. The Irish had one massive peak of arrivals in May, a month not included in MONMAT, whereas the Scottish immigration in 1841 peaked in September and October, two months that were included in MONMAT. MONMAT proved to match better with English arrivals, though it did include the three biggest months, June, July, and October.[16] Either sample provides a more accurate breakdown of immigrants from the British Isles than the official statistics.

Few significant differences were apparent between the five-month sample and the one-in-five sample with respect to occupations (see table 18.7). The larger differences may be explained by the same underestimation of spring arrivals and overrepresentation of autumn arrivals induced by missing lists in 1831. For example, laborers were underrepresented among the English in MONMAT because the month of December, not in the sample, was the month of largest numbers of arrivals of laborers. One could expect greater variations in the figures concerning the Scots in any case because the numbers were smaller.

Thus I conclude that the five-month sample is fairly good as an indicator of occupations of immigrants, certainly an improvement on the figures published by the U.S. State Department at the time and reissued by the U.S. Treasury in 1902/3. But the systematic one-in-five sample of ships is better. The differences are not great enough to rule out com-

Table 18.6

IMMIGRANT ARRIVALS BY NATIONALITY IN 1841, COMPARISON OF SAMPLES

Nationality	1-in-5		5-month		U.S. Passenger arrivals	
	No.	%	No.	%	No.	%
English & Welsh	4,799	43.3	5,519	43.4	16,188	30.0
Scottish	829	7.5	1,235	9.7		
Irish	5,443	49.2	5,965	46.9	37,772	70.0
Totals	11,071	100.0	12,719	100.0	53,960	100.0
Missing observations	181		304			

Table 18.7

OCCUPATIONS OF IMMIGRANT MALES AGED 20 OR MORE, 1841, COMPARISON OF SAMPLES PERCENTAGE DISTRIBUTION

Occupational Class	English & Welsh		Scots		Irish	
	5-month sample	1-in-5 sample	5-month sample	1-in-5 sample	5-month sample	1-in-5 sample
Agriculture	18.0	20.9	21.8	16.9	14.1	14.8
Laborers	15.4	12.4	15.9	15.7	54.1	57.6
Preindustrial tertiary	2.0	2.3	.9	1.5	2.1	2.0
Craftsmen	33.7	30.6	27.2	24.6	18.6	15.1
Modern industrial	20.8	22.8	24.0	25.8	6.7	5.7
Modern tertiary	8.5	9.2	10.2	13.5	4.0	3.6
Gentlemen, students	1.6	1.8	.0	1.8	.5	1.2
	100.0	100.0	100.0	100.0	100.0	100.0
N =	2,146	1,848	459	325	2,142	1,943

parisons between the two 5-month samples of 1831 and 1841 as improving our knowledge about the composition of British and Irish immigration via American ports in the period. The conclusion is supported by comparisons between samples with respect to age distribution, mean age, sex ratios, and migrating units.

Two further problems arose in trying to extract the best possible information from the lists included in any of the samples. Family relationships were sometimes stated on the lists as "wife," "mother," "sister," and so forth. More frequently the relationship had to be judged. Many were easy to code, for example, a man and woman with the same surname accompanied by children with the same surname. A man and woman with the same surname without children might, however, be siblings or spouses. It was uncertain whether a woman with a different surname following a family group was traveling alone or was perhaps the mother or sister of the wife. No doubt women have not been attached to the appropriate family groups in all cases because of this reliance on surnames, and the incidence of their traveling alone correspondingly exaggerated. Rules were adopted for making inferences about family relationships when this was necessary. Those about which we were uncertain were coded separately as such and logged. When coding was completed it was found that 98.9 percent of the English and Welsh migrating units had been coded with confidence and 97 percent of the Irish, among whom the problem of distinguishing between siblings and married couples was greater.

Lists that were otherwise good sometimes reported Great Britain as place of origin, a fact that explains the very large numbers returned as "G.B. not stated" in published statistics. I used surname dictionaries to assign nationality in such cases. For the most part only those surnames designated as distinctive, that is, not found in more than one part of the British Isles at the time, were coded as to nationality with confidence. Others were assigned under certain conditions, for example, when a large number of Irish passengers were traveling together, the few passengers with nondistinctive names among them were assumed to be Irish as well. Nationalities were assigned according to rules and coded separately as "probable" when not assigned with perfect confidence. The use of dictionaries of surnames raised the percentage of English and Welsh immigrants in the one-in-five sample by about 3-1/2 percent and reduced that of the Irish and Scots by that amount. I have little doubt that my estimates of the share of each nationality in the 1841 emigration to the United States is immensely better than the portion to be surmised from figures given in the *Historical Statistics of the United States*.

The results of this work on the 1841 census will be published elsewhere. I can do no more than summarize very baldly some of the first gleanings. The share of the English among emigrants form the British Isles is underestimated, and the share of the Irish exaggerated in official returns for this period. A very high incidence of family migration was found among English emigrants of 1831, only slightly diminished in 1841. Welsh emigration was even more familial than the English, and both more so than the Irish and Scots, though Scottish emigration contained more families in 1841 than in 1831.

There is evidence that the timing of emigration was related to the family life cycle, most families leaving at a favorable moment, either before more than one child had arrived, or when there was more than one of an age to enter the labor force immediately. A similar rationality of choice seems evident in decisions about ports of debarkation, especially among the English, with textile workers, for example, favoring Boston, and farmers New York City or New Orleans. Farmers were more likely to be emigrating with family than industrial workers from the modernizing sectors in England, who most frequently went out alone.

The only occupation excessively overrepresented, as compared with the labor force in England, was that of farmer. Laborers, on the other hand, were underrepresented. The emigration of 1841 proved to be, as expected from contemporary comment, more industrial than that of 1831. The share of preindustrial craftsmen was about the same in 1831 and 1841, not significantly greater than their distribution in the English labor force. The increase in the share of industrial workers in 1841 consisted primarily of emigrants from the industrializing sectors, chiefly textile workers and engineers, though the index of representation of these in 1841 scarcely suggested anything like a mass exodus. Indeed, the similarities between the emigrating population and the census population in age, sex, and occupation was noteworthy; and the findings, therefore, suggest that standard descriptions of emigration in this period in terms of the poverty and difficulties of certain groups do not stand up to quantitative tests.

The contrasts between the emigration of 1831 and 1841 on the one hand and that of the 1880s on the other were unmistakable. The English and Scots' emigration had been transformed from one in which a large majority left with other members of their immediate families to one in which there was a great preponderance of adult males; and far more females were traveling alone, in spite of the fact that the percentage of women barely changed among the English though rising quite steeply among the Scots and Irish. The share of laborers had risen very sharply between the two periods as had that of clerical workers, the less-skilled white-collar workers. It makes sense that the availability of steam transport at the same price as sail had once been, as well as rising real incomes, should have made it possible for poorer people closer to the bottom of the occupation scale to have been able to contemplate and embark upon emigration later in the century. However, more is involved in the changes in structure than mere financial capability. There were significant differences between occupational groups in the tendency to travel in families or with dependent children and in the size of migrating units in the early period. Industrial workers in the modernizing industries, who presumably could have afforded to take families, were more likely to travel alone or in smaller family groups than were laborers.

Thus there are a number of unresolved issues in the emigration from

England that a further investigation of passenger lists might help illuminate.[17] Assuming that this structural shift in emigrants, which did not merely reflect changes in the ages and occupations of the parent populations, did take place between the 1830s and the 1880s—an assumption that itself requires further work to verify—when did the changes take place? Were they gradual or somewhat sudden responses to changes in the States or opportunities in other regions of settlement? One would also like to be able to compare troughs and peaks of migration with respect to data accessible in the passenger lists. Production of annual estimates may be overly ambitious in these hard times; but even the sampling of a few more carefully selected years would greatly enhance our knowledge, or at least provide some underpinning for our speculations. Any serious attempt at explaining the emigration from Great Britain requires such improved descriptive data on migration differentials. However, as I have suggested, that data may be collected more confidently by careful sampling than by using all of the lists we hope will be available one day in the databank at the Balch Institute.

Finally, I want to turn briefly to a consideration of the scope for record linkage of passengers with other historical documentation, something in which Professor Swierenga has accomplished so much for Dutch migrants and Ollson, in a different way, for the Swedes.[18] Can one trace passengers from origins to destination and thus secure longitudinal studies of lifetime careers?

If we turn first to the British side of such a proposal, it is evident that the manuscript censuses available from 1841 to 1871, and the civil registers of births and marriages, compiled with increasing completeness from 1837 onward for England and Wales, and 1857 for Scotland, afford tempting possibilities. Other sources such as parish registers, tax records, and local directories have much more limited usefulness.

But the obstacles are forbidding. The Registrar General now insists on a fee of £3.50 for every single birth or marriage certificate, and scholars are no longer permitted to search the registers even when copies survive in local archives. The registers provide quarterly national indexes; but the search for individuals, in the absence of precise place of origin from the passenger lists, would be a daunting and uncertain chore, never mind the expense. This want of information as to place of origin, as well as an absence of indexes, militates against linkage with census records. Michael Anderson's project on the 1851 census consists of samples, and thus will not provide the comprehensive base one would need for linkage with passenger lists.[18] The case would seem to be hopeless.

Yet I can see certain possibilities and will give one example. Nick Tiratsoo has recently completed a dissertation on Coventry that, among other things, examines family strategies in the face of the difficulties of the silk industry in the 1850s and its collapse in the 1860s.[19] He has used census manuscripts in order to trace families and individuals who remained in Coventry during these decades. The disappearances might be checked against death registers. Since those who failed to appear in a subsequent census consist of far too many young people to be accounted for by deaths, they must constitute a large part of those who migrated internally or overseas. The different family position and age of the nonpersistent in the two decades also suggests that the role of overseas migration may have varied as between a slowly growing and a declining industry. Access to an alphabetical listing of English emigrants during these years might make matching possible, especially in that in this case one would have several variables to match, not only Christian names, but sometimes wives and even children, as well as ages and occupations. At least one could get some idea of the extent to which emigration to the most popular field for English emigration in the period offered a way out of the town's distress and the social and familial composition of those groups who sought and were able to take this step. It would be an interesting test of the hardship, or push, theory of emigration, but will not be feasible without the datafile of passenger lists.

Linking English migrants on passenger lists with U.S. records also offers particular problems, partly because, unlike the Dutch, the English scattered to so many destinations within the United States. It would be hard to think of any place where one might begin with a significant or typical English settlement that might warrant a census search and subsequent attempt to link cases with passenger lists. Paterson, New Jersey, Fall River, Massachusetts, or East Liverpool, Ohio, might be possibilities. Unfortunately such linking could not easily open up a way into the English sources.

If we want to try to compile life histories of English emigrants to the United States in quantity, clearly another means of understanding the movement away from the world's most industrial nation to a less-developed one, the place to begin, I suggest, is with county histories. Admittedly the subjects of biographies appearing therein are not selected randomly, and the quality of brief lives varies; but one can select counties to be examined according to explicit criteria, and the biographies contain clues for U.S. census and directory linkages. They also usually give at least the year of emigration if not the actual ship. Indexes to passenger lists would greatly facilitate identification therein, and in turn lead to English sources that in this case would be usable, if expensive, because place of birth or marriage or even intermediate migrations are so frequently given in the county histories. Longitudinal studies of such migrants, not quite élite but clearly more successful than the ordinary migrant, would yield much food for thought, and the passenger lists could help in their compilation when they become more easily accessible as a result of the work now being carried out in Philadelphia.

Notes

1. C. J. Erickson, "Who Were the English and Scottish Immigrants to the U.S.A. in the 1880s?" in D. V. Glass and R. Revelle, eds., *Population and Social Change*, E. Arnold, London, 1972, p. 371.

2. M. A. Jones, "The Background to Emigration from Great Britain in the Nineteenth Century," *Perspectives in American History*, VII, 1973, pp. 35–36. Terry Coleman, *Passage to America*, Hutchinson, London, 1972, pp. 71–72, 213, 216.

3. R. P. Swierenga, "Dutch Immigrant Demography, 1820–1880," *Journal of Family History*, Winter 1980, p. 393, where he asserts that "for all of their flaws and occasional omissions [the U.S. passenger lists] provide a more trustworthy record of immigration into the United States than do foreign passport journals or municipal emigration or population registers." N. W. Olssen, *Swedish Passenger Arrivals*, Acta Bibliotecae Regiae Stockholmiensis, 6, Stockholm, 1967, p. xiii. R. P. Swierenga, *Dutch Immigrants on U.S. Passenger Lists: An Alphabetical Listing*, Kent, Ohio, 1978, R. P. Swierenga and H. S. Stout, "Dutch Immigration in the Nineteenth Century, 1820–1877: A Quantitative Overview," *Indiana Social Studies Quarterly* 27, 1975, pp. 7–34.

4. Joel Mokyr and Cormac Ó Gráda, "Emigration and Poverty in Prefamine Ireland," Unpublished paper, Northwestern University, October 1981. Joel Mokyr, *Why Ireland Starved: A Quantitative and Analytical History of the Irish Economy, 1800–1850*, Allen & Unwin, London, 1983.

5. Olsson, *Swedish Passenger Arrivals*. Mokyr has analyzed Olsson's material to use as a control in his study of Irish emigration.

6. Erickson in Glass and Revelle, eds., *Population and Social Change*, pp. 354–55. C. J. Erickson, "Emigration from the British Isles to the U.S.A. in 1831," *Population Studies* 25, July 1981, pp. 175–97.

7. The sample from good ship lists produced an estimate of 29.5% of laborers among adult male immigrants from England and Scotland, 1885–88, although the statistics compiled by the U.S. Treasury gave even higher estimates—47% in 1882 and 35% in 1888, 38.9% for the years 1885–88. (Erickson in Glass and Revelle, eds., *Population and Social Change*, pp. 363, 380, 381.)

8. Cf. R. P. Swierenga, "International Labor Migration in the Nineteenth Century: the Dutch Example," Paper presented to Session C.10 of the *Seventh International Economic History Congress*, Edinburgh, Scotland, August 13–19 1978. R. P. Swierenga, *Journal of Family History*, Winter 1980, p. 390. R. P. Shaw, *Migration, Theory and Fact*, Philadelphia Regional Social Science Institute, 1975, p. 21. B. Kronberg and T. Nilsson, *Stadtsflyttare, Industrialesering, migration och social mobilitet med utgångspunkt från Halmstad, 1870–1910*, Studia Historica Upsaliensla, 65, pp. 270–71.

9. J. R. Jeffery and N. H. Carrier, *External Migration, A Study of the Available Statistics, 1815–1950*, General Register Office, *Studies on Medical and Population Subjects*, no. 6, London, HMSO, 1953. U.S. Treasury Department, Bureau of Statistics, *Immigration into the United States . . . 1820–1903*, HR 57c, 2s, Doc. no. 15, part 2, Series 1902–3, *Monthly Summary of Finance and Commerce of the United States*, May 1903. W. J. Bromwell, *History of Immigration to the United States*, New York, 1856. For the emigration census, see *Census of Great Britain, 1841: Abstract of Answers and Returns*, British Parliamentary Papers, 1843. The census is discussed in Jones, *Perspectives*, 1973, pp. 45–47 and in Arthur Redford, *Labour Migration in England*, Manchester University Press, 1926, p. 78.

10. S. C. Johnson, *A History of Emigration from the United Kingdom to North America, 1763–1912*, George Routledge and Sons, London, 1913, pp. 40–41, 44–45, 48–49, 50–59. W. A. Corrothers, *Emigration from the British Isles*, P. S. King, London, 1929, pp. 172–73, 180–82. W. S. Shepperson, *British Emigration to North America, Projects and Opinions in the Early Victorian Period*, University of Minnesota Press, Minneapolis, 1957, pp. 26–27, 67–68, 76–78, 80–81. M. A. Jones dismisses the plight of the handloomweavers and enclosures as sources of emigration (Jones, *Perspectives*, 1973, pp. 43–45). But see also ibid., pp. 6–9, 37–40, 88–90.

11. Harry Jerome, *Migration and the Business Cycle*, National Bureau of Economic Research, New York, 1926, pp. 240–41. Brinley Thomas, *Migration and Economic Growth*, NIESR, Cambridge University Press, Cambridge, 1954, pp. 92–94, 159–60.

12. A. D. Gayer, W. W. Rostow, and A. J. Schwarz, *The Growth and Fluctuation of the British Economy, 1790–1850*, Clarendon Press, Oxford, 1952, vol. 1, pp. 276, 285, 286, 288, 290, 294–95. The writers cite Thomas Tooke, who noted that in the first months of 1841 there was "a general feeling of hope prevalent that a revival of trade was about to take place." But as the summer advanced it became clear that continued high prices of corn and cattle, together with the scarcity of employment "precluded any material improvement for the present; and reports from the manufacturing districts grew gradually more gloomy than ever." Not until 1842 did good weather break "the spell of the previous four years of 'dearth'." (Ibid. p. 277, n. 8, and 277–78.)

13. Ray Boston, *Chartists in America, 1839–1900*, Manchester University Press, Manchester, 1971, pp. xiii, 17–18, 21–35 and Appendix A, pp. 88–97.

14. No lists survive from Baltimore in 1831, but it can be shown that Baltimore was not a significant port of entry at that time for British and Irish immigrants. (Erickson, *Population Studies*, July 1981, p. 180, n. 21.)

15. Tables comparing the two samples according to age distribution, sex ratios, and migrating units are included in my Final Report to the SSRC, British Lending Library, pp. 22–23.

16. W. S. Shepperson suggested that an autumn peaking of departures indicated that industrial workers were departing, since agriculturists usually chose the spring and early summer (*British Emigration to North America*, p. 81). Both he and M. A. Jones concluded from other sources that industrial workers (not craftsmen) constituted a larger share of British emigrants during periods of cyclical depression such as 1841–42 (ibid., p. 81; Jones, *Perspectives*, 1973, pp. 45–47).

17. See the summary of literature relating migration to structural change in R. P. Shaw, *Migration, Theory and Fact*, p. 29.

18. Scholars who have linked New Zealand and Australian passenger lists with the U.K. census include Rollo Arnold, *The Farthest Promised Land*, Victoria University Press, Wellington, 1981, and Ross Duncan, "Case Studies in Emigration; Cornwall, Gloucestershire and New South Wales, 1877–86," *Economic History Review*, Second Series, vol. 16, no. 2, December 1963, pp. 272–89.

19. N. Tiratsoo, "Coventry's Ribbon Trade in the Mid-Victorian period: Some Social and Economic Responses to Industrial Development and Decay," Ph.D. diss. (University of London, 1980).

19

Internal Migration and the Changing Structure of Employment in the United States in 1900: Machine Readable Census Samples as a New Source for Historical Research

Ann R. Miller

The crucial importance of migration in the economic development of the United States and in the structural transformation of employment from agricultural to nonagricultural activities is an accepted fact of history. But we have only minimal direct empirical evidence of the links between population redistribution and structural change. This essay adds to that evidence by utilizing newly available data on age and occupation of native-born migrants. The data are from a recently developed Public Use Sample [6] constructed from the manuscript returns of the 1900 Census of Population, and a major purpose here is to suggest the great potential of such a source.

Two interrelated questions are posed for empirical investigation: (1) what part does migration play in effecting changes in the structure of employment? and (2) how do migrants differ from the nonmigrant population? In terms of the newly available data these strip down to two sets of questions.

Do migrants contribute disproportionately to the growing sectors of the economy? This is related to but not identical with the economists' framework that regards migration as an equilibrating mechanism and (therefore) expects migration flows to be from areas of declining to areas of expanding economic opportunity. For example, one could hypothesize that local residents move into growth sectors and migrants take the place of those locals in the less prosperous sectors. Indeed, much migration literature has posited such a model, arguing that migrants come in at the bottom of whatever occupational hierarchy prevails. Such a situation can obviously occur within an overall equilibrating framework, since even the bottom of the hierarchy in area A may present better income opportunities than those available in area B.

Simplifying, we can say that migration can contribute to a structural change in employment either indirectly by "freeing" nonmigrants to make the necessary adjustment or directly by the entrance of migrants to the expanding sector. A third possibility, of course, is that the structural role of migration is random, i.e., that no differences exist in the employment distribution patterns of migrants and nonmigrants. In this case, the functional role of migration is to shift the location of employment rather than to affect its structure. Strictly speaking, this occurs only when (in the aggregate) the employment distribution of migrants is identical to that of nonmigrants in both the area of origin and the area of destination since a deviation from either of these distributions will affect the "global" structure.

This essay will be confined to the examination of these three variants but, logically, several other possibilities exist. For example, if 5,000 farm workers move from area A to area B, employment structure in both areas will be affected, but the total (national, let us say) structure will not show an immediate change. If productivity in B is greater than productivity in A, however, this migration contributes to economic growth and can be expected eventually to result in a changed distribution of employment in accordance with the resulting changed structure in the demand for goods and services. The shift of agricultural workers westward in the United States may be generally assumed to have functioned in this way.

The opposite situation may also obtain: migrants may be randomly selected from the area of origin and be randomly employed in the area of destination so that the structure (although not the level) of employment is unaffected in either area but the total structure is altered, the mechanism being the association of migration with occupational change on the part of the migrants. This assumption, in fact, appears to underlie much migration analysis that, in the absence of information on the occupation of migrants, must rely on population rather than on worker flows.[1] A deficiency in this model, which cannot link migration and structural change, is that it ignores (i.e., does not permit consideration of) the function of migration in the dispersion of structural change, an important correlate—and perhaps an essential component—of modern economic growth. Nevertheless, the arithmetic of the situation, the rapidity of the shift out of agriculture in some parts of the country, suggests that occupational change must have been significantly associated with migration even if, as we must in this analysis, we exclude persons moving from rural to urban areas of the same state from participation in the migration process.

The consideration of occupational change leads quite naturally to the second aspect of migration noted—the extent to which migrants differ from the nonmigrant population. In the present essay this consists merely of looking at the same data from a different viewpoint, although later we will explore other available microlevel variables.

That migration is selective is a pervading theme in that body of the migration literature that has concerned itself with the characteristics of migrants—primarily the contributions of sociologists and demographers. One aspect of selectivity, the high incidence of migration in the young adult ages, has been adopted into the economic literature on migration also, since it fits nicely into the human capital framework that has dominated recent work by economists. But the selectivity issue of more general concern is whether migrants are somehow "better" (or "worse") than nonmigrants.

Twenty years ago Simon Kuznets proposed, with due caution, that one could reasonably assume that migrants include "a greater proportion of adventurous and independent individuals" and that "the personality characteristics . . . involved in such selectivity make for long-term prospects of greater productivity and efficiency" with the result that the "process of selection . . . promises an extra gain of productivity over and above the assumption of unselected migration" [2, p. xxxii]. More recently it has been suggested that migrants may be selected from the more advantaged segments of the origin population, that is, that they come from families with above average economic status in the area of origin, with the concomitant effect of reducing the "risks" of migration [5, p. 15]; according to this hypothesis, premigration status rather than personality is the underlying selector.[2]

The present data set cannot be used to support or refute either of these hypotheses since we know neither the personality traits nor the premigration status of the migrants. Nevertheless, as we shall see, migrants do differ from nonmigrants and, if one is willing to concede that white-collar work is accorded high social status, have, on average, higher status occupations than nonmigrants in the United States as a whole and, generally, in the region of destination; whether one interprets this as indicating that they start out with higher status or that they achieve higher status by more energetic effort depends on one's own predilections.

The Data

The basic data come from a national sample of the 1900 Census of Population. The sample was chosen from the manuscript returns, with all household and individual characteristics collected in that census for the 100,000 persons in the sample put in machine-readable form (see table 19.1). Although I hope eventually to incorporate data for the black population and for white women, the present essay uses only a file for gainfully occupied white men aged twenty years and over in 1900. The age cut-off—that is, the exclusion of gainful workers under age twenty—is chosen in an attempt to increase the probability that the migrants in our study are "decision makers." A lifetime migration measure—the only measure available in the 1900 Census—obviously tells us nothing about the timing of migration and an assumption that a high proportion of migrants under age twenty are what are known as "tied" migrants, moving in company with their parents under a decision made by the parents, seems reasonable. Clearly, some persons in all age groups are migrants by reason of a parental decision, but the proportion is likely to be lower in the adult ages.[3]

Three age groups are distinguished. One purpose is to control for age, which here represents the "exposure to risk" period. In fixed-interval migration research, controls for age are ordinarily introduced because the incidence of migration is so highly concentrated in the young adult population, with the consequence that comparisons among general proportions between populations with different age composition may be distorted. The lifetime migration measure is cumulative and also subject to distortion, but in this case the effect comes from differential concentration in older ages. An example of this appears in table 19.2: the interstate migration proportion for the total number of individuals twenty years of age and over among the Northeast born is higher for farm than for manual workers, but this is not true for any of the individual age groups; it has occurred because nearly half the farm workers are over forty-five, i.e., in the high exposure group, while only a little over a fourth of manual workers are in this age category and half are under thirty-five, i.e., in the low exposure group. To conclude, on the basis of the top panel of table 19.2, that, among the Northeastern born, farmers are more likely to make interstate moves than manual workers would clearly be inaccurate.

A second purpose in presenting the age groups is to introduce a rough control for structural changes in employment over time. The hypothesis, generally supported by what empirical evidence we have, is that new

Table 19.1

GAINFULLY OCCUPIED WHITE MEN, TWENTY YEARS OF AGE AND OVER, BY OCCUPATION, AGE, AND *REGION OF RESIDENCE IN 1900* BY LIFETIME MIGRATION STATUS

Age and occupation in 1900	Region of residence in 1900 (N)					Percent born outside region of residence (including foreign-born)				
	United States	Northeast	North Central	South	West	United States	Northeast	North Central	South	West
Gainfully occupied 20 years of age and over	22,895	7,350	8,761	5,173	1,611	36	37	40	15	79
White collar	4,325	1,604	1,555	851	315	34	28	37	22	80
Manual and service	8,232	3,771	2,751	1,048	662	45	43	46	23	84
Farm	8,212	1,146	3,592	2,996	478	26	17	35	10	74
Laborers, not specified	2,126	829	863	278	156	49	56	47	18	74
Gainfully occupied, 20–34	10,478	3,372	3,973	2,443	690	28	34	27	12	67
White collar	1,918	706	695	385	132	24	24	22	15	64
Manual and service	4,025	1,887	1,338	519	281	37	39	33	19	75
Farm	3,435	368	1,509	1,361	197	17	15	19	8	59
Laborers, not specified	1,100	411	431	178	80	38	48	33	14	62
Gainfully occupied, 35–44	5,553	1,808	2,166	1,155	424	39	41	42	17	82
White collar	1,111	399	415	210	87	37	28	40	27	85
Manual and service	2,164	945	749	272	198	50	49	50	23	86
Farm	1,807	264	802	635	106	24	14	33	10	75
Laborers, not specified	471	200	200	38	33	56	64	50	10	75
Gainfully occupied 45 and over	6,864	2,170	2,622	1,575	497	46	38	60	19	94
White collar	1,296	499	445	256	96	45	33	58	27	98
Manual and service	2,043	939	664	257	183	55	46	66	33	96
Farm	2,970	514	1,281	1,000	175	37	19	56	13	89
Laborers, not specified	555	218	232	62	43	64	63	71	*	*

	Percent foreign-born					Percent native interregional migrants				
Gainfully occupied 20 years of age and over	26	34	28	6	36	11	2	13	9	43
White collar	20	23	22	8	27	14	4	16	13	53
Manual and service	35	41	34	12	42	10	2	13	12	42
Farm	16	15	23	3	35	10	1	12	7	38
Laborers, not specified	40	55	37	9	35	8	1	10	9	39
Gainfully occupied, 20–34	20	31	19	3	30	8	3	7	8	37
White collar	14	19	13	4	19	10	5	10	11	45
Manual and service	29	36	26	8	37	8	2	8	11	38
Farm	10	13	14	1	29	7	2	5	7	30
Laborers, not specified	31	47	28	6	25	7	1	5	8	38
Gainfully occupied, 35–44	28	38	30	8	38	11	3	12	9	45
White collar	22	23	25	11	36	14	5	15	16	49
Manual and service	38	46	38	12	38	11	3	12	11	48
Farm	15	12	21	4	42	9	2	11	6	34
Laborers, not specified	48	63	42	*	*	7	—	8	*	*
Gainfully occupied 45 and over	31	36	38	9	45	15	2	22	10	49
White collar	27	29	33	12	31	18	4	26	14	67
Manual and service	42	44	44	19	55	13	2	22	13	42
Farm	22	18	35	5	39	15	1	21	8	50
Laborers, not specified	52	61	52	*	*	12	1	19	*	*

Source: 1900 Public Use Sample
*Percent not shown where base is less than 75 cases
—Less than 0.5 percent

341

Table 19.2

GAINFULLY OCCUPIED NATIVE MEN, TWENTY YEARS OF AGE AND OVER, BY OCCUPATION, AGE IN 1900, BY REGION OF BIRTH AND LIFETIME MIGRATION STATUS

Age and occupation in 1900	Region of birth (N)					Percent out of state of birth in 1900				
	United States	Northeast	North Central	South	West	United States	Northeast	North Central	South	West
Gainfully occupied 20 years of age and over	17,037	5,736	6,023	4,922	356	33	30	38	31	26
White collar	3,456	1,460	1,157	769	70	38	35	43	39	*
Manual and service	5,373	2,534	1,749	975	115	33	28	39	37	28
Farm	6,938	1,296	2,601	2,913	128	30	31	35	27	20
Laborers, not specified	1,270	446	516	265	43	31	25	36	32	*
Gainfully occupied, 20–34	8,352	2,500	3,284	2,326	242	26	22	30	24	27
White collar	1,651	614	618	366	53	31	26	34	35	*
Manual and service	2,849	1,278	1,004	491	76	27	21	30	33	32
Farm	3,095	375	1,335	1,302	83	22	20	27	18	23
Laborers, not specified	757	233	327	167	30	25	17	33	22	*
Gainfully occupied, 35–44	3,974	1,319	1,472	1,101	82	35	30	42	32	23
White collar	864	360	305	184	15	40	36	48	38	*
Manual and service	1,333	582	457	262	32	37	30	47	37	*
Farm	1,533	288	599	620	26	30	25	36	28	*
Laborers, not specified	244	89	111	35	9	34	28	40	*	*
Gainfully occupied 45 and over	4,711	1,917	1,267	1,495	32	44	41	52	42	*
White collar	941	486	234	219	2	50	47	59	47	*
Manual and service	1,191	674	288	222	7	44	39	58	45	*
Farm	2,310	633	667	991	19	42	39	48	39	*
Laborers, not specified	269	124	78	63	4	45	40	42	*	*

	Percent intraregional migrants					Percent interregional migrants				
Gainfully occupied 20 years of age and over	19	11	24	20	20	14	19	13	11	6
White collar	21	14	27	26	*	17	21	16	13	*
Manual and service	17	13	23	19	19	16	15	16	18	9
Farm	18	4	24	20	19	12	26	11	7	2
Laborers, not specified	17	7	24	18	*	14	18	11	14	*
Gainfully occupied, 20–34	16	11	19	16	21	10	11	11	7	6
White collar	19	13	22	24	*	12	13	13	11	*
Manual and service	15	12	18	19	24	11	9	13	14	8
Farm	15	3	18	14	20	8	17	9	4	2
Laborers, not specified	16	8	21	13	*	10	9	12	8	*
Gainfully occupied, 35–44	19	11	27	19	15	15	19	15	13	9
White collar	22	16	29	21	*	19	20	19	17	*
Manual and service	18	12	28	17	*	18	17	19	20	*
Farm	19	4	26	20	*	11	21	10	8	*
Laborers, not specified	20	10	30	*	*	14	18	10	*	*
Gainfully occupied 45 and over	23	11	35	28	*	21	30	17	14	*
White collar	25	15	38	33	*	25	31	21	15	*
Manual and service	21	14	36	23	*	23	24	21	22	*
Farm	23	5	34	27	*	19	34	15	12	*
Laborers, not specified	20	5	29	*	*	26	35	13	*	*

Source: 1900 Public Use Sample
*Percent not shown where base is less than 75 cases
Note: Data for United States in this table differ from those in table 19.1 because this table excludes the foreign-born.

Table 19.3

GAINFULLY OCCUPIED WHITE MEN BY AGE AND
OCCUPATION IN 1900—UNITED STATES

Occupation in 1900	All workers (age in 1900)			Nonmigrant workers (age in 1900)		
	20–34	35–44	45 and over	20–34	35–44	45 and over
Total (N)	10,478	5,553	6,864	6,206	2,592	2,627
Total percent	100	100	100	100	100	100
White collar	18	21	19	18	20	18
Manual and service	39	38	30	34	33	25
Farm	33	33	43	39	41	51
Laborers, not specified	10	8	8	9	6	6

entrants to the labor market make the structural adjustments required by changes in the demand for labor. Under this hypothesis then the occupational distribution of each age group becomes a crude approximation of the structure of demand for labor at the time that that group entered the labor market; and differences among the age groups are, in turn, a crude approximation of changes in the demand for labor over time. The crudity of such an indicator is obvious. Nevertheless, as table 19.3 indicates, the procedure does capture the decline in farm and the increase in manual workers for both total and nonmigrant men.

The fact that no trend emerges for white collar workers is somewhat surprising in view of previous estimates that have suggested a substantial increase in the share of retail and wholesale trade in the last decades of the nineteenth century [3, p. 53]; the anomaly may occur because of the fact that retail trade—in particular, when it is carried on primarily by small independent proprietors—is a sector into which older workers are likely to move, in contradiction to the general hypothesis already proposed.[4]

In any event, since both the incidence of lifetime migration and the occupational distribution vary among the age groups, it is obviously desirable to hold age constant if we wish to compare migrants and nonmigrants. I might also note that, more or less fortuitously, the youngest group are those born after the Civil War, the oldest those born before.

Four occupational categories are shown in the tables, but only three enter into the discussion, the omitted category being "Laborers, not specified." This occupational title appears in the censuses of 1870 through 1900 and has plagued scholars trying to develop historical series for decades [4, pp. 383–85]. The primary issue is how to estimate its agricultural and nonagricultural components. We hope eventually to throw further light on the issue by doing a microlevel analysis of individuals classified to the category, but for the present it seems wisest to carry them as a separate group. I might add, however, that our preliminary assessment is that most should be included with manual and service rather than with farm workers.

The remaining three occupational categories are the major broad groupings that have come into use over the last forty years. The manuscript entries on the 1900 Census schedules were coded to the 1950 detailed occupational classification system[5] in the process of developing the sample, and these groups are aggregations of that system. They are comparable with similar groupings from the 1940 through 1970 censuses and with the historical series for the 1900–1950 period developed by Kaplan and Casey [1] for the country as a whole, although obviously our inability to distribute the "Laborers, not specified" category at this point introduces some incomparability in the relative proportions.

An objection may be made to regarding an occupational distribution that includes only one segment of the labor force, white men, as indicating structural change in the demand for labor. This is a valid objection, but several aspects of the situation in 1900 suggest that the distribution for white men may be particularly responsive to expanding employment opportunities. Occupational segregation of blacks and of white women generally had the effect of preventing their movement into expanding sectors. Clerical work, which provides the jobs accounting for much of the spectacular increase in women's employment in the twentieth century, is by far the smallest of the white collar categories in 1900 and at that date less than a fourth of clerical workers are women. Further work, incorporating all groups, will indicate whether this use of the distribution of white men is reasonable.

Two simple measures are used for the preliminary exploration of these data: (1) the proportion in-migrants are of the total in the area of destination (table 19.1); and (2) the proportion out-migrants are of the total origin population (table 19.2). The first is a measure of the impact of migration; the second is commonly referred to as the probability rate of out-migration. In both cases, differences between the proportion for a given occupation and that for the total gainfully occupied in the particular age-region category may be interpreted as differences in incidence: for example, among gainfully occupied men aged twenty to thirty-four living in the Northeast in 1900 (table 19.1), 34 percent were born outside the region; if migrants were randomly distributed among all occupations we would expect each of the figures in that set to be 34. But, in fact, only 15

percent of farm workers are in this category, while the figure for manual
and service workers is 39 percent; migrants are, therefore, disproportionately concentrated in manual and service occupations.

In both tables, the upper left bank shows the base population (sample
size) on which the percentages are computed, and the two lower banks
show the component parts of the upper right bank summary percent (as a
result of rounding the components are sometimes one point off from the
summary). The reader is reminded that in 1900 only occupation is available
so the data in table 19.2 are correctly interpreted as the probability that (for
example) Northeastern-born men in a given occupation in 1900 were living
outside their state (region) of birth at that date.

The Contribution of In-migrants

In 1900, well over a third (36 percent) of adult white male workers in the
United States had been born outside the region in which they were living
at this date, that is, either in another region or abroad. Differences among
the regions are much as one would expect: the South recruits only 15
percent of its white male workers from outside; the West is almost entirely
dependent on outsiders, particularly among older workers; while the
proportion of outsiders in the Northeast and North Central states are at
roughly the national average. There are, however, significant differences in
age patterns between the latter two regions: the proportion of outsiders is
relatively constant among the three age groups for the Northeast, but rises
steeply in the North Central region. Older workers, among whom the
majority (60 percent) are out-born, reflect the situation in the settlement
period of the North Central region, when the picture was probably much
like that in the West in 1900, while the relatively low proportions among
younger workers may be associated with a decline in the North Central's
attraction (and retention) power, a hypothesis we will investigate further
later in the essay.

Interesting—and consistent—differences are apparent among the
broad occupation groups. Farm workers are least likely to have come from
outside, regardless of the region (or the age group) under consideration.
Even in the West, with its overwhelming proportion of outsiders, this
holds true. Disregarding the category "Laborers, not specified," who the
new evidence suggests are most likely to be nonagricultural manual workers, the manual-service worker group includes the highest proportion of
out-born; white-collar workers are in an intermediate position.

What these consistent differentials among the three occupation
groups suggest is that migrants were recruited primarily into the expanding sectors of the economy. Farm workers as a proportion of total em-

ployed are declining in all regions except the West by 1900 [3, p. 82] and in the Northeast even the absolute number is decreasing [3, p. 41]. On the other hand, white-collar jobs are probably on the increase, and the post-Civil War development of manufacturing, transportation, and other users of manual workers is having a sharp impact on the demand for blue-collar labor.

What were the respective roles of native-born interregional migrants and the foreign-born in contributing to these developments? Despite high levels of interregional migration, it is the international flow that provides the dominant component. For the country as a whole, 71 percent of these long-distance movers are from abroad; in the Northeast, in-movement from other regions is negligible, and the region depends almost entirely on the foreign-born for its "outside" recruits. Even in the South, 40 percent of the low level of outside recruits consists of foreigners, although the proportion falls sharply (from nearly half to 29 percent) among those born after the Civil War (i.e., those aged twenty to thirty-four in 1900).

Again, there are differences among the occupation groups. The probability that white-collar recruits are internal migrants is generally greater in each region than is the case for the blue-collar group; but only one in six of the recruits are native in the Northeast, and the proportion remains less than half in the North Central region also. In future work I plan to examine the extent to which literacy—presumably necessary for many white-collar jobs—may be associated with the lower white-collar job holding of the foreign-born. The next step here, however, is to compare the interregional migrants with persons who remained in their region of birth or made interstate moves within the region.

The Current Occupation of Out-Migrants

In the aggregate the probability of interregional migration is much higher for the Northeastern-born than for natives of other regions. If the migrant measure is interstate rather than interregional movers, however, workers born in the Northeast are the least mobile segment of the work force.[6] Natives of the North Central region are substantially more likely to change state of residence and even the Southern-born are marginally more mobile than Easterners. The difference, obviously, arises from the extent of intraregional movement: in the North Central and Southern regions nearly two-thirds of interstate movers remain in the region of birth, in the Northeast the proportion is only a third.

For the United States as a whole at both the interstate and interregional level, the differences in migrant proportions for the three occupation groups are in accord with findings on current (1970) differentials—

white-collar workers are more likely to have moved, manual and service workers have intermediate proportions, and farmers are least likely. The 1970 differences among the three groups, however, are substantially greater than those that the 1900 data reveal.

Among the three regions several notable deviations from the consistent pattern occur. These presumably reflect both past settlement patterns and current (1900) structural differences.

For the Northeast-born the proportion of interregional migrants among those who are farm workers in 1900 is higher than for either of the other two occupations in each age group. For older workers one feels safe in assuming that this reflects earlier agricultural settlement of the North Central region (where most of these farm workers are in 1900) by migrants from the Northeast. Its occurrence among the twenty- to thirty-four-year-olds is more ambiguous. Since we know nothing about the timing of the move we cannot know whether these young migrants are the children of older migrants who happened to be born before their parents moved or whether there is a continuing flow out of the Northeast by young men seeking opportunities in agriculture.[7]

If farm workers are most likely to have left the Northeast, manual and service workers are most likely to have stayed. An interesting contrast emerges in the pattern of interregional migration of Northeast- and Southern-born workers. Southern-born men who are manual workers in 1900 are more likely to be out of the South than are those in other occupations, while those who are farmers are least likely to have left—that is, the differences are exactly opposite the pattern among the Northeast-born. These regional contrasts are, of course, in conformity with differences in what we may call the opportunity structure in each region. The interpretation that suggests itself is that expanding opportunities inhibit out-migration of natives who wish to pursue work of a given type and accelerate in-migration of those from other regions where similar expansion is not taking place. The appeal of this interpretation is somewhat lessened, however, by the fact that for both occupation groups and for both regions of origin the dominant destination of migrants is the North Central region (see table 19.4).

Only among the small group of young (twenty to thirty-four) Southern-born out-migrants in white-collar occupations in 1900 is there any indication that the Northeast is a destination of preference at least equal to the North Central region (data not shown).

The fact that flows of workers (in all occupations) from both the Northeast and South are predominantly to the North Central region can by no means be interpreted to mean that the North Central states are only

Table 19.4

INTERREGIONAL MIGRANTS AMONG GAINFULLY
OCCUPIED NATIVE WHITE MEN, TWENTY YEARS OF AGE
AND OVER: REGION OF BIRTH, OCCUPATION, AND AGE IN
1900, BY REGION OF RESIDENCE IN 1900

Region of birth, occupation, and age in 1900	N		Region of residence in 1900 (Percent)			
			Northeast	North Central	South	West
Total (U.S.)a	2,448	100	8	45	19	28
Northeast	1,103	100	—	67	13	19
North Central	797	100	11	—	39	50
South	526	100	17	68	—	15
White collar	595	100	12	41	19	28
Manual and service	841	100	11	41	15	33
Farm	835	100	2	52	25	22
20–34	829	100	11	34	25	31
35–44	609	100	9	43	17	31
45 and over	1,010	100	4	56	15	24

a Includes men born in West and "Laborers, not specified," not shown separately.
Source: Tables 19.1 and 19.2.

receivers of workers. As table 19.2 makes clear, there is a substantial outflow from this region also. In the aggregate one could almost say that the North Central region functions as a sort of distribution center in this period, receiving workers from the two older regions and sending them out to the newest development area, the West. Differences among the three age groups are particularly instructive: among those forty-five years of age and over, the number of in-migrants to the North Central region is two and a half times as great as the number of out-migrants from the region; for young workers, the volume of in-migration is only about 75 percent of the volume of out-migration. What we may have captured here is a turning point in the growth of the North Central region through net internal migration—from high positive growth in the pre-Civil War period to negative growth in the last decades of the nineteenth century. The negative contribution of internal migration, however, is more than offset by a continuing high rate of natural increase and, as we have seen earlier, by high proportions of foreign-born workers in the North Central region.

Nor is the flow out of the North Central states entirely to the West. Roughly half the workers leaving go West, but a substantial proportion go

Table 19.5

LIFETIME MIGRANT WORKERS PER 1,000 TOTAL WORKERS:
NATIVE WHITE MEN, TWENTY YEARS OF AGE AND OVER,
UNITED STATES, 1900 AND 1970

	Age at census date							
Occupation at census date	20 years and over		20–34		35–44		45 years and over	
	1900	1970	1900	1970	1900	1970	1900	1970
All occupations[a]	144	184	99	162	153	190	214	197
White collar	172	220	122	192	186	225	248	236
Manual and service	157	163	113	143	185	166	230	178
Farm	120	78	76	73	109	71	188	82

[a] Includes "Laborers, not specified" in 1900 and "Occupation not reported" 1970, not shown separately.

Source: Table 19.2 and 1970 Public Use Sample

South also; in fact, out-migrant farm workers from the North Central region are predominantly in the South in 1900, presumably reflecting the development of agriculture in Texas and other West South Central states in this period.[8] Although the West is growing rapidly, it is not yet attracting workers from the rest of the country—even the North Central region—at rates anywhere near those that occur later in the twentieth century. Moreover, there are only minor differences in these findings among the three age groups, suggesting that little acceleration in the West's drawing power is taking place in the last decades of the nineteenth century.

Summary and Conclusion

The empirical evidence makes clear that migrant workers are not randomly distributed whether they are compared to workers in their region of origin (among internal migrants) or their region of destination (for both internal or external migrants). Moreover, at the national level it is clear that they are more likely than the average worker to be in the expanding nonagricultural sector, as white-collar or manual workers, and less likely to be in the declining agricultural sector. Further, migrants are also more likely to be in the high-status, white-collar jobs, although differences between manual and white-collar workers are considerably less than they are for 1970, as the following data make clear (see table 19.5).

The differences between the two censuses, for both occupation and age groups, are most intriguing and are in accord with a hypothesis proposing that migration becomes increasingly selective of upper socioeconomic groups once the urban, nonagricultural society is fully established [5, p. 15]. But the data cry out for a series rather than two isolated dates. Fortunately, within the next few years public use samples similar to that for 1900 will become available for the 1910, 1940, and 1950 U.S. Censuses, and one can hope that eventually data for the crucial 1920 and 1930 dates will also be produced.

The relation between migration and structural change is considerably more complex to assess at the regional level. One has, first, to establish the nature of structural change in the regions and then to examine the inter-regional flows and the flows from abroad in this context. State estimates for agricultural and nonagricultural workers are available for each census in the period 1870–1950 [4, table L–4]. I have chosen the interval 1880–1900 as the most relevant for summarizing regional changes that may have affected the opportunity structure for the lifetime migrants in our study population, although obviously there is a strong arbitrary element in this choice (see table 19.6).

Except in the West, nonagricultural jobs are everywhere expanding very much more rapidly than those in agriculture, and the share of agriculture is consequently declining. In this context, summary data from the present study suggest that migration has indeed been a force in this change (see table 19.7).

1. Native white men who remained in their region of birth have a higher proportion in farm occupations in 1900 than the regional

Table 19.6

AGRICULTURAL AND NONAGRICULTURAL GAINFUL WORKERS, TEN YEARS OF AGE AND OVER, U.S. BY REGION 1880 AND 1900

| | Number (in 1,000s) | | | | Percentage of total in nonagriculture | | Percentage change 1880–1900 | |
| | Agricultural | | Nonagricultural | | | | Agricultural | Nonagricultural |
Region	1880	1900	1880	1900	1880	1900		
United States	8,591	11,288	8,802	17,785	51	61	+31	+102
Northeast	1,213	1,194	4,097	7,386	77	86	−2	+80
North Central	3,068	3,855	2,557	5,726	46	60	+26	+124
South	4,092	5,736	1,608	3,474	28	38	+40	+116
West	218	503	539	1,200	71	70	+130	+123

Source: [4], table L–4.

Table 19.7

PERCENTAGE OF GAINFUL WORKERS IN FARM
OCCUPATIONS BY LIFETIME MIGRATION STATUS:
REGIONS OF THE UNITED STATES

	All workers 10 years of age and over		White men, 20 years of age and over in 1900			
	1880	1900	Live in region of birth, 1900	Live in region in 1900, born outside		Born in region, live outside in 1900
				Foreign	Native	
Region	(1)	(2)	(3)	(4)	(5)	(6)
Northeast	23	14	21	7	8	31
North Central	54	40	44	34	39	35
South	72	62	61	30	44	41
West	29	30	38	29	27	*

*Percent not shown where base is less than 75 cases.
Source: (1) and (2) from [4], table L–4; (3)–(6) from 1900 Public Use Sample.

structure would predict (column 3 is higher than column 2). The
exception in the South occurs because columns 1 and 2 include the
large black component that is almost entirely in agriculture in 1900.

2. In-migrants, both foreign- and native-born, are substantially below
the expected level in agriculture in the Northeast and South (columns 4 and 5 are lower than column 2). Native-born in-migrants are
not significantly below the expected level in the North Central
region because the relative volume of migration to the North Central
region has been falling so that these in-migrants reflect responses to
earlier rather than current structural changes. Among interregional
gainful worker migrants twenty years of age and over in 1900, 51
percent in the North Central states are forty-five and over, as compared to 35 percent in the West, 33 percent in the South, and 23
percent in the Northeast.[9]

3. In-migrants to the West are in farm occupations at about the expected levels (columns 4 and 5 are about equal to columns 1 and 2), in
accordance with the similarity in growth rates for farm and nonfarm
occupations in this region.

4. Native-born out-migrants from the North Central and Southern
regions are less likely to be in farm occupations than workers in their
home regions in 1900, while those leaving the Northeast are more
likely (comparison between columns 6 and 2). This is associated with
a general tendency for migrants in specific flows to fall midway
between the area of origin and the area of destination (data not
presented). But the point mentioned previously should also be

noted: The rapidity of the decline in agriculture in the Northeast probably put strong pressure on those who wished to be farmers to leave the region.

Evidence on the other question raised in the introductory section—the relative status of migrants and nonmigrants—is both simpler and less satisfactory (see table 19.8).

Among native white men, both in-migrants to and out-migrants from each region are more likely to be in white-collar jobs in 1900 than those who stay in their region of birth. But, as noted, whether they achieved this status after migration or before remains an open question. The situation in the Northeast is particularly interesting. It is clearly the most "developed" section of the country at this date and as such provides proportionately more white-collar opportunities. Although, as we have seen earlier, the interregional flow to the Northeast is small, it includes a substantially higher proportion of white-collar workers than the flow to any other region.[10] Is this because the opportunities to achieve white-collar status are greater in the Northeast, in particular because the large flow of foreign in-migrants are unable to respond to these opportunities, or is it because "high" status migrants have a (relative) preference for this "developed" region? The high proportion of white-collar workers among the foreign-born in the South—in contrast to their status in other regions—probably reflects their contribution to retail trade, as proprietors and sales workers; trade is a much greater proportion of the nonagricultural sector in the South than in any other region [3, p. 70] in the later decades of the nineteenth century.

Table 19.8

PERCENTAGE OF GAINFUL WORKERS IN WHITE-COLLAR OCCUPATIONS IN 1900 BY LIFETIME MIGRATION STATUS

	White men, twenty years of age and over in 1900			
	Live in region of birth	Live in region in 1900, born outside		Born in region, live outside in 1900
Region		Foreign	Native	
Northeast	25	15	38	27
North Central	19	14	22	23
South	15	23	24	19
West	19	15	24	*

*Percentage not shown where base is less than 75 cases.
Source: 1900 Public Use Sample.

Lifetime migration data have many drawbacks, but they are all we have historically and, properly exploited, they can add substantially to our understanding of the processes of change. The present essay has examined only the most superficial manifestations of their potential, but I hope it has illustrated the value of constructing microlevel samples from what are undoubtedly the most comprehensive bodies of quantitative data available to scholars concerned with historical trends—the national censuses. The development of continuous series will add even more to their value. For example, when the 1910 sample becomes available we may be able to use a survival ratio technique to estimate the role of rural-urban migration in changing structure (we cannot do this now since we have the urban-rural designation only for residence in 1900).

The potential of the computer as a tool for historical migration research has so far been primarily confined to the use of local data such as parish registers or local censuses. Valuable as such research is, it lacks reference points to the overall framework of change. Knowledge of the general context in which local developments are taking place can serve further to enrich their analysis.

Notes

1. The present essay also must face up to this analytical problem in part, since only the occupation after migration (i.e., in 1900) is available; I will deal with this further.

2. These hypotheses are not necessarily contradictory, of course, since "personality" may select within the "advantaged" group.

3. Occupational outcome for such "tied" migrants is not without interest but it is not relevant to the focus of this essay.

4. Later work with these data will test this possible explanation.

5. No attempt was made to deal with the "laborers, not specified" problem, however.

6. The sample is too small to permit analysis of migrants born in the West; the region is, therefore, omitted from discussion of place or origin data.

7. Some clue may be offered by the fact that the young farmers are somewhat less likely to be in the North Central region than are those past forty-five—but the differences are small. Future analysis of household data may throw additional light on this problem.

8. The number of agricultural workers in Texas increased by about 75 percent between 1880 and 1900, compared to an increase of just over 30 percent for the country as a whole [4, p. 609, 619].

9. Among the foreign-born this proportion is consistently 27–28 percent in each region.

10. The same situation can be observed for native white men in 1970.

References

1. Kaplan, D. L., and M. C. Casey, *Occupational Trends in the United States, 1900–1950*. Washington, D.C.: U.S. Bureau of the Census, Working Paper No. 5, 1958.

2. Kuznets, S. S., Introduction, in H. T. Eldridge and D. S. Thomas, *Population Redistribution and Economic Growth, United States, 1870–1950*, Vol. 3, *Demographic Analyses and Interrelations*. Philadelphia: American Philosophical Society, 1964.

3. Kuznets, S. S., A. R. Miller, R. A. Easterlin, *Population Redistribution and Economic Growth, United States, 1870–1950*, Vol. 2, *Analyses of Economic Change*. Philadelphia: American Philosophical Society, 1960.

4. Lee, E. S., A. R. Miller, C. P. Brainerd, R. A. Easterlin, *Population Redistribution and Economic Growth, United States, 1870–1950*, Vol. 1, *Methodological Considerations and Reference Tables*. Philadelphia: American Philosophical Society, 1957.

5. Miller, A. R. Interstate migrants in the United States: some social-economic differences by type of move, *Demography* 14:1 (February 1977), pp. 1–17.

6. 1900 Public Use Sample. See S. N. Graham, *1900 Public Use Sample User's Handbook* (Draft version), prepared at The Center for Studies in Demography and Ecology, University of Washington, Seattle, Washington, July 1980.

20

Geographic and Social Mobility in France in the Nineteenth and Twentieth Centuries

Jacques Dupâquier

In France in the past twenty years the study of migratory movements has progressed at a much slower pace than the study of population structure or fertility despite the efforts of J. P. Poussou.[1] This delay is due in part to objective causes: the French have contributed much less to the field of international migrations than their neighbors; however, there exist no specific sources for the study of migration in France—no *status animarum* for the seventeenth and eighteenth centuries, no registers of population for the nineteenth and twentieth centuries.

One is, therefore, reduced to rough estimates based on migration balances, or to detailed studies of existing sources (passenger lists, passport registrations). But aggregate statistics do not give a complete view of the migratory phenomenon. They describe certain material aspects of migration but do not permit direct comprehension of the problem. They serve only as a basis for explanatory hypotheses, which in the end generally prove to be partial and fragile. In order to go more deeply into the problem one must resort to microanalysis, which offers two possibilities for research; the study of migration through comparison of successive nominative lists[2], and genealogical reconstitution of families.

As a rule, French demographic historians seem to have all the necessary tools for microanalysis of migrations, since the method of family reconstitution was developed in France. In fact, for over twenty years this orientation has diverted them from serious study of migration.

The method employed by Louis Henry consists of collecting on a fiche all information on a couple that can be matched with data in civil registers: place and date of birth, marriage and death of parents and children, remarriage of the surviving parent, and so forth. One can obtain from these data statistics concerning the marital status, legitimate births and deaths within the framework of a village, a group of villages, or a small town.[3] Supplemented by rigorous techniques and carefully controlled observation, the method of family reconstitution has made possible major progress in the study of the history of population. More than 500 parish histories have been completed, and a major study launched by the National Institute of Demographic Studies and based on a large population sample has made it possible to reconstruct the history of French population between 1670 and 1829.[4]

Unfortunately, the family fiche, as conceived by Louis Henry, did not permit serious study of geographic and social mobility. In fact, the focus of the monographs is always a village or a group of villages. As soon as a family member leaves the village he automatically escapes observation, which limits, in local studies, the possibility of analysis of migration. But it is obvious that social mobility and geographic mobility are connected: in rural areas, possibilities for upward social mobility in the same locale are very limited. The parish monographs only permit the listing of stable families: they, therefore, create an impression of social immobility. "The immobile village" is also the subtitle of one of the most famous of such monographs, conducted more in a historical than demographic spirit.[5]

In theory, one can evaluate the mobile part of the population by comparing, period by period, the number of completed family fiches with fiches that are incomplete (those where either the beginning or the end of the observation is missing). While this provides us with a global evaluation, it does not give us information on the characteristics of the mobile population.

One can learn more about migration by combining information from civil registers with nominative data from the census lists. Thus one can determine in an approximate way the date at which a family enters or leaves the village and, above all, at which intervals children leave the family, information very useful for the study of the family cycle. But unfortunately destination remains unknown and a serious study of migration must, therefore, be based on other sources.

In order to make the method of family reconstitution useful for the history of migration, one has to introduce a radical change of perspective, that is, to move from a territorial to a genealogical framework.

In fact, genealogical studies have the advantage of following individuals in their geographical movements. They permit analysis of problems such as demographic changes between town and countryside in traditional societies, rural exodus, matrimonial dislocations, family migrations, and so forth.

If they are based only on the examination of civil registers, genealogical studies are problem prone as individuals are identified only in terms of family events: birth, marriage, divorce, death; birth, marriage, and death of the children. One can follow more easily the movements of married couples (and especially couples with children) than of single persons. Therefore, one has to supplement the sources with information on the civil state with available nominative lists (electoral lists, tax lists, nominative census lists), and other types of serial data from social history (notarial, military, and religious archives).

There are various kinds of genealogical studies. Not all of them can provide the same service for the history of migration. Let us leave aside the linear genealogies limited to the study of filiation. The best example is offered by the gospel of St. Matthew: "Abraham begat Isaac; Isaac begat Jacob; Jacob begat Judas and his brothers . . ." Scientific interest is very limited, even nil if age and birthplace are not given. By contrast, family trees can make an important contribution to our subject.

One can distinguish two types of family trees: ascending genealogies (the more frequent case), which give tables of all ancestors of an individual, including both the maternal and paternal line; and descending genealogies, which are limited to presenting all the descendants of the same ancestor. Ascending genealogies permit comparison of place of birth, marriage, and death in the same generation or chronological period, and the measurement of movement from one generation to another. The most serious drawback in this type of genealogy is that it is not representative; on the one hand, because the individuals who make up the genealogical tree are not representative of the entire society, and, on the other, because contemporary man is not descended in equal parts from all elements of the earlier population. To take a concrete example, an Englishman who wishes to establish his genealogy would have little chance of finding ancestors who were emigrants. Microanalysis, therefore, should be based principally on descending genealogies.

Descending genealogies do not entirely escape the risks mentioned above. In fact, available genealogies do not emerge by accident. In almost all cases they concern royal, aristocratic, or bourgeois families where the family has always been of great importance. In almost every case, the ancestor chosen by the genealogist is distinguished by fortune or talent from common mortals. For the study of migration, therefore, descending genealogies must be formed from a sample of ancestors representative of the population to be studied.

In addition, it must take into account a difficult problem: completeness. While in an ascending genealogy gaps can be seen at a glance (the entire line in which an ancestor is missing is blocked), in descending genealogies gaps easily go unnoticed. The gaps may be due to infants who die at an early age or to persons for whom we have birth certificates but who disappear in later life. The first type of gap presents difficulties for the study of fertility and mortality but not for migration. The second type presents an obstacle for the study of geographic mobility. It is, in fact, indispensable to be able to trace an individual from birth to death in order to measure his movements.

But it is very difficult, in fact, to trace an individual when starting only from a birth certificate. Countries in which individual moves are recorded are very rare. In most states birth certificates give no clue as to the ultimate destination of the migrant. In France it is only since 1897 that marriages have been recorded on birth certificates. The same is true for deaths since 1945. For the nineteenth century, therefore, finding migrants from the enormous mass of material in the civil registers might seem an impossible task despite the existence of decennial alphabetical tables for each of the 38,000 communes. For each individual it would mean "looking for a needle in a haystack." That is why the laboratory for demographic history at the Ecole des Hautes Études en Sciences Sociales has decided to launch an inquiry on an entirely different basis in order to study geographic and social mobility in contemporary France (nineteenth and twentieth centuries).

This involves studying a representative sample of 3,000 couples constituted during the First Empire and tracing their male descendants to the present day. It would have been very desirable to trace the descendants of the female line as well; unfortunately the introduction of new combinations in each generation, if descendants of females were included, would have doubled the size of the sample every 30 years: starting with 3,000 couples, one would have ended up with 100,000. This would have made the inquiry most difficult if not impossible. Moreover, as the main objective is to trace migrants, there was no other solution than to choose all couples according to alphabetic criteria in order to avoid social discrimination and to facilitate research. Decennial tables from the civil registers are available since the Revolution. By choosing all surnames in the same "alphabetical zone" (from the occurrence of the letters TRA, which is represented in all European ethnic groups), it is possible to undertake systematic research on all individuals observed in the course of the first reconstitution. If French women keep their family name as a personal name after marriage, this allows us to trace them up to marriage and even to death; but they do not transmit family names to their children. This would have rendered the constitution of integral descending genealogies very long and very difficult.

The dimensions of the sample were established after consultation with specialists: with 3,000 couples dispersed over an entire territory, the sample will remain representative on a national scale, even if several hundred branches in each generation die out. Furthermore, in order to ensure territorial distribution in each department one couple per 10,000 inhabitants present at the census of 1806 was chosen within the administrative confines of the time.

Given the natural rate of growth of the French population, one should have 3,400 couples in the second generation (around 1835), 3,800 in the third (around 1865), 4,000 in the fourth (around 1895), 4,100 in the fifth (around 1925), and 4,900 in the sixth generation (around 1955), which would give us a total of 23,000 family fiches. As a matter of fact, one would expect to have less than 20,000 fiches considering that French population growth since 1800 is due in large part to a longer life expectancy, and especially to the fact that a not inconsiderable fraction of the current population consists of foreigners and descendants of foreigners. For immigrants and their descendants, a special study should, therefore, be made, the results of which would then have to be taken into account in the inquiry.

This is how the research has been organized and how the difficulties have been overcome: since civil registers for the last hundred years were generally not available to the public, it was necessary to obtain special permission from local government bodies that permitted departmental correspondents to consult the series preserved in the archives. As the elaboration of these records involved a very considerable amount of work, it was necessary to find help. This was provided by genealogists under the

aegis of their societies and their federation. Numerous (explanatory) meetings have been held in the provinces, and a newsletter (with the title "3,000
Families") appears regularly. Many genealogists realized that the inquiry
was a unique opportunity for their discipline and offered the possibility to
establish genealogy as an auxiliary science in the field of social history.

It was necessary first of all to establish the main corpus of the material
and to choose the sample. In the first stage, one has systematically recorded from the decennial tables (births, marriages, and deaths) data for
all persons whose last names begin with the letters TRA, for each department for the period 1803–1902. In order to ensure the representativeness of
the sample at the social level, one must proceed alphabetically, giving
priority to married couples between 1803 and 1902 whose last name begins
with the letters TRAB, then TRAC, TRAD, and so forth.[6] If the number
of marriages cannot provide the necessary number of couples, we return to
the birth and death certificates in the same period. In this way the sample
satisfies the criteria of stratification (at the geographic level) and of random-
ness (at the social level). To eliminate the effects of clustering, we reject
couples that already have a relative in the sample. For each of the retained
couples we now fill out a new family fiche, which involves research on
birth certificates (or baptismal records) of the spouses, death certificates,
birth, marriage, and death certificates of their children (recorded on the
fiches). The marriage licenses of young males give rise to a new fiche and
so on. The work is carried on in the departmental archives where the series
have been kept for more than one hundred years.

It would be necessary finally to continue the research in the archives
of the departmental district. From 1897 on, the work will be greatly
facilitated by comments on birth certificates, indicating date and place of
marriage—and divorce—and, even better, from 1945 on deaths are given
detailed reports. At this stage, we pass to the level of the department for
research on persons for whom we have found a birth certificate or a
marriage license, but not a death certificate. This research will be conducted primarily through the registration service, as the future of children
is generally known at the time of inheritance. Finally, at the departmental
level, we will try to trace reconstituted families in the nominative lists of
the census. These references will help to trace children for whom we have
insufficient information and to find out at what age they left the family.

From research on the decennial tables we can record systematically all
the references made concerning families with the last name TRA, even if
these families are not linked to the departmental sample. These records
will be of great service to the inquiry.

Once the research at the departmental level is completed, we will have
to proceed to a general inquiry in order to find all the persons in the

sample who have left their departments of origin without leaving a trace (such a case will be very rare in the twentieth century, thanks to the annotations on the birth certificates).

For each of these persons, the correspondent will start a research fiche containing a maximum amount of detail. These fiches will permit us to create an alphabetical list at the national level. A first step will focus on registers of the regional capitals and their suburban communes (for example, Caen for the "missing persons" from the Manche), then in those of Paris and the Seine regions, where the work should be facilitated by the large number of persons in the French *Who's Who* and also in the annual telephone directories. This operation should reduce the number of unknown cases by at least one thousand. Then we can ask for help from all the departmental correspondents—following the techniques employed by the bulletins for the exchange of genealogical information—in order to reduce the number of unknown cases by at least one hundred.

As the principal object of the examination is the study of social mobility, I will refrain here from giving details on the kinds of demographic, economic, and social data that we hope to collect. I will only indicate in a summary fashion what we can hope to learn from the study of migration. In the majority of cases, the study could be made by comparing nominative lists. This involves two kinds of approaches: a geographic approach (that is, the study of distances covered) and a chronological one (where migration is studied as an aspect of demography, starting with the initial population after correcting for the disturbance effect caused by deaths). One could then construct migratory tables by generation where the migratory quotient at each age will be given by the following formula.

$$mx = \frac{2\,Mx}{Px\,(2 - qx)}$$

mx = migratory quotient at age x

Mx = absolute number of moves at age x

Px = number present at birth of x

qx = mortality quotient at age x

From the calculation of the migratory tables by generation, one could proceed to the calculation of time tables according to classical methods of demographic analysis. In cases where we do not have nominative lists, we will proceed through comparison of places named in the civil registers.

For single persons, information is particularly weak. We can only compare place of birth and place of death. We can, therefore, classify death by age and by place of birth (or, more precisely, by the residence of the parents at time of birth), thus making it possible to construct a table like table 20.1.

For the study of the migration of married people, we have to take into account that because of custom, the marriage ceremony is often celebrated at the residence of the parents of the spouse, which may not necessarily correspond to the residence of the new couple. The residence of the new couple should, therefore, be considered to be the birthplace of their first-born child. This, in effect, will exclude from the study any sterile couples (their cases will be dealt with along with those of singles).

The observation is concluded at the dissolution of the marriage, be it by death or divorce. The migration is then defined as a variation in the location of the demographic events of the family; the date of the migration will be defined as the average of the dates of the same events.

In this way we can construct a table of migratory quotients analogous to fertility tables by length of marriage (see table 20.2).

After having studied the cohorts of marriage, we repeat the analysis according to the date of birth of the father and of the mother. This will allow us to correlate these migratory tables with those of single persons. Similarly, we will be able to construct migratory tables for widows and divorced persons after the termination of the marriage.

Thus the study of a representative sample of descending genealogies should allow a complete evaluation of internal migration. Unfortunately, it will be far more difficult to utilize the sample for the study of international migration, particularly for a country such as France, where international migration is of relatively minor importance. With a sample of 3,000 families we can only hope to find a small number of persons on the

Table 20.1

MIGRATION TABLE BY AGE AT DEATH AND
PLACE OF BIRTH

Age of deceased (A)	Total deaths (B)	Deaths occurring outside the place of birth (C)	Migratory quotient (D) = (C)/(B)
0	1,211	27	0.022
1–4	718	36	0.050
5–9	204	13	0.064
etc.			

Table 20.2

MIGRATION TABLE BY DATE OF MARRIAGE

Marriage cohort	Time elapsed since the first birth (years)					
	0–4	5–9	10–14	15–19	20–24	25–29
1880	0.071	0.081	0.080	0.079	0.072	0.064
1885–89	0.073	0.084	0.083	0.081	0.075	0.067
1890–94	0.077	0.087	0.085	0.081	0.075	0.069
etc.	—	—	—	—	—	—

passenger lists. As for those that have left France by land rather than by sea, they will probably escape observation.

It remains only to place migrants in their family setting. Microanalysis should allow us to understand in what way migrants differ from those around them, to know their age, birth order, size of family; to calculate on an individual basis, distance of migration, subsequent mobility, frequency of return; to compare demographic behavior of migrants and their socioprofessional characteristics with those of nonmigrants; to study the links between geographic and social mobility; in short, to discover new models and methods of research in migration history.

Notes

1. J. P. Poussou, Les mouvements migratoires en France et a partir de la France de la fin du XVᵉ siècle au début du XIXᵉ siècle. Approches pour une synthèse. *Annales de démographie historique* 1970, p. 11–78.

2. V. Blayo, La mobilité dans un village de la Brie vers le milieu du XIXᵉ siècle. *Population*, 25,3, mai-juin 1970, pp. 573–605.

3. L. Henry, *Techniques d'analyse en démographie historique*. Paris, Editions de l'INED, 1980.

4. Results for the period 1740–1829 have been published in a special number of *Population:* "Démographie historique," nov. 1975.

5. G. Bouchard, *Le village immobile. Sennely en Sologne au XVIIIᵉ siècle*. Paris, Plon, 1972.

6. For practical reasons, to avoid possible errors in spelling, I have placed name combinations beginning with TRAE, TRAI, TRAM, TRAN, TRAO and TRAU at the end of the list.

21

A Cartographic Approach to the Problem of Internal Migration in Sardinia in the Eighteenth Century
PART ONE
John Day

The purpose of this essay is to determine, on the basis of changing population densities and characteristic economic activities, the pattern of internal migration in Sardinia in the first half of the eighteenth century. The cartographic materials, prepared and elucidated by Serge Bonin, are intended to serve as instruments of comparative analysis.

We have concentrated on a period when birth and death rates probably did not vary significantly from region to region. There were no major epidemics reported, and only two harvest failures (in 1728 and 1735), neither, it seems, of famine proportions. The phenomenon of mass emigration was two centuries in the future, and immigration, despite the growing conviction that it constituted the ideal solution to the problem of chronic underpopulation, was limited to the modest influx of Corsican herders in Gallura. For all these reasons, local population movements that are at variance with the general rates of natural increase (+ 9 percent between 1688 and 1698, + 23 percent between 1698 and 1728, + 13 percent between 1728 and 1751) are assumed to reflect internal migrations. (see table 21.1)

Figure 21.1: The Regions of Sardinia

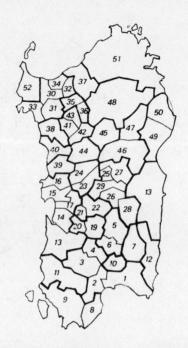

CAMPIDANO DI CAGLIARI
1 Campidano
2 Decimo
3 Gippi
4 Nuraminis

SIURGUS
5 Siurgus

TREXENTA
6 Trexenta

GERREI
7 Gerrei

SULCIS
8 Nora
9 Sulcis

PARTIOLLA
10 Dolia

IGLESIENTE
11 Cixerri

SARRABUS QUIRRA
12 Sarrabus Quirra

OGLIASTRA
13 Ogliastra

WESTERN CAMPIDANO
14 Bonorzuli
15 Campidano Maggiore
16 Campidano Milis
17 Campidano Simaxis
18 Monreale

MARMILLA
19 Marmilla
20 Parte Montis

ARBOREA
21 Parte Usellus
22 Parte Valenza

TIRSO VALLEY
23 Parte Barigadu
24 Parte Cier

BARBAGIA
25 Austis
26 Barbagia Belvi
27 Barbagia Ollolai
28 Barbagia Seulo
29 Mandrolisai

REGION OF SASSARI
30 Flumenargia
31 Coros
32 Montes
33 Nulauro
34 Romangia

LOGUDORO
35 Figulina
36 Oppia

ANGLONA
37 Anglona

MONTELEONE
38 Monteleone

MONTE FERRU
39 Montiferro

PLANARGIA
40 Planargia

MEILOGU
41 Cabudabbas
42 Costavalle
43 Meilogu

MARGHINE
44 Marghine

GOCEANO
45 Goceano

REGION OF NUORO
46 Bitti
47 Dore

MONTACUTO
48 Montacuto

LE BARONIE
49 Orosei
50 Posada

GALLURA
51 Gallura

NURRA
52 Nurra

Table 21.1
POPULATION CHANGES IN SARDINIA 1688-1711
(percent)*

	1688–1698	1698–1728	1728–1751	1688–1751
Sardinia	+ 9 (− 3)	+ 23 (+ 3)	+ 13 (− 1)	+ 52 (− 1)
Regions				
Campidano di				
Cagliari	− 8 (+ 1)	+ 35	− 7 (− 1)	+ 17
Dolia	+ 5	+ 29	+ 11	+ 51
Trexenta	+ 12 (− 1)	+ 21 (+ 1)	+ 5	+ 43
Siurgus	+ 6	+ 9	+ 6	+ 22
Gerrei	+ 3	+ 71	+ 18	+ 109
Sulcis	+ 37	+ 420 (+ 2)	+ 34 (+ 2)	+ 857 (+ 4)
Cixerri	+ 19	+ 21 (+ 1)	+ 14	+ 63 (+ 1)
Sarrabus	+ 26	+ 15	+ 53	+ 121
Ogliastra	+ 34	− 21	+ 101	+ 113
Western Campidano	+ 27	+ 32	+ 2	+ 71
Marmilla	− 3 (− 1)	+ 26 (− 1)	− 9 (− 1)	+ 11 (− 3)
Arborea	− 16	+ 33 (+ 1)	+ 18	+ 33 (+ 1)
Tirso Valley	+ 6	+ 15	+ 6	+ 30
Barbagie	+ 2	+ 26 (− 1)	+ 29	+ 60 (− 1)
Region of Sassari	+ 27	+ 13 (+ 1)	+ 15 (+ 1)	+ 64 (+ 2)
Logudoro	− 1	+ 51	+ 8 (− 1)	+ 61 (− 1)
Anglona	+ 15	+ 49	− 15	+ 41
Monteleone	− 1	+ 24	+ 11	+ 37
Planargia	− 10	+ 5	+ 28	+ 21
Monte Ferru	0	− 3	+ 49	+ 44
Meilogu	+ 2 (− 1)	+ 14	+ 19	+ 39 (− 1)
Marghine	− 13	+ 101	+ 22	+ 114
Goceano	+ 119	+ 10	+ 17 (− 1)	+ 195 (− 1)
Region of Nuoro	+ 14 (− 1)	− 31	+ 92	+ 51 (− 1)
Montacuto	+ 32	+ 33 (− 1)	+ 17	+ 105 (− 1)
Baronie	− 4	+ 52	+ 26	+ 83
Gallura	+ 28	+ 36	+ 12	+ 95
Towns				
Cagliari	− 27	+ 34	− 1	− 3
Iglesias	+ 29	+ 28	+ 9	+ 81
Oristano	+ 14	+ 47	+ 7	+ 79
Sassari	+ 24	+ 22	− 5	+ 43
Alghero	+ 56	+ 5	+ 34	+ 120
Bosa	− 9	+ 7	+ 34	+ 30

Source: F. Corridore, *Storia documentata della popalazione del Regno di Sardegna, 1479–1901.*
Turin, 1902
*In parentheses: changes in the number of inhabited localities.

Scattered data on infant mortality confirm that the death rate was declining in the eighteenth century: 48.9 percent of all deaths in the sample were children under ten in 1730–39, compared to 43.9 percent in 1750–59 and 36 percent in 1790–99. A study of the parish registers of 30 localities in different parts of the island indicates that the number of marriages and births also declined between 1700 and 1750, from 12.1 to 9.6 and from 46.3 to 36.7 per 1,000 inhabitants. On balance, however, the death rate declined faster than the birth rate, resulting in a 50 percent increase in the number of taxable hearths between 1688 and 1751.

A harvest and livestock census dating from 1771 has served to determine the "vocation" of the different regions corresponding to medieval provinces *(curatorie)* later known as *encontrade*. These seemed better suited to our present purpose than the confused patchwork of feudal divisions of the Spanish and Piedmontese period, the more so because the right of all subjects to migrate "from village to village and from fief to fief" was sanctioned by the Crown.

The Sardinian population was unusually mobile in the first half of the eighteenth century. Based on a sample of 14 localities, "exogamous" (intervillage) marriages constituted about 20–25 percent of the total in this period (but the percentage varied widely from village to village), compared to 15–20 percent in the second half of the century. At the same time, the number of consanguineous marriages was insignificant—1.40 percent compared to 1.82 percent in 1790–94, 3.51 percent in 1810–14, and a record 6.71 percent in the year 1880.

A high degree of mobility is further suggested by the fact that important population losses in one period were usually made good in the next (Parte Montis, Parte Usellus, and Marghine in 1688–98 and 1698–1728; Ogliastra, Posada, the region of Nuoro in 1698–1728 and 1728–51). The principle of equilibrium or optimum population density that seems to have been at work in these instances also operated in the opposite sense. Gippi and Bonorzuli experienced a sharp rise in population in 1698–1728, followed by a major exodus (or a Malthusian leap in the death rate) in 1728–51.

If the six urban centers are considered apart, no consistent pattern of migration emerges in the first half of the eighteenth century. The populations of Cagliari, Sassari, and Bosa fell behind the average rate of natural increase, while Iglesias and Oristano posted modest gains. Only Alghero, where the population more than doubled between 1688 and 1751, seems to have attracted immigrants from the countryside. In this instance, paradoxically—judging by the proportion of livestock to population in 1771—urbanization and pastoralism went hand in hand.

In 1728–51, the demographic balance in Sardinia tilted in favor of the pastoral districts, most of which seem to have attracted settlers from other parts of the island, especially from the farming areas. A similar pattern emerges when one considers the period as a whole. The pastoral or agropastoral regions of Sulcis, Gerrei, Sarrabus, Ogliastra, Baronie, Gallura, Montacuto, and Marghine more than doubled their population while the agricultural regions of Campidano di Cagliari, Siurgus, Marmilla, and Arborea fell between 20 and 40 percentage points behind the average rate of natural increase.

A comparison between a livestock census of 1756 and the corresponding figures for 1771 (table 21.2) indicates that the switch to stock raising and, presumably, the migrations to the pastoral villages continued for another generation. The number of plough oxen remained practically stationary at around 100,000 head while other kinds of stock increased by half, from 1,315,330 to 1,949,385. The seed banks *(monti frumentari)* and other reforms introduced in the 1760s and 1770s to encourage the spread of

Table 21.2
RÉSUMÉ OF THE HARVEST AND LIVESTOCK
CENSUS OF 1771[†]
Active population (over 10 years of age)—335,926

	Wheat	Barley	Vegetables	Total
Seed	314,557 st.	99,450 st.	64,094 st.	478,197 st.
Harvest	1,639,420 st.	561,340 st.	259,131 st.	2,459,891 st.
Percentage	66.6%	22.8%	10.6%	100.0%
Average yield	5.2 :1	5.6 :1	4.0 :1	—
Per capita	4.88 st.	1.67 st.	0.77 st.	7.32 st.
Land under crop	5.7%	1.3%	0.4%	7.4%

	Domestic stock	Per capita	Range stock	Per capita
Oxen	100,093	0.30		
Cows	12,745	0.04		
Calves	8,457	0.02		
Cattle			233,453	0.69
Horses	33,863	0.10	31,310	0.09
Pigs	35,572	0.10	130,777	0.39
Sheep			979,142	2.91
Goats			383,975	1.14
Total	190,728	0.56	1,758,657	5.24

Number of *starelli* of crop land per ox team: 8.9 (ca. 3.5 ha)

[†] *Starello* (grain measure) = ca. 50 liters
Starello (land measure) = ca. 40 ares

cereal cultivation seem to have reversed this trend toward pastoralism until the crisis of the 1790s ushered in by a new cycle of deficit harvests.

References

Anatra, B. "Di barone in barone," *Almanacco della Sardegna*. Cagliari, 1973, pp. 9–13.

Anatra, B., and G. Puggioni. "Dinamica demografica e mobilità matrimoniale in Sardegna tra il Settecento e il primo quarto dell'Ottocento." *Annali della Facoltà di Scienze Politiche dell'Università di Cagliari*, vol. 5, 1980, pp. 1–28.

Bonin, S., I. Calia, and J. Day. *Atlas historique de la Sardaigne aux XVIIᵉ–XVIIIᵉ siècles*. Ecole des Hautes Études en Sciences Sociales, Paris, forthcoming.

Bulferetti, L. "Gli orientamenti della politica demografica in Sardegna durante il regno di Vittorio Amedeo III," *Archivio Storico Sardo* 24, 1954, pp. 237–67.

Corridore, F. *Storia documentata della popolazione del Regno di Sardegna (1479–1901)*. Turin, 1902.

Day, J. "L'insediamento precario in Sardegna nei secoli XII–XVIII," *Atti del Colloquio Internazionale di Archeologia Medievale*. Palermo, 1976, pp. 228–42.

———. "Villaggi abbandonati e tradizione orale: il caso sardo." *Archeologia Medievale*, 3, 1976, pp. 203–39.

Doneddu, G. "Il censorato generale," *Economia e Storia*. 1980, pp. 65–94.

King, R., and A. Strachan. "Patterns of Sardinian Migration," *Tijdschrift voor economische en sociale geografie* 71, 1980, pp. 209–22.

Loddo Canepa, F. *La Sardegna dal 1478 al 1793. I. Gli anni 1478–1720*. G. Todde, ed., Sassari, 1974, pp. 93–106.

Moroni, A., et al. "La consanguineità umana nell'isola di Sardegna dal secolo XVIII al secolo XX," *Ateneo Parmense*, 8, suppl.1, pp. 69–92.

Ortu, G. G. *L'economia pastorale della Sardegna moderna*. Sassari, 1981.

Pino Branca, A. *La vita economica della Sardegna sabauda*. Messina, 1926.

Rudas, N. *L'emigrazione sarda*. Rome, 1974.

21

A Cartographic Approach to the Problem of Internal Migration in Sardinia in the Eighteenth Century
PART TWO
Serge Bonin

The cartographic representation of historical data should be regarded as an instrument of discovery and analysis. The comparison of separate phenomena at the same or at different times as well as the comparison of changes occurring within a single phenomenon can be represented by maps and diagrams containing all the essential information. Such documents constitute in fact extremely versatile tools of research that are too often ignored or misunderstood by the historian.

In the present case patterns or changes in the geographical distribution of the different demographic or economic elements suggest a number of hypotheses concerning problems of internal migration. The cartographic approach, if it cannot claim to resolve such problems unaided, can undoubtedly contribute in important ways to their solution.

The demographic data (population densities, number of inhabited localities) for the years 1688, 1698, 1728, and 1751 are represented by a series of computerized maps (figure 21.2). The economic data (a harvest, livestock, and population census for 1771) have been subjected to a matrix treatment (figure 21.3) which is reproduced schematically in figure 21.4.

The same data have been broken down on a series of analytic maps (figure 21.5). Detailed information is available in both cases for 51 regions of Sardinia (Nurra was uninhabited). A minicomputer H.P. 9825 was used to compose the maps in figures 21.2 and 21.5.

A Cartographic Treatment of the Demographic Data (1688–1751)
(figure 21.2)

Population densities: The first set of four maps utilizes a common scale (the maximum number of hearths or households per km^2 are in black, the minimum in white). A general increase is especially marked along the NW–SE axis, which was already characterized by maximum population densities at the beginning of the period. The second set of four maps are drawn to proper scales. The visual values range from black to white (the two extremes) as in the previous case. The distribution of population at each of the four dates emerges more distinctly and in greater detail thanks to the use of proper scales. By differentiating between the positive and negative evolution of population densities it is possible to apprehend at a glance two aspects of the same phenomenon. One is struck by a marked negative evolution in several regions between 1698 and 1728 compensated by a positive evolution in the succeeding period, and by the weak positive (or even negative) evolution along the NW–SE axis between 1688 and 1698 and between 1728 and 1751.

Number of Villages: The positive and negative variations in the number of inhabited localities are relatively minor and affect in general the same regions in every period.

A Cartographic Treatment of the Economic Data (1771)
(figures 21.3–21.5)

A wide range of economic data exists for each of the 51 regions (see table 21.2.). Harvest and livestock figures have been expressed in terms of population, crop land in terms of total land surface, plough teams in terms of crop land. On the reorderable matrix (figure 21.3) each vertical band stands for a different region and each horizontal band for a different variable. In the latter case the data have been transcribed in eleven gradations ranging from white (the minimum value) through various combinations of white-gray-black to black (the maximum value). The bands have been arranged so as to group together as far as possible regions with similar economic activities. The result is a regional typology of Sardinian agriculture in the second half of the eighteenth century.

On the matrix a marked economic structure as defined by groups of

Figure 21.2: Population Densities and Inhabited Localities 1688–1751

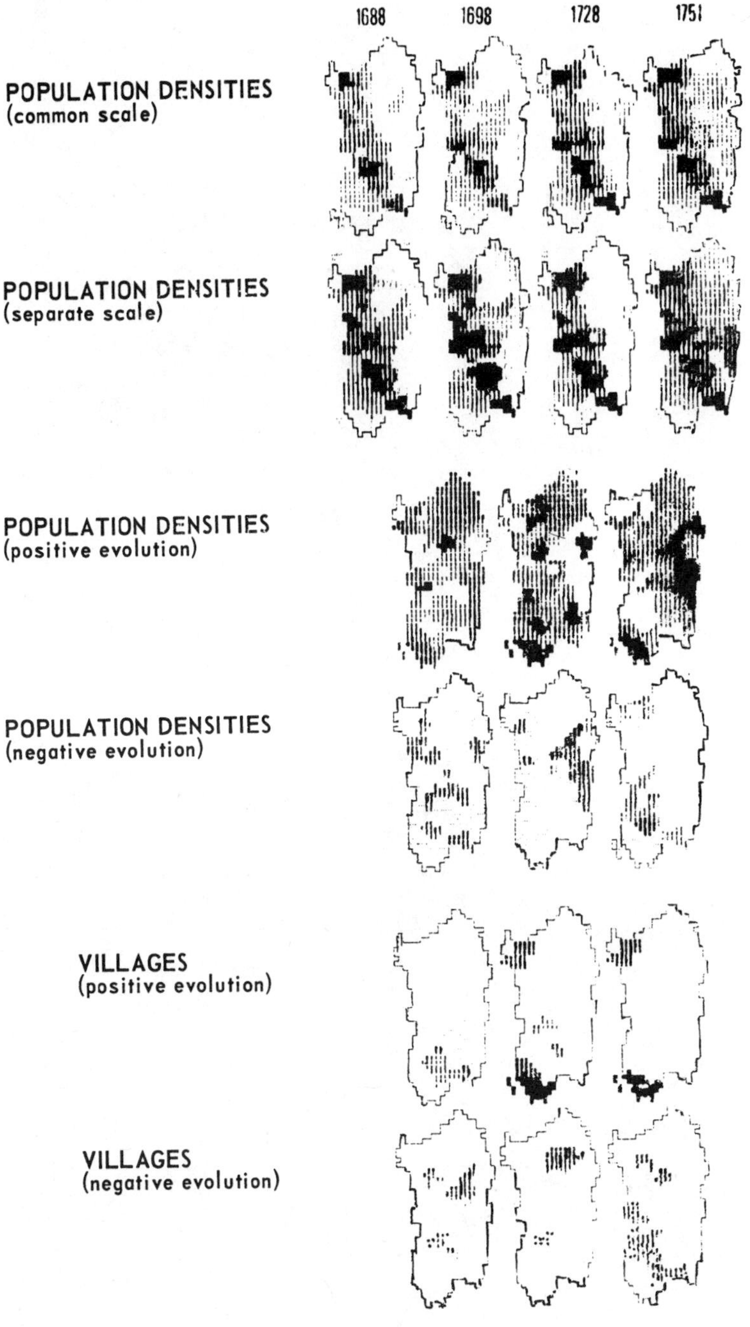

Figure 21.3: Matrix of Harvest, Livestock, and Population, 1771

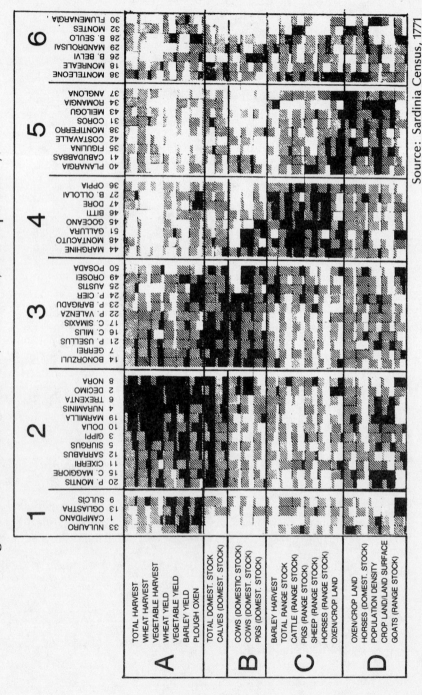

Source: Sardinia Census, 1771

374

variables A, B, and C exists for the regions in groups 1 through 5. The regions in group 6, on the contrary, and the variables in group D, do not fit into this system of classification. At this stage the data have been organized and the main groupings defined. But because no details have been omitted, it is difficult to extract the principal relationships.

Simplification and Interpretation Based on a Matrix Treatment
(figure 21.4)

The visual and thematic simplification, which is closely related to an interpretation of the results of the previous operation, leads to the determination of the most important relationships, to the mastery of the mass of information at our disposal. One has to decide what is essential, what will prove to be relevant to the problem at hand. In short, it is at this stage that one must choose the significant divisions between groups of variables and groups of regions. It is the most fruitful step in the procedure for it involves the considered elimination of details that are irrelevant at the higher level of comprehension. The details are preserved in the matrix (figure 21.3) and of course one can always consult the original data. To concentrate on a single detail is to concern oneself with one item out of hundreds. In figure 21.4 the different groups have been transposed to a map of the island by means of a legend. The result is a synthetic picture of relationships involving 1,122 elements (22 variables × 51 regions). This representation of the agricultural geography of Sardinia in the eighteenth century can serve as a basis of comparison with other cartographic material (cf. figure 21.2), and as a point of departure for further reflections on the problem of internal migration.

Analytic Maps
(figure 21.5)

Of the 22 variables on figure 21.3, eighteen are represented by separate computerized maps. The matrix enables one to establish relationships between groups of economic variables and groups of geographic regions, but it tends to obscure spatial affinities in individual cases. Thanks to a series of analytic maps following the same groupings as the matrix, it is possible to determine the geographic situation of the different variables, but it is no longer possible to visualize the relationships involving the series as a whole. One is here concerned with an intermediate level of perception where a certain number of details serve to complete the general picture provided by the matrix.

If one wishes to study the phenomenon of migration in the absence of direct sources one must possess tools of analysis capable of raising ques-

Figure 21.4: Schematic Representation of Harvest, Livestock and Population, 1771

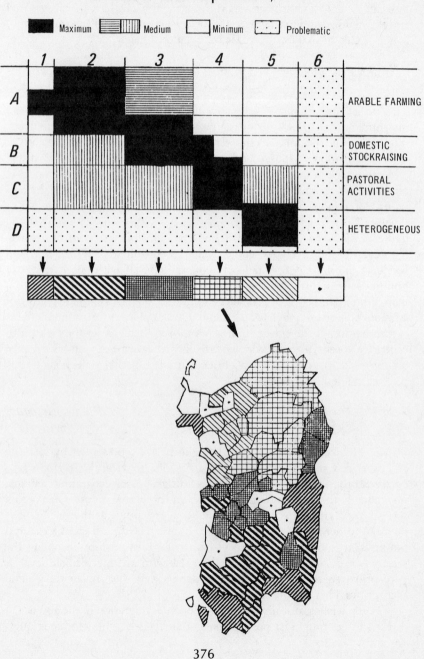

Figure 21.5: Analytic Map of Harvest, Livestock and Population, 1771

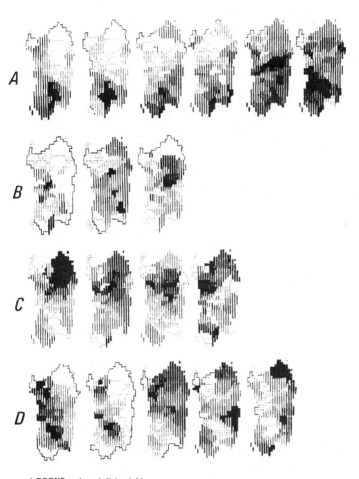

LEGEND : from left to right

A Wheat harvest - vegetable harvest - wheat yield - vegetable yield - barley yield - plough oxen -
Remarks : strong concentrations in the south, extending towards the center.

B Domestic stock (cows) - domestic stock (pigs) - barley harvest.
Remarks : heaviest concentrations generally in the center.

C Range stock (cattle) - range stock (pigs) - range stock (sheep) - range stock (horses).
Remarks : strong concentration in the north.

D Population density - crop land - domestic stock (horses) - oxen/crop land - range stock (goats).
Remarks : the distribution is problematical. However, population densities correspond in general to the amount of arable.

377

tions and suggesting hypotheses. One must consider the geographic distribution of the variables destined to figure in the final interpretation. Finally, one must master the general relationships. I have tried to present here a series of documents that will help the historian to reflect on the problems he wishes to resolve.

LOOKING AHEAD

22

An Agenda for the Future

M. Mark Stolarik

The papers presented in Budapest, and published in this volume, represent three main approaches scholars have recently taken to studying patterns of migration: the traditional (socioeconomic) approach, the current statistical (cliomatric) path, and the new (socio-psychological) explanation for this phenomenon.

Among the traditional essays I would place those by Avraham Barkai, Ivan Čizmić, A. J. H. Latham, and Frank Spooner. Barkai reminds us that most immigrants, like German Jews in the nineteenth century, moved within the borders of their own country before they left for another one. Ivan Čizmić, while focusing on the economic causes of Croatian emigration, laments the fact that most of his countrymen who returned home invested in land and not in industry. The same could be said of migrants returning to other countries of Europe. A. J. H. Latham, while focusing on migration in Southeast Asia in the nineteenth century, paints a picture of "push" and "pull" factors that were remarkably similar to those operating in the transatlantic migrations of the same period. Frank Spooner, meanwhile, in looking at Batavia in the period 1673–1790, points to the incredible ethnic diversity of that Dutch colony, the discrimination felt by the ethnic Chinese, and the ultimate failure of Europeans to plant permanent colonies in the Far East.

A second group of scholars used the more recent methods of statistical analysis of their survey of migration patterns. Cormac Ó Gráda, in constructing a profile, in eight tables, of who left Ireland before 1850, when and why, found no pat answers. Charlotte Erickson, meanwhile, concluded that the U.S. passenger lists were more reliable in recording the ethnic origins of migrants than either British or American census records. Walter D. Kamphoefner illustrated how German migrants to the United States could be traced forward and backward by using German emigration lists plus American census and other records. Ann Miller, in studying a sample of the 1900 U.S. Population Census, found that newly arrived emigrants did, indeed, "push upward" older arrivals and that also the newcomers provided much-needed labor for growing American industry. Jacques Dupâquier, meanwhile, broke with his French colleagues and showed that it was, indeed, possible to study the demographic patterns of French geographical mobility after 1829 and up to the present.

A third group of scholars at the Budapest conference suggested that the best approach to studying migration was social-psychological. Robert C. Ostergren reminded us that the Uppsala group studied Swedish emigration in a systematic manner in the 1960s and 1970s and concluded that not economic but individual and psychological reasons mattered far more in determining whether or not a person moved. Kristin Ruggiero, in focusing on the Waldensians of northern Italy, agreed. She concluded that emigration appeared to be a product of certain cultures and mentalities and that, even at the village level, some people were expected to move and others to stay put. Robert J. Kleiner and his colleagues called for the adoption of a theoretical framework in the study of migration, one that would look at the migrants' community of origin, the trip itself, the community of destination, and that would be studied with the help of social-structural, social-cultural, and social-psychological data for the same period of time.

It seems to me that these essays cry out for an organizing principle for migration studies. We need to agree on methods, sources, and approaches to be used. Since not all of us share the same expertise, whether it be linguistic, statistical, psychological, economic, or any number of others, we should create a five-year plan of sorts, one that would break down the tasks required of us and assign them to appropriate people. Once we have agreed on what we should do, how we should do it, and who will do it, we should get busy, stay in touch, share our findings, refine our methods and, eventually, publish the results. In other words, we need to create another "Uppsala group," but this time an international one to study migration as a world process, which it really is. That will necessitate regular conferences, perhaps on an annual basis, and the development of a true community of scholars that will go beyond national boundaries and work in an international framework.

Contributors

Avraham Barkai is at the Leo Baeck Institute, Jerusalem, Israel.

Serge Bonin is at the U.E.R. de Geographie, Histoire et Sciences de la Societe, Paris, France.

Ivan Čizmić is at the Matica Iseljenica Hrvatska, Zagreb, Yugoslavia.

Odd Stefan Dalgard is at the University of Oslo, Norway.

John Day is professor at C.N.R. and at the University of Paris, France.

Luigi De Rosa is Dean of Faculty and professor of Economic History, University of Naples, Naples, Italy.

Luigi Di Comité is Professor at the Institute of Economics and Finance, Faculty of Law, University of Bari, Italy.

Dale Drews is in the Sociology Department, Temple University, Philadelphia, Pennsylvania.

Jacques Dupâquier is professor at the Ècole Historique et Sciences Sociale, University of Paris, France.

Jana Englová is at the Charles University, Prague, Czechoslovakia.

Charlotte Erickson is professor in the Faculty of History, Cambridge University, Cambridge, England.

Ira A. Glazier is professor of Economics and History and Director, Temple–Balch Center of Immigration Research, Philadelphia, Pennsylvania.

Walter D. Kamphoefner is in the History Department, University of Miami, Florida.

Robert J. Kleiner is professor in the Sociology Department, Temple University Philadelphia, Pennsylvania.

A.J.H. Latham is senior lecturer in the Department of Economic History, University College, Swansea, England.

Deirdre Mageean is on the Faculty of Social Sciences, The Open University, Milton Keynes, England.

Ann R. Miller is professor in the Department of Sociology, Center for Population Studies, University of Pennsylvania.

Torbjøorn Moum is at the University of Oslo, Norway.

Cormac Ó Gráda is in the Department of Political Economy, University College, Dublin, Ireland.

Robert C. Ostergren is professor in the Department of Geography, University of Wisconsin, Madison, Wisconsin.

Julianna Puskás is at the Institute of History, Hungarian Academy of Science, Budapest, Hungary.

M.S.A. Rao is professor in the Department of Sociology, University of Delhi, India. (Just prior to publication, Professor Rao passed away.)

Kristin Ruggerio is professor in the Department of History at St. Lawrence College, New York.

Tom Sørenson is at the University of Oslo, Norway.

Frank Spooner is professor in the Department of Economic History, University of Durham, England.

Shaul Stampfer is in the Department of History, Hebrew University, Jerusalem, Israel.

Mark Stolarik is president of the Balch Institute, Philadelphia, Pennsylvania.

Robert P. Swierenga is professor in the Department of History, Kent State University, Ohio.

Rudolph J. Vecoli is professor of History and Director, Immigration History Research Center, University of Minnesota, St. Paul, Minnesota.

DATE DUE

JAN 3 1 1991			
FEB 2 0 2001			